The Methuen Drama Book of Post-Black Plays

The Methuen Drama Book of Post-Black Plays

The Methuen Drama Book of Post-Black Plays

Bulrusher
Good Goods
The Shipment
Satellites
And Jesus Moonwalks the Mississippi
Antebellum
In the Continuum
Black Diamond

edited by
Harry J. Elam, Jr. and Douglas A. Jones, Jr.

Methuen Drama

Methuen Drama

Methuen Drama, an imprint of Bloomsbury Publishing Plc

1 3 5 7 9 10 8 6 4 2

Methuen Drama
Bloomsbury Publishing Plc
50 Bedford Square
London WC1B 3DP
www.methuendrama.com

ISBN 978 1 408 17382 4

A CIP catalogue record for this book is available from the British Library

Available in the USA from Bloomsbury Academic & Professional, 175 Fifth Avenue/3rd Floor, New York, NY 10010.

Harry J. Elam, Jr. is the Olive H. Palmer Professor in the Humanities, and the Freeman-Thornton Vice Provost for Undergraduate Education at Stanford University. He is author of *Taking It to the Streets: The Social Protest Theater of Luis Valdez and Amiri Baraka*; *The Past as Present in the Drama of August Wilson*, winner of the Errol Hill Award; and co-editor of *African American Performance and Theater History: A Critical Reader*; *Colored Contradictions: An Anthology of Contemporary African American Drama*; *The Fire This Time: African American Plays for the New Millennium*; and *Black Cultural Traffic: Crossroads in Performance and Popular Culture*. His articles have appeared in *American Drama*, *Modern Drama*, *Theatre Journal*, *Text and Performance Quarterly* as well as journals in Israel, Belgium, Poland and Taiwan and also in several critical anthologies.

Douglas A. Jones, Jr. is Cotsen Fellow in the Princeton Society of Fellows at Princeton University, where he teaches in the Department of English. He has published several articles and book chapters that span a wide array of issues in (African) American cultural and literary history, race and performance, and American dramatic literature. His first book, *The Captive Stage: Black Exception, Performance, and the Proslavery Imagination of the Antebellum North*, is forthcoming from University of Michigan Press. In fall of 2013, he will join the English faculty at Rutgers University.

Acknowledgments

We editors extend our sincere gratitude to our eight authors for their willingness to have their works anthologized in this collection. We thank our own editors at Methuen Drama, Charlotte Loveridge for accepting this project and Anna Brewer for seeing it through to fruition. We are most appreciative of Lisa Bilgen for her efforts at editing and proofreading. We thank David Goldman, Alex Mallory, Dominic Taylor, and Harvey Young for their help in identifying plays and playwrights. Credit also goes out to Isaiah Wooden, Jennifer Brody, and Radiclani Clytus for their constructive suggestions on the notion of the post-black. Michele Elam's support and insight as always proved invaluable, and Tirzah Enumah provided bracing encouragement throughout the process.

Contents

Introduction

What we call the beginning is often the end
And to make an end is to make a beginning.
The end is where we start from.

–T.S. Eliot, *Four Quartets*

those who cannot forget the past are destined to remix it

–Evie Shockley, 'duck, duck, redux'

Post-Black. . .

First and foremost: our decision to classify the plays collected in this volume, all written between 2005 and 2011, as 'post-black' does not mean that we believe American society in the twenty-first century is post-racial. To be sure, the academic, economic, and political successes that African Americans have achieved only obscure the fact that in certain social fields, as legal scholar Michelle Alexander has persuasively shown, 'something akin to a racial caste system currently exists in the United States.'[1] Instead, we use the term 'post-black' as an aesthetic and historiographical designation, a marker of the way in which a cadre of playwrights and other artists intellectually and ideologically reared after the Civil Rights and Black Power movements – and not all of whom are black – render the pleasures and perils of blackness that are particular to their era. Their efforts mark a departure from, though indebtedness to, the dominant ideological sensibilities and representational modalities of segregation-era and Black Nationalist cultural production, especially those of the Black Arts Movement. They do not necessarily move past any connection to race or racialized meanings but, rather, travel beyond older definitions of blackness that delimit creation or predetermine the social and political thrust of their artistic efforts, such as collective racial uplift. To that effect, post-black artists are virtuosos of what Ralph Ellison called the 'appropriation game,' they are cultural provocateurs who are decidedly cosmopolitan in their approach because the realities of black American life that they seek to delineate are just as multiple, overlapping, divergent, and often contradictory as their very cosmopolitanism.[2]

At stake in their work, and perhaps ironically so given that they are post-black, is the very definition of blackness. As curator and art critic Thelma Golden of the Studio Museum explains, post-black is 'characterized by artists who were adamant about not being labeled as 'black' artists, though their work was steeped, in fact deeply interested, in redefining complex notions of blackness.'[3] These definitions took hold in the artistic, performance, and literary worlds of the early 2000s, and, as Golden famously declared, 'Post-black was the new black.'[4] While scholars and cultural critics continue to debate how to periodize and even label this new era of black arts and letters, there is clear consensus that contemporary artists and writers enjoy unprecedented freedom in their explorations of blackness and all its multiplicities and valences.[5] This freedom, as literary critic Kenneth Warren reminds us, rests on the expansion of American democracy and the sociopolitical achievements of the second half of the twentieth century. Unlike the texts and practices that African Americans and their allies produced as means to 'change or repeal laws that significantly shaped black social and political life from the late 1890s through the 1960s,' Warren writes, 'contemporary black political and cultural inquiry, by its own admission, is not similarly oriented.'[6] However, the expressive latitude that the post-Jim Crow U.S. affords those working to redefine blackness is not without complication. These artists and writers must also confront, implicitly or explicitly, an ethical quandary seemingly less prescribed than it was for their predecessors: What, if any, should be the social and political ends of our artistic efforts?

A recent explosion of critical literature, both popular and scholarly, coheres around this question.[7] These writings grapple with the difficulty of how we remember the past but remain guided by the present and oriented towards the future. Eddie S. Glaude, Jr., a philosopher of religion and intellectual historian, explains how and why contemporary (cultural) politics must be just that, contemporary, and unmoored from the ideological and strategic assumptions of the past, particularly those of the 1960s:

> In the end, my point is simply this: those who struggled in the 1960s did not have the symbolic weight of 'the 1960s' to contend with. We do. Old strategies and personalities continue to define how we engage in race-based politics. Yet, these old strategies and leaders stand alongside new problems and personalities that are not reducible to that moment of struggle. We live in a different time, a moment made possible by the extraordinary efforts of past generations. But our task is different because the conditions have changed.[8]

The historical, sociological, and epistemological conditions that Glaude lays out here animate the necessity for what he calls a 'post-soul politics for the twenty-first century;' they are also the very conditions of the post-black. Thus, the post-black, in our view, does not simply identify those who do not 'feel obliged to refer to ethnicity or racial history in their work,' as art critic Holland Cotter suggests.[9] Rather, the term designates an artistic and cultural moment and movement with its own historicity, a set of shared aesthetic and ideological sensibilities that, tautologically, came *after* a previous set.

We use the expression 'post-black' for the plays in this volume, then, to emphasize the dichotomous ways in which these works incorporate but also diverge from what have become normative dramaturgical formations of black drama. Perhaps more than anything else, these plays are like other contemporaneous literary and artistic works by and about African Americans that do not 'contribute demonstrably to some social end' or stand in as 'proxies for the status or the nature of the race as a whole.'[10] Instead, they function as dramatic ruminations and accountings of the tumultuous, though productive differences surrounding racial experiences in the twenty-first-century U.S.

Thus, an overriding preoccupation of these plays, and of post-black aesthetics generally, is the problem of identity.[11] The question of who we are, *now*, dominates the thematics of these artists and critics. In answering this question, they respond to the ways in which not only new socio-cultural circumstances, but legacies from the African American past, shape African American identities in the present. Asian American playwright Young Jean Lee, whose work *The Shipment* we have anthologized here for how it responds to post-black imperatives, argues for the need for playwrights of color to interrogate traditional renderings of race. As she puts it, 'It's almost become part of the dominant white power structure to have identity-politics plays about how screwed-over minorities are. It's such a familiar, soothing pattern . . . It's become the status quo.'[12] According to Lee, representing identity politics can prove stultifying and even reactionary. Her play, like others anthologized in this volume, seeks to disrupt such ideological and affective norms. Instead, these artists strive for the unfamiliar, the unsettling, and the uncanny as means to offer progressive renderings of black identities structured by the unfamiliar, unsettling, and uncanny nature of our contemporary moment.

To do this, post-black playwrights often manipulate dramatic, theatrical, and performance conventions. Lee, for instance, uses the structure of 'identity-politics plays' and their stock renderings of white oppression, racial stereotyping, and thwarted strivings of minorities to her advantage: she parodies them, showing how stale and antiquated they are.[13] In fact, the mode of parody is one of the most effective strategies of post-black artists and writers, though surely not their only one, because it allows them and their audiences to understand themselves in contradistinction to what and who came before. As literary theorist Carolyn Williams maintains, 'Parody, although by no means a modern mode, is a powerfully *modernizing* one. In taking up its models, parody . . . casts them back into

the past, treating them as outmoded relics compared with itself. Parody turns on its models, but also internally turns against them and away from them, moving beyond them in the novelty of the present, recasting them as outworn and old-fashioned.'[14] In parody, therefore, the past becomes the vehicle with which to escape the past itself.

Given the considerable symbolic purchase that the 1960s continues to hold on the cultural imagination, the forms and figures of the period are essential fodder for post-black parody. One of the most mordant, though illustrative of these efforts is comedian Baratunde Thurston's semi-autobiographical text, *How To Be Black* (2012). The book, a sort of manifesto for post-black cultural politics, aims to debunk notions of essential blackness and, as its title suggests, make clear how blackness is contingent and performative. For example, in his attempt to show how contemporary black identity must be understood outside the terms and conditions of the 1960s, Thurston parodies the assumptions of the era. In a 'list of ten ways one can celebrate the contributions of African-Americans to these United States, carefully designed with the non-black person in mind,' he includes: 'Change the wallpaper on your computer or mobile phone to an image of a slave plantation;' 'Know the key people' (Thurston offers Martin Luther King, Rosa Parks, Malcolm X, Muhammad Ali, and J.J. from *Good Times*, among others); 'Hum a Negro spiritual;' and 'Read *The Autobiography of Malcolm X*.'[15] If one completes these and the other six activities, he is 'an official friend of black America' and receives, among other awards, 'the right to attend two secret Black Meetings a year.'[16] Thurston's parodic treatment of civil rights history and heroism, Afro-centrism, and Black Nationalism reveals the ways in which inter- and intra-racial understandings of contemporary black American life refracted through the 1960s are limiting, that the personal and collective dynamics of race today are markedly different than those of the past.

And yet, post-black parodies such as Thurston's also preserve something of the past. As Williams writes, 'The modernizing effects of parody . . . are conservative as well as progressive, preserving the forms of the past even while mocking, overturning, twisting, or updating them . . . Parody performs the conservative function of historical preservation, effectively creating repaired continuity while making a break from the past.'[17] Indeed, the use of parody in post-black cultural production is in some ways ironic because it archives the very past from which it seeks to deliver us. When read against the grain of its parody, Thurston's list of ways to celebrate African Americans does, in fact, preserve signal moments in black history. In this way, *How to Be Black*, like several of the plays in this volume, deploys a signal strategy of post-black art, literature, and culture: the turn *to* the past in an effort to turn *from* the past. Put simply, the post-black is very often retrospective, and it is this working through and against the past that allows its practitioners and audiences to contemplate the present.[18]

To be sure, the retrospective gestures in post-black praxis are not all parodic or satirical. They are also often philosophical, reverent, mythic, or magical. In either case, the appropriation and subsequent reshaping of the (black) past yields new visual, discursive, and critical lexicons with which to grapple with the problems of contemporary identity, thus redoubling the irony of the post-black. As the poet Evie Shockley neatly puts it, '*those who cannot forget the past are destined to remix it*.'[19] Remixing the past is a dominant representational practice in post-black aesthetics, and Shockley's own poetry is an exemplar in this regard. Her recently published collection of poetry, *the new black*, is a haunting exploration of the constitutive dynamism of racial, sexual, and class identity in the twenty-first century. Yet it is also a haunted one insofar as she does not allow her readers and listeners to ignore how the past contributed to that dynamism. But the past does not encumber Shockley either. Instead, she remixes it in order to account for where we are in our contemporary moment and where we have left to go.

Thus Shockley's poetry instantiates several of the formal, representational, and even political concerns of the post-black, even though she is 'wary' of the term.[20] Similarly, literary critic Bertram Ashe's theorization of the post-soul, his preferred label, offers a particularly useful way to understand the historical and aesthetic intervention of the post-black. He writes, 'These artists and texts trouble blackness, they worry blackness; they stir it up, touch it, feel it, and hold it up for examination in ways that depart significantly from previous – and necessary – preoccupations with struggling for political freedom, or with an attempt to establish and sustain a coherent black identity. Still, from my vantage point, this "troubling" of blackness by post-soul writers is ultimately done in service to black people.'[21] The playwrights anthologized in this volume do just what Ashe describes here in that they offer heterogeneous and heterodox renderings of blackness that are grounded in the contexts and conditions of today. This is the animating principle of the post-black. As such, the post-black does not signal the end of blackness, but a potentially new and vibrant beginning.

What is a post-black play?

While one can certainly locate traces of contemporary post-black dramaturgy in earlier plays, the eight plays we have collected here evidence critical developments in black theatre and black arts more generally during the first decades of the twenty-first century. These plays form part and parcel of a concerted movement to 'complicate the discourse around black art,' as art critic Mary Schmidt Campbell puts it. She goes on to say that post-black visual artists 'didn't reject an ethnic designation for themselves; they rejected an ethnic label for their work. Ethnic designations were a limitation on the way others viewed them – at best, a form of provincialism, at worst, a way of slapping on a label and shelving the art without giving the work the careful attention it deserved.'[22] Post-black playwrights, like the other artists, critics, and scholars who make up this movement, have recognized the need to develop new visual and rhetorical vocabularies that delineate the politics of race and identity that they experience. Visual artist Kori Newkirk explains the aesthetic approach he shares with his post-black compatriots: 'We're all making work that can be difficult sometimes, with an incredible investigation into materials and strong basis in conceptual art . . . I would say we're all making work that doesn't hit people over the head with the race conversation anymore. It's juicy conceptualism.'[23] Conceptualism, however juicy, with its sometimes reactionary politics does not represent the hallmark of post-blackness. Rather, the Newkirk quote acknowledges the desire of this new generation of artists to experiment with form as well as content as they compel reassessments of how and what we label as 'black art.'

Observing an equally 'juicy conceptualism' that 'doesn't hit people over the head with the race conversation' in contemporary (African) American theatre has prompted us to reconsider within and through this volume what constitutes a black play. This query harks back to George C. Wolfe's explanation for the genesis of his groundbreaking, irreverent satire, *The Colored Museum* (1986). Wolfe quips, 'People kept asking for a 'black' play. I kept asking, 'What's a "black" play? Four walls, a couch and a mama?' I can't live within those old definitions.'[24] With *The Colored Museum*, Wolfe smashes icons of the black theatrical past and celebrates the contradictions inherent in black experiences. Now, over twenty years later, we repeat and revise Wolfe's dramaturgical declaration of independence as we consider the post-black play. That is, the spirit of possibility found in post-black drama flows from the interventions of Wolfe and others made in the 1980s, while potentially troubling the classification of the black play even further.

The plays in this volume emerge in an era when some critics and commentators have proclaimed the end of race as we have known it.[25] In a cultural moment, where advocates for and scholars of mixed race have challenged the traditional ways we talk about race, where the lines between the American pop culture mainstream and black

musical genres have become irrevocably blurred, post-black playwrights have created diverse and complex works that embrace and exploit the freedom and fluidity of the moment. What Michele Elam argues about the artists and writers she explores in her study of contemporary mixed-race aesthetics, *The Souls of Mixed Folk*, holds just as true for the plays we include in this collection: they 'offer up capacious racial identities fully consistent with heterogeneity, postmodernity, and self-examination . . .'[26] Accordingly, the definition of the post-black play must necessarily be contingent and variable, flexible enough to accommodate the ever-shifting parameters of blackness.

While the period of post-black drama marks a new beginning, it unfolds amid a moment of profound loss within American theatre history: the death of playwright August Wilson in October 2005. The two-time Pulitzer Prize-winning playwright died after completing the final play of his ten-play cycle, *Radio Golf* (2005). In the cycle, for which he wrote a play set in each decade of the twentieth century, Wilson explores the triumphs and perils that have constituted black life and reflects on the choices African Americans have made in order to survive. In sum, he has created an epic history out of the mundane stories and experiences of ordinary black people. The most produced playwright in the United States during the decades of the 1990s and the 2000s, Wilson, in many ways, came to personify black theatre. Indeed, when regional theatres around the country mounted a black play at this time, they generally chose one of the plays in Wilson's cycle. Hence, theatre practitioners, critics, and scholars not only mourned his passing, but also pondered who would pick up Wilson's mantle and what direction black theatre would subsequently take.

In part, post-black drama surfaces as a rejoinder to these queries regarding Wilson's legacy as well as to Wolfe's earlier interrogation of the black play. Pulitzer Prize- and MacArthur Award-winning playwright Suzan-Lori Parks recognizes this in her essay 'New black math,' which she wrote in response to the question 'What is a black play?' for a special 2005 issue of *Theatre Journal* on black performance. She asserts:

> What is a black play? The definition is housed in the reality of two things that occurred recently and almost simultaneously: 26 August 05, playwright scholar poet king August Wilson announces he is dying of cancer, and hurricane Katrina devastated the Gulf Coast. It feels like judgment day. What I'm talking about today is the same and different.[27]

Signaling the implicit connection of black plays to black life, Parks posits Wilson's announcement of his terminal illness and Hurricane Katrina as foundational events in the direction of contemporary black dramaturgy, two dramatic and devastating scenes that drew the nation's attention to blackness and its meanings in that moment. Each of the crises produced a complex interchange of emotions, from feelings of futility to frustration and anger, from racial pride to racial outrage. The flood waters of Katrina, with the spectacle of black bodies struggling against the turbulent currents and huddled en masse in the perilous hull of the Superdome, revealed the blatant neglect of the Bush Administration and state and local authorities, showcased the media's mislabeling of black victims as refugees and looters, and uncovered the racial inequities that continue to shape the present. Wilson's divulgence of his cancer similarly summoned memories of his compelling dramaturgical achievements, but also portended uncertainty as to what would follow. Consequently, Parks' definition for black plays conjoins the personal and the political. Parks references dichotomous circumstances and imagines the conjunction of old and new. Using August Wilson and Hurricane Katrina as reference points, Parks' 'new black math' offers an understanding of the black play that is 'the same and different,' dependent on the current contexts and conditions of African American existence but also responsive to past circumstances.

Extrapolating from Parks' 'new black math' then, any calculation of post-black drama must recognize its direct relationship to the exigencies of the times as well as its connection to previous paradigms of black cultural production. This definition makes the post-black the 'same and different' from its African American theatrical antecedents. The Black Arts Movement of the 1960s and 1970s, with its expressions of black pride and black consciousness, certainly functioned as response to the urgencies of its day. Empowered by the burgeoning frustrations and insistent demands for change emanating from black communities, Black Arts activists directly linked their theatrical efforts to the agenda of the Black Power movement. They imagined their theatre as fundamentally a mechanism to achieve social ends. Thus, collaborative attempts to articulate a unified artistic vision, to create a political black aesthetic, and to promote black liberation through performance characterize this earlier movement, its dramaturgy, and its playwrights. In contrast, however, the post-black represents a time and temperament decidedly removed from these convictions. Post-black playwrights, like the artists of the Black Arts Movement, do express dissatisfaction with the status quo and exhibit the desire to remake black theatre practices on their own terms. But post-black playwrights do not attempt to cultivate a singular artistic perspective, nor do they envision themselves and their art as most principally part of a collective. Rather, each of the playwrights within this volume has had a decidedly distinct response to how they situate themselves and their work.

Moreover, the evolving politics of representation in the early twenty-first century have had a profound impact on the plays in this anthology. The long-held sentiment that black plays require black producers, black venues, and black audiences has waned. Notably, in 1926, W.E.B. Du Bois stated that 'a real Negro theatre' must be 'About us, By us, For us, and Near us.'[28] Similarly, the Black Arts Movement in the 1960s and 1970s espoused a doctrine of theatrical separatism. In fact, in 1965 the Black Arts Repertory School in Harlem attempted to prohibit white patrons from attending the theatre. And although a white director, Todd Kriedler, mounted August Wilson's final one-man show, *How I Learned What I Learned* (2003), and Tony Award-winning white director Bartlett Sher, with the permission of Wilson's widow, Constanza Romero, staged a Lincoln Center revival of Wilson's *Joe Turner's Come and Gone* (1988) in 2009, Wilson, in the late 1980s, would not allow his Pulitzer Prize-winning play, *Fences* (1987), to be made into a film without a black director. Re-animating Du Bois' earlier dictates for a 'Negro Theater,' Wilson, in his much-discussed 1996 speech to the Theatre Communications Group (TCG), *The Ground on Which I Stand*, calls for the establishment of a culturally specific and distinct black theatre in order to cultivate and nurture the efforts of black playwrights. With idealism and urgency, Wilson's TCG speech encourages black playwrights to act as racial activists: 'We can be the spearhead of a movement to reignite and reunite our people's positive energy for a political and social change that is reflective of our spiritual truth rather than our economic fallacies.'[29] On the whole, post-black playwrights have neither taken up Wilson's directives nor espoused such an ethos of black particularism. Black particularism, as articulated by Harold Cruse, functions as a strategy of situational separatism. It serves as a response to a dominant society that diminishes 'the validity of other kinds of cultural values that might compete with its own standards – whether in the social sciences, the arts, literature, or economic activity.'[30] Wilson challenges black playwrights and champions the establishment of black theatrical institutions on these terms. While post-black playwrights may not have responded directly to Wilson's black activist appeal, they have certainly benefitted from his groundbreaking efforts to open up the potential for regional theatres to embrace the work of black playwrights.

Altering expected racial customs, an increasing number of predominantly white regional theatres have not only produced post-black plays but engaged white directors to stage them. Previously, the unwritten rule of racialized theatrical practice presumed that regional theatres would hire black directors to mount the one black play that they included within their theatrical seasons – often the work of August Wilson. In the post-black theatrical world, however, this policy appears to no longer be a necessity or a foregone conclusion as artistic directors of regional theatres as well as post-black playwrights themselves have turned more and more to white directors. The reasons for this are complex, but the implication is that white artistic directors, no longer compelled by cultural mandates to choose a black director, believe that the preferred white director is best artistically suited for the project. Aesthetic interest now possibly trumps racial affinities. Yet an unequal racial playing field still figures within this equation. Discussing the ethics of white directors and the August Wilson cycle, Charles Dutton, who starred in August Wilson's *Ma Rainey's Bottom* (1984) and *Piano Lesson* (1990) on Broadway, remarks, 'August told me himself that the reason he did not want white directors was because if one ever had a chance to do one of his plays on Broadway, it would be very unlikely that a black director would ever be chosen again to direct his plays on that level.'[31] What Dutton underscores is not a divergence in talent between white and black directors, but rather the difference in access to the mechanisms of power that still determines directing opportunities on Broadway and off.

Even as selected African American playwrights in the contemporary period have received promising creative opportunities, a racialized power structure – the authority to produce and commission theatrical work – remains in the hands of a select white majority and this has political as well as commercial consequences for post-black drama. During the 1980s and 1990s, regional theatres around the country, from Arena Stage in Washington D.C. to the Mark Taper Forum in Los Angeles, offered focused workshops and training programs for playwrights of color. Significantly, most of these programs have since closed. On the one hand, this has limited the avenues for these playwrights to develop their work. On the other hand, a number of contemporary African American playwrights such as Lynn Nottage – winner of the Pulitzer Prize for *Ruined* (2009) – and Tarell Alvin McCraney – whose highly acclaimed trilogy, *The Brother/Sister Plays* (2009), has garnered productions all across the country – have succeeded largely without designated programs for minority playwrights. Due to the broad critical and commercial acclaim of their work, they have received commissions from such mainstream institutions as the Goodman Theatre in Chicago, the Royal Shakespeare Company in London, and the Manhattan Theatre Club in New York.[32] A number of them have also trained at top-tier institutions such as Yale University, Brown University, and New York University. Still, this does not mean that the need for particularized support for African American playwrights no longer exists. While we applaud these artists for their achievements, we must recognize the hierarchies of power that are in place as well as the conditions that regulate mainstream theatrical production and impact the advancement of black playwrights.

We must also acknowledge that the ability of post-black playwrights to break barriers and to form effective interracial theatrical partnerships does indicate that, in significant respects, the racial climate has in fact changed; specifically, they have emerged in the context of the United States electing its first black president in 2008, in what might be called 'the age of Obama.'[33] Obama's election has caused some to conjecture that, by and large, race no longer matters in American life – for if it did, how could a black man have ever been elected to the nation's highest office? Moreover, Obama and his team employed a new approach to electoral politics, foregoing the traditional, 1960s-style formulas of black candidates for the presidency such as Jesse Jackson or Al Sharpton. Their decision to reject older coalitions, rhetorical styles, and campaign strategies made good electoral sense because it reflected the sweeping changes in American attitudes towards race: opinion polls of younger voters under age 30, who overwhelmingly voted for Obama, reveal that they perceive race much more positively than earlier generations. In a 2012 interview with *Rolling Stone*, the President himself notes:

> I've seen in my own lifetime how racial attitudes have changed and improved, and anybody who suggests that they haven't isn't paying attention or is trying to make a rhetorical point. Because we all see it every day, and me being in this Oval Office is a testimony to changes that have been taking place . . . you shouldn't also underestimate the fact that there are a whole bunch of little white girls and white boys all across the country who just take it for granted that there's an African-American president. That's the president they're growing up with, and that's changing attitudes.[34]

Thus, the cultural, political, and institutional conditions within which post-black playwrights work are clearly in a state of flux, allowing them to approach blackness from diverse angles and to pursue venues outside black communities willing to mount their plays.

Emboldened by the ideological latitude and the more liberal cultural current, post-black playwrights have taken calculated risks in their explorations of black identity. Young Jean Lee's *The Shipment* (2009) directly assails her audience with exaggerated images of blackness. At the beginning of the play, an abrasive black comedian unleashes a profane diatribe on racial politics, firing off salacious jokes composed of derogatory stereotypes of both blacks and whites. Lee's distortion of black humor and her theatrical flirtation with racial taboos seeks to provoke the audience and challenge spectators' racial perceptions. She muses, 'For centuries, from minstrel shows to stand-up comics, white Americans expected black people to entertain them . . . Now that the president is black, are some people thinking in the back of their minds, "Oh, there's this black guy on television every day, why isn't he singing and dancing for me?"'[35] Evident in the subversive strategies of Lee and others is the refusal to be trapped in or by past significations and expectations of blackness.

Even as they have sought to escape past limitations, post-black playwrights have also sought to explore African American history. Examining the African American past through new eyes and from new perspectives has proven another critical project for post-black dramatists. Consider, for example, Eisa Davis's play *Bulrusher* (2007), which takes place in 1955. Rather than situating the play in the south where the injustices and second-class citizenship of Jim Crow are most readily associated, Davis sets the play in Boonville, California, a town with only two black residents. The characters briefly discuss the lynching of Emmitt Till, its aftermath, and other examples of southern racism. But the distance of these acts from Boonville highlights the particularities and multiplicity of black experiences; instead of the expected narratives of black oppression of the 1950s, the play focuses on the socially naïve title character, Bulrusher, and her journey into sexual and racial awareness. In disrupting normative renderings of the racial past, post-black dramatists, like W.E.B. Dubois and August Wilson before them, challenge assumptions regarding what histories should get told and who gets to tell them.

Furthermore, through certain works, post-black playwrights ask: Why are certain historical narratives, images, and ideas held as too serious, too sensitive for humor, satire, or irreverence? Challenging the process of history-making itself, they detach past institutions and events from their traditional representations and conventional meanings. Marcus Gardley's *And Jesus Moonwalks the Mississippi*, a poetic and at times cheeky Civil War drama, features, as the title suggests, a figure of Jesus who performs Michael Jackson's signature dance, the moonwalk. It tells the story of an escaped slave, Damascus, who is lynched and subsequently converted into the goddess Demeter. The play queries the legacy of black captivity and the meanings of freedom; slavery, lynching, and other historical atrocities committed against African Americans previously protected as sacrosanct in the black dramaturgical imagination are open to re-interpretation, myth, and distortion in the post-black imagination.[36] The result is an enlarged and even revisionist understanding of the past – if not new paths to personal and social change – as well as a broadening of the possibilities of (African) American theatre.

Yet, what might be most striking about post-black plays are the formal complexities and challenges the texts offer audiences, critics, and students. In fact, it is through form that these playwrights have most commonly reinvested in the question of what constitutes a black play, exploring how dramaturgical shape, size, and structure function as the inner logic of new content. Robert O'Hara's *Antebellum* (2009) traverses time and space, with disparate but intersecting settings in prewar Nazi Germany and in Atlanta, Georgia at the time of the premier of the film *Gone with the Wind*. Similarly, Christina Anderson's *Good Goods* (2010) turns conventional realism inside out to reveal how the supposedly otherworldly are very much a part of our day-to-day lives and relationships. As Anderson puts it in an interview with the director of the Yale Repertory Theatre's 2012 production of *Good Goods*, Tina Landau: 'I really do want to tell a good story. And I also want to open the play-world, and the stage-world, and the audience to possibility, and being able to, like, travel to these mystical places even though we never actually leave the shop [i.e., the play's setting.]'[37] This is the poetical thrust of *Good Goods* and *Antebellum*, and both use the dynamism of such temporal and spatial disorder to probe the connections of race, sexuality, and spiritualism. As these plays and the others collected in this volume show, post-black dramaturgy does not conform structurally to any codified or prescriptive formal aesthetic but, instead, it relishes the freedom to cultivate what Suzan-Lori Parks terms the 'new territory' of black drama.[38]

Certainly, diversity of expression marks the 'new territory' of post-black drama. Still, readers of this volume will find thematic affinities and formal resonances across the eight plays. Evident within these works are the ways in which they are 'the same and different' from black theatre of earlier generations and movements. We have divided this anthology into four sections, each containing two plays and organized around a decisive characteristic or preoccupation of post-black dramaturgy. Collecting these plays together in this anthology places them in productive dialogue with each other and around the representation and meanings of blackness. The plays contained inform the ever-evolving discussion of how to define a black play.

Section I: Homecomings and Goings

The first section, 'Homecomings and Goings,' explores the shifting, multivalent definitions of what constitutes the home. Drama theorist Una Chadhuri argues, 'The privileged setting of modern drama is the family home. The domestic interior contains the history of a process, begun in the nineteenth century and still unconcluded as the twentieth century nears its end, a way of filling the signifying space of theatre with an *environment*. This kind of environmentalism [serves] . . . as a factor of knowledge and a code of representation.'[39] As the plays in this section demonstrate, the environment of the home maintains a significant hold in the dramaturgical imagination of the early twenty-first century, allowing post-black playwrights to weigh how it shapes the dynamism and complexity of black adolescence, families, and generational relationships. Refusing traditional ways of representing the home and black family life on the American stage, particularly the strictures of domestic or kitchen-sink realism, these plays cultivate poetically rich and theatrically vivid meditations on the interplay of race, intimacy, and domesticity.

Eisa Davis's Pulitzer Prize-nominated play *Bulrusher* (2006), set in 1955, is a coming-of-age narrative in which the title character, abandoned as a baby and taken in by strangers, navigates a world where she finds herself increasingly outside the mainstream of Boonville, California, the small country town where she was raised. When a black visitor from Alabama arrives in the town, Bulrusher begins to confront the norms and attitudes that she and those in her town take for granted. Through her encounter with this young black woman from the south, Bulrusher comes into a new sexual and racial consciousness. Eventually, she even learns the identity of her mother and father. Bulrusher undergoes her own kind of psychological, intellectual, and emotional homecoming throughout the play – although she never leaves Boonville. Through *Bulrusher*, Davis asks us to consider how we might locate home, its significance in the making of identity, and who constitutes 'family' in the first place: those with whom we are reared or those who accept us without condition or pretense.

Unlike Bulrusher, the protagonist of Christina Anderson's *Good Goods* (2009), Stacey Goods, physically returns to the black south, where he tends to his family's general merchandise store that his father has recently abandoned. Rather than the store's sole employee, Truth, assuming the store's proprietorship, Stacey seizes the reins, setting up a battle between the two men. The play also follows the homecoming of Patricia, who is Stacey's partner in their touring cabaret act and grew up in the same town as him, with her new companion, a runaway bride named Sunny. *Good Goods* uses Stacey and Patricia's return to their childhood homes as the occasion to interrogate the terms of inheritance, filial obligation, and parentage. At the same time, the play traces how much we change outside the environs of those homes and, consequently, differ from those who stayed behind. At first glance a tale of small-town intrigue, *Good Goods* explodes its realistic trappings to explore the philosophical dimensions and mystical contingencies of the home, prompting reconsiderations of the significance of race and individual personhood in domestic, familial, and sexual relationships.

Section II: Post-Blackness by Non-Black Playwrights

The second section of this anthology, 'Post-Blackness by Non-Black Playwrights,' purposefully complicates the question of what constitutes post-black drama by offering two plays that foreground concerns of black identity formation but were not written by African Americans. In the post-black era, an increasing number of non-African American playwrights have created works featuring black characters and exploring issues of blackness. This is not wholly new, however: from the stages of the early national period, to the era of blackface minstrelsy, to the first decades of the twentieth century with writers such as Eugene O'Neill, Dubose Heyward, Ridgely Torrence, and Paul Green, white playwrights and performers defined how blackness signified on the American stage. (A significant element of the black dramaturgical and theatrical enterprise has been to rectify these representations.) Still, what we are suggesting with the plays in this section is that something very different is happening with the post-black. That is, the way in which these non-black playwrights stage blackness speaks to the expansive representational politics of the movement and its conduciveness to the portability and fecundity of blackness. These two works also reflect how post-black drama attempts to trouble black-white binaries and, as a result, complicate what it means to be African American.

With *The Shipment,* Korean American playwright Young Jean Lee admittedly sought to create what she calls a 'black identity politics show.'[40] With a title that conjures images of African human cargo on slave ships, drugs travelling to inner cities, and a rap song by the group The Coup, Lee's highly experimental play presents a confluence of black stereotypes and holds them up for careful examination. The play's exaggerated and stylized representations challenge contemporary meanings of blackness and the audience's expectations. *The Shipment* does not stop there, however: the play's two structurally distinct sections facilitate Lee's examination of what it means to 'act white' and perform race more generally.

Satellites (2006), by Korean American playwright Diana Son, employs a more conventional realism to probe the intersections of race and class. An interracial family composed of an African American husband, Korean American wife, and their baby, has just moved into a previously predominantly black inner-city neighborhood. The personal dynamics of family and childbearing have decidedly political ramifications as the parents confront issues of gentrification, mixed-race identity, and language difference. Son foregrounds the husband and wife's attempt to reconcile their relationship (and that with their newborn daughter) with their struggles over love and intimacy, employment, and familial obligation. Through these private concerns, Son engages broader social categories and contexts – race, class, and culture – that surround her characters and the play.

Section III: Re-Imagining Pasts

The third section brings together works that call attention to the ways in which multiple pasts accumulate and amalgamate to shape black subjectivity in subsequent presents. Specifically, these plays show how the seemingly immaterial of passed acts, actors, and events remain very much material in the making of contemporary racially and sexually diverse identities. While the other plays in this anthology also explore the intersections of race and sexuality, what sets 'Re-Imagining Pasts' apart are the time-bending and space-shifting aesthetics of its plays. They exemplify the formal innovation and historiographical irreverence that marks much of post-black dramaturgy. The historical and logical distortions that the playwrights in this section forge serve to create dramaturgically novel and theatrically generative works that are both epic and contemporary.

In Marcus Gardley's *And Jesus Moonwalks the Mississippi* (2007), the world of the Civil War provides the setting in which Greek myth, talking trees, singing rivers, and a moonwalking Jesus combine to interrogate the politics of sex and the body. By disregarding and distorting sacrosanct narratives and images of Christianity and American history, Gardley pushes us to rethink the lessons and limitations of these institutions vis-à-vis our contemporary moment. His inventive and brazen formal approach not only prompts such re-evaluations, but also frames an affecting story whose essence is one of longing, redemption, and forgiveness.

Likewise, Robert O'Hara's *Antebellum* bridges continents to highlight the intractability of love and the power of desire. Set in 1939, amid the cabarets and concentration camps of prewar Berlin and the plantations of post-Civil War Atlanta, the play uses seemingly unrelated historical events to explore the dynamic interplay of race, sexuality, and religion in the production of identity. *Antebellum* employs a complex yet stirring hodgepodge of dramaturgical techniques, ranging from naturalistic to Brechtian, that evidence the formal complexities and heterodoxy of post-black dramaturgy. Even more than he did in his earlier play *Insurrection: Holding History* (1996), O'Hara seamlessly melds the personal and the political to create a world that, by his own admission, is intimately connected to his own 'relationship to life and to love' but remains expansive and generous enough that his audiences might recognize and learn something about their own.[41] Indeed, the expansive and plural pasts constructed in *Antebellum*, as well as those in *And Jesus Moonwalks the Mississippi*, instantiate the retrospective gestures that post-black playwrights favor as means to account for the now.

Section IV: Re-imagining Africa

The question of how to imagine, summon, and construct a connection to an African past has been one that has captivated black Western artists, scholars, activists, and ordinary people since the landing of the first slave ships in the New World. In the theatrical formations that African Americans have crafted, for instance, Africa has functioned as a romanticized site of origin as well as an aspirational vision of a liberated future. Accordingly, these representations have often said more about African American politics and identities than they have about those of Africa. In the post-black era, the form and function of Africa within American theatrical imagery has become increasingly complex. Post-black playwrights, impacted by the very real and pressing social matters plaguing the African continent, as well as the powerful symbolism of an African American president who is the son of a Kenyan father, probe the ties that bind African and African Americans with far less idealism. They favor, instead, a far grittier look at how the realities of AIDS, ethnic genocide, government corruption, devastating poverty, and global indifference continue to link black diasporic communities.

In the Continuum (2005), by Nikkole Salter and Danai Gurira, provides a minimalist, yet profound exploration of the interconnectedness between the United States and Africa. The play stages the lives of two women who, although continents apart, with one in Zimbabwe and the other in Los Angeles, share the same life-altering event: their respective male partners have infected them with HIV. Through intersecting scenes, *In the Continuum* depicts the particular sociocultural and gender dynamics that these women must endure as they confront the new knowledge of their infections. Even as these women live in distinct sociopolitical and economic environments, they are both 'in the continuum,' attempting to survive and make sense of a world in which everything, and yet nothing, has changed. In innovative and haunting ways, Salter and Gurira show how disease and prejudice know no geographical, class, ethnic, or personal boundaries.

In *Black Diamond* (2007), J. Nicole Brooks interrogates contemporary connections and discontinuities between the Africans in Liberia and African Americans in the United

States. Set in 1999, the play opens in the middle of the second Liberian civil war, which eventually resulted in the overthrow of brutal despot Charles Taylor and his arrest as a war criminal. At issue in this drama is the question of what should be the responsibility of the United States to this war-torn African state racked by genocidal atrocities and human rights violations. After all, Liberia has a unique bond to the United States, beginning in 1827 when former black slaves from the United States attempted to settle Liberia. At the center of her drama, Brooks places an African American journalist sent by the BBC to cover the war story. As Americans and the world turn a seemingly deaf ear toward the suffering in Liberia, this journalist faces his own life-altering questions as to his duty to his profession and his obligation as a black man to this intra-racial conflict. Like the previous play, *Black Diamond* foregrounds questions of women's agency. The title character is the leader of a band of women freedom fighters. Brooks complicates conventional feminist readings to the degree that Black Diamond and her troop are activists who slaughter without conscience in the name of liberation as well as victims of rape and crimes against women. Fast-paced and episodic in structure, *Black Diamond*'s eclectic form also rubs up against convention, assaulting the audience's senses as moments of flashback clash against burlesque enactments, docudrama narrativization, and rap music interludes. The play's structure informs its content. The contrasts and incongruities in style underscore the contradictory cultural politics at play within this catastrophic African struggle. By depicting rebel soldiers that associate their own brutality and swagger with the urban cool of African American hip hop, Brooks' play showcases the complications and ambiguities of black cultural traffic, the flow and, importantly, the friction of black imagery. With its structural hybridity and diverse representations of blackness, *Black Diamond* enacts the post-black.

The eight plays in this volume evidence a wide range of ideological and formal innovations for the American theatre. They suggest that post-black aesthetics and the 'new territory' they detail will be an important and formative contributor to American cultural production in the new millennium. By gathering them within one collection, we hope to provide a critical retort to the assessment theatre critic Ed Siegel of the *Boston Globe* offered in response to August Wilson's passing: 'Mr. Wilson's death leaves a major hole in the American theater.'[42] Whether or not they intended to do so, post-black playwrights are filling that hole and more. Indeed, they have charted new and important directions for (African) American dramaturgy, theatrical production, and performance aesthetics.

Harry J. Elam, Jr. and Douglas A. Jones, Jr.

Notes

1 Michelle Alexander, *The New Jim Crow: Mass Incarceration in the Age of Colorblindness* (New York: The New Press, 2010), 2. Alexander's study of incarceration and the sociopolitical stigmatization of convicted felons is the most compelling account of the contemporary racial caste system in the U.S.
2 Ralph Ellison, 'The Little Man at Chehaw Station,' in *Going to the Territory* (1986; reprint, New York: Vintage, 1995), 28.
3 Thelma Golden, 'Introduction' to *Freestyle* (New York, NY: The Studio Museum in Harlem, 2001), 14.
4 Ibid.
5 See Bertram D. Ashe, 'Theorizing the Post-Soul Aesthetic: An Introduction,' *African American Review* 41.4 (Winter, 2007): 609–23.
6 Kenneth W. Warren, *What Was African American Literature?* (Cambridge: Harvard University Press, 2011), 96.
7 Two of the most insightful and provocative of these works are Baratunde Thurston, *How to Be Black* (New York: Harper), 2012, and Kevin Young, *The Grey Album: On the Blackness of Blackness* (Minneapolis: Graywolf Press, 2012).
8 Eddie S. Glaude, Jr., *In a Shade of Blue: Pragmatism and the Politics of Black America* (Chicago: University of Chicago Press, 2007), 149–50.
9 Holland Cotter, ''Black' Comes in Many Shadings,' Arts and Leisure, *New York Times*, August 13, 2004.
10 Warren, 13.
11 Ibid., 107.
12 Quoted in Hilton Als, 'By the Skin of Our Teeth: Young Jean Lee's Irreverent Take on Racial Politics,' *The New Yorker*, January 26, 2009.
13 This was the approach with *The Shipment*, which she calls her 'black identity-politics play.' Young Jean Lee, Untitled Talk presented at

'"Enabling Violations": Race, Theater, and Experimentation,' Princeton University, 2012.
[14] Carolyn Williams, *Gilbert and Sullivan: Gender, Genre, Parody* (New York: Columbia University Press, 2011), 9.
[15] Thurston, 4–8.
[16] Ibid., 10.
[17] Williams, 9.
[18] See Warren, 42–3.
[19] Evie Shockley, 'duck, duck, redux,' in *the new black* (Middletown: Wesleyan University Press, 2011), 58.
[20] See Bertram D. Ashe et. al, 'These – Are – The "Breaks": A Roundtable Discussion on Teaching the Post-Soul Aesthetic,' *African American Review* 41.4 (Winter, 2007): 787–90.
[21] Ashe, 614.
[22] Mary Schmidt Campbell, 'African American Art in a Post-Black Era,' *Women & Performance: a journal of feminist theory*, 17.3 (November 2007): 319.
[23] Kori Newkirk, quoted in Jori Finkel, 'A Reluctant Fraternity, Thinking Post-Black,' *New York Times*, June, 10 2007.
[24] George C. Wolfe, quoted in Jeremy Gerard, '"Colored Museum" Is Author's Exorcism,' *New York Times*, November, 6 1986.
[25] For a representative example of this literature, see Debra J. Dickerson, *The End of Blackness: Returning the Souls of Black Folk to Their Rightful Owners* (New York: Pantheon Books, 2004).
[26] Michele Elam, *The Souls of Mixed Folk* (Palo Alto: Stanford University Press, 2011), 21.
[27] Suzan-Lori Parks, 'New black math,' *Theatre Journal*, 57.4 (December 2005): 576.
[28] W.E.B. DuBois, 'Krigwa Little Theatre Movement,' *Crisis* , XXXII (July 1926):135.
[29] August Wilson, *The Ground on Which I Stand* (New York TCG Press, 1996 2001), 40.
[30] Harold Cruse, 'The Integrationist Ethic as a Basis for Scholarly Endeavors,' 12.
[31] Charles Dutton quoted by Patrick Healey, 'A Director's Race Adds to the Drama for August Wilson Revival,' *New York Times*, (April 23, 2009): A18.
[32] While attending a 2010 workshop at Penumbra Theatre in Minneapolis, Minnesota, one of the oldest black theatres in the United States, Yale-trained playwright Marcus Gardley remarked to Dominic Taylor, Penumbra's Associate Artistic Director, that this was the first time he had ever participated in a play development workshop where the participants were predominantly black. Dominic Taylor, Interview with Harry J. Elam, Jr., Minneapolis, Minnesota, 2012.
[33] See Harry J. Elam, Jr., 'Black Theatre in the Age of Obama,' in Harvey Young, editor, *The Cambridge Companion to African American Theatre* (Cambridge: Cambridge University Press, 2012).

[34] Barack Obama quoted by Jann S. Wenner, 'Ready for the Fight: *Rolling Stone* interview with Barack Obama (April 25, 2012).
[35] Young Jean Lee, quoted in Patrick Healy, 'An Evening in Black and White from a Playwright who is Neither,' *New York Times*, January 28, 2009.
[36] This is not to say, however, that writers and artists have never satirized, burlesqued, or ironized horrors committed against African Americans. What distinguishes those works and the thematically and stylistically related ones produced in our contemporary moment is not only the historical and experiential distance, or lack thereof, between artist and event, but also signal differences in approach, production, audience, and intention. See Glenda Carpio, *Laughing Fit to Kill: Black Humor In the Fictions of Slavery* (Oxford: Oxford University Press, 2008).
[37] Christina Anderson, 'In Rehearsal with Christina Anderson and Tina Landau at Yale Rep' Interview with Tina Landau. New Haven: Yale Repertory Theatre, 2012.
[38] Suzan-Lori Parks, 'An Equation for Black People Onstage,' in *The America Play and Other Works* (New York: Theatre Communications Group Press, 1995), 21.
[39] Una Chadhuri, *Staging Place: The Geography of Modern Drama* (Ann Arbor: University of Michigan Press, 1995), 6.
[40] Young Jean Lee quoted by Charles Isherwood, 'Off-Center Refractions of African American Worlds,' *New York Times* (January 13, 2009): C1.
[41] Robert O'Hara, quoted in Michael O'Sullivan, '*Antebellum* at Woolly Mammoth Theatre,' *Washington Post*, March 27, 2009.
[42] Ed Siegel, 'Playwright August Wilson Dies at 60,' *Boston Globe*, October 3, 2005.

strong argument concerning the signif-icance of the play's title

Section I
The New Black Family

Eisa Davis

Bulrusher

Bulrusher was first developed in readings at New Dramatists directed by the author and, later, by Seret Scott. Subsequent readings were hosted by The Cherry Lane (directed by Leah C. Gardiner), Hartford Stage (directed by Kate Whoriskey), Musefire (directed by Lorraine Robinson), and San Francisco Stage and Film (directed by Mark Routhier). Portland Center Stage workshopped the play in its JAW/West Festival, where it was directed by Valerie Curtis-Newton, with dramaturgy by Mead Hunter.

In March 2006, *Bulrusher* received its world premiere at Urban Stages/Playwrights' Preview Productions in New York (Frances Hill, Artistic Director; Sonia Koslova, Managing Director; Lori Ann Laster, Program Director; Stanton Wood, Development Director). It was directed by Leah C. Gardiner.

Cast

In order of appearance

Bulrusher	*Zabryna Guevara/Donna Duplantier*
Madame	*Charlotte Colavin*
Logger	*Guiesseppe Jones*
Schoolch	*Peter Bradbury/Darrill Rosen*
Boy	*Robert Beitzel*
Vera	*Tinashe Kajese*

Scenic Design and Video/Projection Design Dustin O'Neill
Lighting Design Sarah Sidman
Costume Design Kimberly Ann Glennon
Sound Design Jill BC DuBoff
Original Songs Composed by Eisa Davis
Original Score Composed and Performed by Daniel T. Denver
Additional Guitar Music by Robert Beitzel
Choreography Jennifer Harrison Newman
Fight Choreography Denise Hurd
Stage Management and Board Op Jana Llynn, Leisah Swenson, Sonia Koslova, Holly M. Kirk
Assistant Stage Manager Stephen Riscica
Assistant Director Ronald Francis Brescio

Characters

Bulrusher
Madame
Logger
Schoolch
Boy
Vera

Setting

Boonville, California, a small town in the Anderson Valley of Mendocino County, north of San Francisco, 1955. The set can be realistic, suggestive, or a combination of both. Water, live guitar, real oranges and apples are necessary.

Notes

Actual Boonville residents developed their own dialect of over 1,300 words and phrases at the turn of the last century. The language, called Boontling, was primarily devised to discuss taboo subjects and keep outsiders out. But Boontling also functioned to document town history, create unexpected value from the strange, and satisfy the residents' overriding love of inventive talk.

The characters imagined here do not have a contemporary self-consciousness. They speak with energy and assuredness, in the rhythms of the self-made.

Act One

In the dark, the sound of dripping water – leaky faucet into a steel washtub. Then, a spot on Bulrusher, entirely wet, looking up into the sky. She wears a green dress. She talks to the river, reciting her first memory.

Bulrusher I float in a basket toward the Pacific, hands
blue as huckleberries. This air is too sweet,
this cold water a thin, foul milk.

The woman who bore me wrapped me,
gave me to the green of the Navarro,
named me silence. She prays

this river has studied time
and will never turn back
her secret skin, the mark

that stretched into life.
Forgiveness is an insect
that may one day draw my blood.

Catch me, I ask the power lines,
defying the fog's quiet shroud. What is
a motherless daughter but pure will?

The river hears me and turns to molasses.
With a sharp bank through high shams,
I am born into a new language.

More drops falling quickly, becoming gradually slower as lights darken.

Madame It's gonna happen.

Lights up on the back parlor of a brothel. **Madame, Logger**, *and* **Schoolch** *are in the parlor.* **Madame** *wears a crucifix.* **Schoolch** *drinks tea. It is the Fourth of July.*

Logger Oh you're just sayin that.

Madame I'm gonna leave here, I tell you.

Logger Say that every summer.

Madame I mean it too.

Logger What about your business? What about alla us?

Madame Come the Apple Show, I'll stay through the prize giving and then I'm a leave.

Logger Not even stayin for the dance? You love the dance.

Madame It don't love me. End up hobbin by myself cause no one's got the beans to say they know me. You, you don't come and Schoolch dance too fancy. What's for me.

Logger The music. They hire that band from Frisk to show all the Boont tunesters how it's done.

Madame You never even been to the Apple Show dance!

Logger I heard it's nice.

Madame From me! I'm the one told you it's nice. But I can't stay out my years here, Apple Show dance or not. Feel rain comin?

Logger Can't smell it.

Madame We'll ask Bulrusher when she get here what the river say.

Logger I want me sweet Michelle today.

Madame Sweet Michelle is flattened with the influenzy.

Logger Then young Elinor.

Madame She don't like you.

Logger You don't like me with her 'cause she do like me.

Madame Elinor ain't the only one.

Logger Well I asked for sweet Michelle. Who else you got? Cory?

Madame Her flag's out. She ain't workin today.

Logger You call yourself a businesswoman? Never give me what I want 'cause you like to see me scramble. You like watchin the screw turn.

Madame Lucky I let you in here at all. You could have to go all the way into Ukiah for your geechin.

Logger Who left?

Madame Well. I suppose I could let you burlap Reina.

Logger That Mexican gal. She so set in her ways. I like to experiment, move things around some. Don't like it the same way all the time.

Madame We make the rules around here. Do it the way we like or you can go to Ukiah.

Logger I ain't got the gas.

Madame Then take it here the way we say! And you know you only get bahl girls here. Everybody says it and we know it's true. We are the best, because we do it our own way. You don't got no stringy hair and wrinkle socks here. If you want some low quality diseased moldunes head up the pike and cool off in the oaks. But we are the softest madges you goin to find. So is it the Spanish moss or my witch's butter?

Logger I'm tryin to enjoy myself. I'm tryin to buy me some heel scratchin. I got money and you got girls, so why you got to rout me each time?

Madame So you'll appreciate what you're gettin. Reina's up front with the rest of the girls; let me tell her you want her.

Logger I never said I wanted her.

Madame You didn't have to. She's the quiet one, don't harp much at all. And I can see you ain't in the mood for any more talkin.

Logger That's earth. You sure sulled me.

Madame Get your money together. You're payin up front today.

Logger Aw girl –

Madame No more credit for you. Can't have you old dehigged jackers tryin to dish me. Makes me can-kicky.

She exits.

Logger When we gon get you a girl up there Schoolch?

Schoolch *is silent, but* **Logger** *converses with him anyway, waiting for his responses in the pauses below.*

Logger Let go a that teacher's English, talk a little how we talk. Harp the ling, and you can take one of these women for a ride. (*Pause.*) No? Well it's a shame you won't cause they all love it. (*Pause.*) You seein' the fireworks later? Nice out in the buzzchick field. Open view. (*Pause.*) You got any kids goin on to high school in the fall? I thought goin on to the upper school would be real special with all the readin of books and poetry; get you some right romantic material. Only finished middle school myself but my daddy was awful proud. He ain't had but a little education so I read the Dunbar and Wheatley to him at night.

Schoolch *looks quizzical.*

Logger Negro poets. Colored. Bookers who could write poems. (**Schoolch** *is unconvinced.*) They did. A whole bunch of em. Long poems too.

As **Madame** *re-enters:*

Madame Reina's in her room.

Logger (*continuing, to* **Schoolch**) I feel poetical all the time 'cause I keep they verses in my head. (*To* **Madame**.) When you gonna get Schoolch in with one of your girls? He can't be a silent seeker all his life.

Madame He won't sleep with none of them, says he's waiting for me. I just think he's scared to roll somebody he taught long division to. Time to pay up now, Lucas.

Logger (*to* **Madame**) You ever heard of the colored poets they had in slavery days and right after?

Madame It's ten dollars. Don't try to shike me.

Logger Wait now, ten dollars? I just got a phone line put in, so I'm watchin my budget. How much a that do I get to keep?

Madame Pardon?

Logger Ten dollars ain't what I pay. Now I spect some change.

Madame I only gave you a break way back when you were goin with me. You go with her, your same money got two mouths to feed.

Logger You always got two mouths and both of em always wide open.

Madame Listen booker tee, ain't no call for that sorta nonch harpin. You can step right out and get your Fourth of Jeel jollies rubbin up gainst some tree.

Logger Hold up, you love my nonch harpin.

Madame Only when I'm working.

Logger Then what you doin right now?

Madame Tryin to get you to give me my ten dollars.

Logger Oh girl, you ain't gonna leave this town.

Bulrusher *enters.*

Bulrusher Evenin Schoolch. Madame. Mr Jeans.

Logger Evenin. (*To* **Madame**.) Take your ten then. I need me a fresh smellin girl right now, fresh as a sprig of mint.

Madame We don't serve any other kind.

Logger *throws down a ten and heads up the stairs.*

Madame Don't tell me, Schoolch, I already know, don't let no booker tee backtalk me. I know that's what you gonna say. He may not be as single-minded as you, but he's a man all the same, ain't no second class citizen. Don't tell me otherwise not on no Fourth of Jeel. What the river say today Bulrusher?

Bulrusher Clear through midday tomorrow, some mornin fog. Then a storm tomorrow evenin.

Madame Rain? Now? Well that does my garden no good. All the rows I planted are already dead from heat.

Bulrusher Your ground cover and wildflowers should take to it. This kinda rain, they'll grow right over the bald patches.

Madame That river tells you everything, don't it. Schoolch, do you realize how much money you have lost over the last eighteen years letting this girl keep her future readin skills to herself? No excuse, just plain bad business. You raised her and won't let her pay you back. And you're not even religious! You don't even go to church! This is the only place you come to with any regularity besides the schoolhouse. You come here, don't even sleep with the beautiful whores I got workin here, you just come and sit and drink tea with the madame of them all. You ain't a Christian, and you ain't a good businessman. Just a waste. And the real shame is that you never get your sexual release. It ain't nothin like tea-drinkin, I tell you.

Bulrusher Supper's in the oven, Schoolch. I done ate so you go head on, I'll see you back at the house.

Schoolch *looks at* **Bulrusher**.

Bulrusher I'm just gon sit out a while, keep the sunset in view.

Schoolch *exits.*

Madame You still know how to tell people's futures?

Bulrusher I haven't for some time.

Madame I suppose everyone in this town asked you to read their bathwater by now. No fortunes left to tell.

Bulrusher I've never read your water.

Madame And that's how it'll stay.

Bulrusher Yes'm.

Sounds of lovemaking from upstairs.

Madame Alright, time to set yourself spinnin.

Bulrusher Alright then.

Bulrusher *exits and lights change. She sits, looking into the sunset.*

Boy *enters. He looks at* **Bulrusher**, *then looks away. She opens a book.*

Boy Well we can't just sit here and not say nothin.

Bulrusher I'm readin.

Boy No you're not, you're ignorin me.

Bulrusher Just 'cause it's the Fourth of July don't mean we gotta talk.

He is quiet for a moment, then flares.

Boy I'm done with women! They don't tell you what they mean! Hide the truth of they feelins, sweeten it up with rosewater perfume, then just outta nowhere, plop. Splat. You are thrown over and no land for miles.

Bulrusher You didn't care about her no way.

Boy What do you know?

Bulrusher She knew things weren't goin nowhere with you and took the words outta your mouth.

Boy You know who I'm talkin about?

Bulrusher You was goin with the McGimsey girl.

Boy She said somethin bout me to you?

Bulrusher You know nobody talk to me.

Boy You did some a your fortune tellin on me, that's how you know?

Bulrusher I ain't never touched your water. I just used my eyes.

Boy Ain't got no one to go to the fireworks with tonight. Out here talkin to you instead.

Bulrusher I told you, we ain't gotta talk. (*Pause.*) You ain't never talked to me before.

Boy No one talk to you 'cause all you got is hard truth for people. If you was nice and not cocked darley all the time you might have you a pal.

Bulrusher Don't need no pal. Got the river.

Boy Well I like bein stuck on someone, I don't care how unnatural *you* are.

Bulrusher Let's make this our first and last conversation.

Boy *looks at her and smiles.*

Boy You're gonna be my new girlfriend.

He exits. Fireworks.

Bulrusher *slams the book closed and talks to the river.*

Bulrusher They want to know who I am.
I don't. I want to swing, swing
over the scrub pine, the hens.

They want me to lend them my eyes.
I won't. I want to snake like ice grass,
thick as a future I can't see.

But at five, I knew it all,
I read it in their bathwater;
I met them in front of the general store.

I want to swing, swing
over the scrub pine, the poppies: be a meteor,
a perfume, love the fly on my tongue.

Next morning. **Schoolch***'s house.*

Bulrusher I packed a lemon for you to bring over to Madame, for tea. It's in your lunch basket.

Schoolch *is silent.*

Bulrusher Heard the Gschwends say Darlin ain't gonna make it to the library to help you today. He almost lost a thumb launchin rockets in the field last night.

Schoolch *is silent.*

Bulrusher Have a good day now.

Schoolch *picks up his books and basket, exits.*

Bulrusher *plays with his water glass. Is about to put her fingers into it, then tosses the water out the window. She steps out onto the porch.*

Boy *is stumbling down the road, hung over, trying to keep the sun out of his face. He gets to her porch and sinks onto it to rest. He doesn't acknowledge her as she looks at him a spell. Then she walks to the pump and pumps some water into a bowl. She sets it by him on the step.*

Boy *splashes water onto his face, drinks some, then plays in it, slapping it like a baby.* **Bulrusher** *sits on her chair.*

Boy Where'd you get that moshe?

Bulrusher I ain't talkin to you.

Boy Your truck. Where'd you get it. Where'd you get it?

Bulrusher While back I got it.

Boy I want me a truck. Always hitchin a ride to see my ma in Mendocino – I want me a truck a my own.

Bulrusher Yeah, well.

Boy You got one. I can do as good as you, or better. Get me a new one. Goddamn I need a cigarette. You got a cigarette?

Bulrusher You want a cigarette?

Boy Yeah.

Bulrusher They're inside the house.

Boy Wait. I forgot. You my new girlfriend. I gotta be nice. I pretty please pretty face need a pretty cigarette. Please.

Bulrusher I'm getting em anyway. I'm headed into Cloverdale, pick up my oranges.

She goes in, but peeks out at him through the window.

Boy (*sings*) Thorn, spine and thistle
Bramble, pennywhistle
Poisoned flowers on a vine

Sticky cockleburrs and pine
Sap that's sweet but never kind
Stuck like so much gristle.

Calls to her.

I made that one up. What kinda perfume you use?

Bulrusher (*off*) I don't.

Boy There's a smell I smell when I come near ya.

She comes back onto porch. She has no cigarettes.

Bulrusher Orange rind.

Boy No, sweeter.

Bulrusher Algae.

Boy Come on now, say something pretty.

Bulrusher Fresh out.

Boy No pretty words and no cigs? Well. Just looking at you smokes me.

Bulrusher Be seein ya.

Boy Every Monday you head into Cloverdale. Pick up your oranges, sell em to the town. You must make you a lot of money. What you do with it?

Bulrusher Well I ain't givin none to you. I'll be gettin on the road.

Boy The pike!

Bulrusher *Road.*

Boy *Pike.* You harp the ling, maybe people would like you.

Bulrusher They buy my oranges. That's enough.

Boy Schoolch won't let you talk the way we all talk, huh.

Bulrusher Don't need to.

Boy You can't find out anything bout anyone in this town if you don't harp the ling. Like last night. I found out why that McGimsey girl went mossy on me – she's been bilchin Tom Soo, and his ma is Chinese! That ain't so bad, but Tom Soo? Tom Soo from *Philo*? She ain't had a taste for any tarp but boarch, so I'm glad she got ink-standy with me. Can't have no applehead ruinin my track record, sunderin my reputation. I'm a standin man.

Bulrusher I reckon.

Boy I ain't afraid a talkin to you. Hey, I just splashed in this bowl a water.

Bulrusher Yeah.

Boy Means my fortune's in it. You could stick your fingers in there and tell what's gon happen to me. What's my life gonna feel like? What's it gonna feel like when I touch you?

He reaches for her arm. She lets him touch her, then pulls away.

Bulrusher I only tell the weather now. Ain't read nobody's bathwater in years. After the May Bloyd incident.

Boy It was you brought that on May Bloyd?

Bulrusher I just told her it was coming.

Boy And you never read nobody since.

Bulrusher Sometimes I get a little taste by accident. Like in the general store and one of the twins hand me a coke got beads of water on the bottle.

Boy Con-den-sa-tion is the proper name.

Bulrusher Con-des-cen-sion, I'll try to remember that.

Boy So you're smart too.

Bulrusher Don't try to school the schoolteacher's girl.

Boy You're so smart, you oughta tell fortunes again. Get you a booth at the Apple Show.

Bulrusher I said I ain't done it in years.

Boy So you can't do it anymore.

Bulrusher I'm at the peak of my perception! I can call rain a whole week off from it coming down. I'm the best I ever been.

Boy And keepin it all to yourself. People come from all over the county for the Apple Show. You could make a name with folks you never even met. You need you a manager, to publicize all your ventures. You could really make a killing.

Bulrusher For what?

Boy I don't know. Why you think you got that power in the first place?

Bulrusher *starts to go.*

Boy Look, you could just tell my fortune then.

Bulrusher I ain't putting my fingers in there. Or your bathwater.

Boy What about spit? That's water, right? If you just kiss me you'll know everything there is to know.

Bulrusher One of your friends put you up to this? You messin with me just 'cause everyone thinks you're cute? Just 'cause you can?

Boy Tiger lily, manzanita, you're my girlfriend. (*Sings.*) Oh my girl –

Bulrusher If I'm your girlfriend, prove it. Give me something.

Boy I ain't got much to offer a girl except my sensuality. We could take a walk through Fern Canyon, watch the salmon run –

Bulrusher It's summertime, ain't no salmon running the river.

Boy There's always trout. Steelhead trout.

Bulrusher Take me somewhere where there's people and put your arm around me. Take me to the Anyhow.

Boy The Anyhow Saloon? I just came from there.

Bulrusher And I'm leavin here.

Bulrusher *opens the door to her truck and slams it.*

Boy Bulrusher, be my fortune.

Boy *dumps the bowl of water on his head.*

(*Sings.*) Oh my girl, with the cattail curls, be mine, be mine, all mine.

Rain. **Bulrusher***'s truck is now filled with oranges. She sees a girl walking.*

Bulrusher Hey.

Vera Hey.

Bulrusher You want a lift?

Vera 'Preciate it.

Vera *gets into the truck with her suitcase, exhausted and soaking wet. She has covered her head in newspaper. When they see each other's faces, they are instantly struck but try to maintain their ease.*

Bulrusher You walked all the way from Cloverdale in this storm?

Vera I didn't know what else to do. Gone so long without sleep can't tell night from day, rain from dry. I come all the way from Alabama on a Jim Crow train.

Bulrusher Is that a new model?

Vera Afraid not. You never heard a Jim Crow?

Bulrusher Separately, but not together. Where you going to?

Vera (*removes newspaper*) Some tiny town where my uncle live.

Bulrusher Got his name? I know everybody round here.

Vera Don't care what name he answer to long as he give me a place to lay my head. Conductor wouldn't give me a berth for nothing. Southern route.

Bulrusher Why not?

Vera If you don't know the answer to that I am pleased to meet you.

Bulrusher We'll find him. Where in Alabama you from?

Vera Birmingham. The Magic City.

Bulrusher What's there?

Vera Church. Iron ore. And a Vulcan that forges everything with fire.

Bulrusher You like it there?

Vera Can't stand it and I can't stand rain. Guess I'm outta luck.

Bulrusher It'll stop tomorrow morning.

Vera Hope so, I gotta find me some work in a jiffy. (*Realizes.*) How do you know the rain'll stop?

Bulrusher The river told me.

Vera Huh. (*She takes this in.*) My name's Vera Blass.

Bulrusher Bulrusher.

Vera What's your family name.

Bulrusher Ain't got family.

Vera Dead?

Bulrusher Don't know. Was born somewhere far from where I live. And my mother tried to drown me when I got born, but I guess I wasn't ready to go.

Vera She changed her mind?

Bulrusher No. She sent me down the Navarro River but someone found me in the weeds. The bulrushes.

Vera Like Moses.

Bulrusher No. Like me.

Vera You can have *my* mother if you want – she's too concerned with being a model Negro citizen to drown anyone. (*Yawns.*) Forgive me, I can barely keep my eyes open. You in school?

Bulrusher Naw. But I like books. Got learnt at home.

Vera What are all these oranges for?

Bulrusher Sellin.

Vera So there's a street got colored merchants here? 'Cause I am howlin hungry. Ain't had a thing to eat since Texas. Would love a plate of fried fish and biscuits, cornbread and greens, ooh. (*Looks into sideview mirror.*) Look at my hair, oh Lord! I can't meet no one like this. Wrong as a wet cat. Why didn't you tell me?

Bulrusher You look beautiful to me.

Vera Really.

Bulrusher Yeah.

Silence.

Vera What kind of beauty shops in your town?

Bulrusher Mazie does hair.

Vera Our kind of hair?

Bulrusher No. I do my own.

Vera Looks . . . nice. But ain't no colored women to do it for you?

Bulrusher I'm the only one.

Vera (*panicking*) What? My uncle live in a all-white town?

Bulrusher He look like you?

Vera I don't know. I just know he's colored.

Bulrusher A logger lives downriver from the general store, maybe he's the one you mean.

Vera He's the only Negro besides you?

Bulrusher Yeah. What's wrong? (**Vera** *is silent.*) Well how bout some Indians? We just passed the reservation. (**Vera** *is silent.*) If you hungry, I got an orange –

Vera (*suddenly*) Let me out.

Bulrusher We're almost to Boonville.

Vera Please.

Bulrusher You gotta find your uncle.

Vera Let me out.

Bulrusher You can't walk back.

Vera Don't tell me what I can't do.

Bulrusher Let's at least get you fed and dry.

Vera I can take care of myself –

Bulrusher I can ride you back to the train station in the morning when the rain clears. Just get some rest tonight.

Vera *is silent. She leans her head back on the seat and closes her eyes. They ride.*

Bulrusher Alabama, huh. So is the dirt really red there?

Vera Yeah.

Silence.

Bulrusher That must be confusing to all the honeybees. You got bees right?

Vera Mm hm.

Silence.

Bulrusher 'Cause you know they like red. Huh. Red dirt. You come from a place where the dirt looks like flowers?

No response from **Vera**. **Bulrusher** *turns to look at her* – **Vera** *is asleep.* **Bulrusher** *talks to the river, rapt. The storm rages.*

Bulrusher Newspaper over
her head with the ink
just about run off.

In this dark light, I see her,
and build a pedestal
of water. She is the one,

the only one, nothing is caught
between us but my throat.
I want to say this

is a dream but it is true.
Do I know her? Is she the wet sight
of home?

The brothel. **Madame, Logger, Schoolch**.

Logger (*to* **Madame**) I'll get Tuttle's tree up for you, but not tonight. It's a roger out there and I'm gittin back to my mink. This Michelle gives me the fiddlers! (*Calls up the stairs.*) Michelle, I'm comin to put in on you! Yes, I'm ready for my ricky chow!

Logger *heads up the stairs.*

Madame His tree just fell on *my* property. And Tuttle has the nerve to say it is *my* responsibility to lift that log up. Isn't my tree, it's *his* tree – and I try my best to be patient – but the last time one of his trees fell in my yard, he left it layin there for three whole months! I had to plant my flower garden around it. What sort of look is that? I try to build a little civilization here, I try. But people don't have the work ethic I do, they don't understand that adherin to standards of behavior and so forth is fortifyin to the morals. And I got morals. Keep the whole of my brothel with its eye on discipline. If you don't have that, you don't have nothing divine in your life. If you can't get up regular as the sun each day, no matter what sort of cloud is cloudin ya, you ain't fit to meet God. And I'm a meet him. God will be my final savior and I will be comforted, and it won't be because I chose to give my body over to the menfolk, it won't be because I'm a businesswoman like Mary Magdalene – and Jesus *loved* her – but because I am disciplined and godlike in my approach to all things. I have nothing if not that foundation to stand upon. And so I will be revealed. And still you judge me. What can I do to make you happy, Schoolch? How is it I can do right by God but never can do right by you? I gotta find a way to sell this place and leave this town for good. I have to see my mother's grave again. I gotta smell the grass growin there.

She goes to the window.

Bulrush here with somebody. Ooh, but it is pearlin out there.

Schoolch *looks as if he is getting ready to say something.* **Vera** *and* **Bulrusher** *enter.*

Bulrusher Evenin Schoolch, Madame.

Madame Evenin. Who's this now?

Bulrusher This Vera. She's looking for a relative of hers.

Madame Is it a man relative?

Bulrusher Uh huh.

Madame He ain't here.

Bulrusher What about the logger Mr Jeans? If he ain't the man, he might know him.

Madame (*to* **Vera**) Where you from?

Vera Well, it's a little browner than here.

Madame Is it.

Vera I'm from Alabam. We lost the war.

Madame We try to forget about that stuff round here. You'll get used to it.

Sounds of **Logger** *and* **Michelle***'s lovemaking.*

Madame Well you can't stay here. No offense darlin, but I don't take in no strays.

Bulrusher Schoolch, you go on home and eat – I'll make sure she's got a place to stay for the night.

Vera It's alright.

Bulrusher If we can't find the logger you can have my bed.

Schoolch *looks at Bulrusher.*

Bulrusher It's my room. If she hasn't got a place to stay, I'm giving her my room.

Schoolch *looks.*

Bulrusher I'm eighteen now Schoolch, I got majority.

Schoolch *exits.*

Madame Ooh, he's upset. Well, let me call out to the logger's house then. It *is* late, you know. He most likely ain't in.

Vera You don't have to call him. I'll find him on my own.

Madame It's raining child. The phone is drier and has a little less pride.

Vera *goes out and sits on the porch.*

Bulrusher (*calling to her*) Sit under the awning so you don't get wet.

Madame (*to herself*) I'll be. Another piece of cut cabbage in this town. (*To* **Bulrusher**.) Tell her to stand on the side. Don't want her affiliated with my business.

Madame *picks up the phone, pretends to dial, harried.*

Bulrusher You got any fried fish or biscuits, cornbread or greens?

Madame There's a plate a biscuits in the kitchen. None a that other stuff. What's it for? You can't eat my food for free now.

Bulrusher It's for Vera. I'll get it.

Madame The butter and preserves are in crocks by the icebox. But don't mess up the place now, and don't get any crumbs on the counter!

Sounds of ceramic bumping around.

Madame Don't doll around in there I said! Slice a ham in the box if you want it – but put the lid back on the container, don't let it go bad. (*Pretending to 'end' her phone call.*) Well I just rang the logger and he ain't home. You all might want to hit that hotel.

Bulrusher *comes back out with a plate for* **Vera**.

Bulrusher (*calling to* **Vera**) I got some biscuits and ham for you Vera if you want to step in and have it at the table.

Madame No, you better wrap that gorm up and walk down to the hotel now; it's getting on into the night, wanna make sure she can get a room without any fuss. It's really not good for my business havin you two round here on a rainy night like this.

Bulrusher Vera, don't bother bout comin inside, I'm headed out there.

Madame That's right, use that common sense.

Logger *enters from a room upstairs. He wears only a woman's Chinese silk robe.* **Bulrusher** *sees him and stops.*

Logger Heard some talk about biscuits –

Madame Oh limpin Jesus –

Logger – and had to get right up out of that bed and see what you was hiding from me. You know geechin gets me scottied. Better give me some of those flories so I can go another round with Michelle –

Madame I just called you.

Logger No you didn't, I didn't hear you say my name. Did you holler up to me, say, Lucas, come on down, I need you?

Bulrusher She called you on the phone. Called your house.

Logger (*proud*) Yeah, I just got me a telephone. (*To* **Madame**.) But you knew I was here.

Bulrusher She did, huh.

Logger Yeah. What you want me for? (*Takes a biscuit from* **Bulrusher**.) Think I'll have this biscuit right here.

Bulrusher I got a person for you to meet. Vera! Come inside and meet a Negro.

Logger I always say colored. That other one's too easy to mispronounce.

Vera *comes inside*.

Bulrusher This Vera.

Madame She just came to town. I didn't want to disturb you.

Vera Your name is Lucas?

Logger Yes ma'am. Lucas Jeans.

Vera I'm Ina's daughter Vera.

Logger You Vera? (*Exuberant.*) Oh my goodness. Let me get my pants on. I didn't know you were coming here. Just let me splash a little water on and cleanse myself –

He runs upstairs. **Vera, Bulrusher**, *and* **Madame** *stand in silence as he fumbles around, noisily picking up his clothes. He runs down the stairs, still dressing, and hugs* **Vera**.

Logger You look like Ina round the eyes, but you shaped different. I ain't seen your mother since we was kids. She here with you?

Vera No, I'm by myself.

Logger How is she?

Vera She's doin her best.

Logger And did your daddy keep his job as a porter on the railroad?

Vera He's at the steel mill now.

Logger Well, you can only go so long bowing and scraping for people before it breaks your manhood, that's just how it is. I wish I'd a known you were comin.

Vera Didn't my mother send you a telegram?

Logger Huh. Reckon she sent it to the sawmill. It's closed now, logging days are done. I just do odd jobs now, pickin apples and hops, herdin sheep and trainin horses. But Lord you just in, you don't need to hear all this. Let's get you some food and into a warm bed.

Vera Thank you.

Logger You already grown, land's end. Why don't I drive you back over to my region. Make a pallet for myself and you can have the ticking and boxspring, alright? You got your things, suitcase somewhere?

Vera In Bulrusher's truck.

Logger You got Vera from the station?

Bulrusher Saw her walking the road and gave her a lift.

Logger My goodness, but that was Christian. I won't forget that, girl. Thank you for your trouble.

Bulrusher Alright. (*To* **Vera**.) Here's the food if you still want it.

Logger (*to* **Madame**) Let me give you toobs for it.

Bulrusher No, I got it. Here's a quarter.

Madame Let Lucas pay. He owes me a belhoon for leavin early anyway.

Logger You always trying to rooje me.

Madame You woulda spent at least that much on horn and chiggle if'n you kept your normal hours.

Logger You ain't got one straw of kindness in that heart of hay do ya? I just want a tidrey of love. Just a tidrey.

He throws a dollar on the pool table and leaves with **Vera**. **Bulrusher** *walks out with them.*

Logger Vera, that woman ain't representative. Got a lot of honest two handed folks around here, they'll be happy to meetcha. Thanks again Bulrusher. You done a bahl thing. (*To* **Vera**.) You know I was the one told Bulrusher she was colored. She was five and didn't even know. My moshe is over here, I'll jape you home.

Vera I don't know what that means.

Logger You don't have to. Just another part of the scenery.

He takes her bag to his car.

Bulrusher If you need anything.

Vera How bout an orange.

Bulrusher *throws her one.*

Bulrusher You gonna stay?

Vera *waves goodbye.* **Bulrusher** *stands and watches her go in the rain. Suddenly she realizes how wet she is and smiles. Heads inside.*

Madame Don't track mud in here, you're all wet.

Bulrusher You lied on the night of the only rain of the summer. The logger was here all the time.

Madame It's a habit Bulrusher. Think I would jenny on a customer that's got a woman asking for him? Woulda lost this madge house long ago if I was that tuddish. If you going to be a businesswoman – and I see you are enterprising with them oranges – you gotta be wise. Think on both sides of your head. Don't be afraid of anything anyone can ever say to you.

Bulrusher You woulda had us over to the hotel wasting good money on a room when he was here all the time.

Madame I woulda told him soon as you were out the door. He'd a come and found you – and didn't he? Find you? Don't judge me for what never happened.

Bulrusher I don't like to argue with Schoolch.

Madame When has he ever stayed mad with you? He can see what's going on.

Bulrusher What.

Madame You ain't never had a – a friend. You ain't never had somebody you can see yourself in.

Bulrusher I ain't like other folks, don't need no friends. I was born to read. Born to read water.

Madame Go see Schoolch before he goes to sleep. He'll steam you but you can take it.

Bulrusher I need a beer first.

Bulrusher *exits.*

Madame You left crumbs on my pool table.

Bulrusher *enters* **Schoolch***'s house. She is tipsy. Moves around the kitchen, soaking some beans. Distracted, she knocks over a bowl and it breaks.* **Schoolch** *comes down the stairs.*

Schoolch You'll replace that with your orange money.

Bulrusher Yes sir.

Schoolch Careless. But you eighteen! Got your majority! Telling me how old you are. I know how old you are. You are alive because of me.

Bulrusher Yes sir.

Schoolch You broke that on purpose to make your point?

Bulrusher No sir.

Schoolch Well you must want an ear settin after all the backtalk you gave me tonight. In front of a stranger at that.

Bulrusher No sir.

Schoolch Then what's all this somersettin for? I never expected to see you acting like this.

Bulrusher Yes sir.

Schoolch Like all the other children when their comb's gittin red. I thought I trained you so you'd never jump track on me.

Bulrusher I've been good. I done everything you said. I stopped readin water and tellin fortunes, did all my lessons here at home so I wouldn't be 'taminated by the children at the school. I don't harp the ling with anybody and I save up all my money steada spendin it in Cloverdale or Fort Bragg. All I do is show my 'preciation.

Schoolch More backtalk? My house, my rules. Break them, and you can leave here. But you won't. How many times do I have to tell you? When you were a baby, when you were just a few days old, your mama sent you down the river, sent you floating down to the brine. Wanted nothing to do with you. But you got yourself caught in some weeds and the Negro Jeans found you, brought you to the brothel tied up in his suede duster. Put you on the pool table and there you were, kicking up the smoky air. You didn't blink or cry under that hanging lamp, you just lay there kicking for your life. Madame, she ain't the kind to take pity, wasn't going to risk her business taking you in. But even if she said she wanted you, she would have had to fight me. I saw you and I felt like you had answered a question. Your eyes, the clay color of your legs, the curly hair on your head – you seemed like family, like mine. That if I had you, I'd be alright. And if you had me, you'd be alright. I knew I could protect you, I knew that you weren't supposed to be alive, that you weren't supposed to belong to me at all and that's why I needed you. That's why you fit. So there's no separating us Bulrusher, we are just like our names, bound to what we do and what's been done to us. Our names are our fates and our proper place. Don't forget that.

Pause.

Bulrusher Gotta clean this up.

Schoolch *starts up the stairs.*

Bulrusher Schoolch, I was Christened at the church, right?

Schoolch *stops.*

Bulrusher Did the reverend give me a name when he tapped me with the water? I got a Christian name, don't I?

Pause.

Schoolch Once we had another name for you, but I forget it now. You're Bulrusher to me.

Next morning. **Logger***'s house. He is tending a fire in the wood burning stove. He puts a few pieces of bread and a pot of water over the flames.* **Vera** *comes into the kitchen in a nightgown. It's too large; she has to pick up the hem to walk. The hem is splattered with a little mud.*

Logger You look like you still sleep. (**Vera** *frowns, squinting.*) 'Ere sleep comes down to soothe the weary eyes.' That's Dunbar. You like the morning? (**Vera** *mumbles.*) Your mother would stay in bed all day if she wasn't colored. I can't imagine what she look like now, grown and running a house. See I was always the one up and getting breakfast on. She liked to sit in the bed and play with the strings from her blanket, talk a little bout her dreams from the night before. Stare out the window like a princess waiting for some magic. My sister.

Vera It's cold.

Logger Yeah, mornings are cool here then it heats up by midday – lot different than Birmingham. I tend to ride in the mornings, but I thought I'd stay in today, hear your news. (*A brief pause, then*) I hope you brought a comb with you. I've tried not to say anything since we're just meeting but your hair looks like the burning bush.

Vera Well if nobody does hair around here I don't know what I'm a do.

Logger You don't do your own hair?

Vera Mother always does it.

Logger (*looking at her*) And it's thick too. Huh. I ain't got a pressing comb but I can plait it for you.

Vera That's alright, I'll just get some rollers and smooth it down that way.

Logger But you can't go in the store to buy rollers looking like that.

Vera I'll wear a scarf.

Logger Didn't Ina tell you always wear clean panties case you have an accident and have to get operated on in the hospital?

Vera Yes.

Logger Well why would you walk out the house with clean panties and a nappy head? That defies all reason, makes my mouth hurt to say it. I'm gonna plait your hair up before you even think about goin outside. Sit down here. And bring the comb and grease from the dresser.

He sits on a chair and opens his legs. **Vera** *stands stock still.*

Logger Come on. I don't care if you tenderheaded, it's gotta be done.

Vera You gon braid my hair? You a man. You ain't sposed to do that.

Logger Used to do Ina's every Saturday night, with clean square parts. What am I doing explaining myself to you! Just set down.

Vera You gon be careful?

Logger No.

Vera I'll just wear a scarf –

Logger What did I just say to you? Now set!

Vera *gets comb and grease.*

Logger Questioning your elders, mmph. I don't know how Ina raised you but no sellin wolf tickets round here. You got you a job and your own place to stay, *then* we can put our conversation on an even plank.

Vera *is afraid to sit down.*

Logger I ain't tellin you again.

Vera *sits between his legs. He begins to comb and part* **Vera***'s hair.*

Logger I'm gonna do it so you don't need no rollers. If you wet it and let it dry like this, when you take it out you'll have all the pincurls you need.

He goes to work on two french braids. Silence.

Vera I do want to find me a job while I'm here.

Logger Well, what can you do?

Vera Type. File. Take minutes.

Logger Nobody need none of that fingernail polish stuff round here. We'll find you something you can put your back into.

He combs. She looks out the window.

Vera That Bulrusher girl said it would clear up this morning.

Logger She's always right about the weather. You oughta pay her a visit today, thank her for her kindness.

Vera Is she really the only Negro this way? I don't want to work for white people.

Logger Used to be more of us here during boom time, but once the sawmills closed, everybody went south. Oakland, Fresno, Los Angeles.

Vera But you stayed.

Logger Keep your head still.

Vera You like living with all these ofays?

Logger It's alright. Indians are the colored folk here, what's left of em. They got it *bad*. All their land got took, they ain't allowed to go to school, and some of em can remember when they was legal slaves. So don't go lyin and sayin you're part Cherokee.

Vera White folk just don't have no morals. And easy women too. Never thought I'd see a town a crackers let a buck into their bordello.

Logger *yanks her head to the side. She yells.*

Logger I know we're just getting to know each other, but I have to ask. Why you here, Vera?

Vera Mother sent me.

Logger By yourself. In the middle of the summer.

Vera She needed to get me off her hands for a while.

Logger Lean forward. You done with school?

Vera Graduated Parker High. I'm going to college.

Logger (*excited*) That's all right! (*Hugs her head.*) Oh Vera, I'm proud. Proud of ya.

Vera I just need a job so I can save up.

Logger College! Pretty soon you'll be a teacher yourself, huh.

Vera (*with real hope*) Maybe.

Logger Don't sell yourself short, now, you can do anything you put your mind to.

Vera Mother always talks so fondly of you. Said you cut down fifty foot trees all by yourself. That white men look up to you in California.

Logger How is Birmingham doin these days?

Vera They only bomb our houses every *other* Sunday.

Logger Yeah, I like these ofays a lot better than those. Listen Vera, you are family and you are welcome to stay. We'll find you a job, that's earth.

Vera I won't be no trouble.

Logger Love braidin hair.

Bulrusher *talks to the river.*

Bulrusher She has tiny burns on her arm and on her ear and on her forehead near her hairline. Thin feathery scars, with crosshatching that looks like the teeth of a comb. All hot and fried and ironed – her smell begins with that – her hair, her clothes – all of her seems to have been cooked with corn oil and a strip of metal. Is it the smell of Birmingham, the steel pressing against her, burning her skin? Is that where her scars are from? I want to dream of her.

Schoolch*'s porch.* **Bulrusher** *is cleaning her shotgun.* **Vera** *enters.*

Bulrusher Hey.

Vera Hey. It stopped raining.

Bulrusher Yeah. You sleep good?

Vera No. After the rain it was too quiet. Silence in my ears all night.

Bulrusher You don't like it?

Vera I just never heard darkness before. Is it too early to visit?

Bulrusher No. I been up, out in the woods, catching some dinner.

Vera You used that gun?

Bulrusher Mm hm. Want to see what I shot?

Vera That's alright.

Bulrusher Sure? I ain't cleaned her yet –

Vera It's alright. Thanks again for helping me last night. Hope I didn't get you in trouble.

Bulrusher Well, Schoolch never speaks to me otherwise so I think of it as a special occasion.

Vera I don't want to step on anybody's toes. Especially when I got to find a job.

Bulrusher I never even seen anyone like you.

Vera We look just the same.

Bulrusher No we don't. You're pretty, like the kind you feel inside of yourself when you go to the movies and think you're in it?

Vera Yeah? You never seen another colored girl before?

Bulrusher No. I had to drink some beer just to get over you.

Vera Beer? But that's only for men! You'll grow hairs on your tongue you keep that up.

Bulrusher I been doin it since I was twelve! Are there hairs?

Bulrusher *opens her mouth.*

Vera Let me see your – open wider. (*She looks.*) Looks clean, but your tongue is real long. You have to be careful.

Bulrusher But I don't like whiskey. What else am I gonna drink at the Anyhow?

Vera The Anyhow?

Bulrusher Saloon.

Vera They let you drink at a saloon?

Bulrusher Something wrong with that?

Vera And you walk right in the front door?

Bulrusher Ain't no other door.

Vera I used the front door once at Pizitz. Department store. We supposed to use the back entrance, in the alleyway, by the trash – but I strode right in the front.

Bulrusher Why are you supposed to use the back?

Vera I went to buy some doughnuts and they came to throw me out. Back door, they said. My pocket got caught on the door handle when they were pushing me, and the whole front panel of my dress just came off. Came off right in this cracker's hand. And he got so red when he saw my stockings, he just walked off real fast. The bus wouldn't pick me up. Had to walk all the way home holding myself with newspaper.

Bulrusher *looks at her.*

And it's the dark that scares me, huh.

Bulrusher You gonna stay?

Vera If you'll be my friend.

Bulrusher I'll take care of you, whatever you need.

Vera (*smiles*) So what do y'all do around here? For fun?

Bulrusher Drink. The Apple Show is coming up though. Big dance for that.

Vera Applesauce, huh.

Boy *enters.*

Boy Whoa, seein dubs. Whose sneeble are you?

Bulrusher *aims her gun at* **Boy***'s crotch.*

Vera Bulrusher!

Bulrusher Show her some manners.

Boy That thing ain't even loaded, you just cleaned it.

Bulrusher She ain't nobody's sneeble. Introduce yourself proper.

She pokes him with the gun.

Boy Pleased to make your acquaintance.

Vera I'm Vera, pleased to meet you.

Bulrusher Say *your* name.

Boy Damn Bulrusher, take that highgun offa me!

Bulrusher Say it.

Boy I'm Wilkerson, enchanté.

Bulrusher Your whole name.

Boy Streebs Wilkerson –

Bulrusher Streebs, which means strawberries –

Boy Don't tell her that –

Bulrusher – 'count of the red birthmark he got on his balls.

Boy You supposed to be my girlfriend, don't go spreading lies. (*To* **Vera**.) She ain't even seen my privates.

Bulrusher Don't need to, as much as you talk about em. He says I'm his girlfriend but he didn't even talk to me last night at the Anyhow.

Boy We're in the early phases of love. You all kin?

Bulrusher	**Vera**
She kin to Mr Jeans.	I'm kin to Mr Jeans.

Vera From Birmingham.

Boy My great granddad died over you, tryin to keep the Union together.

Vera You think us colored folk are worth it?

Boy What?

Vera Death.

Boy Haven't really sized up the race as a whole.

Bulrusher Yeah. We are.

Boy You ain't colored, you a bulrusher and a fortune teller. And you my girlfriend.

Bulrusher Just 'cause you say something don't make it true. Get off my porch 'fore I load up this gun and use it.

Boy Aw, manzanita –

Bulrusher Off.

Boy I'll stack your oranges for you nice and tight.

Bulrusher What did I say.

Boy Don't be so teet lipped. Leavin me all dove cooey. I just wanna see your golden eagles.

Bulrusher *chases him off. As he exits, he yells:*

Boy You can't get rid of me, doolsey boo, no no! I'm gonna geech you!

Vera What's a sneeble?

Bulrusher Like a snowball. It's the funny way to say Negro.

Vera And you'd point a gun at a white man for that?

Bulrusher He's a boy. I won't have him treat you wrong.

Vera Fred – my boyfriend at home – he'd never do what you just did. He fears the Lord God. He did steal me a pickle dipped in Kool-Aid powder from the store once, but that's about it. Sneebles. Why's everyone talk so funny here?

Bulrusher They're harpin the ling. Folks made it up a while ago to tell jokes and secrets, to make everything they talk about something they own. I can harp it but I don't. Made up my own way to talk instead, a way to talk to the river. I tell stories, make poetry, like I'm writing my own book. I tell things over and over so I can understand em. Hey, you really want a job?

Vera Yeah. Need one bad.

Bulrusher I'm thinking of expanding my business. Summertime and all, oranges always do good, but I thought I might sell some lemons.

Vera *laughs.*

Bulrusher What? If lemons don't please you, we could try pineapples. Or bananas.

Vera You want my help?

Bulrusher Sure. We could split our yield clear down the middle.

Vera You sure? All I done is office work.

Bulrusher I'll teach you what you need to know. How to choose the ripe ones, how much to charge on the road versus my regulars buy crates. You're smart enough; you won't have to pay me no mind after the first day.

Vera (*laughing*) Applesauce *and* lemonade. And I thought California didn't have nothing else in it but movie stars and palm trees.

Bulrusher You don't want to work with me?

Vera Of course I do, I was just kidding you. It's how I say thanks.

Bulrusher I got a twang in my stomach when you walked up today. Then it spread all over. Still feels like there's turpentine under my skin. You did all that to me. Wait till I tell the river.

Vera You something else.

The brothel porch. A month and a half later. **Logger** *sings.* **Boy** *accompanies him on his guitar.*

Logger (*sings*) Oh she caned me with her look
She slayed me with her eye
But I had her sweet jerk once
And for it I would die
And for it I would die
And for it I would die

She turned me like a horse
She reined my wildness in
But every time she pats my rump
Oh Lord I want to sin
Oh Lord I want to sin
Oh Lord I wants to sin.

Boy That's an old song from the mill ain't it. Pa sang it different. You changed the words.

Logger Naw, the song changed on *me*. I can't sing it like we used to 'cause I don't feel it that way anymore. I mean, they got electric saws now.

Boy What's the electric saw got to do with a girl?

Logger I'm saying! I mean, I came out here from Birmingham when I was about your age and that whole field in front of you was a stand of conifers. Used to ride my Appaloosa over that ridge with your pa, just take in the country. Built my own house. Not with siding, not with half logs. Tongue and grooved my own cabin all from redwood I felled myself. Now you're lucky if you see a pygmy tree.

Boy Where's the girl in that?

Logger Right! All through the valley, up and down the coast, the trees are gone and so is my youth – I have nothing left to destroy. Nothing fallin around here but apples on sheep.

Boy Yeah, I'm kinda weary of doing what all everyone else do. I mean I'm not different from nobody, I'm just not always the same. Hey, I got a new song to keep me company. You wanna hear it?

Logger Not one of them lonesome tunes now.

Boy Oh I can't write those. I just missed the draft to Korea, got all my days in front of me, so I think I got a right to be happy, to sing a happy song.

Logger Alright. Ply it for me. But soft now. I don't want to get jangled. Too pretty an evening for nothing loud.

Boy It's in a new key I found, real sweet. (*He plays a chord.*) Isn't that bahl.

Logger See what'n all you got jacker, ply your song.

Boy (*sings and plays guitar*)
Twelve nights of hard liquor
Sent Rowan to his grave
He saw the lights of Galilee
And Mary just the same

And if you call for Rowan now
The road'll answer back
He's twelve nights gone to perfidy
Spread on a burlap sack

Oh save me in my nightly walk
Save me in my days
Don't want to go like Rowan Hale
I'll keep my goodly ways

Oh save me in my nightly walk
Save me in my days
Don't want to go like Rowan Hale
I'll keep my goodly ways
I'll keep my goodly ways.

Logger Huh. That's your happy song? You got kinda loud at the end there.

Boy I didn't know what I was sayin for a minute and I sang with my full power to get me through.

Logger And you made that tune up.

Boy Most of it.

Logger Clearly, you been inspired – but stop that loud singing. It sounds like you wanna hurt somebody. Don't you got a gal?

Boy Yeah, I'm getting her.

Logger Well what you doing about it? You need to marry and set up house. That's what you oughta do since you ain't in the service or a travelin man. Need you a wife.

Boy You ain't had one.

Madame *enters with glasses on, reading a letter.*

Madame Are you comin in today or are you just tryin to hoot on me by sittin on my stoop?

Logger If you got any vision in that pinchy face of yours, you could see I am whittlin and warblin with this yink here.

Madame Yes but I don't see either a y'all payin my loiterin fee. If you gonna porch up and tell jonnems and wess all day, fine by me but you have got to give up some rent.

Logger 'There is a heaven, for ever, day by day,
The upward longing of my soul doth tell me so.
There is a hell, I'm quite as sure; for pray,
If there were not, where would my neighbours go?'

That's some Dunbar for ya Madame, Paul Laurence. Better get you some compassion 'fore you die.

Boy I was playin some songs on the guitar. You want to hear another one I wrote, Jeans?

Logger Well, just play some chords, what all you strummed on that last one. None of them words, just the strings vibratin. That's all I want to hear.

Boy Airtight.

Boy *strums.*

Logger Madame, you ain't been honest with me.

Madame What now.

Logger You ain't always been this hard. You used to be another kind of woman, kind got gentleness swaying out her like a breeze.

Madame I am the same woman you have always known, Lucas, I still got wind for ya.

Logger You would hold me before; before you wouldn't let me go with the other girls.

Madame (*evasive*) There's more paperwork now, I got more things to take care of.

Logger You put me out. You had me in your arms and then you shunted me like I had the tuberculosis.

Madame Well, I started to lose my business sense with you comin so regular – I had to draw a line just to clarify.

Logger I ain't happy with the way my life looks. With Vera here got me thinking. I'm a forty-six year-old grizz and I don't know what is ahead of me. Like this tweed here. He's comin into his manliness and he got all sorts of gals to choose from for to make a future. My future is done. All I got left is the past.

Madame You still active in your daming. You don't miss a weekend here.

Logger And that ain't appealin to me no more. It feels like I'm just eatin the same Thanksgiving meal over and over – I get all stuffed up and nothing tastes good enough anymore to be thankful for.

Madame So that's it? Tradin in your riding crop for a chastity belt?

Logger I just want to settle myself into somethin more wholesome. I want to feel someone. The same someone every night.

Madame Pay me and I'll hold your hand.

Logger I don't want it that way. I want it for real. I know Schoolch has been on you for the same thing but –

Madame What you askin me, Lucas.

Logger I don't know. You've been good to me, more than any other woman I know – I just want a real home and a quiet con*tent* in the evenings steada all this skee swillin and boisteration. I don't got a ring or nothin like that –

Madame Oh you have lost your skull fillin now.

Logger I just want to give something over. I want to smush myself into you.

Boy There's another song I got – I can play just the chords to that. Kinda gettin tired of this one –

Logger Well pluck another song then.

Boy That's what I'll do.

He strums another song.

Madame Lucas, I can't marry you.

Logger That's just your knee jerking.

Madame Apple Show almost here. Just got this letter from someone who wants to buy this place, make me rich. How can I marry you when I'm leavin?

Logger You didn't even think about it.

Madame I have – for longer than you want to know.

Logger You've been wanting this?

Madame I don't run my life by what I want, Lucas. That ain't my way.

Lights shift to **Bulrusher** *and* **Vera**. **Bulrusher** *talks to the river as* **Vera** *sings*.

Bulrusher She is a mirror.

Vera (*singing under* **Bulrusher**'*s words*) For all we know

Bulrusher A mirror. Schoolch never allowed any mirrors in the house.

Vera This may only be a dream

Bulrusher I always think about touching her skin. It's just like mine only smoother.

Vera We come and we go, like the ripples on a stream

Bulrusher She says that I am beautiful. She says she wants to stretch herself over me like taffy so everyone can see my sweetness. But I want to do that to her.

Vera So love me tonight, tomorrow was made for some

Bulrusher I don't care about anything else.

Vera Tomorrow may never come, for all we know

Bulrusher We sell fruit.

Vera (*speaking to unseen customer*) They're sweet. Nickel a piece.

As the scene continues, they do not speak to each other, but continue to be in their own separate worlds.

Bulrusher I eat with her every day, pick her up from her uncle's house by Barney Flats.

Vera I have never been served food by a white woman before. I sat at the table with my napkin folded in my lap and she poured milk into my glass.

Bulrusher I take her with me to Cloverdale and we buy oranges and lemons and bananas and she sings next to me in the truck. Once she put her fingers on my knee and spelled my name up my thigh.

Vera Bulrusher, why don't we go to the beach? Can't you see us running along the sand and tearing off our stockings?

Bulrusher One day she kissed my cheek to say goodbye. I grabbed her hand.

Vera I'm saving up my money. And I eat anything I want. Sometimes just bread with mustard.

Bulrusher She wants to go to the ocean with me but I don't like the ocean. That's where my mother wanted me to die. You're my river. I'll bring Vera to you instead.

The river. **Bulrusher** *and* **Vera** *now talk to each other.*

Bulrusher (*to* **Vera**) I guess I can tell everybody else's futures because I don't know my own past. I was supposed to die, but I didn't, so I think I got an open ticket to the land of could be.

Vera You like reading water?

Bulrusher Only if the person want to know the future. If she don't then it's all garbled up, can't read a thing. Image gets blurry, blinds me even. (*She picks up a twig and turns it on* **Vera**.) Sometimes I wish I did water witching instead 'cause no one ever minds finding water and water never minds being found.

They laugh.

Have you ever tried wild blackberries? Here.

Vera They're sour.

Bulrusher They're almost ready.

Vera What about these?

Bulrusher Poison.

Vera And these? They smell like being sick.

Bulrusher Just juniper berries. If you're sick, you need these eucalyptus leaves. They'll cure anything that's hurtin your chest from inside.

Vera This water'll cure me!

Vera *takes off her clothes and jumps into the river in her slip.*

I just want to be clean. I'm clean here, right? You can see I'm clean.

Bulrusher Yeah, I can see.

Vera Then why aren't you getting in?

Bulrusher I don't know.

Vera There're fish!

Bulrusher Stand in the sand.

Vera It's deep.

Bulrusher There's a branch above you, hold onto that.

Vera Nobody else come down here?

Bulrusher Only me. This is my secret place on the river.

Vera Your river. It's your diary, your church, your everything.

Bulrusher Yeah, has been.

Vera Well, your river is making me cold, so you should get in.

Bulrusher It's not cold, you're in the sun.

Vera I don't want to die in here.

Bulrusher Why would you die?

Vera Because it's quiet. Everything's so quiet. It makes me want to cry.

Vera *laughs.*

Bulrusher The river holds you. Anything that you are scared of, it'll hold for you. I asked the river to save me when I was a baby girl, and it held me.

Vera Is that why you won't get in? You're scared your luck will run out?

Bulrusher I've just never taken anyone down to this water. I always come here alone to talk and listen and I don't know how to do that with you here too.

Vera *starts to get out.*

Bulrusher No, you stay, I just can't get in with you.

Vera I'm done. I got in and I'm gettin out.

Bulrusher Stay in longer, it's only been a minute.

Vera Nothing to do if you're not in with me. Can't splash, can't play – and I don't hear the river saying things like you do so I suppose I'm just a little less entertained.

Bulrusher Wait – don't get out. I'll put my feet in.

Vera I'm naked as a plucked chicken in an apron! You take off your clothes too.

Bulrusher Why?

Vera Because we're here together. So we're gonna do the same thing.

Bulrusher *takes off her shoes. She takes off her shirt and then* **Vera** *pulls off her trousers for her.* **Bulrusher** *is startled then begins to laugh. She dives in wearing her undershirt and bloomers.*

Vera You don't wear a bra?

Bulrusher What's that?

Vera For to keep your chest up. They'll start draggin in the dust if you don't strap those things.

Bulrusher I didn't know you were supposed wear anything else.

Vera You have been raised by wolves and none of em female.

Bulrusher *touches one of* **Vera's** *tiny scars.*

Bulrusher What are these scars?

Vera From my mama tryin to straighten my hair with a hot comb. But I'm a country girl now. Can get my hair wet as I want. Handstand!

When **Vera** *comes up,* **Bulrusher** *touches* **Vera**'*s neck. Vera holds* **Bulrusher's** *hand to her wet neck and collarbone.*

Vera Have you ever noticed that white people smell like mayonnaise?

Bulrusher You don't want to go back to Birmingham.

Vera Some days I could kill them all.

Bulrusher You're scared.

Vera White folks are the ones should be scared 'cause we ain't takin what they're servin much longer. If they'd just read the Bible sometime they'd see what's coming for em.

Bulrusher Your mother misses you; she will cut her finger on the edge of a letter. But it isn't from you, it's a notice from a contest at the radio station.

Vera I entered it in May.

Bulrusher You'll win a year supply of Dixie Peach Pomade and a subscription to *Jet* magazine. What's all that?

Vera *takes* **Bulrusher***'s hand off of her neck.*

Bulrusher I'm sorry.

Vera You didn't ask if you could do that.

Bulrusher I didn't mean to.

Vera That wasn't fair. I can't see *your* future.

Bulrusher It just happened. I couldn't read if you didn't want me to. I just wanted to touch your skin – like you wanted me to.

Vera So what? So my mother didn't send me here. So I came here on my own. But that isn't all you saw.

Bulrusher No.

Vera Then say it. Say what I already know.

Bulrusher It doesn't matter.

Vera I wanna hear you say it.

Bulrusher I said I'd take care of you, that ain't gonna change now.

Vera Say it.

Bulrusher I'll start tellin fortunes again, make us some more money – you don't have to worry bout nothin.

Vera You can't fix everything! Some things are just wrong and always will be.

Bulrusher Not you.

Vera Yeah me.

Bulrusher So that's why you're here.

Vera Don't make me explain. Just say it. Say it.

Bulrusher You're gonna have a baby. A boy.

Vera A boy?

Bulrusher But I won't let you stand up to work, I'll do all the lifting. You can just sit and count the money.

Vera I'm not gonna have a boy. Or a girl.

Bulrusher Yes you are. And he's gonna be as pretty as you.

Vera I don't want it. All I need is the money to get rid of it.

Bulrusher He's yours. Don't say that.

Vera Then you don't really want to help me.

Bulrusher Why would you want to get rid of a child?

Vera You don't know where it came from.

Bulrusher But he's in you now.

Vera I don't care 'cause I'll never love it.

Bulrusher You can just give him to me.

Vera No! I never want to see its face! If you don't want to help me, that's fine. That's fine.

Vera *gets out of the water.* **Bulrusher** *follows her, quiet.*

Vera If you tell anybody –

Bulrusher I won't.

Bulrusher *turns away from* **Vera**. *They both put on their clothes in silence.*

Vera Bulrusher.

Bulrusher *turns toward her and* **Vera** *buttons* **Bulrusher***'s shirt.* **Vera** *kisses her.*

Vera I guess I can't hide anything from you, huh.

She kisses **Bulrusher** *again.* **Bulrusher** *is crying.* **Vera** *kisses* **Bulrusher***'s tears, then her lips as the lights fade.*

Act Two

Same evening. The brothel. **Boy**, **Madame**, *and* **Logger** *are drunk by now and* **Schoolch**, *sober, has joined them. Boy continues to play his guitar.*

Logger See this woman is an artisan. Don't you remember when you used to have me in your boudoir, this is years ago, boom time, and serve me some of that pecan coffee cake? Sometimes had raspberries too. 'Course you got the berries from Gowan's since everything dies in your garden, but that made sense to me. Seems if you are running a brothel proper, it should look real inviting but not feel like you could really live there. The kinda place you can't wait to get back to but so intense you can't stay? That's 'cause you are an artisan. And trained all your women good.

Madame Well I also train the men. If he's afraid of the woman in front of him, if he thinks he makes the rules, if he don't listen, he can't get nowhere with me. If I see a man got potential, I'll send him to one of the other girls, watch how he touch her. If he is the slightest bit distracted, that is his downfall. I'll tell him. You're distracted. Downfall of mankind! I'll come out and show him what he ought to do and how. Most men ain't used to that – having someone take enough of an interest to increase their skills. But I'm an artisan and on occasion a man can arouse me into my creativity.

Logger You never had to teach me nothin.

Madame Yeah, you were probably practicing on them horses.

Logger I'm a natural, honey, and you know it. Why? Because I know how to talk. And I know how to listen. You used to take me in, 'stead of sendin me with the other girls, 'cause with me you could empty yourself out. Tell me all kinds of stories bout yourself. And after that, I'd slip you out of your bodice and let you lay there. I could see all your moles and freckles, the streaks and scars and blushes. I wanted to turn your bright skin red, from inside. Have it run at top speed, have your heart race your own curves. You were open and draped in those smooth sheets – and I don't know if I was feelin love, but when I look back, I sure want to call it that.

Madame Huh. You hear that, Schoolch? And this is the one talking bout marrying me. Bragging on himself steada begging on his knees.

Boy How bout we sing 'The Wabash Cannonball'?

Logger Ain't braggin. Tellin the truth. You want me so much it makes *my* bones ache.

Madame Ha! I don't want you! I'm sellin and I'm gone. I'm like Schoolch here – kept my feelings in the cupboard so long I don't need em. You're just like old china. Never gonna use you.

Boy You know Schoolch actually taught us 'The Wabash Cannonball' in class, stood up on his desk and looked right at us and his eyes filled up when he sang. He sang so strong, his hair moved, like he was standing on the top of a real cannonball train. And if that train was real, I figured my daddy had to be on it, that he'd left me and my ma on a machine so fast people had to sing about it.

Logger Oh I miss your pa. You know I was there when you were born. Your pa cut your umbilical with my barlow when the midwife got ridgy. Yeah, we felled plenty pine together. How's your ma?

Boy Still working at the hotel in Mendocino.

Madame When you gonna get yourself grown and start taking care of her?

Boy I don't know.

He strums his guitar. As **Vera** *and* **Bulrusher** *enter:*

Boy If I had me a wife, I could do anything.

Logger If I had me a wife.

Madame Where you two been?

Bulrusher Went swimming down on the river.

Boy (*almost singing, to* **Bulrusher**) If I had me a wife . . .

Madame Well, you look distracted. And you don't need to stand that close to each other.

Logger Like two redwood saplings. Vera here going to college, and Bulrusher got her business? They *should* stand close to each other.

Bulrusher I like standing here.

Pause.

Vera I'm feeling pretty tired.

Logger Well then we'll say good night to Madame here. And don't slip and call her Madam – 'cause she will curse you out in French.

Bulrusher I can take Vera home.

Logger That's alright. It *is* on my way. So Madame, you think about what I asked you.

Madame I told you, I'm signing this place away. Settlin accounts with the girls and leavin soon as the cash is in my palm. None of those plans include you.

Logger You know you ain't left town since that year your mother passed. Unless you got another mother you been hiding from us, you staying put.

Boy Before you go, I want to say something.

Logger I'm sure you do.

Boy It's a public announcement and it's got to be made. (*To* **Bulrusher**.) I'm ready to put my arm around you, Bulrusher.

Logger This a new song you wrote?

Boy I'm gonna put my arm around you where the people can see. I'll take you to the Anyhow and stand by you. I'll never leave you.

Madame See what you started Lucas?

Bulrusher Why? Why you wanta stand by me?

Boy I told you I'm a standin man. I've known you all my life.

Bulrusher But you ain't never talked to me till last month.

Boy I was shy.

Bulrusher You didn't want to put your arm around me because I'm colored.

Boy What? No. I just thought you were a witch! Everybody says you don't have no ma, you just got spit out the river by the devil's tongue.

Bulrusher And who said that about me? White people.

Logger Listen now, you can't say that Bulrusher. You know the reason no one talks to you is 'cause you ain't got no family. Whoever gave birth to you didn't care nothing for you, but this white gentleman Schoolch has cared and cared hard.

Bulrusher So this Boy wants to be like Schoolch, wants to save me?

Boy I figure if he lets me be with you, if you let a bloocher like me into your pasture, that's proof I can do anything in this world.

Bulrusher You don't even know what you want to do.

Boy I want to choose you. You pulled a gun on me. It wasn't loaded, but it was passionate. No girl's ever done that to me before.

Bulrusher I'll do it again.

Boy See? Some people don't need reasons – they just know. They just have hearts and certainty. That's what's happening here. And it may seem strange to you because you ain't inside my heart and feeling it pound, but some things are just for sure. You are that. You are my for sure.

Bulrusher What are you talking about?

Boy I'm choosing you! The witch! Why can't you just be chosen? Sometimes that's all people need. To be chosen, to be the only one. I'm a do that for you. You don't have to do it for me if you don't want to, but I'll make it easy for you to change your mind.

Madame Lucas, you taking notes? This boy's got the goods.

Bulrusher I don't need you. I don't need *you*. I might have, but now I got me this one. I got Vera. And I'm a take care a her.

Logger That's different than what he's talking about Bulrush. She's your friend and he's talking romantic.

Madame But they standin too close together! I've seen this before, two girls stand too close, then they get distracted, and blow apart. If you're a woman, you can't fall in love, not with a man or with your friend. You just can't afford to. Schoolch, tell her.

Schoolch *is silent.*

Bulrusher Vera will tell you. I'm a take care of her. I don't want nobody else.

Logger Vera, what you say about all this?

Vera She's a good friend.

Logger That's all?

Bulrusher She kissed me. That's what I know. She kissed me and that means we are meant for each other, don't it?

Boy You're a witch, a bulrusher, a colored girl, and a degenerate too? Oh I've got to save you with my songs of mercy. You don't want her, I'm tellin you you don't.

Logger Vera, ain't there something you got to tell us?

Vera I don't think so.

Logger I realize it's early on and all so I've been letting you cavort and take in your last bit of childhood, but I know what you come here for. I'm up earlier than you, honey. I know you get tongue-cuppy in the mornings out back, and it's every morning, so I know. But we're still gonna get you to that college, believe you me.

Boy You mean this girl is lizzied? Lews 'n' larmers. Well congratulations to the man who got you heisted. See Bulrusher? That's just what I wanna do with you.

Bulrusher *punches* **Boy**. *They struggle.*

Madame No upper-cuttin on my premises!

Logger Let em fight it out. I wanna see who they are.

Bulrusher *is strong, but* **Boy** *is a more experienced fighter. He pins her arm behind her back and holds her down.*

Boy You still feel like hittin me?

Bulrusher Yes!

Vera Stop it!

Boy I'm asking you true, that's what you want?

Bulrusher Yes!

Boy You think you can hurt me that way?

Bulrusher I hope so!

Boy Then try.

He lets go and lies down, face up. She gets on top of him. A moment of reckoning – then she starts pummeling him.

Bulrusher (*punching with each word*) You. Don't. Want. Me.

Madame Lucas, I'll jump in there myself if you don't!

Bulrusher You. Don't. Know. Me.

Vera He's bleeding!

Bulrusher He's drunk, he won't even notice.

Madame Bulrusher, stop this now!

Bulrusher *continues to hit him, focus intensified.*

Vera Why are you doing this?

Madame You may not listen, but you can feel.

Madame *tries to drag* **Bulrusher** *off of him but* **Bulrusher** *hits* **Madame**, *knocking her to the floor.*

Schoolch Bulrusher.

At the sound of his soft voice, everything stops.

That's enough.

Schoolch *and* **Logger** *both move to help* **Madame** – *an awkward moment that evolves into a silent showdown. Finally,* **Logger** *helps her up.* **Bulrusher** *gets off of* **Boy** *slowly and stands, suddenly aware of what she has done.*

Schoolch Go home, Bulrusher.

Bulrusher *looks at* **Vera**, *then runs out, driving off in her truck.* **Madame** *is already cleaning.*

Logger Madame, you hurt?

Madame I'm mad, that's all. Look at the blood on my floor.

Logger You alright son? Ooh, she Joe Macked you.

Boy Got a tooth loose.

Madame *hands him a hot towel.*

Madame Here's some brandy if you need it.

He drinks some.

Boy I hope Bulrusher will forgive me. You think she will?

Logger I'll take you home, Boy. Let's go Vera.

Madame What do you want a baby for.

Logger Let's go.

Logger, **Vera**, *and* **Boy** *exit*.

Split scene: **Madame** *and* **Schoolch** *continue to talk in the brothel parlor while* **Bulrusher** *talks to the river.*

Madame Damn babies. They grow up and make more. Grow up and serve nothing but hurt. Why did you take that girl in?

Bulrusher I float in a basket toward the Pacific, hands blue as huckleberries.

Madame How did Lucas find her in the weeds? Why did he bring that weese here?

Bulrusher The woman who bore me named me silence.

Madame He knew a baby in a brothel takes away more customers than war. The girls would hear her squall and remember they're women.

Bulrusher Who is a motherless daughter but pure will?

Madame She seemed like she was trying to fit in, but now she's a walking curse. Why did you take her in?

Bulrusher I want to swing, swing, over the green grapes, the fir trees, ride the wind, find my home, go all the way home.

Schoolch When your mother passed, you left town. You left me, you left Lucas.

Bulrusher Home.

Schoolch You stayed away a long time, but you came back.

Bulrusher Home. And I am . . .

Schoolch You know how I feel about you. Why'd you come back? Was it for me? Or him?

Bulrusher Who?

Schoolch Me? Or him?

Bulrusher Who?

Schoolch And who are you leaving now? Me? Or him?

Bulrusher Who?

Schoolch Madame? You answer me!

Long pause.

Madame There's blood on my floor.

Split scene ends – lights out on **Bulrusher**. **Madame** *stoops to clean up the floor with her towel, but* **Schoolch** *takes it and wipes the floor for her. He hands her the bloody towel.*

Schoolch Cory up there?

Madame She's in the front with the men on the monthly plan. What, you want me to send her up?

Schoolch On the Wabash Cannonball.

He throws ten dollars on the pool table and goes up the stairs. **Madame**, *shocked, sits.*

Next morning. **Bulrusher** *enters the brothel.* **Madame** *has not moved since the night before.*

Bulrusher Mornin.

Madame Looks the same to me.

Bulrusher I can open your shades for you.

Madame No thanks. Don't need any more heat in this room. And that sun bleaches my upholstery.

Bulrusher You seen Schoolch? I been worried. Couldn't sleep.

Madame Me neither.

Bulrusher He didn't come home last night.

Madame Don't trouble yourself about him.

Bulrusher You know where he is?

Madame He's here.

Bulrusher Here? Upstairs?

Madame That's right. Historic, ain't it? Schoolch finally getting his equipment serviced.

Bulrusher He – he really –

Madame Yes. It is natural, you know.

Bulrusher It's my fault. I'm sorry.

Madame It ain't your fault. Ain't your fault at all.

Bulrusher He's never gonna come home now. He's punishing me.

Madame You don't know that.

Bulrusher It's because of what I said and did last night that's pushed him over –

Madame No, child, he's punishing *me*.

Bulrusher Why?

Madame We've known each other a long long time. Know things about the other no one else knows. He's just angry that I'm leavin town.

Bulrusher You say you're leavin every summer.

Madame Well maybe he was mad at me for being so easy on you! When you knocked me over, you cracked my porcelain spittoon!

Bulrusher I apologize for that too.

Madame You better!

Bulrusher I mean to work it all off. Maybe I can help you with your business here, take in some clients for you.

Madame What? Work a bed for me?

Bulrusher I mean – well, during the Apple Show – if you're short staffed.

Madame You ain't even had your cherry popped.

Bulrusher What do you mean?

Madame My point exactly. You can't just fling yourself into this profession! It's gotta be part of a plan. And I don't want you disrespecting the solicitors I represent with your lack of training and experience. You'd probably get knocked up, like that Vera girl, the love of your life.

Bulrusher You don't know how I feel about her.

Madame I know she's a girl. And she's pregnant. Soon she'll be a woman, with a baby, and she's gonna need more than you can give.

Bulrusher What can't I give? You think she want somebody who talk all that talk about 'you are my for sure' like Boy did last night? He's probably been practicing them lines on every girl he know for the last ten years. He'd say that to a whore.

Madame*'s look stops* **Bulrusher** *cold.*

Bulrusher (*explains*) You don't know what that Boy and his friends used to do to me.

Madame He's trying to give something to you and she's trying to take something from you. You got to choose wisely.

Bulrusher You're just sticking up for him 'cause you're both white people.

Madame That girl has put so much hate into you. (*Pause.*) You shouldn't see her for a little while.

Bulrusher Did you talk to her?

Madame I talked to Lucas. He called this morning.

Bulrusher What'd he say?

Madame Said you needed to cool off.

Bulrusher I am cool.

Madame You meant to hurt Boy last night, and you did.

Bulrusher But Boy don't care what I do. Nothing I do can change him.

Madame That's just not how you treat people.

Bulrusher I'm sorry. I did it for Vera.

Madame And you better cool offa her too.

Bulrusher Can't I apologize?

Madame Lucas don't want you seein Vera no more.

Bulrusher I don't need to kiss her, that was what she did to me. Once. We can just talk.

Madame He says no.

Bulrusher But I said I'd take care of her and the boy when he's born.

Madame A boy?

Bulrusher I read her water. It was an accident.

Madame What do you want with her baby?

Bulrusher I ain't never had a family. So maybe with her, I can make my own.

Madame I've got to have clean lines in my life, nothing blurry: gotta keep all the food on my plate in separate heaps, can't put on my knickers if they haven't been ironed. Anything unexpected, anything messy, I clean it up. My path has always been clear in front of me . . . but I can't see it anymore. Somebody wants to buy this place for more money than I ever expected to see in my life, and I should be happy, but between that and you and Lucas and Schoolch I feel like something's choking me . . . I want that man, but how can I have him? . . . There's something I'm supposed to do but I don't know what it is. Do you?

Bulrusher You're shaking, Madame.

Madame I feel like I'm having a greeney. I need to know something. I need to know what I'm supposed to do.

Bulrusher Why are you asking me?

Madame *walks into the kitchen and brings back a bowl of water.*

Madame Can't you see it on my face? I'm not breathing right. Nothing I plant ever grows in my garden . . . If I could just smell the grass on my mother's grave, smell the grass growing there –

She plunges her hands into it and splashes it onto her face.

Bulrusher What for?

Madame Read my water.

Bulrusher Schoolch.

Madame I'll worry about him.

Bulrusher I said I wouldn't read again, unless Vera wanted me to.

Madame I need you to tell me what to do. Tell me what to do.

Bulrusher I want to see Vera.

Madame I told you Lucas said no.

Bulrusher I'll read your water if you arrange for us to meet.

Madame You can't love that girl!

Bulrusher Call him. Or I won't read.

Madame *picks up the phone to call* **Logger**. *She begins to cry as she talks.*

Madame Lucas, how you doin. No, I'm fine, was just calling about Vera. She's got to get over to the doctor, you know. Make sure she and that baby are alright. I can take her when I go into Mendocino. No, I'll do it. I've done it before. She needs a woman around for that kind of thing. Enough lying on a cold metal table and showing yourself to a man with bad breath. What? No, nothing's wrong with me. No, I'm not crying. It's just hot in here. I'll call you later.

She hangs up.

There.

She moves the bowl of water to **Bulrusher**.

Bulrusher Don't let Vera get rid of the baby.

Madame Don't push it. I asked you to read my water, not hers.

Bulrusher I can't guarantee I'll see something you want to see.

Madame Just hurry.

Bulrusher This could be like May Bloyd.

Madame May had that coming to her. She wasn't the saint she made herself out to be.

Bulrusher If you cry, cry over the bowl, I'll get a stronger signal that way.

Madame Can you see the past?

Bulrusher Water has a current. I follow where it goes. Hands in the water.

Bulrusher *puts her hands into the water with* **Madame***'s. She closes her eyes. After several beats, she pulls* **Madame***'s hands out, holding them over the bowl.* **Schoolch** *comes down the stairs, unseen.*

Bulrusher Don't see anything but you in a blue hat.

Madame That's it?

Bulrusher Yeah – it just looks all the same from here on. Two pillows on your bed, and a blue hat.

Madame That's how soon from now?

Bulrusher *opens her eyes.*

Bulrusher I don't get time, I get pictures. That's the only one coming through.

Madame How is that supposed to help me? You sure ain't what you advertise.

Schoolch Mornin.

Bulrusher *drops* **Madame***'s hands, drying her own on her clothes.*

Bulrusher Mornin. I came to find you.

Madame Schoolch, she didn't see nothin.

Schoolch You asked her to read when you know she's wiped her hands of fortune?

Madame How can she wipe her hands of themselves?

Schoolch You don't mind them calling her a witch then. Well I do. You ain't never loved her. Never loved anybody. Well I do.

Bulrusher I made you some spoonbread, Schoolch. I didn't know where you were.

Schoolch I was setting myself free. You can't be bound to people who don't know how to love.

Bulrusher You didn't come home. Don't do that again without telling me.

Schoolch *laughs*. **Bulrusher** *smiles.*

Madame Schoolch. I don't know what I'm supposed to do.

Schoolch *pulls out a leather envelope thick with money.*

Schoolch This should help.

Madame (*pulling money from envelope, realizing*) You wrote me that letter? *You* wanna buy me out? Why?

Schoolch I want you to leave. I don't care if it costs my life savings. If you ain't gonna set things right, you gotta leave.

I'm tired of waitin and I'm tired of bein tired. Make up your mind.

Schoolch *and* **Bulrusher** *exit.* **Madame** *sits.*

Lights change. The river. One week later. **Bulrusher** *and* **Vera** *are in the water, making love. In the staging, they are not actually touching, but can feel every movement made by the other.* **Bulrusher** *speaks to the river.* **Vera** *cannot hear her.*

Bulrusher Pampas grass, Swiss chard,
waterfall, chipmunk.
And vines, vines, growing in the hill.

Monkeyflower and jackrabbits,
a roll dipped in apricot jam,
fresh cream turns to butter in the churn.

I swing, swing, over the poppies,
the scrub pine: I'm a meteor, its trail,
hold a star on my tongue.

They come out of the water and begin putting their clothes back on. They are strangely awkward with each other – their lovemaking wasn't what they thought it would be. **Vera** *is a bit faraway;* **Bulrusher** *looks to her for cues.*

Vera Hey.

Bulrusher Hey.

Vera I missed you.

Bulrusher You got a new dress.

Vera Madame gave it to me. I put it on in the doctor's office. I guess I'm supposed to grow into it.

Bulrusher So the baby's . . . ?

Vera Still there.

Bulrusher Good. Does your uncle talk bad about me?

Vera Mainly he sings songs to my stomach. He's been real nice to me.

Bulrusher He's a good man.

Vera He made friends with a long distance operator and called my mother. Now she knows everything.

Bulrusher Are you going back?

Pause.

Vera A white man did this to me. A policeman. I typed reports for him in the front office.

Bulrusher Do you love him?

Vera He raped me. And my boyfriend is studying to be a pastor.

Bulrusher Do you want me to kill him?

Vera That's so sweet.

Bulrusher Then I'll do it.

Vera I don't want him dead, I want him to change. (*To herself.*) All of em gotta change . . .

Bulrusher I thought you wanted all white people murdered. I'd do that for you. As many as I could.

Vera Bulrusher, don't say that. I was just talking.

Bulrusher Maybe the same thing happened to you happened to my mother. Maybe that's why she got rid of me.

Vera No, I can tell you were made from love. So you shouldn't go beating people up.

Bulrusher We've saved up a lot of money. That plus the Apple Show, we can go away somewhere. Drive the truck down to Mexico. No one will know where the baby comes from.

Vera And you'd leave Schoolch?

Bulrusher I'd have food sent to him from the hotel.

Vera But you'd be okay without him?

Bulrusher Mm hm.

Vera He's white, you could just kill him.

Bulrusher I could.

Vera (*laughing*) You couldn't. You sure don't know how to lie.

Bulrusher Is your boyfriend gonna be mad that you ran off with me?

Vera Fred? He doesn't get mad, he prays. 'What you do to the least you do to me', something like that. And sometimes he believes the things he says. At least I hope so. What about Boy? He's gonna be awful teary if you go.

Bulrusher I don't understand him. His friends used to lift up my shirt and wouldn't let me go till I said I had goat titties. Boy wouldn't do nothing but watch and laugh. Now I'm the sparkle of his eye.

Vera Well you probably *did* have goat titties back then. You don't anymore.

Bulrusher Isn't that the same as what the policeman did to you?

Vera You already broke the boy's face in, what else do you want?

Madame *enters.*

Madame You still have your clothes on, that's good news. Wrap it up now, I don't want to put Lucas on the wonder.

Vera Just a few more minutes, ma'am.

Madame You want me to wait until you go into labor? I got things to do.

Vera We won't be long.

Madame I'm going to sit in the car. Don't make me have to come and get you again.

Bulrusher A few more minutes.

Madame *exits.*

Bulrusher Should we take off our clothes again just to show her?

Vera No.

Bulrusher I did get that turpentine feeling under my skin again. But your lips were . . . cold.

Vera What did you see when you kissed me? Did you see my future?

Bulrusher I thought I would, but I didn't. You were blurry, like when a person doesn't want me to read. Maybe kissing makes a different kind of water? 'Cause all I felt . . . was your mouth. Cold.

Vera You didn't like it.

Bulrusher Um . . . I think so.

Vera You didn't. I know you didn't. It's okay though. Find the right person I guess, and everything'll fall into place.

Bulrusher What about you? You could teach me.

Vera There's feeling (*She places her hands over her own and* **Bulrusher***'s heart.*) and touching. (*She palms* **Bulrusher***'s hip.*) Sometimes they both come in the same person and sometimes they don't. I think you like Boy. That's who you're meant for.

Bulrusher He's not pretty.

Vera But he's cute.

Bulrusher And I said I'd take care of you.

Vera Woman of your word.

Bulrusher Everything will be fine when we go away together. We'll just have to find a town with a river.

Vera My mother sent the first *Jet* magazine I won.

Bulrusher And the pomade?

Vera She kept that. There's a picture in here I want you to see.

Vera *shows her the magazine.*

Bulrusher Is that a dead boy?

Vera That's what the headline says.

Bulrusher But his head looks like a football with gravel glued on. There's no nose, eyes, mouth – he doesn't have a face left.

Vera They killed him and drowned him in a river for whistling at a white woman.

Bulrusher This happened in your town?

Vera Close enough.

Bulrusher Why do colored people even live where these things happen?

Vera Because we're done runnin . . . done bein ashamed. We didn't do nothing wrong but get born.

Bulrusher Why didn't the river save him?

Vera I guess so we could save ourselves. When I watched you beat that Boy up, I suddenly knew right then and there that I couldn't undo my own hurt by making more. One day I'm gonna be a teacher and I'm 'n a say what I know. That we can take our hate and let it open us so wide we can love anybody. That we can stand in the face of violence and say I can take that, I'm bigger than that.

Bulrusher Bigger than the white people.

Vera Bigger than our own small fists.

Madame (*calling from offstage*) Vera now, let's move it.

Bulrusher So I'll see you at the Apple Show.

Vera (*laughing*) We'll disappear after the dance. We'll drive off into the sunset, won't we?

Bulrusher And the love songs will come on the radio and they'll be about us.

Vera *is silent.*

Bulrusher Did *you* like it? Kissing me?

Vera This is for you. Got it in Mendocino.

Vera *hands* **Bulrusher** *a small pewter hand mirror engraved with flowers.*

Vera I wanted to kiss you all over from the moment I met you. I don't know why. Never felt like that about a girl, ever. But then when we do kiss, it's like – it's like you said. It's cold, like I'm pressing my lips to a mirror, like it's just me again and again, over and over. I don't know why *that* is either. Each time, cold kisses, cold rain. (*Touches Bulrusher's cheek.*) And we can't do nothin about the weather. (*Stands.*) Just take this – and remember me when you look at your own face.

Bulrusher It's nice, but I don't need it. I'll be seeing you all the time.

Vera Keep it anyway.

As **Vera** *begins to leave, she leans down to the water and whispers to it.*

Vera (*to river, softly*) Thank you.

Bulrusher I'll meet you after the Apple Show dance.

Vera Bulrusher.

Bulrusher What.

Vera Don't learn how to lie.

Suddenly **Madame** *is there.*

Madame (*to* **Vera**) In the car.

Vera *hesitates, looking at* **Bulrusher**. *Then, she goes.*

Madame Bulrush, Schoolch says someone's coming to see you.

Bulrusher Who?

Madame He says he heard from your mother, up by Clear Lake. She wants to do penance. Huh. Bout time. She'll meet you Sunday dusk by Wharf Rock.

Bulrusher My mother? But Sunday is the Apple Show dance.

Madame So? You want to meet her, don't you?

Bulrusher I guess.

Madame Sunday by Wharf Rock.

Lights change. **Bulrusher** *talks to the river as the Apple Show begins. Music.*

Bulrusher Dusk, Sunday.

Dusk, Sunday.
Schoolch says my mother
will meet me: dusk,
Sunday, by Wharf Rock.

What will I do with
my hands? Will she push
me into the ocean?
Throw herself to the tide?

O river,
tell me, tell me:

will I kill her?

The Apple Show. Everyone dances as **Boy** *calls it from the grandstand.* **Madame** *leads* **Logger***, who does not know how to dance, and* **Schoolch** *and* **Bulrusher** *dance with great flourish. Stomping, clapping.*

Boy Headgents give right hands across and balance four in line

Back with the left and don't get lost and mind your steps
and time
Swing your partner halfway round and balance there
again
Swing your partner to her place and those two ladies
chain
Rat a tat tat, rat a tat tat, rat a tat tat
Rat a tat tat, rat a tat tat, rat a tat tat

Logger I told you you'd stay for the dance.

Madame Only because you said you'd come.

Logger Can't believe you actually drug me to a dance. I don't do things I ain't good at.

Madame You're tripping over your shoelaces pretty well.

They dance. **Bulrusher**, *now in her booth, reads water for unseen townspeople.*

Bulrusher It's fifty cents for one image of your future. Please pay before you place your hand in the water sir. Thank you. Relax your arm. Alright. (*A few beats.*) Your sheep are going to be attacked by bobcats. Next.

Boy *walks up.*

Boy Will you tell our future?

Bulrusher Step aside, I'm only taking paying customers. It's fifty cents, ma'am.

Boy I want you to be in my future.

Bulrusher Let me get this bowl refreshed.

Boy I wrote songs for you and everything.

Bulrusher Relax your arm. You will purchase a pair of socks that are very intriguing to a person whose sex is difficult to ascertain. No, thank *you*.

Boy You're still sore over hitting me the other night?

Bulrusher You'd like two dollars' worth of images? Yes sir, I'll give you your money's worth – and add one more for free!

Boy You got my jaw real good. I can't eat any of these crunchy apples.

Bulrusher Very relaxed arm, that's a good sign. Your gonorrhea will clear up and be less of a hindrance in your adultery. You will oversleep and miss your mother's funeral. You will leave the Anyhow Saloon drunk and crash your truck into Petrified Gulch, where your tires will calcify before you can tow it out. You will – you sure? But you get two more, we ain't done. Well at least take a complimentary navel orange.

Boy I know I can't make up your mind for you, but won't you give me a little somethin?

Bulrusher I'm working, Boy. And then I'm leaving.

Boy How bout a dance before you go?

Bulrusher Just stop bothering me! Look, I'm sorry I broke in your face.

Boy I'm sorry for not talking to you till – lately.

Bulrusher And.

Boy I'm sorry for not putting my arm around you in the Anyhow.

Bulrusher And.

Boy I'm sorry for laughing at your goat titties.

Bulrusher So we're square. Listen, I've got to get to Wharf Rock by dusk but I need you to keep an eye out for Vera.

Boy You're still stuck on her.

Bulrusher I'm taking care of her.

Boy That's different. Means I still got a chance. Did you ever read that love letter I wrote you when we was twelve?

Bulrusher I took it to the outhouse and threw it down.

Boy (*smiles*) I always knew you liked me.

Bulrusher Tell Vera to wait for me if you see her.

Boy If you'll give me a dance.

Bulrusher Trade.

Boy (*a whoop*) Eeeee tah! What you going to Wharf Rock for?

Bulrusher To meet my mother.

Schoolch *walks up to* **Bulrusher***'s booth.*

Boy Afternoon. Bulrusher's gonna dance with me.

Boy *walks away.* **Bulrusher** *starts to gather up her money.*

Bulrusher Schoolch.

Schoolch Bulrush.

Bulrusher You mind me reading fortunes?

Schoolch No, never. Just minded what all these people had to say about you when you did.

Bulrusher I can take it.

Schoolch I believe you.

Bulrusher Thanks for taking care of me Schoolch.

Schoolch So you're gonna kill your mother and run off with Vera. You got your majority, you can do what you want. I just wanted to make sure that was your plan.

Bulrusher I was gonna have your food sent from the hotel.

Schoolch Where's the shotgun.

Bulrusher I'll bring it back. I'm just afraid she's gonna try and kill me again.

Schoolch You didn't need that gun when you were a baby.

Bulrusher Why did she say we had to meet by the ocean? That's where she sent me to die. I've never been there and I don't want to go. If I even look at the ocean, it might take away all my river power – it could still kill me.

Schoolch You can tell everybody else's fortunes, but you could never tell your own.

Schoolch *watches* **Madame** *and* **Logger** *dance.* **Madame** *notices him and stops, leaving her hand in* **Logger***'s.* **Schoolch** *bows to her, and exits.* **Madame** *and* **Logger** *begin to dance again with* **Bulrusher** *and* **Boy**.

Madame Fancy footwork, Boy. Keep it loose 'cause she might split your lip on the next beat.

Logger Mm, she's starting to look reformed to me. Got a sense of purpose about her.

Madame You want her to read your fortune?

Logger Nope. Holding it right here in my hands.

Madame *and* **Logger** *dance off the stage.*

Boy Schoolch taught you all this?

Bulrusher Yup. He even gets a periodical sent to him from Kansas City with pictures of the new steps.

Boy Let me hold you like this. (*He puts his hand on her hip.*) Your hip feels kinda hard. Is that all the money you made?

Bulrusher And saved. What. You don't like how hard work feels?

Boy Well maybe if you'd just – dance a little closer. A little slower. Yeah, like that.

Bulrusher *moves in and takes his tempo for a few measures. Fireworks – but this time, inside them. She stops dancing.*

Bulrusher Alright, that's enough.

Boy You liked dancing with me! I could feel it.

Bulrusher Keep an eye for Vera. And Boy –

Bulrusher *kisses him on the cheek. Then she walks away.* **Boy** *hops onto the grandstand.*

Boy And this song is for Boonville's own Bulrusher, who has come out of early retirement to tell our fortunes again. I don't know about you, but doesn't that make you feel more secure? Ain't it swell to know where you're going?

Stomping and clapping again, he calls:

Apples in a pot
Apples in a pot
Skin is getting hot
Skin is getting hot
Lemon
sugar
brown

Wharf Rock. Ocean waves crashing. **Bulrusher** *hugs the shotgun to herself. She is unsteady and chants to tame the ocean of her nerves.*

Bulrusher (*eyes closed*) Seaspray,
dress me in white mist,
hide me from her.

No response from the ocean.

Seaspray, white mist,
clothe me in salt.

No response. She opens her eyes.

You're not like the river. You
won't listen. But you will not have me.
You are the mother I refuse.
I will live, and live,
live, and live,
without the terror of your love.

Madame *appears in a blue hat.*

Madame We don't look nothing alike.

Bulrusher *spins around to her.*

Bulrusher Blue hat.

Madame Is that gun for me?

Bulrusher Madame.

Madame Yeah. Don't call me anything different.

Bulrusher Madame.

Madame A gun. Where'd you get all these violent impulses?

Bulrusher Madame?

Madame Yeah. (*Pause.*) Well don't stand there dumb, let's us have a conversation. Ain't you saved up some questions for me?

Pause.

Bulrusher No.

Madame I know you got some curiosity.

Pause.

Bulrusher When you leaving?

Madame You know I say that every summer when the heat gets to me. Gave Schoolch his money back. I can't leave none a you. So you glad it's me? Coulda been someone you couldn't relate to, somebody lacking morals and accountability.

Bulrusher I just – what you –

Madame Spit it out.

Bulrusher How could – I don't – this ocean air is trying to kill me –

Madame No it ain't. You can talk.

Bulrusher I don't got any questions. I got to go.

Madame Bulrush, hold on. We don't gotta change nothing, let's just talk a while.

Bulrusher I got to go. Vera.

Madame I still have that basket I wove you. Went down and picked it up after Lucas found you. Wove it from reeds and rushes I found near Clear Lake when my ma was sick. You kept growin in me, she passed, then you were born. Thought it would be nice for you to float in that basket and look up at the sky. But I was greedy. I had to spend a while with you before I sent you off; had to see what of Lucas made it into you.

Bulrusher Vera and I are cousins?

Madame Kiss kiss.

Bulrusher I've got to tell her.

Madame Bulrush –

Bulrusher I'm going!

Madame *grabs* **Bulrusher** *by the shoulders.*

Madame Lucas took Vera to the train. She's going back to Birmingham.

Bulrusher I can catch her.

Madame No you can't.

Bulrusher Why not?

Madame The train left yesterday.

Bulrusher What about the baby.

Madame What about it. It's up to her.

Bulrusher *pulls all the money out of her pockets and throws it into the ocean.*

Madame Now what did you do that for?

Bulrusher You made Vera go away.

Madame No.

Bulrusher You sent me down the river like I wasn't nothing but shorn hair. White whore didn't want her colored baby.

Madame I ain't white, my ma's a Pomo Indian. The rest I hope you'll let me make up for.

Bulrusher I always wished you were my ma. But why should I want you now?

Madame You don't have to.

Bulrusher I got plenty of shame. Plenty. And now you want to scrape some more off your shoe and rub it on me. You ain't nothing. Nothing but shame.

Madame That's right. Think my mother wanted me to be a businesswoman? Think I could have kept my business with folks knowing I was Indian? I made my choice, stuck to it by her deathbed. Wasn't going to put you through all that I knew. Wasn't going to have no customer's baby. And I wasn't tryin to lose no customer named Lucas.

Bulrusher You told Lucas the truth, that I'm his?

Madame No, I told him I would marry him.

Bulrusher He wouldn't marry you if he knew about me.

Madame I guess I wanted to clear it with you – see if you want another father.

Bulrusher I ain't givin up Schoolch.

Madame You don't have to.

Bulrusher You already turned Schoolch down. He should have somebody in this world.

Madame He has what he's always had. I wish I wanted Schoolch, 'cause he never wanted to be a customer. And he never used you against me. Raised you with pure intent, followed you like a calling.

Bulrusher *You* didn't follow *me* down the river, I did that by myself.

Madame What do you want me to say?

Bulrusher I want you to apologize for trying to kill me.

Madame I didn't want you dead.

Bulrusher Then why did you get rid of me like that? I was floating for an eternity.

Madame You can't remember that.

Bulrusher Yes I can. Yes I can. I remember floating in the night, the fog and the coyotes – didn't know what that sound was then but I do now. Mr Jeans found me at Barney Flats, but I was there for days. I begged to be found. I talked to the sun with my fingers, kept closing my fist around it every time it went down trying to keep it with me. But the night would always come. And the river was so thin there, deep as a teardrop – but I kept myself alive. Why? To find you? To lose the only one who ever really touched me? Schoolch never did, he doesn't know how. Only told me to sit up straight. Vera touched me, gave me softness and you made her leave. You knew she was going when I saw her last, didn't you. (**Madame** *is silent.*) Of course you did. So is she gonna kill the baby or be the preacher's wife who got raped by a cop?

Madame You're angry with me.

Bulrusher I'm not angry. I'm gonna kill you. I want to kill something. Walk toward the edge of that bluff. Do it.

Madame *doesn't move and* **Bulrusher** *aims her shotgun.*

Bulrusher Back to me. Go to the ocean and look at it.

Madame *walks to the edge of the cliff.*

Bulrusher See it gnashing its teeth? It wants you. Didn't want me. But it still wants to eat. Salt gonna sting your eyes, gonna burn you. All that seaweed down there is gonna grab you and drown you.

Madame Bulrusher.

Bulrusher You already dead, ever since you tried to kill me. You been dead.

Madame Bulrush –

Bulrusher Dead for money. Wanted some damn money steada me. Well go get it. I threw it in there for you. It's all yours.

Madame Bulrusher, I named you.

Bulrusher Bulrusher, caught in the bulrushes, abandoned to the weeds. I'm a weed.

Madame You got a name. You ain't a weed.

Bulrusher Jeans? Whore? Sneeble? Witch?

Madame You got my mama's name. You got your grandma's name just like she wanted you to have it.

Bulrusher Pomo? Indian? I don't want it.

Madame You got her name. It's Xa-wena. Means on the water.

Bulrusher You called me that once. One day.

Madame You remember.

Bulrusher I remember everything.

Madame (*chants softly*) O beda-Xa, a thi shishkith, ometh ele'le'. Xa-wéna ewé-ba ke katsilith'ba ele'ledith. O beda-Xa, a thi boshtotsith.

Speaks.

River water, I ask you, protect her, help her. Take her to your bosom. Save her from the night and cold, river water, protect her. I thank you.

Madame *turns around.* **Bulrusher** *has lowered her shotgun.*

Madame I prayed for you in your basket. And your river listened. She listened. The river's your mother. I throw stones into it everyday to thank her for caring for you.

Madame *kneels and hugs* **Bulrusher***'s legs.*

Madame See? I got softness.

Pause.

Bulrusher Xa-wena.

Madame Yes?

Bulrusher I was just sayin it.

Madame Oh.

Lights fade. **Madame** *exits. Spot on* **Bulrusher** *holding the mirror* **Vera** *gave her. She can barely speak as she tries to find her bearings in the things she knows.*

Bulrusher Chaparral, dust, frogs, cicadas, bay trees, sequoias, pine cones, horse shit, lizards, hummingbirds, ravines, ferns, eucalyptus, woodchips, wild rose, full moon in clouds, exposed roots, skunks, hawks, poppies, driftwood fences, yellow hills, cormorants, spiderwebs, all blown dandelion zero.

Two weeks later. **Bulrusher** *sits on the porch with* **Schoolch**. *During the following lines,* **Logger** *enters and puts his foot up on the porch.* **Bulrusher** *does not talk to the river, but to the audience. She is easy, calm.*

Bulrusher This town is a byway, a traveler's raincoat
folded away from sight. People need
something stop here. They smell it, take it,

and pass through. I sell oranges, balls
of sun. You eat them in sections like a heart
torn from the spine. When they're gone,

I lie in my red flatbed and watch the stars
fall without pity.

Logger (*lively*) So Madame and I talkin bout getting locked real soon, October, when the sun fades some and we can have a party in her garden. Both of you invited of course, I'll even braid your hair special Bulrush if you want me to.

Bulrusher Schoolch and I smoke cigarettes
by the duck pond, I peel bark
from the madrone tree and rub
the smooth beneath.

Logger Schoolch, hope you don't mind that I won Madame after all these years you been courtin. But you know, the woman's got her own mind and well, she made it up. Two pillows on her bed now. And Bulrush, you got every right to stay on here with Schoolch, but you just let me know if you need anything, not that Schoolch wouldn't already have it to give, but you know, if you need anything, uh, the family history and so forth, I got a lot a stories, uh, diseases you might be prone to, uh, and the like, of that nature.

Bulrusher Soon it will be colder than ever.
In the garden my collards will be pregnant with ice.
But an early frost makes the greens taste sweeter.

Logger You woulda died in them weeds if I hadn't found ya. And then Schoolch was good enough to raise you up. Well, can't judge Madame for what never happened. (*Bright.*) Got a letter today, from Birmingham. Your cousin Vera wrote you a note. I hear she's gettin married soon too.

He gives the letter to **Bulrusher**.

Logger Gotta have you a family and a church to lean on in a city like that. It's just been sounding worse and worse down there ever since that boy got . . . what they did to him . . . But you can't just take what pain life has to give you, you gotta make something out of it too. People see you got that kinda strength, they can't deny you. No sirree.

Schoolch When I finally took away Bulrusher's bottle she cried and cried all night. 'I want my bah-ul! I want my bah-ul!' Come the next morning she didn't need it no more. But she had turned and turned so in the crib her hair got matted into chunks. It was like she had a hat on made of steel wool. I tried to comb through it, poured baby oil all over it, dunked her in a big vat of lard, but those tangles wouldn't come out.

Logger Is that the truth?

Schoolch So I had to cut it all off. Cut it all off.

Pause.

Logger Did you. (*Laughing.*) Well Bulrusher you must have cried all that next night too!

Logger *hugs* **Bulrusher** *with one arm.*

Schoolch She did. I sat by her crib. Didn't hold her but she knew I was there.

Bulrusher *looks at* **Schoolch**, *then puts the letter into a bowl of water. She lifts up the paper and lets the ink run. She sinks the letter back in, and tries to get a signal. Nothing. She pulls her hands out, then puts them back in. Nothing. Once more she tries, hands in –*

Logger So how is Vera?

Bulrusher I can't tell.

Her hands are still in the water.

Logger Oh, you don't read off of paper. Uh huh.

Bulrusher No, anything somebody touch I can read from once it's in water. Maybe I can't read *her* anymore. Or maybe I can't read at all.

Logger Now don't say 'can't'. You can do anything you want if you put your mind to it. Schoolch, you thought about installing a phone here? I put one in and now I can't live without it.

Boy *enters, plucking his guitar. He sits next to* **Bulrusher**.

Boy I got a new song for you.

Bulrusher I got a new name.

Boy What is it?

Bulrusher *pulls her hands out of the bowl, turns it onto its rim and lets the water run out. She looks at him gently. Blackout.*

A glossary for the curious

From *Boontling: An American Lingo* by Charles C. Adams, Mountain House Press, 1990

Bulrusher	foundling, illegitimate child
Navarro	Bulrusher's river; main waterway west to the ocean
high shams	thick brush
Schoolch	short for school teacher
hobbin	dancing
flattened	sick
flag's out	menstruating
geechin	penetration
burlap	have sex with
bahl	good
stringy hair and wrinkle socks	an unkempt woman
moldunes	breasts
pike	road
madges	prostitutes
heel scratchin	sex
rout	scold
harp	talk
that's earth	that's the truth
sulled	angered
dehigged	broke, without money
jackers	young men who masturbate
dish	cheat
can-kicky	angry
buzzchick	baseball
bookers	black people
silent seeker	quiet, unobtrusive seducer
shike	beat someone in a deal
booker tee	black man
nonch harpin	dirty talk
Fourth of Jeel	Fourth of July
cocked darley	habitually angry
moshe	automobile

ling	Boontling
mossy	change the subject
bilchin	having sex with
Philo	a neighboring rival town
tarp	pudendum of either sex
boarch	Chinese male
ink-standy	tired
applehead	girl, girlfriend
roger	storm
mink	woman (of easy morals, well dressed enough to afford mink)
fiddlers	delirium tremens
put in on	to court
ricky chow	sexual intercourse
pearlin	raining
cut cabbage	a black woman, the feeling of her vagina
gorm	food
scottied	hungry
flories	biscuits
toobs	two bits, a quarter
belhoon	a dollar
rooje	cheat
horn and chiggle	food and drink (the verb 'horn' means 'to drink')
tidrey	a little bit
jape	drive
jenny	snitch
tuddish	mentally disabled
ear settin	a lecture
somersettin	to become emotionally upset
comb's gettin red	puberty
dubs	double
sneeble	black person
highgun	shotgun
teet lipped	angry
dove cooey	lonely
golden eagles	underwear (made from Golden Eagle brand flour sacks)

doolsey boo	sweet potato
hoot	laugh
whittlin	politicking
warblin	singing
yink	young man
jonnems	tall tales
wess	exaggerate
airtight	no problem, also name for a sawmill
grizz	old bachelor
tweed	child
daming	womanizing
skee	whiskey
barlow	pocketknife
ridgy	from the backwoods, unsophisticated
bloocher	one who chatters aimlessly or masturbates
tongue-cuppy	nauseous, to vomit
lizzied	pregnant
lews 'n' larmers	gossip
heisted	pregnant
upper-cuttin	fist fight
Joe Mack	to beat someone up
weese	infant
greeney	a fit, a strange feeling associated with sudden awakening
locked	married

Pronunciation

Navarro	nuh-VAHR-row
Madame	muh-DAMN
Reina	RAY-nuh
McGimsey	mick-JIM-zee
Philo	FY-low
Ina	EYE-nuh
Ukiah	yoo-KAI-yuh
Pizitz	puh-ZITS
Xa-wena	ha-WAY-nah

Pomo chant (courtesy of Robert Geary):
Oh buh-DAH-hah, ah tee-SHEESH-keeth, oh met eh-LAY-lay. Ha-WAY-nah ay-WAY-bah kay kaht-SEE-leet-bah ay-LAY-lay-deeth. Oh buh-DAH-hah, ah tee BOSH-toe tseeth.

The 'th' sounds at the ends of words are very lightly aspirated.

Permissions

Songs by Eisa Davis, except for 'Apple Show Call' (anonymous), and 'For All We Know', written by Fred J. Coots and Samuel M. Lewis (ASCAP).

Acknowledgments

Deep gratitude to the trees, rivers, and hills of Mendocino County, and to all the people who, voluntarily or involuntarily, served as midwives for this play: Daniel T. Denver, Nicole Ari Parker, Angela Davis, Fania Davis, Emily Morse, Mead Hunter, Leah C. Gardiner, Valerie Curtis-Newton, Ian Morgan, New Dramatists, the Helen Merrill Award committee, Marina Drummer, Robert Geary and his aunt, the last living speaker of Southeastern Pomo, Greg Tate, Adrienne Kennedy, August Wilson, and Sam Jordan. A special thank you to all the actors who brought this play to life, particularly: Robert Beitzel, Peter Bradbury, Charlotte Colavin, Donna Duplantier, Matthew Grant, Zabryna Guevara, Adrienne Hurd, Michelle Hurd, Guiesseppe Jones, Tinashe Kajese, the late Margo Skinner, Keith Randolph Smith, Dale Soules, Ed Vassallo, and Michole Briana White.

Christina Anderson

Good Goods

Players

Stacey *Black American male. Twenty-eight years old. The former straight man in a comedy duo with Patricia. Now he's inherited his father's general store called Good Goods.*
Truth *Black American male. Thirty-five years old. The shop assistant and watch guard of Good Goods.*
Wire (*aka* **Patrick**) *Black American male. Thirty years old. A messenger. Short in stature.*
Patricia (*aka Patty*) *Black American female. Twenty-nine turning thirty years old. Wire's twin sister. Also the other half of the comedy duo.*
Sunny *Black American female. Eighteen years old. A young lady who befriends Patricia.*
Waymon as Hunter Priestess; Factory folk *Black American male. Ageless.*

Time

Between 1961 and 1994. There's a keen sense of hindsight in the characters that places this play on a sliding scale in relation to time.

Place

The side pocket of America. It's a small, unknown city / county / town / village that doesn't appear on any map. You have to know about it to get to it. And even then you have to know somebody who's from there to survive.

Author's note

Given the context of the scene, the =.= indicates an active moment of gesture or a moment of communication between characters that transcends language.

POS·SES·SION

Pronunciation: po\-'ze-shən also -'se-\
Function: noun
Date: 14th century

1a : the act of having or taking into control
1b : control or occupancy of property without regard to ownership
1c : ownership
1d : control of the ball or puck; also: an instance of having such control (as in football) scored on their first two possessions
2 : something owned, occupied, or controlled: property
3a : domination by something (as an evil spirit, a passion, or an idea)
3b : a psychological state in which an individual's normal personality is replaced by another

One

This is what we see:

A panoramic view of the Good Goods shop and connecting room. Starting from stage right we see two or three steps that lead to a back porch that leads to a back door that takes us to a cramped room that functions as the bedroom/kitchen/dining room/study of Stacey Good. This room leads to a curtain that takes us to the Good Goods shop. The shop leads to the front door that takes us to the front porch that leads to two or three steps that takes us offstage. The shelves in Good Goods are stocked with various products: cans of this stuff; bottles of that; sacks; boxes big and small; pots-n-pans; candy bins, etc. Modern items are mixed with antiquated ones (e.g. a neon sign on a wall, kerosene lamps line the shelf underneath it). Two medium-sized boxes are on the front porch.

The sky behind the Good Goods establishment is grey. The air is wet.

A large brick building can be seen in the distance. Some windows are covered with stained glass, others with slats of wood. The battered façade makes it difficult to determine the building's function. No signs or markings identify its purpose.

The only indication that the building is operational is the blue smoke that squirms from its pipes.

The sun attempts to break the grey and light the morning.

The sound of the building's whistle signals the start of a workday. The call is faint, but the presence of labor looms over the shop.

Stacey *enters stage right, carrying a couple of shirts and pants fresh off the line. He wears slacks and a button-down shirt. His tailored clothes are a bit too sleek against the shop's rustic style. He climbs the steps leading to the back porch and enters through the back door into his bedroom. He dumps his clothes on the bed.*

Crosses over to a pile of tapes and shuffles through a few, deciding what he wants to listen to. He picks a cassette and puts it into the tape deck that hangs above his bed. Presses play. As the sound plays from the machine, **Stacey** *starts folding his clothes.*

He folds his shirts, pants in a way that indicates he may have worked retail at some point.

The cassette picks up in the middle of a comedy routine. It's the voice of a woman with a raspy voice (think Moms Mabley or Whoopie Goldberg).

Voice from the tape player (*chuckle*) / Yea, like the other night / I'm goin through the channels / it's late at night / I already put my man to sleep / you know what I'm saying ladies / (*laughter*) / I can't go to sleep after I get down / you know? / I'm ready to BE-BoP / but my man turns into Stepin Fetchet / just passes OUT / (*Laughter, applause.*) / So I'm up late at night after my . . . escapades (*Chuckle.*) / and I'm clicking through the channels / and I stop at this movie / it's called . . . / Devil Do*ll* / (*The solo clap of recognition from an audience member.*) / aw, see, mutha-fucka, I know what you into if you clapping for this freaky shit / (*Laughter.*) / you can always tell who into what when they clap / 'you notice how the smell of ass never really leaves your fingers?' / see? see? this muthafucka here clap, clap, clapping / you know you tellin on yourself, right? / (*Comedienne chuckles.*) / just clap, don't care what I'm bout to say next . . .

Truth, *the watch guard and shop assistant, steps up on the front porch. A worn backpack is strapped to his back. He has a key to the front door, unlocks it. Turns on the lights in the store.* **Stacey** *checks his watch, knowing it's* **Truth**. *The men don't speak.* **Stacey** *continues to fold.* **Truth** *removes his backpack, gets settled. He crosses to the safe, spins the dial three times, stopping at each number in the password. He opens the safe and pulls out the till for the register, counts the bills as:*

Voice from the tape player Devil Doll is about this crazy ass hypnotist-voodoo-ventriloquist-man/ who has this dummy / straight up three foot tall dummy that he props up on his lap and does the / 'what do ya say, mack?' kind of jokes / and then he tells this dummy to walk around / and the dummy hops off his lap and struts around / like he didn't just have a hand up his ass!/ My man put his pinky up there and I'm just – 'no you don't muthafucka! You betta wake me up first! You know you can't wash that smell off!' / You know what I'm sayin ladies? / Anyway . . . I'm watching this movie thinking . . . what the hell is this?? Come to find out he den up and put somebody's soul in the damn doll –

Stacey *shuts off the tape. He puts his clothes away in a cardboard box and slides it under the cot. He exits his bedroom, enters the shop.*

The men banter but a tension remains just below the surface.

Truth Hey, hey now.

Stacey Hey now.

Truth *finishes counting the cash. Then he places each stack of bills in its rightful place in the drawer. Shuts it.*

Stacey =.= (*taking inventory around the shop*)

Truth Who's that you listenin to?

Stacey Wire got it for me.

Truth Sounds funny.

Stacey Not yet. We'll see. She's from out east. She's young. Nineteen, twenty . . . ?

Truth Is she cute?

Stacey With a mouth like that?

Truth It's an act, right?

Stacey She's pretty. Not for you though.

Truth How you know what's for me?

Stacey She can see; that's how I know. One look at you and she'd burn outta here with the quickness.

Truth Pssshh. She ain't goin nowhere. This (*re: his body*) is handcrafted, prime cut, one-of-a-kind –

Stacey . . . assembly-line, off-brand, second-hand, patch-work –

Truth Leave *your* goods out of it –

Stacey You wanna talk all that junk while you bringin in them boxes on the front porch?

Truth (*sarcastic*) It would be my pleasure. Boss.

Stacey *has a slight reaction to being called 'boss' in such a sarcastic tone, but he covers it.*

Truth *exits the shop to the front porch. He grabs a box, brings it in as:*

Truth What's in these?

Stacey Special orders. The Factory Folk asked for some things.

Truth They get some change in they pockets . . .

Stacey And come straight here. Cain't be mad at that.

Truth I shouldn't be . . .

Truth *crosses back onto the front porch. Looks up:*

Truth Might rain.

Stacey (*from inside the shop*) It always looks like rain.

Truth But I smell it.

Wire was sayin it was rainin something awful over yonder.

Rain travels.

Truth *brings in the remaining box.*

If it's raining come lunchtime, them Factory Folk gonna have to crowd on the front porch to eat. Spill over into the shop.

Stacey You sound uneasy about that.

Truth No uneasiness . . . It's just hard keep an eye on things when people clump together. It's hard to keep track of whose hands been where.

Stacey You been worried about they hands before?

Truth No.

Stacey So, why you thinkin you need to keep track of hands now?

Truth =.=

=.=

'Cause people get ideas when things change.

A window of opportunity cracks open when responsibility . . . shifts.

Stacey Well, that's why my daddy kept you here, Truth. To make sure that window you talkin bout is locked. Tight.

Plus, those Factory Folk are good people. They wouldn't take nuthin from the store. Why you suspectin them?

Truth Who else comes through here, Stacey?

Stacey You.

Truth =.=

=.=

Well, well, you livin in that back room. You on the suspect list, too.

Stacey I'ma steal from my own store?

Truth This is your daddy's store.

Stacey Is he here?

Truth It's still in his name, so it's like he's here.

Stacey But he's not in this shop. On this property. He ran away. Skipped out.

Truth Until the paperwork shifts, you stealing from *your daddy's* store.

This is Mister Good senior's establishment until the papers say otherwise.

Stacey Who says I'd steal from anywhere?

Truth Who says I'd steal?

Stacey =.=

Truth =.=

Stacey =.=

Truth Your daddy didn't call me Truth to make a joke.

Stacey =.=

Truth =.=

Stacey =.=

Truth If you start suspecting me –

If *we* start suspecting *each other* . . . this shop gonna go outta business in a day.

Stacey =.=

Truth =.=

Truth *starts unpacking a box.*

Stacey *crosses to the register, re-counts the bank.*

Truth *notices this slight, but doesn't take it in full on. Instead:*

Truth (*under his breath*) Been here a damn week . . .

Stacey (*stops counting*) What's that?

Truth I said, you been back a damn week.

Stacey And?

Truth And I'm just stating a truth. I been here everyday since I was a lil boy. You been back a week.

Stacey =.=

Truth Mm-hm.

Stacey =.= (*Returns to counting*).

Truth =.= (*Unpacks the box.*)

Stacey =.= (*Sounds of him handling the bills.*)

Stacey *finishes the count. Returns the money back in its register.*

Truth Humph.

Second-guessing me . . .

Stacey *exits the shop, enters his bedroom. He crosses to the small writing desk grabs sheets of paper. Exits the bedroom, enters the shop, then hands the papers to* **Truth**.

Wire *enters stage left, climbs the front steps. Puffs on a handmade cigarette.*

Truth What's this?

Stacey It's a list of who ordered what. Check off what's in the boxes.

Truth (*reading the list*) Bunch of junk.

Stacey =.=

Truth Magazines, deck of cards, flipbooks, pocket videogames . . .

Waste of time.

Stacey Keeps the shop in business and money in your pocket.

Truth Yea, yea . . .

Wire Hey hey now.

Wire *puts out the cigarette. Enters the shop.*

Truth Hey now.

Stacey Hey hey.

As the men speak **Wire** *greets* **Truth** *with a slap on the back.* **Wire** *crosses over to* **Stacey** *and shakes his hand. There's a lingering between the two. Slight but weighted.* **Truth** *notices this.*

Wire It's gonna be hot today, ya'll.

Stacey Truth was just talkin bout rain.

Wire That could happen, too.

A hot rain.

There was a horrible storm over in –

Truth I was just tellin him that. He didn't believe me though.

Wire Ya'll running smooth 'round here?

Stacey (*quick*) Yea.

Truth *grunts his disapproval.*

Wire Truth?

Truth For now . . .

Stacey Truth . . .

Wire Oooo, what's goin down?

Stacey Nuthin. Nuthin's goin down.

Stacey (*to* **Truth**) Would you stop talkin mess?

Wire I'd prefer ya'll talk sense than mess –

Truth I was sayin we got to be careful since Stacey's daddy left. People think they can get away with liftin goods now.

Wire Who ya'll think would lift from here?

Truth Stacey claimed it could be me –

Stacey I was makin a point. Truth said it could be me –

Truth Cause he don't wanna believe it could be those Factory Folk.

Wire Why would they lift from here?

Stacey That's what I'm sayin, Wire.

Wire They glad to be workin . . . pays more than liftin merchandise.

Truth Most of them fools don't know left from right, back from front since they started workin in that factory.

These days 'easy' is more appealing than 'backbreakin'. And this store is an easy lift.

Wire You slippin on your job, Truth?

Truth I ain't slippin on nuthin. It's the new management.

Stacey Here we go . . .

Truth Mr. Good senior had a certain posture about him. Stacey is . . .

Wire (*benefit of the doubt*) Figurin things out. Getting used to running a business.

Truth Settlin in has its moments of . . . ignorance, you see?

Stacey (*to* **Wire**) He knows I cain't fire him. That's why he's talkin like this.

Truth That's got-dang right you can't fire me. It's in the paperwork –

Stacey You don't got to tell me what I already know –

Truth But I got to remind hardheaded individuals so they don't forget.

If you fire me, I'ma go right to the mayor's office and report your ass.

(*To* **Wire.**) Mr. Good senior got a clause in the paperwork that says getting rid of me puts the property tax on a sliding scale. However much profit the store makes in a given month, Stacey Good got to give it to the town bank.

Stacey (*to* **Wire**) I'd break even every damn month. Won't ever have extra cash.

Now what kind of sense that make?

My daddy's thinkin is like a plate of eggs. Scrambled.

Truth Your daddy's 'scrambled' thinking is what kept this store running.

(*To* **Wire**.) Fed his scrawny behind and kept grease on his elbows, scalp, and knees.

Stacey (*to* **Wire**) See? He talks all kinds of shit, because he knows I cain't kick his ass out.

Truth Why would you get rid of the only somebody who knows how this shop works?

(*To* **Wire**.) Woulda collapsed the first day he got here if it wasn't for me . . .

Stacey I been in four razor fights, spent two nights in a white man's trunk, and made love to a blind man in a dumpster full of broken glass. If I didn't break a sweat during all that, I ain't gonna collapse running my daddy's shop –

Truth First mistake, Wire: taking special orders.

Stacey Uh-uh, first mistake: not reading the fine print on them damn papers.

Truth He needs glasses, too.

Stacey I need some slack is what I need –

Wire Ya'll serving breakfast?

Truth =.=

=.=

Technically: we ain't open.

Wire But the door's never closed to guests, right?

Stacey You more than a guest, Wire. Help yourself.

Wire *slaps a few bills on the counter as payment. He makes himself a bowl of cereal.*

Stacey You don't have to pay, Wire –

Truth *rings it up. Tucks the money in the register.*

Truth Thank you. Have a nice day.

Stacey Truth –

Wire It's alright, Stacey.

Truth *crosses back to the boxes. He sorts through goods.*

Stacey *exits the shop, enters his bedroom. He sits at the small writing desk. Does paperwork.*

Wire =.= (*Chewing, spoon clanks against bowl.*)

Truth =.= (*Sorting.*)

Stacey =.= (*Reading, shuffling papers.*)

Wire *hums a few notes of 'happy birthday'.*

Wire (*to* **Truth**) I was up in that factory the other day.

Truth Yea?

Wire Yea.

Got me to thinking how old that building got to be. It's older than you. Older than me, too. And I'm twenty . . . thirty.

Aw, that's right. I'm thirty.

=.= (*Waits for* **Truth** *to remember it's his birthday. No luck.*)

Wonder when that building was made. You wonder about that? Important to remember when something or . . . somebody was created. Don't you think so, Truth?

Truth (*concentrating on sorting*) I guess . . .

Wire You guess . . . ?

Wire *hums the last line of 'Happy Birthday'.*

He sighs the final note, realizing no one remembers his birthday. **Wire** *tries to cover his disappointment.*

Wire That, that building is pretty pitiful . . . but the equipment they put in there is nice.

Brand new and *expensive*.

Them Factory Folk got to wash they hands *before* they go on the floor.

They all uppity about it, too.

Mention of the factory animates **Truth**.

Truth I don't know what they got to be uppity about.

Operating the machines ain't nuthin like ownin 'em.

Wire Cain't get down on 'em for doin they job.

Truth Every last one of them jobs is a sign of defeat –

Wire I'm not tryin to talk politics, Truth. Just wanna chat. Tellin you what it's like in there, alright?

Truth (*easing up*) Alright . . .

Wire Alright. I had to deliver a message to the foreman from the C.E.O. himself.

Truth Sayin what?

Wire Eh, a bunch of numbers. Product such-and-such needs a reduction of blah-de-blah to double the intake of uh-huh-yea-yea. But I couldn't get over those machines.

Truth Given that building's heavy history, I'm surprised they still went ahead and turned it into a pencil factory.

Wire What heavy history? That building started out as a prison, then a high school, turned into a hospital, a nightclub, an outlet store, a haunted house in October, a mega church, then a smack pad . . .

Truth What I'm saying is . . . Ivory saw her prophecy in that building.

Wire Aw, that's the heavy history you talking about. You think the men running that factory care about 'some brown gurl's vision'? That don't matter one bit to the men who running that factory today. To them makin money is about makin money. No matter what history is holding.

Stacey *exits his bedroom, enters the shop.*

Stacey Ya'll talkin about Ivory Evans. . .

Truth What you know about it?

Stacey Just as much as you do.

Truth I doubt that. Had to be here to know about it.

Wire None of us was even born when it happened, Truth.

Stacey There's that song about . . .

Uhh . . .

Ivory, my Ivory . . . da, da, da, da –

Truth (*sarcastic*) 'Da, da, da, da . . .' That's how the words go? Glad you cleared *that* up for me . . .

Stacey *dismisses* **Truth***'s sarcasm.*

Stacey Ivory, my Ivory, ... coastin 'long the sea.

Ivory, my Ivory, . . . wonderin who she'll be.

. . . The . . . sun behind her.

The grass below.

She . . . walked until she walked no more.

A mama –

Truth (*cutting in*) – calls . .

A daddy calls . . .

A brother calls . . .

A sister calls . . .

Stacey (*taking it back*) And the . . . Devil answered in Ivory tears.

Brown Ivory's red, red tears.

Ivory stopped and fell to her knees.

She saw her people pulled apart like weeds . . .

The . . . heavens behind her.

The hells below.

She screamed until she screamed no more . . .

Spoken.

She was standing in that building when she thought she saw her whole legacy – past, present and future – wiped out. Family claim she saw all these brown faces smiling at her, then with the wave of a hand death took 'em just like that. Screamed so loud the whole town heard her. (*To* **Truth**.) Told you I know that Ivory Evans story.

Truth Humph.

Blue smoke shoots from the factory pipes.

Wire That family still ain't right because of it.

They a bit off, ain't they, Truth?

Truth Something ain't right in 'em.

Stacey They still over there on the other side of the factory?

Wire Mm-hm. Every single member of the Evans clan – cousins, sons, daughters, mamas, daddies, grands and greats – living in a handful of shacks. Just waiting for Ivory's prophecy to come true. They keep a picture of Ivory on 'em at all times. The whole family does.

Girls got lockets around their necks, the boys got her sewn into their caps.

That's the only way they feel safe when they leave the house.

Stacey Why would anybody wanna carry armageddon on their body?

Wire The Evans family thinkin Ivory is a shield more than a reaper.

Truth Rest of the town thinkin she was possessed. And her prophecy happened right in that building. Now the men in this town are in there whittling blocks of wood. The women are packin 'em in crates. Fifteen hours a day for two dollars an hour and –

Stacey Two dollars?

Wire Minimum wage dropped again awhile back.

Truth (*to* **Wire**) Big baller riding high on his comedy tour missed the goings-on of the everyday citizen.

(*To* **Stacey**.) You see why your daddy didn't do special orders? Hard-earned money on junk.

Stacey They got a right to spend their money however they want to.

Truth Drug dealers talk the same trash, don't they –

Wire (*mediating*) All these stories about possessions and prophecies creeps me *out*. Don't it creep you out, Stacey?

Stacey =.=

Wire Truth?

Truth =.=

Wire I get any request to deliver a message, I make sure I carry as much protection as possible.

Stacey =.= Like what?

Wire I got a friend who's a librarian.

He wrote out armor scriptures from every religious text he could get his hands on.

Said to me, 'Wire, I know you travel all over and sometimes you have to tell people what they don't wanna hear. You need protection from the danger that can fall in your path'. I keep it right here.

Wire *lifts up his shirt. A sheet of paper, yellow from age, is wrapped in plastic and taped to his chest. Words are scribbled on it in blue ink.*

Stacey *leans in to get a closer look. There's a lingering.*

Truth *declines.*

Wire I had my mama and my daddy lay hands on it. Then I took it to the spot where I saw somebody die for the first time.

Stacey And where was that?

Wire Out in front of Lonnie's joint.

Two men got into it. One of 'em had a knife. The other didn't see it comin.

I walked over there and stood where that man took his last breath.

Truth That's awful, Wire. I didn't know you do that.

Wire *winces at this judgment and pulls his shirt down. Tucks it back in his pants. Stacey steps back.*

Wire A lot of things you don't know, Truth.

Stacey Amen to *that*.

Truth Why ya'll tag-teamin me?

Wire I don't like nobody judging my armor.

Truth I'm not judging.

Wire Said it was awful.

Truth That's cause it is.

Wire Being a messenger's a hard job. Especially for somebody my size. Need all the help I can get.

Truth I understand that, Wire.

Wire Well then, don't call how I do things 'awful'.

Truth Alright.

Truth *returns to the goods.*

Wire *finishes his cereal.*

Stacey *exits the shop, enters his bedroom.*

Wire =.= (*Chews. His spoon clanks against the bowl as . . .*)

Truth =.= (*Sorts goods in the box as . . .*)

Stacey =.= (*Reads, shuffles papers.*)

Wire *slurps the remaining milk from his bowl, gets up, goes into* **Stacey**'*s room. Closes the curtain that functions as* **Stacey**'*s door.*

Truth *sees this out the corner of his eye but says nothing.*

Stacey *knows* **Wire** *has entered his room, but says nothing.*

Wire *sits on* **Stacey**'*s bed.* **Stacey** *sits at a small table going over papers.*

Wire =.= (*Breathes as . . .*)

Truth =.= (*Sorts as. . .*)

Stacey =.= (*Reads.*)

Wire *stretches out across* **Stacey**'*s bed in a familiar way. Breathes. Rubs his chest / armor. The plastic that surrounds his armor crinkles.* **Wire** *stares at the ceiling.*

Truth *looks to the curtain. He rises to his feet. Crosses over to the front door. Steps out to the porch. Sits on the stairs. Smokes a cigarette.*

Wire Truth act like he don't believe in anything.

Stacey He believes in the truth. My daddy gave him that name for a reason.

Wire More than one kind of truth. The way he think is narrow.

Stacey =.=

Wire =.=

Stacey =.=

Wire It's my birthday today.

Stacey Today? Oh, happy birthday, Wire.

Wire I figured you didn't remember. You woulda said something by now.

Stacey Well, I just figured it was tomorrow since Patty's –

Wire (*quick*) She was born *after* midnight.

I was born *before*. That's why we have it on different days. Even though we're twins.

Our folks would switch the day we'd have a party every year. You don't remember that?

Stacey I'm sorry I forgot . . .

Wire It's, it's alright. (*But it's not.*)

Ever since you and Patty left. It's usually just my party.

Stacey You have a party every year?

Wire Yea. But I'm usually delivering a message somewhere. So I walk into a bar and just order a shot for myself. Tell the bartender it's my birthday and ask him if he'll plug in my player so I can hear KoKo Taylor's 'Wang Dang Doodle'. You know that song?

Stacey Yea, yea. I know that song. I heard her sing it live.

Wire (*sits up*) You did?

Stacey I did.

I was on the road. Got invited to a party and she showed up. Started jamming with the band.

Wire Oh, wow . . .

Stacey *sings the hook from 'Wang Dang Doodle' by Koko Taylor.* **Wire** *joins in. The men share a laugh of recognition.*

Stacey Yea, man, Wire. I ain't never gonna forget that. It was a small joint, you know? People dancing like they under water. Blue smoke. Red lights. She didn't have a mic or nothin. Was just singing, singing from here.

Stacey *taps* **Wire***'s chest / armor. Plastic crinkles.* **Wire** *touches his own chest just as* **Stacey** *removes his hand.*

Stacey I left outta there with the sunrise. Bright orange. Hanging like a big piece of fruit from a tree.

Wire That ain't nuthin like a party I ever have.

Stacey I smoked some of the best grinds of my life that night.

You ever get goose bumps?

Wire Yea.

Stacey Yea. All over, you know?

Wire Yea.

Stacey Uh-huh. Everybody was dancing.

Wire Dancing . . ..

Stacey And we had a really good show that night. Patty and me. We tore the house down. Had everybody crackin up, laughing. And some nights, when we did a good show, I'd be so down afterwards but that was one of the few times I kept a buzz all night. The goose bumps, the blue smoke . . .

Wire =.=

Stacey =.=

Wire =.= (*Lays back on the bed.*)

Stacey =.= (*Looks at* **Wire** *across his bed.*)

=.= (*A consideration.*)

=.= (*Slowly turns back to his papers.*)

Wire =.=

Stacey =.=

Wire Did you listen to the comedy tape I gave you?

Stacey I started it.

Wire I think she's pretty funny.

Stacey I haven't listened to it all the way through.

Wire That Devil Doll bit is fun-ny.

Wire *mimics the comedienne on the tape.*

'and then he tells this dummy to walk around / and the dummy hops off his lap and struts around / like he didn't just have a hand up his ass!/ My man put his pinky up there and I'm just – 'no you don't, muthafucka! You betta wake me up first! You know you can't wash that smell off!' / You know what I'm sayin, ladies?'

=.= (*Laughs, then sees* **Stacey** *isn't laughing.*)

=.=

I thought it was funny.

Stacey (*turning back to* **Wire**) =.=

=.=

We should have a party for you.

Wire (*sits up*) For me?

Stacey Yea. You got any deliveries you gotta make tonight?

I'll throw you a party.

Wire Really?

Stacey Really.

Wire (*remembering . . .*) Damn.

Stacey What?

Wire *retrieves a small date book from his pocket. Flips through it.*

Wire I gotta deliver a message to a worker in the mines.

Stacey Do it now.

Wire I cain't.

Stacey Why not?

Wire I gotta wait for his woman to have the baby.

Gotta tell the father if it's a boy or a girl.

Stacey Oh. Well, we can have it later. Or earlier. Whenever you want it.

Wire Who we gonna invite?

Just as **Wire** *asks this question,* **Patricia** *steps up on the front porch.* **Truth** *stands up, the cigarette hanging from his mouth. She stands face to face with* **Truth**.

Patricia Hey now.

Truth =.= (*Speechless.*)

Patricia Hey now, Truth.

Truth . . . hey hey now . . . Patricia.

Patricia Aw, now, we know each other better than that.

You call me Patty if I call you Truth, hear?

What's good with you? What's good around here?

Truth What, what you doin back?

Patricia Mr. Good senior took the hospitality with him when he jetted out of town?

Patricia *holds out her cheek.* **Truth** *removes the cigarette from his mouth, leans in and kisses* **Patricia** *on the cheek.*

Patricia (*re: the cigarette*) You got another one for me?

Truth *gives* **Patricia** *a cigarette. He lights it for her. She puffs.*

Patricia Stacey around?

Truth Uhhh, yea.

Patricia How's he managin things?

Truth It's been a week . . .

Patricia You can destroy lives in a week, Truth.

Truth There's a lot to pick up. A lot to learn.

Patricia You helpin him?

Truth I have to. If he sinks this store, I have to work at the factory.

Truth *points to the factory in the distance. Blue smoke fills the sky above it.*

Patricia My lord . . . What's in there now? All that blue smoke . . . before I left it was just a –

Truth Well, it ain't that no more. That's what happens when we lose and they win. 'Stead of marking their territory with flags, they got folks elbow to elbow in there making pencils.

Patricia *They* took it over after the invasion?

Truth Mm-hm.

Patricia I can see why you'd wanna stay working here.

Truth Stacey's doin alright. Cain't tell him that though or else he'll get lazy.

=.=

How you keepin?

Cain't be too good if you showin up here seven days after he left you.

Patricia I'm doin fine.

Has he said anything to you about how he left things with me?

Truth No. But he and I don't really talk like that.

I imagine he just walked out.

Patricia You got a pretty dull imagination.

Truth Patty, I didn't want to bother him. Disrupt y'all. But I had to.

Patricia You had to?

Truth He's in the paperwork.

Patricia We know how you hold on to them damn papers, Truth.

Patricia *puts out her cigarette. She enters the shop, the click of her heels causing both* **Wire** *and* **Stacey** *to stand up. They both know that walk.*

Patricia *looks around.*

Patricia Ain't much changed in here.

Stacey *exits the bedroom, enters the shop.* **Patricia** *turns to look at him.*

Stacey Patty.

Patricia Stacey.

Stacey =.=

Patricia =.=

Stacey =.=

Wire *exits the bedroom, enters the shop.*

Patricia Not much has changed at all . . .

Wire Hey now.

Patricia Hey, hey Patrick.

Wire *winces at this name.*

Wire I didn't know you were in town. Not surprised though. Figured it wasn't a matter of *if* but *when*.

Patricia =.=

Stacey You just got into town?

Wire Mama and Daddy know you're here?

Patricia =.=

Stacey =.=

Truth We got cereal.

Patricia I'm not hungry, Truth. But thank you.

Just stepped off the bus.

And I tore my last pair of stockings.

Truth We carry hosiery.

Patricia Stacey knows my size.

Stacey =.=

Patricia =.=

Stacey *crosses over to the hosiery. Picks out* **Patricia**'*s size. Puts them on the counter as*:

Patricia What's good with you, big brotha?

Wire Most everything.

Patricia Messaging business treatin you well?

Wire Yes, Patricia. Uh-huh. It is.

Especially after that endorsement you made up for me.

Stacey Endorsement?

Wire Oh, yea. When y'all last comedy album took off around these parts, Patty gave me a line to print in the papers:

Patricia (*putting on her shtick*) 'The day we were born, he poked his head back in and gave me the all clear! I've trusted my twin brother to give me the scoop ever since!'

Wire I saw a seventy per cent increase in orders after that ad.

Rest of my competition fell through the cracks. Every single last one of them is working at the pencil factory.

Truth He had to buy a lil book to keep track of his message requests.

Wire Got so many I couldn't just keep 'em in my head anymore.

The phone lines getting knocked out – the best thing coulda happened to me.

Patricia How much I owe you, Stacey?

Truth Nothin . . . don't owe us a thing.

Stacey I'll put it on your tab.

Truth You don't have to worry about us cashing that in anytime soon, Patty.

Whatever you want while you're here . . .

Stacey You can talk to me, and I'll make sure –

Truth To ask me to pull it for you. Don't have to bother with the back-and-forth, Stacey. She can just talk to me. I'll take care of everything.

Patricia Well, however y'all wanna handle it, let me know.

Sunny *steps up on the back porch. She carries a package wrapped in brown paper. Raps on the frame of the door.*

Stacey Who could that be knockin from the back?

Patricia It might be my guest.

Sunny?!

Sunny (*from the back porch*) Yes, Ms. Patricia?

Patricia Come on through.

Sunny *politely steps into* **Stacey***'s room. She looks around the cramped space.* **Stacey** *pulls back the curtain.* **Sunny** *enters the shop. Big smiles. A gap between her two front teeth.* **Truth** *falls in love the moment he sees her.* **Patricia** *lights up, too, and we see her blazing charm.*

Patricia Sunny!

Sunny I got a lil' turned around at the square, but a nice lady pointed me the right way.

I said, 'I'm looking for the Good Goods general store.'

Such a funny name: Good Goods. But I like sayin it. It's easy to walk to the beat of that Good Goods / Good Goods / Good Goods . . .

Sunny *does a little dance, carrying the package. The room watches this little glowing ball of brown beauty.* **Sunny** *stops dancing, slightly winded. She returns the gaze of the room. Smiles. Gap.*

Sunny Hello, y'all.

Patricia Gentlemen, this is Sunny.

Sunny this is Stacey –

Sunny So nice to meet you, Mr –

Stacey Stacey is fine. The first name is enough.

Sunny My daddy has all your albums. He'd always say lines from the 'Stacey and Patty Got to Keep It Real!' CD.

Stacey That was a while ago.

Patricia Not that long ago.

Sunny and I got a hold of each other in the most coincidental way. Life is so funny like that.

Sunny It is.

Patricia I had to transfer buses and the only seat available was up front next to Sunny. We got to talkin and well, ten hours later I talked her into comin here with me.

Sunny I hadn't heard of y'all place before. It was all new to me. And if I have a choice of something familiar or something unknown, I choose the unknown one every time.

Truth Where you comin from, Sunny?

Sunny My mama's house.

Stacey And where is that?

Sunny (*evasive*) About a five-day bus ride from here.

Stacey =.=

Truth =.=

Sunny It's boring. All crazy boring where I come from, but ya'll place is nice. Here. Right now. This shop. These people. I know Black folks live everywhere, but the way Patricia talked about it here . . . knew it was something I ain't never seen before.

Truth It's not all that . . .

Sunny You thinkin that cause you familiar with it.

All new to me.

Patricia extended her hospitality. And she's been a . . . fine companion so far. I mean, I know three more people than I did when I got here. (*Smiles. Gap.* **Truth** *swoons.*)

Stacey Where were you headed originally?

Sunny About a seven-hour bus ride from here.

Stacey =.=

Truth I've been up that way. But it's much nicer here. I think. You'll see prettier things here. I'm glad Patty got you to take a lil detour to our town.

Patricia Well, I had to show her where me and Stacey come from. Shotgun houses and red dirt! Look at us, Stacey, back in the old stomping grounds. And here you are. The new official owner of the town's Good Goods.

On command, **Sunny** *does a baby jig. The room watches her.*

Sunny (*as she dances*) I wasn't rushing to get where I was going. So I decided to come through.

Truth (*watching her body move*) Well, allll-right.

Truth (*to Sunny*) Hey hey now. Hi there. We haven't really met each other yet.

Sunny Hi.

Patricia This is Truth.

Sunny Truth?

Truth That's what I go by 'round here.

Can I take that package for you?

Sunny Actually, it's for the birthday boy . . .

She spins around to **Wire**.

Sunny You got to be Patrick!

Sunny *holds out the package.*

Wire I am . . .

But they call me Wire 'round here.

Sunny =.= (*Holding out the package.*)

=.= (*Holding.*)

Lotta people avoidin they birthnames 'round here.

Wire *takes the package.*

Wire (*to Patricia*) You got me a gift?

Patricia Well, I mentioned to Sunny I was coming down here to celebrate your birthday – well, *our* birthday – and we came up with the perfect gift. Sunny was kind enough to attend to the details.

Sunny I'm sorry it took me so long. That's always the deal with being a stranger in a friendly place.

Wire Well, ever since the invasion folks around here like to know who's who and what's what.

Sunny Invasion?

Patricia (*covering*) Sunny, it's fine that you were runnin a lil behind. We were all just . . . standing around . . . shooting the rind.

Stacey (*backhanded*) Yea . . . just standin around.

Talkin shit.

Patricia =.=

Stacey =.=

Sunny (*breaks out into laughter*) Y'all two are so funny together!

Truth Sunny, are you hungry? We got some cold cereal.

Sunny Oh! That would be lovely. I'm pretty hungry. Patricia shared half her roast beef sandwich with me some time last night, but other than that . . . Thank you, Mr. . . .

Truth Truth. Nothing before or after, please. Just Truth.

As **Truth** *escorts* **Sunny** *to a seat and fixes her a bowl of cereal:*

Sunny I like that. You must've done something incredible to earn that name. Even more incredible to keep it.

Truth Well, it's a name you have to earn. That's for sure.

Wire (*to* **Patricia**) You came all the way here for my – *our* – birthday?

Patricia You sound surprised.

Wire I am.

Patricia Why?

Wire For real?

Patricia =.=

Wire We haven't celebrated together in ten years.

You split outta here. Took Stacey with you. Ain't got a card or present until now. 'Til he come back here –

Patricia I'll admit we haven't seen each other –

Wire Had our birthday together . . .

Patricia . . . I know it's been a minute, but the important thing is we're here now.

I mean, it's about the *next gig*, not the one we just finished. Ain't that right, Stacey?

Stacey =.=

Patricia Oh, cain't talk to him about the past. Can we?

Stacey =.=

Stacey *turns, goes back to his room:*

Patricia Oh, oh, now Stacey, come on . . .

Wire Where you planning on stayin, Patricia?

Patricia I'ma get me and Sunny a room.

Wire You don't wanna stay with Mama and Daddy?

Patricia You still livin there?

Wire I sleep there. Don't live there.

Patricia Well, I'd like to sleep somewhere else.

I don't have answers for all their questions.

Not yet.

Wire You should go by.

Patricia I will. I will. I'll let 'em think I'm strutting around overseas a lil while longer. Did they ask about me with Stacey comin back?

Wire They did. Asked me to ask Stacey what you were doing now that the act is busted.

Patricia *winces when she hears the truth said out loud.*

Patricia And what did Stacey tell you to tell them?

Wire That you had been workin on some solo material. Workin on becoming 'the queen of Black comedy'.

Patricia He used that title?

Wire Yea.

Wire Showing up like this, with no notice . . . I don't have anything for you, Patricia. No birthday present or nuthin.

Patricia Well, on technical terms my birthday's not until after midnight. So . . . you got time.

(*Idea!*) We celebrated our last birthday on my day, so tradition says we have our thirtieth tonight.

Wire Tonight?

Patricia Yea! Were you planning anything?

Wire Well, Stacey was talking about . . .

Patricia *takes off for* **Stacey***'s room.*

Patricia Stacey!

Wire *follows, holding on to his gift.*

Patricia My, my! I just had a hot idea! We should throw a birthday party! For me and Patrick! It can be a 'welcome home' party for you! And, and a celebration that Good Goods is still going strong! A big ol' bash.

Stacey Wire and I were talkin about something chill. Just a lil bitty –

Patricia Lil bitty?! All these things to celebrate and y'all wanna sit on the back porch and drink whiskey out of jars?? Uh-uh.

No, no. We are throwing down! Oh! And we can do something from our act, Stacey!

(**Patricia** *snaps her fingers. Sways to the beat.*)

Something light and easy. Those pencil shavers look for a good time, don't they? Maybe we can charge a lil' something to cover expenses . . .

Stacey That ain't something I wanna do, Patricia.

Patricia =.=

=.=

You don't wanna have a good time?

Why?

Stacey =.=

=.= (*Looking for an excuse.*)

Parties lead to foolishness.

People runnin all through here . . .

Patricia Oh. Well. We can keep it outside. On the porch. Truth can keep an eye on things. He's been the security man since he was a lil boy. He can keep an eye on things. We can get someone to sit at the back porch. We'll perform on the front . . . it's all easy greasy, my Stacey.

How about it?

=.=

=.=

Wire =.=

Stacey =.=

Patricia We'll stop it the moment it gets too rowdy.

Stacey =.=

=.=

Is this something you wanna do, Wire?

Wire

=.=

=.=

Well, I've spent so many birthdays dancing by myself in a bar . . .

It'd be nice.

If that baby arrives, I'll get somebody to drive me over to tell the daddy. Get there and back here as quick as I can.

Stacey Alright.

A short party.

Patricia *is excited. Squeals a little bit.*

Patricia Sunny and I will take care of everything! Ooooooooo, Patrick, this is gonna be a throw-down to end all throw-downs!

She kisses **Wire** *on the cheek. Just as he looks away,* **Patricia** *kisses* **Stacey** *on the lips. She runs into the shop.*

Patricia Sunny! You just about done with your breakfast? We got a party to plan!

Sunny Ooooooo, a party! Oh that sounds fire! When, where?!

Patricia Here. Tonight! We're celebrating. Life and . . . and new beginnings.

Truth (*smiling*) I like both those things.

Patricia And our lovely Truth has agreed to keep the peace.

Truth I have?

Patricia You have.

Truth What if I wanna enjoy the party?

Who's gonna keep Sunny company –

Sunny Let's jump to it, Ms Patricia.

The women prepare to go.

Sunny *stops, turns to* **Truth**.

Sunny Thank you for the cereal and the talkin, Truth.

Truth *just smiles. Unable to speak.*

Green smoke belches from the factory pipes, muscling its way past the blue smoke.

Sunny *and* **Patricia** *exit stage left.*

The men are left silent.

Wire *sits on* **Stacey**'*s bed, the gift pressed to his chest.*

Stacey *sits at his small table, head down.*

Truth *crosses out the front door and stands on the front porch, staring off in the distance at* **Sunny** *and* **Patricia**.

Wire =.=

Stacey =.=

Truth (*to himself*) Sho' 'nuff make Truth holler for relief!

Truth *stands for a moment longer. Looks up. He goes back into the shop humming* **Sunny**'*s 'Good Goods' song. He returns to special orders.*

Wire *sits on* **Stacey**'*s bed.*

Truth *checks his watch.*

Truth (*to* **Stacey** *who's in the bedroom*) This day is movin. That lunch whistle's gonna blow before we know it.

What we doin about these orders?

Stacey (*duh*) We'll hand 'em out.

Truth I know that, Stacey, but how you wanna do that?

I don't think we should let 'em all just run up and through here.

Stacey Do whatever you think is right, Truth.

Truth =.=

=.= (*Thinking about it.*)

=.=

We should . . . have 'em collect out front. Then I'll call out a name. Have the man step forward. Give him his order. And wait for him to step back outside before we call the next name.

Stacey Fine, Truth.

Truth *sets up the orders.*

Wire =.=

Stacey =.=

Wire I need to scrape together a gift for Patty. She got me something. I oughta get her something. Right thing to do.

Stacey =.=

Wire Been a while since I had to think of a gift for somebody.

=.=

=.=

I usually just buy my mama flowers for her days: birthday and Mother's Day.

Buy my daddy smokes for his birthday and Father's Day.

=.=

=.=

Stacey She ain't gonna care one way or the other.

Wire Who?

Stacey Patricia. She ain't gonna care if you get her a gift or not.

Wire But I do. I care.

Stacey =.=

Wire =.= (*Thinking what to buy her.*)

Stacey =.=

Wire *shakes the package. It makes a noise.*

Wire Does that sound expensive to you?

Stacey You gonna break it, shakin the thing like that.

Anxious about that possibility, **Wire** *places it gently on his lap.*

Wire =.=

Stacey I wonder what's the deal with that Sunny gal.

Wire She makes you wanna look at her.

Stacey =.=

Wire Do you know Patty's dress size?

Stacey (*Insert the dress size of the actress playing Patricia here.*)

Wire They'll help me pick a dress out for her at the shop.

Stacey She ain't gonna want some cheap cotton thing from town.

Wire =.=

Stacey =.=

Wire On our sixteenth birthday, I bought her gloves.

Stacey (*lost in thought*) Huh?

Wire I bought her satin-lookin gloves with fur around the end of 'em.

Stacey Oh, yea?

Wire She bought me some suspenders.

Stacey =.=

Wire =.=

Stacey =.=

Wire Maybe some nice paper. For writing letters.

Stacey She don't write letters. She comes up with bits.

Wire =.=

=.=

A notebook then. Like the one I got but a bit bigger.

Stacey She don't write nuthin down cause she thinks folks will steal it.

Wire =.=

Stacey =.=

Wire You keep pissin on my ideas.

Stacey Because your ideas are mess buckets, Wire.

Wire You ain't helpin none.

Stacey Cause Patty ain't gonna care. She's not here to get a gift. She's not here for no birthday.

Wire Well, what she here for?

=.=

Tell me what she here for, Stacey. G'on 'head and let me know.

Stacey You tellin me you trustin her intentions?

Wire I ain't sayin that.

She gave me a birthday gift. I ain't got one in a long while. My folks think I'm too grown for 'em. I'm just returning Patty's gesture. A gift ain't a sign of trust. Ain't a sign of forgiveness. It's just the right thing to do.

Stacey =.=

Wire =.=

Wire *unwraps his gift.*

Stacey You not gonna wait until this evening?

Wire Maybe it'll give me an idea.

Wire *takes the lid off the box.*

Pulls out an African Talking Drum.

Wire This don't help me none.

What is this?

Stacey There's something else in the box.

Wire *takes out a pamphlet from the box.*

Wire (reading) 'A talking drum' . . . ? . . . 'from Africa'. . .

Nobody sells anything from Africa around here.

Where'd those two women find this?

Wire *taps at the drum with his fingers.*

Stacey Who knows . . .

Wire They got instructions written in here.

Reading the pamphlet, **Wire** *learns how to hold the drum. He tucks it under his arm. He takes the beater . . . and lightly taps the head.* **Stacey** *watches him. As the beating persists,* **Stacey** *sits forward.*

As **Wire***'s drumming grows in force a young Factory Folk runs into the shop. Winded.*

Factory Folk Truth! Truth! We need bandages, rags, towels, and a whole bucket of ice.

Stacey *and* **Wire** *rush out of the bedroom, enter the shop.*

Truth What's goin on?

Factory Folk No . . . first aid in the . . . factory. One of the Evans boys . . . Emekah, passed out at the grinder machine. Got his hand caught in it. We gotta wrap him up and take him to the hospital. Lost a lot of blood. Had to use the head of a mop to wrap Emekah's hand in . . .

Truth *and* **Stacey** *snatch up a bunch of supplies. Green smoke bellows from the factory pipes.*

Stacey Keep an eye on the store, Wire.

Wire *stands holding his drum.*

Truth, Stacey, *and* **Factory Folk** *exit out the front door in a rush, carrying rags and supplies.*

Wire *is alone in the shop.*

Wire =.=

=.=

=.=

He taps on the drum.

Wire =.=

=.=

He hears something.

Wire =.=

=.=

Taps again.

Listens.

He taps, this time changing the pitch of the tone.

He continues to tap and listen as the lights fade to black.

Two

Evening of the same day.

In the distance, thin green smoke seeps from the factory pipes into the bruised sky.

Sunny *is on the front porch, decorating it for the party. She wears the same dress she wore in the previous act. She hangs up Christmas lights.*

Patricia *sits in the shop, rolling cigarettes. She wears a very fancy black satin dress. A handkerchief is tucked between her breasts.*

The women sing 'Jump to It!' by Aretha Franklin.

They execute a pretty good remix of this song, breaking into wild laughter.

As they collect themselves . . .

Patricia This is some good shit I got. I can smell how good it is.

Sunny What do you call it again?

Patricia Grinds.

It's Stacey's favorite even though he don't smoke it too often.

Last time I saw him smoke was at this party. He was flyin. He never danced like that with me since. I've seen him dance with other . . . folks (*Meaning men.*) like that, but it was the first and the last with me.

Sunny Y'all dance all the time in your act, don't you?

Patricia Yea, but we're dancing for laughs, for applause.

That night at that party . . . you ever dance real nice with somebody, Sunny?

Sunny Not like the way you talkin.

Patricia Koko Taylor was jamming with this band. And Stacey had a hold of me . . . he pulled up my skirt a lil bit and snaked his leg in between mine . . . he had unbuttoned his shirt, had on a tank top underneath, and I had on this deep scoop-neck cotton number and I could feel the hairs on his chest pressin into my chest . . .

Sunny Oooo, I didn't know y'all got down like that.

Patricia We don't. We didn't. He was high. I was too.

He held on to me until the sun came up and then he let go. We did a show the next night and it was back to:

Patricia *sings a verse of 'How High the Moon' by Ella Fitzgerald.*

Sunny*'s attention is drawn to a scene in the distance. She stands, trying to make it out. As it comes closer* **Sunny** *is shocked and disgusted. She covers her mouth.*

Patricia Oh, Sunny, I need me a good time something awful. Things ain't been as good as they used to be.

I don't like bein by myself . . . Cain't tolerate it.

=.=

I'm glad we found each other, Sunny.

Stacey *and* **Truth** *climb the steps, blood splattered on them like a paint job gone bad. On the porch, they remove their shoes and socks. Exhausted and devastated, they walk past a speechless* **Sunny** *and enter the shop.* **Patricia** *looks up, stands up.*

Truth *walks past her into* **Stacey***'s room and out the back door onto the porch, where he removes all his clothes. He leaves them in a heap on the back porch. He stands in his underwear and washes himself from the basin.*

Stacey Where's Wire?

Patricia What happened to y'all?

Stacey Did he leave the shop empty?

Patricia No, he was here when we showed up to decorate. He had to deliver a message . . . Stacey, what did y'all get into?

Stacey (*a bit dazed*) Somebody got hurt at the factory. We had to help get him to the hospital.

Patricia Did you know him?

Stacey He was a part of the Evans family. Ivory Evans' great-great-grandson.

Emekah Evans.

Sunny *enters the shop. Still speechless.*

Stacey

=.=

=.= (*Unbuttons his shirt.*)

=.=

He's gone.

=.=

=.=

=.= (*Removes his shirt. He wears a tank top underneath.*)

The hospital's a ways away from here.

=.=

=.=

=.=

We was halfway there when he stopped screaming.

We just turned the truck back around and took him to the funeral home.

Truth *finishes washing himself, changes the water.*

Stacey *crosses to his bedroom. Takes off his pants and tank top. Stands in his underwear. Looks at his hands covered in blood.*

Truth *enters* **Stacey***'s room.*

Truth Did I get it all off me?

Stacey (*looks*) Yea.

Truth You got some clothes I could borrow?

Stacey Under the bed. Took 'em off the line this morning.

Stacey *goes to the back porch to clean himself.*

Truth *picks from* **Stacey**'*s clothes. Puts on a shirt and pants. Walks out into the shop barefoot. He crosses to his backpack and pulls out a bottle of whiskey. He takes a swig.*

Truth We was in the bed of the truck with him.

Took all six of us to load him in the back.

All six foot three, two-hundred-and-ninety-five-pounds of him. Solid muscle.

On our way to the hospital . . . blood was –

Sunny (*a bit hysterical*) I don't wanna hear it. Can't take stories like this, Patricia. I'm sorry. Cain't listen to whatever he got to say.

Patricia G'on outside on the porch.

Here. (*Gives* **Sunny** *a smoke.*)

Get this started. I'll be out there in a minute.

Sunny *takes the grind. Steps out on the porch. Paces and smokes.*

Patricia (*to Truth*) Not too loud.

She don't need to know about it anyway.

Truth =.=

=.= (*Drinks.*)

Emekah was knocked out cold for most of the ride, and then his eyes pop open and he starts screaming for his cap.

Ivory's picture is . . . sewn in his cap.

'My Ivory's gone! Where's my muthafuckin cap?! Where's my goddamn cap?! Ivory!'

We find it over in the corner. I reach for it and show it to him.

And, and he takes it with his one hand and puts it over his face.

Ivory's picture is on his face. And he screams.

'You was right. Like weeds. You was right. Oh, Lord. Messiah'. And he was screaming 'Ivory messiah, Ivory messiah' until he . . . stopped.

Patricia *exhales at the end of the story.*

Stacey *enters his bedroom and puts on clean clothes.*

Truth The whole town's gonna be still for a few days.

Until the Evans announce the arrangements.

=.=

=.=

Sunny can take them lights down while she out there.

No party tonight.

Patricia What you gonna do, Truth?

Truth I'ma sit here for a minute.

My legs still loose. Don't know if I'll be able to walk home.

=.=

=.=

What'd you give her?

Patricia Grinds.

Truth Where'd you get that?

Patricia Asked around. You wanna spark?

Truth =.= (*Thinks about it.*)

=.=

It ain't good to get messed up the night somebody you know dies.

Truth *puts the cap back on the bottle and puts it in his backpack.*

Stacey *enters the shop. Sits.*

Patricia (*pandering*) Stacey, honey, I got you a present . . .

Stacey (*cynical*) A present? And it ain't even my birthday?

Patricia *dismisses his tone, shows him the smoke.*

Patricia Truth got some issues with relaxing tonight. But . . .

I know it ain't right to have a party, but we shouldn't spend the whole night propped up like chumps.

Stacey You want some other clothes to put on?

Patricia =.=

=.=

What's wrong with my dress . . .?

Stacey =.=

Patricia What's wrong with it?

Stacey I don't wanna look at you in that dress.

Patricia Why not?

Stacey That's a dress you wear performing. I don't wanna think about performing. And that's what I'ma think about with you skipping around in that damn dress.

Truth You wear that onstage?

Patricia Yes, I do.

Truth That's a nice piece. Very nice.

Stacey Don't encourage her, Truth . . .

Truth It is.

Patricia And Stacey had a white three-piece with a black trim . . . you know what I'm talkin about, Stacey.

Stacey No, no, no! Patricia, I don't wanna hash.

Patricia I ain't hashing with you. I'm describing how it was to Truth.

(*To* **Truth**.) And Stacey and I would do this coming-home-from-a-house-party bit . . .

Frustrated, **Stacey** *goes out onto the front porch with* **Sunny**.

Patricia *continues with* **Truth**.

Patricia He and I are playing like we bout to have a one-night stand, you know?

And we do this whole exchange about how I like to get down and how he likes to get down. He's talkin all big about what kinda lover he is, 'I'ma tear that pussy up . . .' all that talk. But the joke starts when the way I like to get down gets freakier and freakier until he starts gettin scared shitless . . . I'm sayin, 'I'm bout to give you some Kunta Kinte strokes, muthafucka . . .' and he's tremblin, too drunk to run straight for the door. I got him cornered and then I tell him, 'Now take off your clothes and get on your j-o-b'.

Truth *cracks up laughing.* **Patricia** *laughs, too.*

On the front porch . . . **Stacey** *sits with* **Sunny**.

Sunny (*already a little blazed*) This shit is pretty good.

Stacey You sure you need any more?

Sunny You right. You probably right.

Sunny *takes one more big hit then gives it to* **Stacey**, *who puts it out.*

Sunny (*thinking he took a hit*) Isn't that good?

Stacey (*smiles*) Mm-hm.

Sunny =.=

Stacey =.=

=.=

I'm sorry the party is a bust.

Sunny Ain't a bust to me. I been to some shitty parties. This ain't one of 'em.

It ain't the best one I been to but it ain't the worst.

Stacey What's the best one you been to?

Sunny My sixth-grade graduation party.

Stacey That was the best one? Really?

Sunny Mm-hm.

Stacey What made it good?

Sunny I got a new dress. Got a brand new Strawberry Shortcake notebook. And one of them graduation caps. Mine was pink.

What's the best party you been to?

Stacey =.= (*Thinking about it.*)

A birthday party I had. My daddy threw it out here in the yard.

Sunny What was so good about it?

Stacey *smiles. He can't help himself. The memory of it is too good.*

Sunny Ooooo, you musta got some!

Stacey *laughs. It's true.*

Sunny Ooooo. From Patricia?

Stacey No! No. Uh-uh.

Somebody else . . . (*Smiles as he remembers.*) Wire was . . . (*Thinks twice about getting into it.*) well, it was a present. Special for me.

Sunny I bet no gift was the same after that!

Sunny *laughs.* ***Stacey*** *laughs.*

In the shop, **Patricia** *hears this and looks in their direction.*

On the front porch:

Sunny You get any more presents from this somebody?

Stacey No . . . Patty got a letter that offered us our first tour. Opening act gig. We were on a bus heading west later that day.

That was ten years ago. No presents since.

Sunny =.= (*Deciding to tell. . .*)

You wanna know the worst party I been to?

Stacey Yea.

Sunny It's more recent.

Stacey How recent?

Sunny Five days ago.

=.=

=.=

I was supposed to marry this man.

=.=

But I ran away.

Stacey For real?

Sunny Uh-huh. It was an engagement party. Horrible.

Stacey Who is he?

Sunny My father and his father got drunk twenty years ago and promised each other their kids would marry.

I'm the girl. He's the boy. We had to jump. I couldn't say no.

Stacey Why not?

Sunny That's how things go down. Drunk promises are like blood oaths. Especially between the men folk. I was gonna have to marry this bearish dude and have his kids cause my daddy wants to play house.

Stacey So you ran away.

Sunny I ran away. Said I needed to pray by myself.

So I prayed on the way to the bus station. Prayed at the ticket counter. Prayed on the bus and when I opened my eyes Patricia was asking if anybody was sitting next to me . . .

I ain't never going back home. I'ma be myself in my own way just like Patricia.

'Cause if I go back home, I'm a wife, a mother. It's over.

Stacey What is?

Sunny Sunny. I am. Me. I'm over. I'd be Mrs. Leon Moore.

Mrs. Leon Whack. Mrs. Whack.

Stacey But what if your people come looking for you?

Sunny Everybody's poor. They can only afford to carry the shame. Leon'll be alright. Men always have a plan B.

Women ain't allowed such security.

Stacey You made your own plan B.

Sunny (*discovers a pride in this*) That's right. I did.

Patricia is so cool.

Stacey Yea . . . cool as a cobra.

Sunny Awww, I know y'all having issues . . . but you cain't deny how glamorous she is. I been watching her live (*As in 'alive'.*) for almost twenty hours now and it's the best show ever.

=.=

=.=

That must've been nice dancing with her.

Stacey On stage?

Sunny Naw, at that Ko Ko Taylor party.

That must've been nice.

Do you remember that? I woulda remembered that . . .

Stacey What'd she tell you?

Sunny Chests pressed up against each other. Legs getting wrapped up. Wang dang DAMN . . . It's hot. Are you hot?

Stacey (*no*) Uh-uh.

Sunny I had to dance with the man I was supposed to marry, and it wasn't nothing like the way Patricia was describing it.

=.=

=.=

You think she'd dance real nice with me?

Stacey (*speechless*) =.=

=.=

Sunny Huh, Stacey?

You seen her dance with . . . folks like me?

In the shop:

Patricia (*to Truth*) Is it too blasphemous in your handbook to play a bit of music tonight?

Truth Not unless you want that Evans boy showing up at the party.

Patricia Aw, now, don't talk no mumbo about souls flying . . .

Truth I don't have to. You already know.

Patricia (*playful pout*) Truth, it's my birthday. You don't want us to have a good time?

Truth Uh-uh. It's Wire's birthday.

And he ain't here no way.

Patricia It's about to be my birthday.

If you don't wanna have a good time with me at least give me a gift.

Truth From where?

Patricia (*duh*) We standin in a store, brotha man!

You can put it on my tab.

=.= (*Smiles.*)

I'ma close my eyes count to ten.

You pick out my gift, put it on the counter, okay?

Truth *chuckles.* **Stacey** *notices this.*

Truth Alright.

Patricia *closes her eyes.*

Patricia

One . . . two . . . three . . . four . . . five . . . six . . .

Truth *looks around the store. He's a bit panicked by the pressure but continues to hunt.*

Patricia . . . seven . . . eight . . . nine . . .

He crosses over and digs out an object from a box. He holds it behind his back, faces **Patricia.**

Patricia Ten!

Patricia *opens her eyes. Looks around.*

Patricia Where is it?

Truth Behind me.

Patricia Show it to me.

Truth You gotta promise me something first.

Patricia Truth, that's a tacky thing. A birthday gift with strings attached.

Truth It's a thin string. Only one. Lotta slack, too. So . . . you don't have to *promise* to make it happen.

Just try to arrange circumstances my way.

Patricia (*a bit wary*) What?

Truth (*intimate*) I'm ready to settle down, Patricia.

Patricia (*wariness grows*) Okay . . .

Truth I been around too many bodies on the brink of death or insanity.

Sittin in the back of that truck watching that Evans boy flail was the final alarm . . .

I cain't spend the rest of my life alone.

Patricia What you expect me to do about that?

Truth (*so as not to be heard from the front porch*) Get me Sunny.

Patricia Sunny?

Truth Uh-huh.

Patricia Truth, she ain't lookin for a –

Truth *reveals* **Patricia***'s birthday gift: a bar of soap in the shape of an airplane. A toy a child would play with at bath time.*

Patricia *is taken aback.*

Truth It's soap. Shaped like a plane. It smells like roses.

Patricia Oh . . .

Truth It's funny, see, cause you travel a lot. Cause you'll be in some faraway land taking a bath with an airplane.

Patricia Thank you . . . Truth.

Truth Take it.

Patricia *takes the gift. A polite smile.*

On the back porch a drunk **Wire** *climbs the steps. His talking drum is slung over his shoulder. He sits on the step. Giggles. Quiets himself.*

Truth So you'll help me?

Patricia I will. But only if you'll help me.

I got offers to play nice houses overseas, but they want the act for the first half then I'd do my solo material for the second. It's good money and lots of exposure for me.

I need help gettin' Wire.

Truth Wire? But I . . . I thought you wanna get . . .

Patricia I do. I do. But he came back only cause of Wire. Stacey don't care about this shop two ways for nuthin.

Truth He don't?

Patricia No.

Truth But, but if I get Wire to leave with you and Stacey follows, the paperwork say the store closes.

I'ma have to go work in the factory. I'ma be a Factory Folk.

Patricia Do you want Sunny or not?

Truth She ain't gonna want me if I'm covered in pencil shavings.

Patricia We'll change the paperwork then. Give the store to you. I'll pay somebody to find a loophole.

Truth Mister Good senior clogged up every crack and hole. When he started getting paranoid, he had Hunter Priestess put a hex on it. Nobody in the town will touch it. Afraid of the bad that comes with it –

Sunny *climbs to her feet. Walks into the shop.*

Sunny (*announcement*) I have to visit the restroom out back.

Patricia How you feeling, Sunny?

Sunny =.= (*Cotton mouth.*)

I'ma need some water.

=.=

But first I have to visit the restroom out back.

Patricia Do you need me to come with you?

Sunny *smiles. Gap.* **Truth**'*s heart melts.* **Sunny** *giggles. Smiles.*

Sunny No, Patricia. I'm, I'll be alright.

Sunny *crosses the shop, she sheepishly waves at* **Truth**, *exits.* **Truth** *is smitten.*

Truth (*to Patricia*) You got a deal.

Sunny *crosses through* **Stacey**'*s bedroom. Enters the back door. She jumps back when she sees* **Wire** *sitting on the steps.*

Wire *looks up. Grins. Smiles.*

Wire Hey hey, Sunny!

Sunny Oh! oh, oh . . . it's just you, Patrick –

Wire Wire.

Oooo, I like my birthday gift. Thank you.

Sunny Uh-huh, but I have to visit the . . .

=.= (*Cotton mouth.*)

My mouth is so dry.

Wire There's some water over there.

Wire *waves his beater in the general direction of the basin and water pitcher.* **Sunny** *crosses over to it. Hovers over the pitcher. Goes in to pick it up, but of course she picks up the basin that Stacey washed himself in.*

She drinks the water with the Evans boy's blood in it. Wire taps on his drum.

Sunny *drinks then puts the basin down.*

Sunny I think there was a bug in that . . .

=.=

Restroom. Now.

Sunny *exits.*

Wire *climbs to his feet.*

Wire (*yells from the back porch*) Hey hey now!

Stacey (*from the front porch*) Hey hey. Birthday boy!

Wire *enters the bedroom.* **Stacey** *enters the shop.* **Wire** *enters the shop all drunk and smiling . . .*

Patricia Looks like he's getting back from a party.

Wire Is it over?

Stacey It never got started.

Truth That Evans boy passed away.

Stacey Emekah.

Wire Oh.

=.=

=.=

That's sad to hear that.

=.=

=.=

Hurt himself that bad, huh?

Stacey Yea.

Wire Bad luck to be drunk the day a man dies.

But I didn't know.

When I left to tell that daddy about his daughter I didn't know nuthin about it.

Patricia Is that where you got all sauced?

Wire Yes, ma'am.

=.=

But I didn't know about Emekah.

Or else I woulda passed when they sent the bottle around.

Would *not* have told them it was my birthday.

Would *not* have played them 'Wang Dang Doodle' . . . (*Sings a line from the hook.*) . . .

(*Spoken.*) They liked my drum, too.

(*To* **Patricia**.) Thank you so much for this drum, Patricia. I'ma trust this gesture is comin from a good place 'cause I like it so much. I know you live and breathe off ulterior motives, but I'ma hope you on a diet from it –

Truth Wire, maybe you oughta go rest on Stacey's bed.

Wire Now, wait a minute now, just cause we lost somebody today don't mean we cain't try to have a good time.

Truth I think that is what it means.

It means exactly that.

Wire Truth, Truth, you are being unnecessarily stupid.

Stacey Okay . . . Wire –

Wire I busted my ass getting back here to spend my birthday with ya'll. Them minin folk were real nice to me. First time in . . . I don't know when . . . that I played my song and other people danced with me. I left all that to come here.

Patricia Uh-uh. Clearly you left there to come back here and get pissy with us.

Wire I came back here cause it's our party. You said you was throwin a party.

Truth And we said a man died tonight.

Wire I'm thirty years old. Patty, you gonna be thirty years old, too.

Patricia I know . . .

Wire Mama had us when she was thirty.

What I'ma have? What you gonna have, Patty, huh?

Patricia The way you carryin on I'ma have a headache –

Wire That new daddy I was drinkin with tonight, he's twenty-two.

Twenty-damn-two! Got a wife and a child, working the mines – a good, steady job.

On my way back here, I was scratchin my head tryna remember: where was my thinkin when I was twenty-two? I wasn't wrapped up in no family, that's for sure. I was wrapped up in waitin. Bidin my time. Just waitin for . . .

(*Looks at* **Stacey**.) Writin letters. My pride kept 'em short. My pride talked about the town but I couldn't write anything about the waiting . . . the yearnin . . . yearnin through my birthdays, through the invasion . . . Waitin through everything. And, and tonight I was standin in front of this brotha who was tearin up over the birth of his daughter. And, and then he was nice enough to celebrate his daughter *and me*. He didn't even know who I was beyond payin me to bring him a message but he celebrated me.

Ya'll know what that's like?

Not for writing a funny joke, or singing a pretty song or stocking a crappy shelf but for being alive. Celebrated for being born.

=.=

=.=

I hate I still wanna give that to you, Patty.

I do.

But it's your birthday – our birthday.

I still want both of us to feel celebrated. Like we used to.

=.=

=.= (*Getting a little sick.*)

I, I, I'ma need some air . . .

Wire *stumbles across the room, heading for the front porch.* **Stacey** *goes to him, but* **Patricia** *holds him back.*

She crosses over to **Wire** *and helps him out onto the porch. She helps him sit.*

Truth *and* **Stacey** *are left in the shop.*

A puff of green smoke shines in the night sky above the factory.

Stacey =.=

Truth =.=

Stacey =.=

Truth Your daddy was the same way as that young cat Wire was talkin bout. He was the same way when I told him about you.

Stacey He didn't know about me?

Truth No, he did. He just didn't know if you were a boy or a girl.

He was stuck in another county negotiating the price for a order of . . . (*Tries to remember.*) hair grease.

I ran there and told him he had a son.

He was so happy. I remember seeing tears. He was young, too. Younger than that cat Wire was talking about.

Stacey Were you?

Truth What?

Stacey Happy.

Truth Hell no. Uh-uh.

Stacey Why?

Truth I was a boy. Around seven or eight. Your daddy was the only daddy I knew.

Stacey I took your limelight . . .

Truth Yea . . . among other things.

On the front porch **Wire** *sits, holding onto his drum.* **Patricia** *stands, leaning against a post. She smokes.*

Wire =.=

=.= (*Tap, tap.*)

This is the worst party I ever been to.

Patricia That's a fine way to deal with things.

Wire You cain't say all this is fun, Patty.

Patricia Nobody said it was, but at least I'm polite enough to keep my mouth shut.

Wire For what?

Who I'm gonna offend with the truth?

Patricia Me. Sunny. Stacey –

Wire Shit, the way Stacey been treatin me . . . he's the one flickin offenses all over the damn place.

Patricia =.=

=.=

=.=

How he been treatin you?

Wire *gives* **Patricia** *the side eye.*

Patricia What?

Wire I ain't that messed up.

You think I'ma tell you all that?

Patricia You don't think I can help?

I been on the road with him for the past ten years . . . I know every crease in his thinkin and every note in his voice.

Wire That don't make you an expert on his heart though.

Patricia =.=

=.= (*This is true.*)

=.= (*Smokes.*)

You right.

=.=

Damn. Mhm.

Wire =.=

=.= (*Tap, tap on the drum.*)

You got issues with me.

Patricia That's the liquor talkin.

Wire That's the truth talkin.

Liquor or not.

We twins. I can feel you; you can feel me.

I got issues with you, too.

You left me.

Left me and took him with you.

Patricia =.=

=.= (*Smokes.*)

This is a party, Wire.

We got lots of other occasions to scratch at each other. Don't have to get into it now.

Wire Who's gettin into anything?

Patricia You tryin to.

Wire Uh-uh. I'm just tryin to have a good birthday . . . ain't you tryin to have a good birthday, Patty?

In the shop with **Stacey** *and* **Truth**.

Truth You did well today. Handlin that Evans ride.

Stacey =.=

=.= (*Surprised by* **Truth**'*s compliment.*)

Thank you.

=.=

=.=

You did, too.

=.=

We need a hospital closer to here.

That Emekah Evans boy coulda been saved.

Truth It's cheaper to bury us than to save us.

Stacey =.=

Truth =.=

Stacey Maybe I'll get into politics. Try to better some things.

Truth Around here?

Stacey Yea.

Truth You really don't know jack about what went down, do you?

Gettin into politics is an early grave.

Stacey So people around here are just givin up? The invasion happens and the fight's over.

Truth Says the brotha who stayed away.

Stacey I didn't stay away.

Truth You didn't come fight.

Stacey Folks in this town can't even get they stories straight about what exactly happened.

Truth Cause when you live through it, there ain't no easy way to explain it.

And you think smoking that shit is gonna help things?

Stacey You know, you ain't that much older than me, Truth.

Why you crickin around here like you Frederick Douglass or something?

Truth Better than bein ignorant all the damn time –

Stacey You wanna talk about somebody being ignorant?

All you know is what's in front of your damn face. You ain't been nowhere.

Ain't carried on a decent conversation with nobody. Now *that's* ignorant.

I know things, seen things you never will, Truth.

Truth Do you know why your daddy had to jet outta town?

Stacey =.=

Truth =.=

=.=

Huh?

Stacey =.= (*He doesn't.*)

Truth He got chased out.

=.=

=.=

And not by no debt or no affair . . .

Not by what you can see, but what you feel.

=.=

=.=

=.=

Said the Devil was after him. Trying to possess his soul.

Said he'd be in bed in that back room just like you do now and he'd open his eyes to the Devil standin over him, pissin fire on his sheets.

=.=

=.=

He stopped sleepin.

=.=

Made me sit up with him thru the night with a rifle in my lap and a .45 in his.

Me. I did that for your daddy.

=.=

He kept getting worse and worse. I couldn't keep a hold of him.

=.=

=.=

You a waste, Stacey. Ain't worth the pot you shit in . . .

Stacey =.=

Truth =.=

Stacey =.=

Truth Disappointment.

Stacey =.=

=.=

Truth You think you funny?

You ain't. Patty makes me laugh. But you, you make me cry. Make a grown man cry –

Stacey Instead of talkin bullshit to me, why don't you go find my daddy? That's what you want, ain't it? To crawl up under my father so you can keep playin house for the rest of your life? Why you hangin around here? I don't need a thirty-five-year-old son –

Truth Cause all this was supposed to be mine!

=.=

=.=

All of this was promised to me and I cain't leave it.

I won't leave it. You were supposed to be a girl! You were promised to me! I was supposed to be your husband! You was supposed to come out a girl and I was gonna marry you and your daddy was gonna give me this damn shop!

When I was six years old he promised me . . . promised me . . . right at that counter. Said I was gonna marry his daughter. Be his son. He said I could add on a house in the back to raise a family in . . .

=.=

I was cryin the whole way when I ran to tell your daddy how you came out. I thought he was gonna be upset. I thought he was gonna be disappointed that he couldn't have me . . . but, but he was happy.

That muthafucka was overjoyed!

=.=

And just like that . . . I ain't got nothin. Or nobody. All I do is watch this fuckin shop day in, day out. Sweep the damn floors, clean the windows. But none of it is mine. Never will be . . . I felt like I ain't had no plan B for most of my life.

'Til today. 'Til that gal walked thru that door with that smile . . .

Just then **Sunny** *climbs up the steps onto the back porch. Her gait altered. Wide stance. Her left hand curled up in a knot. She blows green smoke from her mouth. She sings with a new voice, a different voice, a man's voice . . . a sweet tenor reminiscent of Donny Hathaway or Sam Cooke . . . she sings with the voice of a dislocated soul: Emekah Evans . . .*

Sunny Ivory, my Ivory, coastin 'long the sea.

Ivory, my Ivory, wonderin who she'll be.

The sun behind her.

The grass below.

She walked until she walked no more . . .

Stacey, **Truth**, **Wire**, *then* **Patricia** *face the direction of the voice.*

Wire *and* **Patricia** *enter the shop.*

Sunny *steps into* **Stacey***'s bedroom. She knocks aside anything near her path. She pulls back the curtain, stands in the doorway of the shop.* **Sunny** *looks at the room. The room looks at her.*

Sunny A mama calls . . .

A daddy calls . . .

A brother calls . . .

A sister calls . . .

And the Devil answered in Ivory tears.

Brown Ivory's red, red tears.

Sunny *enters the shop, holds up her knotted hand, offering it to the heavens.*

Sunny Ivory stopped and fell to her knees.

She saw her people pulled apart like weeds.

(*Hushed.*) I saw it, too.

The heavens behind her.

The hells below.

She screamed until she screamed no more.

=.=

Ivory messiah. Ivory messiah. Messiah . . .

=.=

=.=

Spoken. Hey hey now.

Three

Night that same day. In the shop **Sunny/Emekah Evans** *is bound to a chair that's bound to the counter. Everyone in the room breathes heavy. A wrestling match has just ended. The front of* **Patricia**'*s dress is ripped.* **Wire**'*s drum is broken. Clothes are ruffled and ripped. A green haze surrounds* **Sunny**'*s body.*

Truth =.= (*Catching his breath.*)

Stacey =.= (*Catching his breath.*)

Patricia =.= (*Breathing, holding her dress up against her body.*)

Emekah **Sunny** =.= (*Breathing.*)

Wire =.= (*Breathing.*)

Emekah **Sunny** Y'all got to tie a muthafucka up like an animal?

Stacey You act like one, get treated like one.

Wire Coulda been worse.

Emekah **Sunny** Fuck you, coulda been worse.

Shiiiiiiiiiiit . . .

Truth =.=

Emekah [Sunny] =.=

Stacey =.=

Patricia =.=

Wire =.=

Emekah [Sunny] Comin at me like that. Who the fuck y'all think y'all are? . . .

Wire =.= (*Breathing.*)

Patricia =.= (*Looking at* **Emekah / Sunny**. *Turns away.*)

Emekah [Sunny] These ropes are too tight! Y'all den made this shit too . . .

Wire, Truth *and* **Stacey** *look at* **Emekah / Sunny** *squirm. It's clear that the knots are too strong for* **Emekah / Sunny** *to break. The room relaxes a bit in this realization.*

Truth *grabs the bottle of whiskey from his backpack. He takes a swig then passes it to* **Patricia,** *who takes a swig then passes it to* **Wire,** *who drinks then passes it to* **Stacey**. **Stacey** *drinks then returns it to* **Truth**.

Truth *is devastated by the turn of events.*

Patricia (*to* **Stacey**; *hushed*) I'ma need a change of clothes . . .

Stacey In my room. Under the bed.

Patricia *exits the shop. Enters* **Stacey**'*s room. She finds a dress shirt and a belt. Changes her clothes as:*

Emekah [Sunny] This gurl got some nice skin. Why y'all wanna ruin it makin these ropes so tight?

Stacey Cause you punched me, scratched Truth, broke Wire's drum, busted up Patricia's dress . . .

Truth And now you squattin in that poor girl's body . . .

Wire You den created a whole heap of mess in a short bit of time, Emekah Evans.

Emekah [Sunny] You can kiss my black ass, Wire.

All y'all can.

Shit, why y'all ain't askin why I got hurt at that machine?!

Why y'all ain't hollerin at the owner about getting some damn first aid in that factory?

Or, or getting a hospital 'round here? Worried about some damn gal . . . what about *me*?!

Is she even from around here?

Checks out the body.

Got some nice credentials though . . .

Cain't wait to get loose up in here –

Patricia *exits the bedroom, enters the shop wearing* **Stacey***'s clothes.*

Emekah [Sunny] Oooo wee! Patty sweets Patty. Back in town . . . Stacey come back and you come sniffin after him, huh baby girl?

Patricia *crosses over to the bottle of whiskey. As she drinks she flips* **Emekah /Sunny** *the bird.*

Emekah [Sunny] Awww, come on now, Patty baby. You cain't take a joke? That's your job, ain't it? Takin jokes. Long, thick, throbbin jokes? I'm just playin. I'm just messin with you. Don't be mad. I'll make it up to you. Come over here and have a seat on this lap. I'll make you feel all better –

Patricia Rather sit down on a bear trap.

Emekah [Sunny] Damn! Cold-blooded. No wonder you had to cut her ass loose, Stacey –

Stacey What the hell do you want, Emekah?

Emekah Sunny I don't want or need your uppity attitudes, that's for damn sure.

Damn, a brotha dies and still dealin with shit-talkers –

Truth Cause that brotha is bustin in places he ain't got no business in.

Emekah Sunny I got plenty of business. Lots of stuff I need to 'tend to.

You thinkin I knew today was gonna be my last?

I ain't planned for none of this to happen.

Treatin me like a thug.

Truth You cain't stay in there, Emekah.

Emekah Sunny This gal pulled at me . . . ya'll think I'm the kind of man who just pushes his way into some female? I only enter if I'm invited and this invitation landed on me at exactly the right time.

When my body died in the back of that truck, I was sucked out through the belly button and shot out like a bullet from a gun. I was zipping and screaming through the universe. Knowing whatever I was gonna hit was gonna get hit *hard*. Shit, I was going too fast for the landing *not* to be a mess. You heard me? And then I fell plop down into this pretty young thing.

Patricia *drinks more whiskey. Seeing this gesture,* **Wire** *remembers. He jumps up and runs to the back porch to see the empty basin.*

Wire (*yells from the back porch*) The basin is empty. She was thirsty. She was so messed up she musta drank from the basin.

Stacey (*to* **Patricia** *and* **Truth**) And I didn't change the water from the accident . . .

Patricia All that blood . . .

They all vocalize being grossed out.

Wire *enters* **Stacey***'s room, re-enters the shop.*

Patricia We got to get this fool outta her . . .

Emekah Sunny Uh-uh. Cain't do that, Sadity Bop.

I gotta get to my family.

Got to get to my people's house to figure out what I should do.

And I need this body to get me there.

Stacey Why you got to get back to your family?

Truth What does it matter?! He cain't stay!

Emekah Sunny Cause I wasn't supposed to go flyin. Wasn't supposed to zip and scream.

Ivory was supposed to be there.

She was supposed to meet me when I left my body but instead I just went flying. That ain't how it's supposed to happen. My ancestor is supposed to take me in her arms. Supposed to bless me. Walk me to my paradise.

Stacey So you sittin up in Sunny cause Ivory was runnin late?

Emekah Sunny You got jokes! Fuck you, Ms. Stacey.

Stacey What'd you say to me?

Emekah Sunny Get me to my family.

Stacey I'ma get you uh ass-kickin if you –

Patricia Don't put a hand on her, Stacey, don't!

Stacey *steps back.*

Truth You ain't takin her nowhere, Emekah. Especially not to that Evans property.

Ain't no tellin what your people gonna do to her tryin to get you to Ivory.

Emekah Sunny I'm not leavin this body.

Truth I heard your dumb ass, but you gettin out anyway.

Truth *grabs a plastic sandwich bag from a box that rests on a shelf.*

Truth Wire, come on out here . . .

Truth *crosses into* **Stacey***'s room* **Wire** *follows.* **Truth** *grabs a pencil and paper. Goes out onto the back porch. He removes his handkerchief, swabs the inside of the bowl, folds it and puts it in the sandwich bag, gives it to* **Wire**. *Then he writes on the piece of paper.*

In the shop **Patricia, Stacey, Emekah / Sunny**.

Emekah Sunny Patricia and Stacey, keepin it real! (*Chuckles.*)

There was some funny shit on that album.

Most of it was alright, but some of it was funny.

Patricia You talkin all this mess cause you know these men don't hit women.

Crawl up in Truth and see if Stacey don't smack you around then.

Emekah Sunny I heard they was talkin bout givin y'all the key to the town.

Patricia (*instantly diverted*) Really?

Stacey (*not now . . .*) Patricia . . .

Patricia (*to* **Stacey**) Did you know about this?

Stacey Yes.

Patricia And you wasn't gonna tell me?

Emekah Sunny (*to* **Patricia**) Wasn't gonna say a damn thing, gurl –

Stacey Shut up, Emekah.

(*To* **Patricia**.) Ain't no point in talkin about it.

Patricia You didn't turn it down, did you?

Stacey Of course I turned it down.

Emekah Sunny Mhm. Woulda been a nice ceremony, too.

Glazed ham . . . wine coolers . . . brass band . . .

Patricia You up and said no without hearin word from me?

Stacey The last set of words you gave me was a 'fuck' and a 'you'.

And that's after you slapped me.

You expect I'ma write you about some damn key to the town?

Patricia That's how we do, Stacey.

We yell and bitch at each other and then one of us walks away.

But we always make up when we step on stage.

It's how we do.

Stacey Uh-uh. Ain't how we do. Not no more.

Emekah Sunny Oooooo –

Patricia and **Stacey** Shut up!

On the back porch **Truth** *finishes up his note. Folds it up. Gives it to* **Wire**.

Truth Take this note and that sample to Waymon Davis. Over yonder. Tell him to get here as fast as he can make it.

Wire Y'all gonna be alright?

Truth We'll be fine. Gone to him.

Wire *zips through* **Stacey***'s room, into the shop, grabs his broken drum, runs out the front door, jumps off the front porch.*

He's gone.

Truth *trails behind at a much slower pace. He enters the shop as:*

Emekah Sunny That sonofabitch Wire is quick! Runnin out like a jug of liquor.

Speakin of which . . . (*Smacks his/her lips.*) y'all was passin that around and forgot me.

Patricia We didn't forget.

Emekah Sunny Well, I'm askin.

Stacey No, Emekah.

Emekah Sunny Do y'all Sadity Bops realize what I been through today?

I don't think y'all really know . . .

Truth Uh, I think we do. I was holdin your head up when you took your last breath, Emekah.

Emekah Sunny (*taking pause*) Oh, oh . . . really?

Stacey And I had your, your nub in a bag of ice . . .

Emekah Sunny Oh.

=.=

=.=

So, so I guess y'all do know.

=.=

=.=

Y'all tried to help save me?

Stacey Yes.

Emekah Sunny =.=

Huh.

=.=

=.=

Y'all muthafuckas did a whack-ass job of it!

Emekah / **Sunny** *laughs.* **Sunny***'s breasts catch* **Emekah***'s eyes. Laughter subsides.*

Emekah [Sunny] (*re Sunny's breasts*) Oooo, these are nice. Real nice . . . damn!

Emekah *jiggles her chest.*

Truth Man, you betta keep them eyes glued to the wall in front of you or –

Emekah [Sunny] Or what?

What is wrong with you, Truth? A brotha cain't *look* no more. *Lookin* is a crime, security man?

Suddenly:

Sunny [Emekah] (*as if coming out of a deep sleep*) Hello? He, he, hello?

=.= (*Registering the ropes.*)

What did ya'll do to me? Why am I all –

Patricia Sunny?

Sunny [Emekah] Patricia!

Why am I all tied up like this? Did I mess up the outhouse?

Patricia No, no. Listen to me, Sunny. Something . . . happened.

Sunny [Emekah] To me?

Stacey To you.

Patricia That boy that died today . . .

Truth Stacey and I got covered in his blood . . .

Patricia And you got some of that in you . . .

Stacey Got some of him in you . . .

Emekah [Sunny] Got me all up in your gooshy shit!

Sunny [Emekah] Who is that?

Patricia That's what we tryin to tell you, Sunny –

Emekah [Sunny] Sunny . . . that's a nice juicy name –

Sunny *screams.*

Emekah [Sunny] Shit, this girl can holler the skin offa a catfish –

Sunny *screams.*

Truth Sunny. Sunny, now, now calm down. We gonna fix this –

Sunny Is this what y'all do in this town? This why everybody wanted to know who I was?

This is what Wire meant when he was talkin about an invasion –

Emekah *covers* **Sunny***'s voice.*

Emekah [Sunny] I, I ain't very good at this body squattin. I don't really know how to keep her quiet – AHHHHH! That gurl den bit me –

Sunny [Emekah] Patricia! Patricia! You got to help me –

Patricia I will! We are!

Sunny *and* **Emekah** *wrestle in* **Sunny***'s body. Her screams spin with his grunts. There's a great big gasp from them both followed by a free-fall type yell then suddenly* **Sunny***'s body goes limp.*

Patricia =.=

Stacey =.=

Truth =.=

Stacey What the hell was that?

Truth Sunny?! Sunny!

Patricia Sounds like they fell from something –

Stacey What could they fall from? The gurl's five foot three!

Truth *sneaks closer to* **Sunny***'s body. Can see her chest rise and fall.*

Truth She's still breathing. Maybe we oughta let 'em stay out until Davis comes.

Stacey Waymon Davis?

Truth Uh-huh. I sent Wire for him.

Patricia What is he gonna do about this?

Truth He's gonna pull Emekah out of her. Bring Sunny back to her senses.

Stacey Since when does Waymon Davis handle lost souls?

Truth Since Hunter Priestess died and he volunteered to make room for her in his body.

She can come down in him, through him, whenever she wants. Folks got a soul to deal with, they call him and he channels her . . .

Stacey For a fee though, right?

Truth Of course, but –

Patricia and **Truth** I'll pay it.

They look at each other.

Truth I'll pay it, Patty. Let me do it.

Patricia (*backing down*) Okay. Alright.

Stacey I figure Davis don't care *who* the money comes from as long as it comes, right?

Both of y'all can put in half. Everybody feels good about saving Sunny.

Patricia =.=

Truth =.=

Patricia No, no. That's alright. Truth says he'll pay. Let him pay.

Stacey What's wrong with y'all?

Patricia Nuthin.

Truth Patricia and I just have a understanding . . .

Patricia (*trying to cover her tracks*) No understanding, Truth. You just said you want things to go down a certain way. And I respect that.

Stacey Uh-uh. You don't respect nuthin unless you get some benefit from it.

Patricia What are you gettin pinched up about, Stacey? Please dump your mistrust in the shit pot.

There was some concern about method of payment and now it's smooth. Alright?

Truth *exits the shop.*

Patricia Where you goin?

Truth That whiskey ran right through me.

Truth *goes through* **Stacey***'s room onto the back porch down the steps. He's gone.*

Stacey He got a bladder the size of a crock-pot. He don't have to pee.

What are you hustlin him in to?

Patricia Don't you get tired of snoopin?

Stacey =.=

Patricia The brotha had to use the bathroom, Stacey.

Ain't no more to it.

Stacey =.= (*Easing up.*)

Patricia =.= (*Easing up.*)

Stacey =.=

Patricia sighs a genuine breath of exhaustion. **Stacey** *looks at* **Patricia**.

Stacey =.=

=.=

You been takin care of yourself?

Patricia Are you askin me how I been keepin?

Stacey Whether you speak on it or not I know *how* you doin.

I can feel you.

I'm askin you if you takin care of yourself.

Patricia You don't know a damn thing about me.

Ain't how we do, remember?

Stacey I know a lot of things.

Patricia You don't know shit.

Stacey I know Sunny's in love with you.

Patricia What?

Stacey =.=

Patricia How you know that?

Stacey She told me.

Patricia When?

Stacey On the porch. Earlier.

Patricia (*looking at Sunny's limp body*) =.=

=.=

She loves me?

Stacey She *thinks* she does.

Patricia You don't think somebody could love me?

Stacey =.=

Patricia I can do other things besides pine.

=.=

I can be *pined for*, Stacey.

Stacey =.=

Patricia =.=

Patricia *crosses to* **Stacey***'s room.*

Stacey Where you going?

Patricia None of your damn business.

Patricia *enters the back porch. She paces.*

In the shop, **Stacey** *looks at* **Sunny***'s limp body.*

Truth *steps up on the back porch. He sees* **Patricia**:

Truth I didn't say anything, Patty. *Won't* say nuthin. I'm sorry.

Patricia I'm breakin the deal, Truth.

Truth What? Why?

Patricia I just cain't help you. I won't help you.

Truth Tell me why?

Patricia Cause . . . Cause . . . It ain't something I'm interested in doing anymore.

=.=

=.=

=.=

She loves me.

=.=

Sunny.

Truth =.=

=.=

=.=

How you know that?

Patricia She told Stacey.

Truth How you know Stacey tellin the truth?

Patricia He cain't lie about love. He can *deny* it hella good but he cain't lie.

Truth Do you love her?

Patricia (*answering 'no'*) She loves me.

Truth *exhales as this thought seeps into his mind.*

Truth Well, well then I cain't help you no more either.

Patricia I understand.

Truth *slumps down, sits on the steps.*

Truth =.=

=.=

=.=

I ain't got no plan c . . .

Patricia *leans against the post.*

Wire *jumps on the front porch, enters the shop, winded. His drum is slung over his shoulder.*

Wire Where is Truth and Patty?

Stacey Outback.

Wire (*re. Sunny*) What happened to her?

Stacey We don't know. She still breathin though . . . we gonna wait for Waymon Davis.

Wire He's on his way. He told me to leave him alone so he could call Hunter Priestess.

Stacey You sweatin the mess outta yourself . . .

Wire *wipes his sweating brow with the back of his hand.*

Wire Sweatin is a part of my job. Truth told me to make it quick.

Stacey *removes his handkerchief from his back pocket.*

Wire I think I lost my handkerchief at that baby party.

Stacey *wipes* **Wire***'s* face. *It's a casual gesture that quickly takes on an intimate and delicate tone.*

Stacey (*wiping Wire's brow*) How did Waymon end up sharin his self with Hunter Priestess?

Through the following, **Stacey** *wipes* **Wire***'s temples, his jawline, under his chin, reaches around, wipes the back of his neck, behind his ears . . .*

Wire Waymon was lonely.

He went to Hunter Priestess when she was alive to ask her to conjure him a lover.

She did but he wasn't impressed. He had a high taste. He wanted more thighs, less butt, more brains, less poetics.

He wanted his money back.

They got to fighting about it. After the fighting came the talkin.

They found out they were soul mates.

=.=

She got skinned alive during the invasion. Died some hours later.

Waymon was devastated.

He went through her writings, learned how to call her to him.

And they came up with the present-day situation.

Stacey Must needed her bad to make room for her like that.

Wire Folks need people. That's the way life is.

Stacey I know that first-hand. You do, too.

=.=

=.=

Patricia *enters* **Stacey**'*s room. She's about to enter the shop but stops when she hears:*

Stacey I been back a week now and . . .

I, I don't know what to do now that the waitin's over.

You talkin bout waitin all those years . . .

All I know how to do with you is wait.

Been back here a week . . .

We finally with each other . . . and I don't know what to do.

Cain't settle in. Don't know how.

Wire *takes* **Stacey**'*s handkerchief. He places* **Stacey**'*s hands on his chest / armor. The plastic crinkles.* **Wire** *and* **Stacey** *breathe deep.* **Patricia**, *curious about this long moment of silence, peeks into the shop from* **Stacey**'*s bedroom. She looks in just as* **Stacey** *and Wire* **kiss**. **Wire** *lets go of his drum. It crashes to the floor, but he remains connected to* **Stacey**. *Immediately after they separate:*

Stacey Patricia needs to get . . .

Wire . . . gone.

Patricia *hears this and quietly steps away from the curtain. What is she going to do now?*

Wire We'll get Sunny right, then they need . . .

Stacey . . . to get gone.

Wire They'll be alright on they own.

Stacey More than alright. She's in love with her.

Wire Who's in love with who?

Stacey (*gesturing to* **Sunny**) She's in love with your sister.

Wire Sunny tell you that?

Stacey I could hear it in her voice.

Wire Does Patty know?

Stacey Uh-huh.

I told her.

Wire You told her?

Stacey Yea.

Wire Why?

Stacey Cause Truth was barkin about Sunny being his wife.

Sunny wasn't gonna be his wife.

Truth cain't be nobody's husband.

Wire How you know?

Stacey For a man like that . . . love is tied up with owning things. He don't care who the woman is. He's just lookin to corner somebody.

Wire And how is any of that your business?

Stacey =.=

Wire Why you tellin Patty what Sunny told you?

It ain't your business keepin Truth from being somebody's husband –

Stacey But it wasn't gonna happen –

Wire Well, if it wasn't gonna happen, it means you don't need to meddle in it.

Stacey Why you gettin all pinched at me?

Wire 'Cause you kickin up dirt, stirrin pots that ain't yours –

Stacey Pots that ain't mine? Patty and me been –

Patricia *goes back to the curtain that leads to the shop.*

Wire Don't talk that 'you and Patty' shit, Stacey.

Stacey You actin like I ain't got a right to –

Wire You actin like a history with somebody gives you a right to hold on to 'em.

It don't.

All that matters is who's got a hold of what's in here. (*Slaps his own chest, plastic crinkles.*)

Stacey And she ain't got a hold of that in me –

Wire But you keepin a grip on hers.

Stacey =.=

Wire You been layin up with her while you was on the road?

Stacey No.

=.=

=.=

She cain't function without some man tellin her how she is or how she oughta be. She held on to your daddy 'til she got too big for it then she moved on to you and then she ended up needing me. I'm the only man she got left. She cain't do no better than me.

Patricia *pulls back the curtain. Steps into the shop.*

Wire *and* **Stacey** *break away from each other.* **Wire** *takes* **Stacey***'s handkerchief and stuffs it in his pocket.*

Patricia *crosses over to* **Sunny**, *who is still breathing.*

Stacey Wire said Waymon Davis is coming.

He's conjurin up Hunter Priestess then he'll be on his way.

Patricia Uh-huh.

=.=

=.=

Wire (*to* **Stacey**) You got a fresh shirt for me?

I'm stinkin this one up . . .

Patricia There's a box of fresh clothes under his bed.

Stacey =.=

Wire =.=

Patricia (*to* **Stacey**) Am I lying?

Stacey Naw . . .

Wire *crosses into* **Stacey***'s room. Takes off his shirt, grabs* **Stacey***'s handkerchief and wipes his back, armpits, around his armor. Stuffs it back into his pocket. He finds one of* **Stacey***'s clean shirts.*

In the shop, **Patricia** *talks to* **Stacey** *but speaks loud enough so that* **Wire** *can hear her.*

Patricia I love my brother.

He's scared of me though.

=.=

Can only do the big talk when I'm out of sight.

Certain types of men is built that way . . .

Wire *reacts to this but remains silent.*

Truth *rises to his feet on the back porch. He enters* **Stacey's** *room. Sees* **Wire**. *He speaks quietly enough so that* **Wire** *is the only one who can hear him.*

Truth Wire, Wire, I'm glad it's you.

Wire (*taken aback*) Got-damn, Truth! You was out there?

Truth Look, I got something I need to talk to you about.

Stacey You don't act like you love him.

Patricia Neither did you until Truth told you you had to come stand in your daddy's shoes.

Truth Do you need some extra help with your business?

Wire (*distracted, trying to listen to* **Patty** *and* **Stacey**) What?

Truth Do you need help?

I know how to drive – automatic and stick.

Can swim a long ways.

Learned hand-to-hand combat for the invasion.

And you know I know how to keep things in order . . .

Stacey You think I only came back cause this shop?

Patricia I know you had your reasons, Stacey.

Just like I got my reasons for comin back.

Stacey You only got one reason, Patricia.

Patricia And what is that?

Stacey Me.

Patricia You? (**Patricia** *laughs*.)

Negro, please.

Truth (*to* **Wire**) I'm thinkin I might leave the shop.

For good. Thinkin maybe I could work for you.

Patricia You and Wire really think I need ya'll, don't you?

Stacey =.=

Patricia I don't.

I don't *need* anybody.

Just choose to have people around me cause I like folks.

And they like me.

Truth I need you to seriously consider this, Wire.

Wire Truth, I ain't in the state of mind to consider anything right now.

Truth I need to cut loose from all this.

Got my soul busted too many times.

But I cain't go to that factory . . .

Patricia I came back for Wire's birthday.

I came back to see how you were doin.

And . . .

Wire *steps out of* **Stacey***'s room wearing his shirt, carrying his handkerchief. Everyone, except* **Sunny**, *is dressed in* **Stacey***'s clothes.*

Truth *follows* **Wire**. **Patricia** *looks at him.*

Patricia I got a few gigs after I leave here, houses that want me not the act, so I cain't stay long . . .

It'd be nice to have some company.

Stacey I'm sure Sunny'll go with you once we get her right.

Patricia I'm sure she will.

But I'm talkin bout takin somebody who can maintain books, handle money, and other matters.

What you think about travelin around, Truth?

The whole room stops, eyes on **Truth**.

Truth Travelin? With you?

Patricia With me.

Stacey You cain't be for real –

Patricia Why not?

Truth Why cain't she be?

Stacey (*to* **Truth**) You cain't be serious bout goin?

Truth (*defiant*) Why the hell not?

Wire Stacey, maybe it's a good idea . . .

Stacey What the hell kind of bullshit is ya'll on?

Truth cain't leave. He's in the papers. I'm about to own this shop, which means I'm about to own hi –

Truth You gonna own who?

Stacey (*backtracking*) He'd be on the road with two women, he ain't even spent as much time with his own mama.

He don't know how to act around women.

Plus, plus he's in love with that girl. She ain't never gonna love him back.

Truth Why do you care one way or the other?

Patricia He don't.

He just cain't stand for you to be happy without him –

Stacey (*to* **Patricia**) You cain't stand for me to have my shit together without you.

Patricia What shit you got together? It took you a week to kiss Wire –

Wire (*to* **Patricia**) You snoopin on me now, Patty?

Patricia It's just a damn curtain up at that doorway. What you expect?

Truth Ha! Busted!

(*To* **Patricia**.) You ain't gonna be in my business like that, are you, Patty?

Patricia You ain't got no business to speak of, so no.

Commotion. **Patricia, Wire, Truth,** *and* **Stacey** *get wrapped up in a shouting match. Insults spin from every mouth, confessions are made, truths are told but no one hears anybody cause everybody is cussing somebody out.* **Sunny**'s *body remains limp.*

Waymon Davis as Hunter Priestess *climbs the steps onto the front porch, carrying a toolbox and tambourine. He wears overalls stained with mud and dirt, worn workman boots and a soiled undershirt. He wears the clothes of a sharecropper. The purple haze that surrounds him is the only indication that he's carrying the skills needed to harness an unruly soul. He stands on the porch looking in at the chaos.*

Waymon as Hunter Priestess *puts down his box and delivers a series of rolls with his tambourine.*

Everyone continues to argue.

Waymon's *rolls transform into a beat. It's a slow groove that snakes its way into the room and wraps around everyone's hips one by one. His flourish and dexterity with this instrument surprises those who have seen* **Waymon as Hunter Priestess** *play for the first time. This big, burly man can beat the tears out of the Devil with the way he handles this thing.*

Suddenly, **Patricia, Wire, Truth,** *and* **Stacey** *emerge from their argument and start to sing a melody in time with the tambourine beat. They enter a trance one by one until they have joined* **Waymon**'s *soulful spin. The four of them turn to* **Waymon Davis as High Priestess,** *who continues to play. He enters the shop.* **Truth** *crosses out to the porch, brings* **Waymon**'s *box inside.*

Waymon as Hunter Priestess (*sung*) Children got a soul they cain't set free?!

Patricia and **Truth** and **Stacey and Wire** (*sung*) Yeeeeeeesssssss! Yea! Yessssssssssssss!

The four of them sway, slide, and roll to **Waymon as Hunter Priestess***'s beat.*

Waymon as Hunter Priestess (*sung*) Children got a soul they cain't set free?!

Patricia and **Truth** and **Stacey and Wire** (*sung*) Yeeeeeeesssssss! Yea! Yessssssssssssss!

Waymon as Hunter Priestess (*sung*) Send that soul to Hunter Priestess!

Send that soul straight unto me!

Send that soul to Hunter Priestess!

And that soul will soon be free!

They repeat the song again and again, improvising words, sounds, and feelings.

Waymon as Hunter Priestess *orchestrates the brown bodies in the room with various trills and rolls of his tambourine. An unconscious* **Sunny** *remains limp against the counter.* **Patricia, Wire, Stacey,** *and* **Truth** *sing and clap, supporting* **Waymon***'s rhythm.* **Waymon** *does one final trill then stops.* **Waymon***'s purple haze settles against the green haze that surrounds* **Sunny***'s* **body***.*

The sky is black, swallowing the pipes and the smoke that seeps from them.

Everyone is silent. Only breath.

Patricia, Stacey, Truth, *and* **Wire** *anchor one side of the room.*

Waymon as Hunter Priestess Hey hey now.

The four of them stagger their responses.

Patricia Hey hey . . .

Truth Hey now hey . . .

Stacey Hey now now . . .

Wire Hey hey now . . .

Waymon as Hunter Priestess (*to Sunny's body*) Emekah Evans!

The room waits.

Patricia, **Truth**, **Stacey**, *and* **Wire** *get low to the ground. They beat a quiet rhythm against the floor.*

Waymon *pulls a small bottle of liquid from the bib of his overalls. He pops the top and drinks the concoction. He plays a quiet rhythm on the tambourine that serves as a pace for him to walk with. He squats down right in* **Sunny**'*s face and blows . . .*

Sunny *snaps awake, gasping for air. The others stop their rhythm.*

Waymon *shakes his tambourine.*

Sunny *locks eyes with* **Waymon as Hunter Priestess**.

Sunny =.= (*Breathing.*)

Waymon as Hunter Priestess =.= (*Looking.*)

Sunny Who, who are you?

Waymon as Hunter Priestess (*smiles*) You, my darling, are lookin at Mr. Waymon Davis.

However, you're speakin with Mizzzzz Hunter Priestess.

Now, who am I speakin with?

Sunny This, this is Sunny talkin.

Waymon as Hunter Priestess That's a pretty name, Sunny.

Sunny Thank, thank you.

Waymon as Hunter Priestess I got word you got company in there with you . . .

Frightened. **Sunny** *nods.*

Waymon as Hunter Priestess (*caressing the side of* **Sunny's** *face*) Emekah?

Sunny *nods.*

Waymon as Hunter Priestess Where is he now, Sunny?

Sunny He's passed out. Over in the corner of me.

I can see the shape of 'em out the side of my eye . . .

Waymon as Hunter Priestess That's how we want him. He's just as scared as you . . . don't know what he doin. A soul that don't know his powers yet is one that's easy to take down.

You know what you can do for me?

Sunny What?

Waymon as Hunter Priestess If you look the other direction out the corner of your eye, you see that corner.

It's empty, ain't it?

Sunny *nods.*

Waymon as Hunter Priestess Crawl over in that corner and don't come out until I tell you to, alright?

Sunny Okay.

=.=

=.=

Is Patricia still here?

Waymon as Hunter Priestess *turns to the group.* **Patricia** *starts to say something.*

Waymon as Hunter Priestess Don't say nuthin. Just let her see you.

Patricia *raises up in* **Sunny**'*s line of sight.* **Sunny** *smiles sheepishly. Sighs.* **Waymon as Hunter Priestess** *shoos* **Patricia** *down.* **Patricia** *gets back low.*

Waymon as Hunter Priestess Now crawl over yonder in that corner Sunny, okay?

A series of sounds escape **Sunny***'s body as she crawls to a corner in her body.*

Sunny (*in the distance*) Okay.

Waymon as Hunter Priestess *pulls another small bottle from his back pocket. He pops the top, drinks the concoction. Then he blows into* **Sunny***'s face again.* **Emekah** *wakes up. Gasps for air:*

Emekah Sunny =.= (*Breathing, wild-eyed.*)

Waymon as Hunter Priestess *shakes his tambourine.*

Emekah Sunny *locks eyes with* **Waymon as Hunter Priestess**. **Emekah** Sunny scoots back frightened.

Waymon as Hunter Priestess Hey hey now.

Emekah.

Emekah Sunny What the fuck is this shit?!

What you want?

Waymon as Hunter Priestess Aww, now, you know what I want, Emekah.

Emekah Sunny (*yelling to the others*) I told y'all I wanted my family! I want to go to my mama's house! Y'all den up and called Hunter Priestess and her, her man sack –

Waymon as Hunter Priestess We callin folks out of their names? Is that how it is, Emekah?

Emekah Sunny I want my people –

Waymon as Hunter Priestess I heard about your accident, Emekah.

Ivory told me it was gonna happen.

Emekah Sunny She did?

Waymon as High Priestess *nods.*

Emekah Sunny Where was she? Why'd she leave me hangin then?

Waymon as Hunter Priestess I cain't answer that for you. Got to ask her yourself.

Go to her and talk to her yourself.

Emekah Sunny (*shaking her head*) I ain't leavin this girl, Priestess. Soon as I leave her no tellin where I end up.

Only get one shot to make it to the ancestors. I already spoiled mine.

Waymon as Hunter Priestess You cain't stay where you are, Emekah Evans.

Emekah Sunny You cain't force me out.

Waymon as Hunter Priestess What makes you think that?

Emekah Sunny This lil body of brown sunshine. No scratches, nicks, or dents, Mizzz Priestess. Gotta leave it how you found it. And I heard you don't do clean sweeps. Which means I'm stayin high and dry.

Waymon as Hunter Priestess I usually don't do clean sweeps when I'm dealing with pricks.

But you're a good boy, Emekah Evans.

Emekah Sunny Don't call me boy.

Waymon as Hunter Priestess You ain't gonna be a prick, are you, boy?

Emekah Sunny Well, you actin like a cunt which means I'm bout to be a prick.

Waymon as Hunter Priestess *stands up, steps back. This is going to be harder than anticipated . . .*

Waymon as Hunter Priestes (*quietly to* **Truth** *and* **Stacey**) I'ma need you to come over here and untie her . . .

Truth *and* **Stacey** *give a 'who? me?' look.* **Waymon as Hunter Priestess** *nods. Yes, you.*

Wire *and* **Patricia** *barricade the front door and the door leading to* **Stacey***'s room.* **Wire** *holds a can of soup,* **Patricia** *holds her high-heel shoe – weapons on the ready for defense.*

Truth *and* **Stacey** *untie* **Sunny***'s body.*

Emekah / Sunny *remains calm . . . too calm. Suddenly,* **Emekah / Sunny** *springs to her feet and runs for the front door.* **Waymon as Hunter Priestess** *catches* **Emekah / Sunny** *in mid-air, spins her around and gently places the body on the ground, using his bodyweight to stifle her.* **Emekah / Sunny** *settles down.* **Waymon as Hunter Priestess** *rises up, crosses over to his toolbox. The tambourine goes down with great care. The cymbals hardly make a noise.*

Emekah / Sunny *springs again, this time on all fours. He scurries and scampers for an exit but* **Patricia**, **Truth**, **Wire**, *and* **Stacey** *have him trapped. He's stumped.*

Everyone in the room is ready to pounce.

Hunter Priestess *opens his bag. Pulls out a worn red bandana stitched diagonally with a blue bandana. He places it on the ground. He kneels on it.*

Waymon as Hunter Priestess I'ma sit down here, Emekah Evans.

I'ma sit here.

And I'ma ask you some questions.

Emekah [Sunny] I don't give a shit what you do.

Waymon as Hunter Priestess =.=

=.=

Waymon as Hunter Priestess *removes a pouch from his pocket. He places a pinch of powder on the back of his hand. Sniffs it up one nostril. Places another pinch on the back of his hand. Sniffs it up the* *other. He dumps the rest of the powder in his mouth. He mixes it up with his saliva. He swishes around his mouth. He swallows. He waits.*

He exhales in **Sunny***'s direction, surrounding her body in a purple haze. An invisible force shapes and shifts the body as if animated by a puppet master.* **Waymon as Hunter Priestess** *laughs. The force places* **Sunny** *on top of the counter and places her in a very ladylike position – legs crossed, hands draped across the lap, head tilted slightly to one side, a vapid expression rests on the face.*

Patricia What is she doin to her?!

Waymon as Hunter Priestess She's a very pretty gal. Mm-hm. She sho' nuff is . . .

Emekah Sunny You don't scare me a damn bit, Priestess.

Waymon as Hunter Priestess *exhales in the body's direction.* **Sunny***'s body very slowly uncrosses her legs and sits wide-legged on the counter, gathering her skirt between her legs. The body leans towards* **Waymon as Hunter Priestess***, showing off its cleavage. A titillating sway back-and-forth puts a smile on* **Waymon***'s face.*

Waymon as Hunter Priestess Ahhhhhhh . . . (*Laughs.*)

Emekah Sunny You think this shit is funny, bitch?

Waymon as Hunter Priestess Oh, Emekah Evans, I seen you sit on the steps right outside this shop and holler at the gurls who walked by . . . Cain't blame me, can ya?

EmekahSunny Ain't right for you to be doin it to another woman . . .

Waymon as Hunter Priestess Waymon gave his body to me to wrestle with you.

I ain't breakin your rules of how things supposed to work in this body, Emekahhhhhhh (*Laughter.*) . . .

Waymon as Hunter Priestess *ogles the body. Just as* **Sunny***'s about to raise her dress –*

Truth Ain't that enuff, Priestess?

Waymon as Hunter Priestess Don't question me.

=.=

=.=

I know when it's enuff.

Sunny *stops from raising her skirt, but continues to pose à la pin-up girl, flashing a smile.*

Waymon as Hunter Priestess *stands and bangs his foot twice on the floor.* **Sunny***'s body returns to the ladylike pose.* **Sunny***'s body executes 'ladylike' mannerisms and gestures as* **Emekah***'s voice bellows from the mouth.*

The following exchange is rapid-fire:

Waymon as Hunter Priestess What do you consider a revolutionary act, Emekah Evans?

Emekah^Sunny^ What the fuck you talkin bout –

Waymon as Hunter Priestess A revolutionary act, Emekah Evans. Name four.

Emekah^Sunny^ Fuck you.

Waymon as Hunter Priestess That's one. You really want that to count as your first one?

Emekah^Sunny^ You tryin to psych me out or some shit?

I'm not leavin this body!

Waymon as Hunter Priestess That's two.

Fuckin me is one.

Stayin in that body is two.

What's three?

Emekah^Sunny^ This is a bunch of bullshit –

Waymon as Hunter Priestess Disengagement. Very nice. Lazy but necessary.

Fuckin me.

Stayin in that body.

And emotional detachment.

Those are three revolutionary acts.

Emekah[Sunny] This is the muthafucka y'all called to deal with me?

Crazy-ass cat talkin about revolutions?

Waymon as Hunter Priestess Where were you during the invasion, Emekah Evans?

Emekah[Sunny] Where were you?

Waymon as Hunter Priestess Waymon was strapped to a tree and whipped across the back three hundred times while salt was poured on his wounds.

I was forced to crack the whip. Pour that salt across his back.

Where were you?

Emekah[Sunny] I was here.

Waymon as Hunter Priestess Where?

Emekah[Sunny] With my people.

Waymon as Hunter Priestess Locked up at your house.

Emekah[Sunny] So what?

Waymon as Hunter Priestess So what!!!?

Sunny*'s body is locked in a ladylike position.*

The rest of us was tryna fight to keep our town, but the Evans were awol.

Deserters. Chicken-dick cowards.

Emekah[Sunny] Fuck you. We thought it was all over. The end of our people –

Waymon as Hunter Priestess (*mocking*) Yea, yea, yea . . . you thought the invasion was when your people were gonna get pulled apart blah-blah-blah.

Emekah[Sunny] Don't 'blah-blah' that shit, man. We thought it was over.

Waymon as Hunter Priestess (*mocking continues*) Sittin in your cul-de-sac shacks, the Evans clan thought the prophecy was gonna be fulfilled.

Emekah[Sunny] You a heartless skank –

Waymon as Hunter Priestess So your fourth revolutionary act is sittin in your house on your goddamn ass until y'all got the all-clear. While they invade our town. Claim our land. Break our skin, our bones, our flesh, our spirits.

Emekah[Sunny] Y'all a bunch of weak-ass muthafuckas to begin with –

Waymon as Hunter Priestess They twist our laws to hustle us, beat us, bust us. And the Evans are hiding out, pissing they pants.

Emekah[Sunny] You can suck my dick, Hunter Priestess.

Waymon as Hunter Priestess Right after you grow some balls, young blood.

Emekah[Sunny] You wanna see what I'm packin?

Waymon as Hunter Priestess Waymon is packin a bigger sack than you and every other damn man in that Evans clan.

Lettin some woman curse your line –

Emekah[Sunny] She ain't 'some woman'!

Elder Ivory Evans was the start of our line –

Waymon as Hunter Priestess She was sick –

Emekah[Sunny] Shut up!!

Waymon as Hunter Priestess Twisted in the head like a white man chasin brown tail –

Emekah[Sunny] SHUT UP!

Waymon as Hunter Priestess Heard voices.

Emekah[Sunny] She had visions!

Waymon as Hunter Priestess Boogie man pullin at her skirt.

Emekah[Sunny] Got harassed for being redbone –

Waymon as Hunter Priestess Kept scratchin at the veins in her wrists.

Emekah[Sunny] She's takin us to the promise land.

Waymon as Hunter Priestess Wasn't no name for what she had back then but we all know what it is now.

I know what to call it.

But y'all Evans a lil bit sensitive about it –

Sunny'*s body begins to shake, but the head remains still.* **Emekah** *is full of rage that bubbles out of the pores of* **Sunny**'*s skin.*

Emekah[Sunny] You dirty raggedy piece of shit! Talkin about my people . . . talkin bout Ivory . . . you don't know shit about my people . . . she wasn't crazy . . . *we* ain't crazy. They, they, they made her that way. Made us this way . . . you, you talkin out your, your stank ass, Hunter Priestess.

Waymon as Hunter Priestess Uh-uh, Emekah Evans. Ivory was sick in the head. Needed help. Not a congregation.

Waymon as Hunter Priestess *turns to* **Patricia, Wire, Truth, Stacey**. **Emekah** *doesn't hear this because he's steeped in such rage.*

Waymon as Hunter Priestess (*hushed*) Close your eyes.

Cover your ears when I say the word.

He's gonna come after me then try to hide in one of y'all.

Emekah[Sunny] Dried-up piece of pig dick . . . stupid tar baby . . . black ignorant . . . piece of fuckin . . . you don't know my people . . . she wasn't crazy . . . they, they made her that way. Made us that way. They was tryin to kill us off . . . tried killing all of us.

Waymon as Hunter Priestess Your Ivory Messiah was a, a . . . para.noid schizo.phrenic, ain't that right, Emekah?

She was a para.noid schizo –

The spirit of **Emekah Evans** *shoots out the bottom of* **Sunny***'s feet. It ricochets across the room.* **Sunny***'s body falls limp, passed out on the counter.*

Waymon as Hunter Priestess (*yells to* **Patricia**, **Stacey**, **Truth**, **Wire**) Close EM UP!

The four of them cup their ears and close their eyes. A dark shadow bursts past **Waymon**, *knocking him off his stool.* **Waymon** *wails as if being punched and kicked.*

A blur as **Emekah***'s soul tries to find another body to crawl into, but* **Patricia**, **Stacey**, **Wire** *and* **Truth** *are shut tight. Objects are knocked around, thrown across the space as* **Emekah** *blindly searches for a way to survive. He goes to* **Sunny**, *her body shakes but she's locked up, too.*

Waymon *crawls to his tambourine. Grabs it and shakes a long trill.* **Waymon as Hunter Priestess** *plays a series of staccato jabs with the tambourine.*

Emekah*'s spirit spins and spins and spins, arms flailing in a violent manner. Pats himself as if putting out a fire all over his body. Holds his hands up to the heavens, reaching, reaching. Jumps. Jumps. Jumps as if trying to get at the only fruit on the highest limb. On the final jump a roar erupts from him and* **Emekah***'s soul disappears.*

The air is still. The sky is grey. No smoke from the factory pipes.

Four

Dawn the following morning.

The shop is still a mess from **Emekah***'s furious eruption.*

Patricia *and* **Sunny** *are in* **Stacey***'s bed.* **Patricia** *holds* **Sunny** *and gently caresses her.* **Sunny** *breathes deep, having a fitful sleep.*

In the shop, **Truth**, **Wire**, *and* **Stacey** *sleep on the floor.* **Stacey** *holds* **Wire**, *who sleeps deep. The men stopped responding to* **Sunny***'s whimpers hours ago.*

Waymon *climbs the steps onto the back porch, carrying a basin of fresh water. He places the basin on a pedestal, splashes his face and the back of his neck. He takes several deep breaths. Dries his face and neck on a towel. He enters* **Stacey***'s room.* **Patricia** *looks at him.* **Waymon** *is meek and mild-mannered. He's nothing like the person who stepped on the front porch earlier as Hunter Priestess.*

Waymon =.=

Patricia =.=

Sunny =.= (*whimpers in her sleep*)

Waymon She'll be alright.

It's just the residue.

She's gotta work through it.

Waymon *places a bottle on the writing table.*

Rub some of this on her lips.

And just under her nose every four hours.

It'll help flush it out faster.

=.=

=.=

=.=

Hunter Priestess says y'all be fine together.

=.=

=.=

And she apologizes if she got outta hand.

=.=

=.=

A part of the job.

Patricia Thank you, Waymon.

Waymon *nods, enters the shop.* **Stacey** *wakes up at the sound of his footsteps.*

Stacey You want a fresh shirt?

Waymon Naw, I'ma be alright.

The air'll do me good.

Priestess can choke me up sometimes. Feels good to be loose when she lets go of me.

Truth *snaps awake. Looks around. Sees* **Waymon**.

Truth Waymon?

Waymon Yea, it's me. Priestess let me loose.

Truth Alright . . .

Truth *climbs to his feet. He digs for his wallet, pulls money from it, gives it to* **Waymon**.

Truth That it?

Waymon *counts it.*

Waymon That's it.

The men shake hands.

Truth Priestess don't play.

Waymon No, she don't.

Cain't do without her though.

=.=

=.= (*Starts packing up his things.*)

(*To* **Truth**.) Hey, hey, you goin home?

I can walk back yonder with you.

Truth Yea, yea. I just need a minute . . .

Truth *crosses into* **Stacey***'s bedroom.* **Stacey** *watches him. Looks at the curtain.*

Stacey (*to* **Waymon**) You hungry?

We got some cereal 'round here . . . (*Taking in the mess.*) somewhere . . .

Truth *stands before* **Sunny** *and* **Patricia**.

Truth How's she doin?

Patricia She ain't no worse.

Waymon gave me something to help her.

Truth Good.

=.=

Patty, I'm acceptin your offer. Is it still on the table?

Patricia It is.

But you gotta be sure you're comin with me for the right reasons, though.

Don't do it to piss off Stacey or keep tabs on Sunny.

Truth It's for me. I'ma try doin this for myself.

After Hunter Priestess freed Sunny,

I felt like I got free, too.

My small way of thinkin, bein, got pulled right out of me.

And I never thought I'd go overseas . . .

Patricia Well, overseas probably won't happen for a while.

No duo, no foreign lands.

I'm a solo act now, which means starting back at the bottom.

Truth That's alright. That's fine. We'll get you over them seas soon enough.

A whimper seeps from **Sunny** *that's a bit edgier than what we've heard.*

Patricia Hand me that bottle on the table.

Truth *gives the small bottle to* **Patricia**. *She unscrews the top, dabs some of the potion on her finger and intimately, delicately wipes it on* **Sunny***'s lips, just under her nose.* **Truth** *quietly exits the bedroom, enters the shop.*

Waymon (*to* **Stacey**) Order some sage and burn it all over, everywhere . . . chase any and everything out.

Stacey I'll do that first thing.

Truth I'll be back by to help clean up.

Need to be in my own clothes, sleep in my own bed.

Stacey Alright . . .

What about after Patricia and Sunny leave?

You gonna be around then?

Truth No.

Stacey =.=

Truth Ain't nobody here for me, Stacey.

Truth *puts on his shoes. Grabs his bag.* **Waymon** *grabs his bag. The two men step out the front door, climb down the front steps.*

They're gone.

Stacey *looks down at* **Wire**. *Looks back at the curtain to his bedroom. Looks around the shop.*

Stacey (*to Patricia*) Did you hear that?

He said, 'ain't nobody here for me'.

Patricia (*holding* **Sunny**) I can understand that.

Patricia *wipes* **Sunny***'s brow.* **Sunny** *slowly opens her eyes, looks up at* **Patricia**. *When it registers who's holding her,* **Sunny** *kisses* **Patricia**.

Immediately after they separate:

Patricia Stacey, I'm gonna be fine without you.

Sunny *closes her eyes. Snuggles up to* **Patricia**.

Stacey Okay, Patricia.

Patricia You don't believe me?

Stacey Truth'll be good for you.

Patricia Truth'll be good for his self.

Stacey =.=

Patricia =.=

Stacey Patricia . . .

Patricia . . .

Patricia Hm?

Stacey =.=

=.=

Patricia What is it, Stacey?

Stacey (*doing the beginning of their comedy routine*) Tell the people how you feelin this evening . . .

Patricia (*not getting it*) What?

Stacey We rode all the way here to this lovely county, let these people know how you feelin tonight . . .

Patricia (*a slow realization*) Oh . . . Oh . . . For real, Stacey?

Stacey For real.

Just for now. This moment.

Patricia (*performing the routine*) Well, Stacey, I'ma have to be real with 'em.

I gotta be real wit y'all tonight.

Stacey Gone 'head and tell 'em.

I shouldn't be the only one who's sufferin . . .

Patricia It's that time of the month, ladies.

Y'all know what I'm sayin'.

And Stacey don't wanna help a sista when she wrestlin wit some fierce pussy demons.

Stacey Uh-uh. No. No. You got to fight the good fight on your own . . .

No way, Jack. I will see you on the other side of next week, you feelin me?

Patricia See?

But I do get mean around this time. I do. Don't I, Stacey?

Stacey She does.

Patricia I do. Mm-hm. Get so mean you hafta take two planes, a train, and a boat just to get to my good side. So mean I throw vegetables at fat kids. So mean I showed up at Satan's door and he said, 'Oh, hell no. Not you!'

Patricia *and* **Stacey** *chuckle from this shared memory.*

Blue smoke starts to pump out of the factory pipes. The work whistle blows in the distance to signify the start of another workday. The sun blossoms a bright orange like a piece of fruit in the sky.

Stacey =.= (*Holds* **Wire**.)

Wire =.= (*Sleeps.*)

Patricia =.= (*Holds Sunny.*)

Sunny =.= (*Sleeps.*)

As lights fade:

Stacey Ladies and gentlemen, I got a song I'd like to dedicate to Ms. Patricia tonight.

Patricia What you gonna sing for me?

Stacey *sings 'Happy Birthday' to* **Patricia**. *The song is a gift of sincerity from Stacey to* **Patricia**.

Patricia (*touched, but covers it*) You got some nerve talkin bout birthdays, boy . . .

Black.

Section II
(Post-) Blackness by Non-Black Playwrights

Young Jean Lee

The Shipment

Production history

The Shipment *premiered in January 2009 at The Kitchen in New York City. It was co-commissioned by the Wexner Center for the Arts at The Ohio State University and The Kitchen, and produced by Young Jean Lee's Theater Company (Young Jean Lee, Artistic Director; Caleb Hammons, Producing Director). It was written and directed by Young Jean Lee. It was produced by Caleb Hammons. The set design was by David Evans Morris, the lighting design was by Mark Barton, the costume design was by Roxana Ramseur, the sound design was by Matthew Tierney and the choreography was by Faye Driscoll. It was performed by:*

Dancer 2, Sidekick Michael, Crackhead John, Bad Cop 2, Sashay, Omar *Mikéah Ernest Jennings*
Dancer 1, Drug Dealer Desmond, Record Company Executive, Singer 2, Desmond *Prentice Onayemi*
Rapper Omar, Singer 3, Michael *Okieriete Onodowan*
Stand-up Comedian, Grandpa Joe, Paul the Extreme, Bad Cop 1, Thomas *Douglas Scott Streater*
Mama, Drug Dealer Mama, Video Ho, Grandma from Heaven, Singer 1, Thomasina *Amelia Workman*
Stagehand 1 *Joseph John*
Stagehand 2 *Foteos Macrides*

An earlier version of The Shipment *premiered in 2008 at the Wexner Center for the Arts in Columbus, with the same production team. It was performed by:*

Dancer 2, Sidekick Michael, Crackhead John, Bad Cop 2, Sashay, Omar *Mikéah Ernest Jennings*
Dancer 1, Drug Dealer Desmond, Record Company Executive, Singer 2, Desmond *Prentice Onayemi*
Rapper Omar, Singer 3, Michael *Jordan Barbour*
Stand-up Comedian, Grandpa Joe, Paul the Extreme, Bad Cop 1, Thomas *Douglas Scott Streater*
Mama, Drug Dealer Mama, Video Ho, Grandma from Heaven, Singer 1, Thomasina *Amelia Workman*
Stagehand 1 *Edward Hawkins*
Stagehand 2 *Joe McCutcheon*

Author's Note

The show is divided into two parts. The first half is structured like a minstrel show – dance, stand-up routine, sketches, and a song – and I wrote it to address the stereotypes my cast members felt they had to deal with as black performers. Our goal was to walk the line between stock forms of black entertainment and some unidentifiable weirdness to the point where the audience wasn't sure what they were watching or how they were supposed to respond. The performers wore stereotypes like ill-fitting paper-doll outfits held on by two tabs, which denied the audience easy responses (illicit pleasure or self-righteous indignation) to racial clichés and created a kind of uncomfortable, paranoid watchfulness in everyone. The second half of the show is a relatively straight naturalistic comedy. I asked the actors to come up with roles they'd always wanted to play and wrote the second half of the show in response to their requests.

A bare stage. Stark lights. Ominous white noise in the background.

Sudden lights down.

Sound of footsteps.

Sound of shoes clattering against the floor as Dancer 1 begins his dance in the dark.

A rock song – Semisonic's 'F.N.T.' – begins.

Lights up on Dancer 1 mid-jump, his arms and legs sprawling. He is wearing a black tuxedo with a white shirt, black suspenders, black cummerbund, and black bow tie.

Dancer 1 performs a series of bordering-on-goofy choreographed moves that are unidentifiable in genre. Occasionally we'll see a flash of possible minstrel reference – a gesture, a bit of footwork. Sometimes Dancer 1 is smiling, sometimes not. It's difficult to tell what his relationship is to what he's doing and to the audience.

Dancer 2 enters and watches Dancer 1, looking bemused. He is wearing a black suit, white shirt, flowered vest, red tie, black flower lapel brooch, and white shoes.

He starts to shake violently, still smiling. The two Dancers take turns doing herky-jerky movements and then flail wildly back and forth across the stage, sometimes syncing up to flail in unison. It's reminiscent of a tap routine, except that neither of them has any coordination and they look as if they are about to fall.

They break out of the flailing and walk in a square pattern around the perimeter of the stage, stopping downstage to stare at the audience. Then they move upstage to do a partner dance that involves Dancer 2 shaking violently in place while Dancer 1 twirls around him, grabbing hold of Dancer 2's stiff, jerking hands as he dips and spins.

For the big finish, both Dancers take turns doing fancy spins with their arms out. Dancer 1 breaks the pattern to do a goofy little jump. Dancer 2 does an even goofier move. Dancer 1 runs up to the back wall and touches it with his butt. Dancer 2 follows suit. Both

Dancers push themselves off the back wall and collapse onto the floor downstage, standing up crookedly to do a little half-smiling hat-tip to the audience before walking offstage.

'F.N.T.' lyrics:
Fascinating new thing
You delight me
And I know you're speaking of me

Fascinating new thing
Get beside me,
I want you to love me

I'm surprised that you've never been told before
That you're lovely and you're perfect
And that somebody wants you

Fascinating new thing
The scene makin'
Want a temporary savior

Fascinating new thing
Don't betray them
By becoming familiar

I'm surprised that you've never been told before
That you're lovely and you're perfect
And that somebody wants you

I'm surprised that you've never been told before
That you're priceless and you're precious
Even when you are not new.

I'm surprised that you've never been told before
That you're lovely and you're perfect
And that somebody wants you

I'm surprised that you've never been told before
That you're priceless
Yeah, you're holy
Even when you are not new

Fascinating new thing (fascinating new thing)
Fascinating new thing (fascinating new thing)
Fascinating new thing (fascinating new thing)
Fascinating new thing (fascinating new thing).

A rap song, Lil Jon's 'I Don't Give a Fuck', *begins as the dance ends.*

Announcer *(into offstage mike)* (*Name of city!*) Please put cho mothafuckin' hands together for the one, the only, (*Name of actor playing Stand-Up Comedian!*)

Stand-up Comedian *runs onstage to the music. He is wearing a black tux with a white shirt and skinny black tie.*

He stops downstage left and mimes having sex doggy style while facing the audience. He mimes wiping his imaginary partner's crotch from the rear, smells his fingers, makes a disgusted face, and kicks her away as he goes into a 'superman' dance move.

He runs downstage center, turns his back to the audience, looks coyly over his shoulder at them, starts jiggling his ass, and then drops his booty like a stripper.

He runs downstage right and does the 'tootsie roll' dance, ending with his fist in the air as he spins around and grabs his mike from its stand offstage right.

The music stops.

Stand-up Comedian (*Name of city!*) (*Name of city*) mothafuckin' (*Name of state or country*) up in this! Wassup, bitches?! Where (*Location appropriate reference such as 'Brooklyn' or 'My Bears Fans' or 'The Parisians'*) at? (*He calls out the name of a rich neighborhood in the city he's in*)

The cast backstage makes woofing noises à la The Arsenio Hall Show.

See, that's my shit y'all. I'm a (*Name of rich neighborhood in city*) nigga born and bred – that's right! GOOD to be back in (*Name of city*). GOOD to be back. Got some good memories about this place here. Some real shit.

Had these two little girlfriends when I was seven. One white and one black. Never gave me the pussy though. Never. Used to let me watch. They'd come over to my house and start rubbin' they pussies together, and one of 'em used to fuck herself with a pencil! Yeah! Used to fuck herself with a number two pencil until she came, or as she liked to call it, 'Passed her test'. That bitch had straight A's when it came to that shit!

He gives the audience a 'What's your problem?' look.

What! This mothafucka be lookin' at me like, (*He singles someone out in the audience and imitates a white guy voice.*) 'That man is a pedophile!' I ain't no pedophile, nigga! YOU a fuckin' pedophile for thinkin' 'bout it in a pedophiliac way!

Kids be some nasty-ass freaks, man! Oh, don't act like you ain't neva seen a three-year-old humpin' a sofa cushion! (*He humps the air and smacks an imaginary sofa cushion as if it's an ass.*) 'You take that, sofa cushion! Take that, TAKE THAT.'

Now if black mama see that shit? Maaan, you betta hope that kid get to keep his dick! Black mama be like, (*He makes violent hitting noise and gesture*) 'Mothafucka, you KNOW we rented this shit! Now put some ice on yo' eye and get dressed. We gotta go to church and pray for yo' little demon ass!' And that's how putting plastic on furniture got started.

Now, a white mama? White mama don't know how to deal with this shit! White mama be like, 'Chad? Do you know why Daddy and I always smell like wet dog? It's because we fuck goats.' And that's how syphilis got started.

Now, I know some a you thinkin', 'Why do black comedians still do those, "White people are like this, and black people are like that" jokes?'

Well, I'm a tell you why. Now I don't mean to be offensive by sayin' this, but – white people be evil.

He gives the audience a deadly serious look.

Naw, I'm just playin' witch'all. Most white folks ain't evil – they just stupid. White people be some a the stupidest mothafuckas on the planet. You think I ENJOY talkin' 'bout race? I wanna talk about POOP, mothafucka!

Shit, there ain't nothin' funnier to me than poop. When I'm at home that's practically all I wanna talk about. My wife, she can't take it. Finally it got to be too much for her and she started threatenin' to stop suckin' my dick, so I had to stop. But I still needed an outlet to express my feelins, so I came up with the poop FACE.

He makes the poop face.

Now, I'm not allowed to talk about poop in my wife's presence, but when I make the poop face, she KNOW what I'm thinkin' 'bout.

He makes the poop face.

But I can't talk about poop. Nope. I gotta talk about RACE because white people be some stupid-ass mothafuckas.

[*To be added in applicable countries outside the United States:*] And don't think I'm just talkin' 'bout Americans, neither. (*Imitating local accent.*) 'Ha ha ha, those stupid Americans. We do not have such race problems here in (*Name of country.*). So y'all don't got no race problems in (*Name of country.*)? Mothafuckas, you KNOW your shit is fucked-up, too! (*Name of city.*) got plenty a niggas – y'all just call 'em (*Name of ethnicity.*). And y'all be like, 'For us it is not about race, it is about nationality and religion.' But the fact that y'all don't SOCIALIZE with YOUR darkies don't mean you ain't racist, it just mean you even MORE fucked-up! Shee-it, I been called a nigger in every major city in (*Name of country*). And some a y'all think you bein' FRIENDLY by callin' me that!

And all a you people who consider yourselves to be 'color-blind'? Y'all are the WORST mothafuckin' offenders. What is that shit? Color-blind. That's some bullshit right there.

He gestures to his face.

Does this look like a TAN to you, mothafucka?

Speakin' a tans, my docta told me I needed to exercise. Now,that gym shit freaks me the fuck out. All a them white folks hatin' theyselves for havin' a little bit a belly fat. Shit, black folks ain't like that. Once we past our skinny phase we just hurry up and get married so we don't have to worry 'bout that shit. 'Pass me the mothafuckin' PORKCHOPS – I know I'M gettin' pussy sometime next WEEK!'

He singles out an audience member with a knowing look.

And I might even get my asshole licked, too!

Naw, I can't handle the gym. What I like to do is run on railroad tracks. For some reason, ever since I was a kid that's what I liked to do, is run on the railroad tracks. Now, the funny thing about railroad tracks, and this shit happens to me all the time, maybe it's happened to you – have you ever had the experience where you standin' by a railroad track, and you hear the train comin', and you get a strong desire to step onto the railroad track, get hit by the train, and die?

White people don't like to hear black people whine. They want black people to take some personal responsibility and shut the fuck up. But white people be some a the whininest mothafuckers out there! Seriously, you ever heard a white person whine? 'I don't know what I'm doing with my life.' 'I hate feeling fat all the time.' 'Argh, I didn't get anything done today!' 'That's reverse racism!'

And white folks always gotta be beastin'. Y'all know that term? 'Beastin''? Well, you can add it to your repertoire of semi-ironic hip-hop lingo. 'Beastin'' is when I call you out on your racist bullshit and you turn around and say that I'M the one that's got the problem. THAT'S beastin', just bein' a beast. So I'm gonna say what I gotta say, and fuck it. If you don't like it, leave! This is MY show! If you don't like it, leave! A bunch a crackas stupid enough to give me a show, and my show is what they gon' get!

Oh yeah, I said 'cracka'! White people don't like it when they get called 'cracka.' They be like, 'If I can't call you a nigger, then you can't call me a cracker.' I like to call it the principle of 'Even Steven.' White people be all into Even Steven. The idea behind Even Steven is: If I got this much stuff (*He gestures high.*) and you got this much stuff (*He gestures low.*) and someone give us a cookie, then we gon' split that cookie EVENLY down the middle to be Even Steven. Now, I'm not sayin' it's nice for me to go around callin' white people cracka, but the fact of the matter is that no one ever called anyone a cracka before lynchin' 'em. So take that, cracka! Whatchu gon' do?

So I been talkin' shit 'bout white folks for a while. Now it's time for me to go after some niggas. Black people be some of the stupidest, forty-drinkin', hot-wing-eatin', check-cashin', Tyler Perry-watchin', R. Kelly-listenin', dice-shootin', electric-slidin', money-mismanagin', Newport-smokin' mothafuckas in the WORLD.

Now, a lotta white folks in the audience just came.

He mimes jerking-off and coming while moaning the following:

Even Steven, Even Steven!

If I was to take a shit onstage, use my own shit as blackfacepaint, fuck a human brain until I came, suck my come back out of the brain, and spit it at the audience . . . I don't really know where I'm goin' with this.

Anyway, it ain't just white folks that's clueless. White, Asian, Latino, black. To be honest, I'm scared to walk into a room full a niggas! Anyone who ever seen me do an interview know I don't talk the same way onstage that I do in real life. I even been accused a playin' a stereotype to cater to a white audience. Well, that's true, but mostly I talk this way because I'm fuckin' terrified a black people!

(*Imitating thug voice.*) 'Yo, who that nigga think he is, tryin' a sound like a white man an' shit! Let's fuck that nigga up!'

Shee-it! Bein' black can be fuckin' inconvenient! And white folks are always the ones who feel persecuted! I never met no black person who felt as persecuted as the white people I've met. Black people be like, 'Man, fuck that shit!' and go about our business. See, we used to that shit! But for white people, the sense of persecution festers. They feel PERSECUTED when people call them out on their racism. That's like if I took a SHIT in yo FACE for three hundred years and then felt persecuted when you didn't swallow!

And in the event that you actually manage to convince a cracka that white privilege exists, they be like, 'But what can I do? How can I get sick enough to make another person well?' Well, I ain't advocating for any great political movement. And nobody expect you to feel guilty about slavery – you didn't do that shit! JUST ACKNOWLEDGE THE SYSTEMATIC RACISM THAT IS EMBEDDED IN OUR COUNTRY (*Outside the U.S.: 'CULTURES'*) AND TRY TO MAKE THINGS BETTER BY NOT CONSTANTLY ASKING ME TO PROVE THAT WHAT I EXPERIENCE IS REALLY RACISM OR REFERRING TO THE FACT THAT I'M BLACK OR MAKING ASSUMPTIONS ABOUT MY BACKGROUND OR THE KIND OF MUSIC I LISTEN TO OR WHO I DATE, AND WHEN I CALL YOU OUT ON YOUR BULLSHIT, JUST FUCKING SAY I'M SORRY AND TRY NOT TO DO IT AGAIN! I know you think you treat black people the same way you do everyone else, but honestly you don't. You need to watch that subtle shit a little more carefully. Shit, I'm tired a dealin' with the cluelessness of white people, havin' to talk 'bout this race shit when I could be talkin' 'bout tiny pigs flyin' out my cock-hole or fairies that hatch in diarrhea.

He makes the poop face.

Speakin' a diarrhea, have you ever noticed how much shit comes outta newborn babies? People always makin' a fuss over babies like they the greatest thing on earth, when really they the worst fuckin' form a life known to man. Makin' you work for 'em twenty-four hours a day, lyin' there uselessly, shittin' theyselves and screamin'. I'm sorry, but fuck babies! Have you ever been tempted to make a baby stop cryin' by puttin' a pillow over its face and pressin' down till it can't breathe? Sometimes that's the only way!

My boner is hungry!

Old black folks be like, 'Boy, wassa matta witch you? Why yo mouf got to be so dirty? Killin' babies ain't nothin' to laugh 'bout!' Well, I don't believe in taboos! I don't think it's wrong for people to fuck animals. Now, anyone who's ever had a pet knows animals can communicate – so if you some farmer foolin' 'round witch yo cow, and the cow seem into it, then that's some consensual shit right there!

The incest taboo offends me! Listen, if yo' sister want you to fuck her in the ass, and your dick hard, GO IN! Who gets hurt? I'm surprised more siblings don't fall in love! Shit, they got so much in common!

Anyway, now that I've cleansed your palates of all the angry race shit y'all don't wanna hear, lemme give you some more. I don't like it when you call me 'brotha' or try and give me some kinda grip-down when I go to shake your hand. DON'T DO THAT SHIT! Also, don't say, 'Oh, you must think I'm so white right now!' Shit, I LIKE it when white people act white! That ain't nothin' to be ashamed of – that's just keepin' it real.

And for all you white folks out there who walk on eggshells around black people, paranoid about sayin' the wrong thing that's gonna make us uncomfortable . . . shit, I like you. That's it. I like you. We black folks been doin' that shit for y'all since the day we got here! Keep up the good work! YOU my niggas. Peace out.

He starts to leave, comes back.

Oh, I almost forgot. For all you self-hating crackas who feel disappointed that I didn't sodomize you worse than I did – I got a white wife. She got blond hair, blue eyes, and BIG titties. She's also the most wonderful person I've ever known, and I love her and my mixed tan babies more than anything in the world. Good night, (*Name of city*!)

Stand-Up Comedian *exits as* **Mama** *and* **Rapper Omar** *enter.* **Mama** *is wearing a long turquoise evening gown. She will also play* **Drug Dealer Mama, Video Ho,** *and* **Grandma from Heaven.** **Rapper Omar** *is wearing a black three-piece suit, white shirt, and red polka-dotted bow tie.*

Mama *stands and* **Rapper Omar** *lies flat on the floor. In the following series of sketches, none of the performers should put on any kind of 'black-sounding' or 'white-sounding' accent. They should deliver their lines and move as flatly as possible. All props are mimed. They all wear visible wireless mikes. The performers should not hold for laughs until they get to the naturalistic play that closes the show.*

Mama Omar wake up!

Wake up!

You have to go to school so that you can be a doctor!

Rapper Omar I want to be a rap star!

Mama I worked three jobs and raised six children and ten grand-children by myself so that you could be a doctor!

He gets up to face her.

Rapper Omar But rapping is my dream!

Mama I'm mad at you Omar!

He shrinks in the face of her wrath.

Rapper Omar I'm sorry Mama.

Mama You won't do anything I want!

Rapper Omar I just don't like school.

Mama Why?!

Rapper Omar Because it's hard and it's boring and people shoot each other at my school!

Mama Maybe you should try hard like Frederick Douglass.

Rapper Omar Mama, Frederick Douglass was a brain.

Mama I'm not interesting!

Rapper Omar Don't say that Mama.

Mama I'm not interesting nobody is interested in me!

Why do you have to rap?!

Rapper Omar Because rapping is fun and it sounds good and I can express myself.

Mama Okay I understand.

I'm proud of you for following your dreams.

Mama *exits as* **Rapper Omar** *starts rapping.* **Sidekick Michael** *enters dribbling a basketball.*

Sidekick Michael *is played by the same actor who played* **Dancer 2** *and is still wearing his black suit and flowered vest. The same actor will play* **Crackhead John, Bad Cop 2, Sashay,** *and* **Omar**.

Rapper Omar *'raps' by covering his mouth with his hand and swaying his hips from side to side while making clumsy 'beatbox-ing' noises that sound like: 'Puh, puh chuh. Puh, puh, puh chuh.'* **Sidekick Michael** *'dribbles' by jerking his hand up and down flatly in rhythm with an imaginary basketball.*

Sidekick Michael Hi Omar!

Rapper Omar Hi Michael.

Sidekick Michael What are you doing?!

Rapper Omar Practicing my rapping.

Sidekick Michael Hey check this out! Why did the turtle have no head?

Rapper Omar I don't know. Why?

Sidekick Michael Because it got stuck in your butt!

He laughs a fake-sounding, hysterical laugh.

Rapper Omar That wasn't funny.

Sidekick Michael Yes it was.

Rapper Omar No it wasn't.

Sidekick Michael I'm funny!

Rapper Omar Okay.

Pause.

Sidekick Michael Yo.

Rapper Omar What.

Sidekick Michael Yo! Shit! Fuck! Goddamn!

Rapper Omar Why are you swearing so much?

Sidekick Michael Because I'm crazy!

I'm going to go steal a car!

Rapper Omar Why?

Sidekick Michael Because I'm sad.

Rapper Omar Why are you sad?

Sidekick Michael Because my life is depressing.

Rapper Omar I'm sorry Michael, but I don't think you should steal.

Grandpa Joe *enters hobbling on his cane.* **Grandpa Joe** *is played by the same actor who played the* **Stand-up Comedian** *and is still wearing his black tux and skinny black tie. He will also play* **Bad Cop 1** *and* **Paul the Extreme**.

Grandpa Joe Did I hear you boys talking about stealing?

Sidekick Michael No, Grandpa Joe.

Grandpa Joe Back in my day–

Rapper Omar *goes back to rapping and* **Sidekick Michael** *goes back to dribbling.*

Grandpa Joe – stealing was considered wrong!

Sidekick Michael Hey, what's the difference between a testicle and a profiterole?!

Grandpa Joe (*pulling out a condom*) Does either of you know what this is?

Rapper Omar It's a condom.

Grandpa Joe That's right. And do you know what to do with it?

Sidekick Michael *gets hit by stray machine-gun fire and dies.*

Rapper Omar Oh no! A drive-by shooting!

Rapper Omar *runs offstage.*

Grandpa Joe (*sadly*) Nobody cares about what I have to say.

Grandpa Joe *exits as* **Rapper Omar** *and* **Drug Dealer Desmond** *enter.*

Drug Dealer Desmond *is played by the same actor who played* **Dancer 1** *and is still wearing his black tux and bow tie. He will also play* **Record Company Executive**.

Drug Dealer Desmond Hi Omar.

Rapper Omar Hi Desmond.

Rapper Omar *starts his 'rapping.'* **Drug Dealer Desmond** *starts making slight repetitive thug-like motions with his arms and shoulders that resemble the movements the characters in the video game Grand Theft Auto make when they are in their holding pattern. Periodically his arms will cross in front of him to complete the pattern before starting over again.*

Drug Dealer Desmond I'm going to rob people and shoot them and also sell drugs.

You should do it, too.

Rapper Omar But I don't want to be a drug dealer. I want to win this rap competition (*Pulls out flyer.*) and get a recording contract.

Drug Dealer Desmond But how are you going to get to the rap competition? You don't have a car or even money to buy bus fare.

Rapper Omar That's a good point.

Drug Dealer Desmond You could get the money by selling these drugs.

He holds out a packet of drugs.

Rapper Omar I don't want to sell drugs!

Drug Dealer Desmond Sell them!

Rapper Omar No!

Drug Dealer Desmond You better sell these drugs! Don't you want to be a rap star?

Rapper Omar (*taking the drugs*) Okay, but just this once.

Drug Dealer Desmond Great.

You're my best friend and I would die for you.

Rapper Omar Me too.

Drug Dealer Desmond I want to get a cat.

Rapper Omar Why?

Drug Dealer Desmond So I can cuddle with it.

Rapper Omar I don't like cats.

Drug Dealer Desmond But they're so nice and cuddly.

Rapper Omar I don't like them they're from Satan.

Drug Dealer Desmond You're from Satan!

Rapper Omar No I'm not, I'm just allergic. And I don't like their evil eyes.

Drug Dealer Desmond You have evil eyes!

Rapper Omar You have evil eyes! You are actually evil because you just convinced me to sell drugs!

Drug Dealer Desmond I just want a cat and a new gun and a bicycle to ride around the lake in France!

Rapper Omar Is that your dream?

Drug Dealer Desmond Yes.

Rapper Omar That sounds like a white person's dream.

Drug Dealer Desmond Well I am a white person.

Rapper Omar How is that?

Drug Dealer Desmond I just am. I'm white.

Rapper Omar No you're not, you're black.

Drug Dealer Desmond You're black.

Rapper Omar You're black.

Drug Dealer Desmond I can't remember which one of us is talking anymore.

Rapper Omar You're the evil one and I'm the good one. Although now I'm evil too.

Drug Dealer Desmond Cool! High-five!

They high-five – **Rapper Omar** *unenthusiastically.*

Rapper Omar Now that you've ruined me, what will happen?

Drug Dealer Desmond We're going to sell drugs and shoot anyone who gets in our way.

Rapper Omar Why?

Drug Dealer Desmond Because if you don't shoot people, then they don't respect you.

Rapper Omar I need to learn more about the streets.

Drug Dealer Desmond I will teach you.

Rapper Omar *and* **Drug Dealer Desmond** *take a step forward to indicate that they are 'on the streets.'*

Drug Dealer Desmond Hey, do you want to buy some drugs?

Rapper Omar (*waving his hand above his head*) I have drugs!

This sucks. Nobody wants to buy drugs from us.

Drug Dealer Desmond I think something suspicious is going on. Usually everyone wants them.

Rapper Omar What do you think is going on?

Drug Dealer Desmond Let me investigate. Crackhead John!

Crackhead John *enters. He enters in a straight line upstage of* **Rapper Omar** *and* **Drug Dealer Desmond**, *makes a sharp turn downstage, and lands crisply between them before slumping into his* **'Crackhead John'** *pose.*

Crackhead John Yes Desmond?

Drug Dealer Desmond Crackhead John, do you know why nobody wants to buy our drugs?

Crackhead John Yes. But what do I get in exchange?

Drug Dealer Desmond Crack.

Crackhead John (*pathetically*) Yay!

Rapper Omar Crackhead John, why isn't anyone buying our drugs?

Crackhead John It's because there's a new drug dealer in town named Mama. And she told all the crackheads that if they bought drugs from anyone else, she'd shoot them in the face. And then one of them did buy drugs from someone else so Mama shot him in the face in front of everyone and said, 'This is what will happen when you buy drugs from anyone else.'

Drug Dealer Desmond Where is this Mama? She's interfering with my business.

Crackhead John Mama is on the corner of Grove and Elm.

Drug Dealer Desmond Thank you, Crackhead John. Here is some crack for you.

Crackhead John (*pathetically*) Yay!

Crackhead John *exits.*

Rapper Omar (*looking after* **Crackhead John**) Crack is bad.

Drug Dealer Desmond I don't care. I like it.

Rapper Omar Maybe we shouldn't sell crack.

Drug Dealer Desmond You know what's bad?

Rapper Omar What.

Drug Dealer Desmond Caffeine.

Rapper Omar Caffeine isn't bad!

Drug Dealer Desmond Caffeine is really bad!

Rapper Omar Here's your crack Desmond I'm not selling it!

Drug Dealer Desmond But then how are you going to get to the rap competition?

Rapper Omar Oh yeah that's right I forgot.

Drug Dealer Desmond You're a pussy.

Rapper Omar I don't like that!

Drug Dealer Desmond You're a pussy who doesn't want to sell drugs!

Rapper Omar Shut up Desmond you're mean!

Drug Dealer Desmond I am mean! I'm the meanest there is! And I'm going to find that Mama and shoot her in the tit-tays!

Drug Dealer Mama *enters. She, like* **Desmond**, *moves in a Grand Theft Auto-style holding pattern, only her arms cross higher than* **Desmond's**.

Drug Dealer Desmond Hey, Mama!

Drug Dealer Mama I'm going to shoot you both in the face!

Drug Dealer Desmond Not before I shoot you first!

Drug Dealer Mama I'm going to shoot you before you can shoot me!

Drug Dealer Desmond I'd like to see you try!

They shoot at each other and miss.

Rapper Omar Guys, guys! Isn't there some way to settle this without shooting each other?

Drug Dealer Desmond and **Drug Dealer Mama** NO!

Drug Dealer Mama All I want is for everyone to stay off my corners and keep their drugs to themselves!

Drug Dealer Desmond I have customers, and those customers need drugs, and I have drugs to sell! If you shoot my customers in the face for buying drugs from me, then that makes me mad!

Drug Dealer Mama Look at it from my point of view! I'm new in town and don't have any customers! So I need to steal yours!

Drug Dealer Desmond THAT MAKES ME ANGRY!

Rapper Omar It is a seemingly insoluble dilemma.

Drug Dealer Mama I can solve it by shooting you in the face!

Drug Dealer Desmond Not if I shoot you first!

They shoot each other in the face and collapse on the floor at awkward angles.

Rapper Omar Desmond! My best friend Desmond! This is a tragedy!

Bad Cop 1 *and* **Bad Cop 2** *enter.*

Bad Cop 1 What's going on!

Rapper Omar Desmond Desmond!

Bad Cop 2 I don't like black people.

Rapper Omar But you're black!

Bad Cop 2 No I'm not.

Bad Cop 1 (*pointing at* **Rapper Omar**) I arrest you!

Rapper Omar For what?

Bad Cop 1 (*pulling out a packet of drugs*) For dealing these drugs.

Rapper Omar (*pulling out his packet of drugs*) But I only have these many!

Bad Cop 1 (*shaking his packet of drugs*) Now you have THESE many.

Rapper Omar That's not fair! I have to compete in a rap competition!

Bad Cop 2 Rap is for ANIMALS! Your life is over!

The **Bad Cops** *take* **Rapper Omar** *by each arm and push him onto the floor.*

Rapper Omar *sits cross-legged, looking traumatized.* **Bad Cop 1** *turns into* **Paul the Extreme** *and stands upstage right of* **Rapper Omar**.

Paul the Extreme Hey kid.

Hey kid are you deaf or are you mad because you're in prison?

Rapper Omar Leave me alone. My anus is all stretched-out already. You wouldn't like it.

Paul the Extreme Hey kid what's your name?

Rapper Omar Omar. But my anus is all stretched-out.

Paul the Extreme I do not have relations with the anus of a man.

Rapper Omar That's good.

Paul the Extreme My name is Paul the Extreme.

Rapper Omar What do you want from me?

Paul the Extreme I want to teach you.

Rapper Omar I don't want to be brainwashed by your religion. I'm a Christian.

Paul the Extreme Christianity is the white man's filth religion. My religion is the only true way for the black man. Here is my book of religion.

Rapper Omar It's written in gobbledygook!

Paul the Extreme I will teach you.

Rapper Omar But I don't want to learn.

Paul the Extreme You have to!

Rapper Omar No!

Paul the Extreme Why are you doing this to me?

Rapper Omar I just don't feel like learning anything right now!

Paul the Extreme That makes me cry.

He cries.

Rapper Omar Don't cry, Mr. Extreme.

Paul the Extreme (*crying*) You made me cry!

Rapper Omar Please stop!

Paul the Extreme *cries harder.*

Rapper Omar Okay I'll learn your religion.

Paul the Extreme Great.

He opens his book of religion and shows a page to **Rapper Omar**.

Paul the Extreme Saints are getting the tops of their heads sawed off, and the people are laughing. Then they realize they have not been chosen. They are looking back in fear. The angels are all at the top. The people are also elevated. Suddenly something changes. Who are these people? It's actually the pope first. Following the pope, the emperor. Following the emperor, the king. Following the king are the religious people. Following the religious people are the wealthy. There are butterflies flying out of my palms, thanks to our bishop. I need to go away from here. I am longing for a life that is somewhere else. Who made this? (*Accusingly.*) Italian (*Pronounced 'Eye-talian'.*) people.

Rapper Omar I don't understand.

Paul the Extreme I hate white people.

Rapper Omar Why?

Paul the Extreme Because they are mean.

Rapper Omar Oh.

Paul the Extreme With so many white people running loose on the streets, why do we point our gun barrels at each other?

Rapper Omar I don't know.

Paul the Extreme We should shoot the white people instead.

Rapper Omar That's a good idea.

Paul the Extreme Omar, what is your greatest wish?

Rapper Omar To be a rap star.

Paul the Extreme Then you must go forth and rap about killing white people until there are no white people left.

Rapper Omar Okay.

Rapper Omar *walks upstage and turns to face downstage as the other performers run onstage and sit cross-legged facing him, forming an audience of prisoners.*

Fellow prisoners! I rap for you!

He does his accustomed 'rapping' gesture and sound.

Puh, puh chuh. Puh, puh, puh chuh.
Puh, puh chuh. Puh, puh, puh chuh.

Getting more intense:

Puh, puh chuh. Puh, puh, puh chuh!

Getting really intense:

PUH, PUH CHUH. PUH, PUH, PUH CHUH!

I'm the master rapper and I'm here to say
I hate white people in a major way
Whitey honky cracka, I wish you were dead
To get that fruity taste I gotta shoot you in the head!

All the prisoners cheer and run off except for **Record Company Executive**, *who approaches* **Omar**.

Record Company Executive Yo, I'm a record company executive and when we both get out of here in two months, I'm going to make you a star!

Rapper Omar I can't believe it!

Record Company Executive *exits.* **Sashay** *enters, bringing a black cube downstage that* **Rapper Omar** *sits on.*

Sashay Do you want your hair like this or like this for the video?

Rapper Omar I don't know.

Sashay Sashay thinks you should wear your hair like this.

Rapper Omar Who is Sashay?

Sashay Who is Sashay?

He sings and dances awkwardly to the tune of the Jem and the Holograms theme song.

Sashay! (Sashay is excitement!)
Ooh Sashay! (Sashay is adventure!) Ooh!
Glamour and glitter
Fashion and fame

Sashay! Sashay is truly outrageous
Truly, truly, truly outrageous
Oh whoa Sashay! (Sashay!)
The music's contagious! (Outrageous!)

Sashay is my name
No one else is the same
Sashay is my name!
Sashay!

Rapper Omar Nice to meet you, Sashay.

Sashay Omar, would you like to go on a date with me?

Rapper Omar No thank you, I'm married to a woman.

Sashay Let me convert you! Being gay is fun!

He makes a 'being gay is fun' gesture. **Video Ho** *enters.*

Video Ho Hi Omar.

Rapper Omar Hi Video Ho.

Video Ho Do you like my booty?

Rapper Omar Yes.

Video Ho Do you like my boobs?

Rapper Omar Yes.

Video Ho I like expensive things.

Rapper Omar Okay.

Video Ho I'll meet you in your trailer in fifteen minutes.

Rapper Omar Okay.

Video Ho *lifts one hand high over her head and snaps her fingers. Then she leans menacingly toward* **Rapper Omar** *and exits.*

Sashay Ooh, Omar. You are truly truly truly outrageous!

Rapper Omar *does five lines of coke, then shoots up.*

Sashay That's a lot of drugs.

Rapper Omar I need a lot.

Sashay Why do you need so many?

Rapper Omar Because I'm addicted.

Video Ho (*shouting from offstage*) Omar, get in here and do stuff to my booty!

Rapper Omar *sighs.*

Rapper Omar I better go.

Sashay Good luck, Omar! I wish you'd converted. I'm a really nice boyfriend.

Sashay *exits and* **Rapper Omar** *addresses the black cube as if it were a gravestone:*

Rapper Omar Oh Desmond. If only you were here to see me now, in my fur coat, gold chains, and designer sunglasses.

Here I am, with all of my dreams come true, but now my mortality presses upon me and death approaches fast.

I was happier in prison with Paul the Extreme!

I'm tired of eating a different pussy every night. I'm tired of being on drugs all the time. I'm on drugs right now!

It's so boring. I'm bored!

And being famous isn't as good as I thought it was going to be. I have to do all this stuff I don't want to do, like sign autographs until my hand hurts.

I feel that there is nothing to live for except drugs and sex and unhealthy foods. Oh Desmond, I don't even have any friends anymore because I fucked all their wives and girlfriends.

He gets on his knees downstage of the cube.

Dear Lord, I am praying to you now. Please shine down from Heaven and show me the way. I have grown to hate the very rap that I once loved. Sometimes I don't even feel like taking a shower!

Please Lord, show me the way!

Grandma from Heaven *enters and stands on the cube behind* **Rapper Omar**. *He turns to face her.*

Grandma from Heaven Here is a parable from me, Grandma from Heaven:

There were two cranes. And the first crane had one red berry for an eye, which the second crane pecked out and ate. And that berry expanded to the size of a world inside the greedy crane until its crane-flesh burst open and went flying in every direction. And that world-sized berry developed boils the shape of a people, which were red and hungry, and which fed upon each other until the juice was dripping down everyone's faces. And the people walked around with parts of their bodies missing – chunks of ear, a bite out of their backs. And the crane that had been eviscerated began to gather up all its molecules to re-form feathers and flesh and eyes and beak, until it found itself whole and healthy on a planet of red berry earth and flesh. And the crane gorged itself until it was as round and red as the planet itself. And everyone sat around, crippled and maimed and feeding, until the sun went down.

Rapper Omar *helps* **Grandma from Heaven** *off the cube and they become* **Singer 2** *and* **Singer 1**, *respectively. The actor who played* **Drug Dealer Desmond** *enters as* **Singer 3**.

They stand in a line looking around at the audience in silence. They look at the audience for an uncomfortably long time.

As they sing an a cappella rendition of the indie-rock song 'Dark Center of the Universe' by Modest Mouse, they continue to look around at the audience. They don't move or change expression, but they sing with feeling.

Singer 1 (*singing*) I might disintegrate into the thin air if you'd like

I'm not the dark center of the universe like you thought

Singers 1, **2** and **3** (*in unison*) I might disintegrate into the thin air if you'd like

I'm not the dark center of the universe like you thought

In three-part harmony:

Well, it took a lot of work to be the ass I am
And I'm real damn sure that anyone can, equally easily fuck you over
Well, died sayin' something, but I didn't mean it
Everyone's life ends, no one ever completes it
Dry or wet ice, they both melt and you're equally cheated

Well, it took a lot of work to be the ass I am
And I'm real damn sure that anyone can, equally easily fuck you over
Well, an endless ocean landin' on an endless desert
Well, it's funny as hell, but no one laughs when they get there
If you can't see the thin air then why the hell should you care?

Well, it took a lot of work to be the ass I am
And I'm real damn sure that anyone can, equally easily fuck
you over
Well, I'm sure you'd tell me you got nothing to say
But our voices shook hands the other day
If you can't see the thin air what the hell is in the way?

The three-part harmony gets more complex:

I might disintegrate into the thin air if you'd like
I'm not the dark center of the universe like you thought

Well, it took a lot of work to be the ass I am
And I'm real damn sure that anyone can, equally easily fuck
you over
Well, an endless ocean landin' on an endless desert
Well, it's funny as hell, but no one laughs when they get
there
If you can't see the thin air then why the hell should you
care?

Well, it took a lot of work to be the ass I am
And I'm real damn sure that anyone can, equally easily fuck
you over
Well, died sayin' something, but I didn't mean it
Everyone's life ends, no one ever completes it
Dry or wet ice, they both melt and you're equally cheated

Well, it took a lot of work to be the ass I am
And I'm real damn sure that anyone can, equally easily fuck
you over
Well, I'm sure you'll tell me you got nothin' to say
But our voices shook hands the other day
If you can't see the thin air then what the hell is in your way?

The **Singers** *exit as Mary J. Blige's soul/pop song 'Ooh' begins.* **Stagehand 1** *and* **Stagehand 2** *enter carrying dollies. They are both white males over the age of fifty, wearing blue jeans.* **Stagehand 1** wears a lilac hooded sweatshirt and **Stagehand 2** wears a blue T-shirt.

They wheel out a brown leather couch with a large rug rolled up on top of it. They set down the couch and roll out the rug. They bring on a long coffee table/bookshelf that contains books and a baseball in a glass case. Then, a wooden folding chair, a lamp, a stacked side table, a rolling bar cart, and a black leather side chair. They carry on a vase with a ridiculously phallic flower arrangement in it. Then, a plate of salami, crackers and cheese. Also, a bowl of nuts, napkins, and chips and salsa. Everything looks modern, expensive and masculine.

The **Stagehands** *grab their dollies and exit offstage right as* **Thomas** *and* **Omar** *enter stage left.*

Thomas *is played by the actor who played the* **Stand-up Comedian**. **Omar** *is played by the actor who played* **Sashay**. **Desmond** *is played by the actor who played* **Drug Dealer Desmond**. **Thomasina** *is played by the actor who playe*d **Mama**. **Michael** *is played by the actor who played* **Rapper Omar**.

Omar *wears the same black suit/flowered vest/white shoes combo he wore at the top of the show.* **Thomas** *is now wearing a three-piece, charcoal pin-striped suit with a white shirt and striped tie.*

Thomas *and* **Omar** *sit on the couch. They look tense and awkward.*

Thomas What about eggs.

Omar Yes, I eat eggs.

Thomas But no dairy.

Omar No dairy and no meat. But I'll eat fish.

Thomas Just fish or all seafood.

Omar All seafood.

Thomas Do you eat butter?

Omar It's interesting that you would ask me that, because I was eating butter for a while but then I switched to olive oil. Did you know that you can put olive oil on toast?

Pause.

Thomas What about alcohol.

Omar Oh, no! No alcohol, tobacco, drugs, caffeine, sugar, meat, dairy, salt, refined grains . . . I think that's it.

Thomas (*gesturing at the coffee table*) I don't think there's anything here for you to eat. The last time I saw you, you seemed to be eating mostly bacon and potato chips.

Omar *flinches.*

Thomas Are you sure I can't get you anything to drink? Cranberry juice and seltzer?

Omar Uh . . . I'm still on the fence about the whole juice thing.

Maybe later.

Thomas Plain seltzer?

Omar Actually I used to drink four liters of seltzer a day until someone told me it hollows out your bones.

Thomas Hollows out your bones?

Omar They said that drinking seltzer hollows out your bones.

Thomas That can't be right.

Omar I don't know.

Thomas I love seltzer.

Omar Me too. But hollow bones . . .

Thomas That can't be right. I wish you hadn't told me that, Omar.

Omar I'm sorry, but don't you want to know? So you can stop drinking it?

Thomas I don't want to stop drinking it. I want to drink as much of it as I want whenever I want without worrying about whether or not it's going to hollow out my bones!

Omar I'm sorry, Thomas. Maybe it's not even true. You should look it up on the internet.

Thomas (*snapping*) People are always telling me to look things up on the internet, but when am I ever going to have the time? Last night I drank an entire bottle of maple syrup.

Omar What?

Thomas Every night before I go to sleep I drink a bottle of maple syrup and then I eat three candy bars in a row.

Omar You can't be serious.

Thomas Yes I eat three candy bars in a row and then go to bed without brushing my teeth.

Omar How come all your teeth haven't fallen out?

Thomas I don't know. I haven't been to a dentist in over eight years.

Omar *looks disgusted. Pause.*

Omar What time is it?

Thomas 7:30.

Omar Huh.

Thomas What.

Omar Did you invite a lot of people?

Thomas A few.

Omar Hm.

Thomas It's only 7:30. You came at seven right on the dot.

Omar I like to be on time.

Thomas I know, you came right on the dot at seven.

Omar I hate it when people are late. I hate waiting for people.

Thomas I don't mind waiting. Sometimes I meet people. Sometimes people just come up to me and strike up a conversation.

I love it.

Omar I don't like it when people speak to me in public. Strangers. Like on an airplane. When I'm on an airplane I try to emit a force field of unfriendliness so that no one will speak to me, and it works.

I don't like parties, I don't like talking to lots of people. Even if it's all people I like, it stresses me out to see their faces. To see everyone's face all at once. It stresses me out.

Thomas You're at a party now.

Omar No, I like parties. But I prefer one-on-one. Definitely I'm better at one-on-one.

Sound of a buzzer.

Thomas Oh, someone's here. I'll be right back.

He exits.

Omar *practices different ways of sitting, trying to find one that looks cool.*

Thomas *re-enters with* **Desmond,** *who is wearing the same black tux/cummerbund/bow tie outfit he wore at the top of the show.*

Thomas Desmond, this is Omar. Omar, Desmond.

Omar Nice to meet you.

Desmond *doesn't respond.*

Thomas Can I get you something to drink? I can get you a scotch, cranberry and vodka, gin and tonic, rum and Coke, beer, wine.

Desmond I'll have a tequila sunrise, please.

Thomas *looks taken aback.* **Desmond** *goes to the leather side chair and sits.*

Thomas Uh, I'll be right back.

Thomas *exits. Pause.*

Omar So how do you know Thomas?

Desmond (*looking at* **Omar** *expressionlessly and then turning away*) We work together.

Omar Do you live around here?

Desmond No.

Omar Are you married?

Desmond Yes.

Omar Do you have any children?

Desmond No.

Omar Why not?

Desmond Because I don't want any.

Thomas *re-enters with tequila and starts making drinks.*

Thomas So, Desmond, how are things with you?

Desmond Fine.

Thomas I heard things got a little sticky for you the other day.

Desmond (*sharply*) Who told you that?

Thomas Thomasina.

Desmond Thomasina told you that things got a little sticky for me the other day?

Thomas She didn't go into detail, she just mentioned it lightly, in passing.

Desmond Is Thomasina coming here tonight?

Thomas I invited her.

Omar Who's Thomasina?

Thomas Thomasina is our friend from work.

Desmond, I didn't mean to offend you. I didn't know it was all so serious.

Desmond (*very seriously*) It's not serious. It's not serious at all.

Thomas Here's a tequila sunrise for you, and a cranberry juice without seltzer for you.

Omar (*panicky*) Oh no thank you. I don't feel like drinking anything right now!

Thomas (*irritated*) Well at least let me put it in front of you in case you get thirsty later.

Omar All right.

Desmond What is this?

Thomas It's a tequila sunrise.

Desmond It doesn't taste like a tequila sunrise.

Thomas What does it taste like?

Desmond It tastes like iodine.

Thomas Well I don't have any iodine in the house so I don't know why it would taste like that. It's just tequila and orange juice and little bit of grenadine. Maybe it's the grenadine. I buy the generic brand.

Omar I always buy generic! Everything in my house is generic! I never buy name brands, ever!

Desmond I don't think it's the grenadine.

Thomas Well I don't know what it could be, then. It's good tequila. Do you want me to fix you something else?

Desmond No.

Pause.

Thomas Desmond, do you want to take a look at that thing I was talking about?

Desmond I don't think so.

Thomas But that thing – I thought you wanted . . .

Do you want to go look at that thing?

Desmond Oh!

All right.

Thomas Omar, would you excuse us for a minute? We'll be right back.

Omar Sure.

Thomas *and* **Desmond** *exit hurriedly.* **Omar** *stands up and paces around. He stares at the food on the coffee table. He puts his face very close to the food and starts inhaling deeply and trying to waft the scent toward his nose with his hands. He starts sucking at the air above the food in a disturbing way.*

Thomasina *and* **Michael** *enter and stare at* **Omar**.

Thomasina *is wearing a champagne-colored satin cocktail dress with a princess skirt.* **Michael** *is wearing brown pants and a tweed jacket with elbow patches. Under the jacket he wears a blue button-down shirt, brown V-neck sweater, and tie.*

Thomasina Hello.

Omar (*startled*) Hi. How did you get in?

Thomasina The door was open. Is Thomas here?

Omar He's in the other room doing coke with Desmond.

Thomasina *and* **Michael** *exchange looks.*

Thomasina I'm Thomasina, and this is Michael.

Omar Hi, I'm Omar.

Michael Nice to meet you, Omar.

They sit awkwardly.

(*To* **Omar**.) You know, it's funny, but you look just like my cousin Freddy.

Omar Really?

Michael Yeah, you two even dress the same. Very stylish.

Thomasina It's true. I love your vest, Omar.

Omar Thank you!!!

Michael I've never been able to understand how stylish people can be so stylish.

Thomasina What are you talking about, Michael? You dress really well!

Michael Anyone can go out and buy a jacket, but I would never be able to put together an outfit like that. That kind of thing requires an artistic eye.

Omar I don't know what to say!!!

Thomasina Oh Omar, you're embarrassed. That's so cute!

Omar Hey, would you two like to come watch the Oscars at my house this Sunday?

Pause.

Thomasina Uhh . . .

Michael Uhh . . . let me check my calendar.

He reluctantly checks his calendar.

It looks like I'm free that evening, so . . .

Omar Great!

Thomasina Michael, I'm so excited for you to meet Thomas.

Michael Me too.

Thomasina I'm sorry I've been so busy.

Michael Oh, don't even worry about it.

Thomasina How's Shannon?

Michael (*unconvincingly*) She's fine.

Thomasina *gives him a look.*

We've been having some problems.

Omar Really? What kind of problems?

Thomasina You don't have to tell us anything, Michael.

Michael No, it's not a big deal, I don't mind talking about it. It's just we got into a big fight the other day.

Omar Mm, what happened?

Michael Well, we were having a conversation about our exes . . .

Thomasina Augh, why?

Michael I don't know, because we're idiots. And she admitted that if her ex Paul who broke her heart were to hit on her again, she would feel tempted to sleep with him.

Omar What?!

Thomasina You mean Paul from her work Paul?

Michael The Paul whom she sees every day, goes on business trips with, and talks to constantly on the phone.

Omar Fuck!!!

Thomasina What did you do?

Michael I got really upset and walked out, and didn't call her for like a day, but then she called and I picked up.

Thomasina What did she say?

Michael Well, that's the thing. I wanted her to apologize and say something reassuring, like, 'I love you and you're so much better than Paul is and have a way bigger cock,' but instead she was like, 'Michael, I'm with *you*. What I'm talking about is purely sexual. I would feel that way about *any* of my exes.'

Omar That's really really really fucked-up!!!

Michael And then I felt like a jealous freak, so I was like, 'Okay, I understand.'

Thomasina Michael, I know I'm not supposed to do this, but I'm going to be really honest with you.

Michael Shit.

Thomasina You deserve better than this, Michael. You are like the world's most perfect boyfriend and this behavior you're describing is completely shitty and unacceptable.

Michael I know she's difficult, but she's like a genius. If we broke up I don't think I could find anyone better than her.

Thomasina Now Michael, you know I will support you in anything you do, but honey I'm telling you that there is someone out there for you whom you can be madly in love with and who won't do fucked-up things to you.

Omar Michael, I want to be honest with you as well. Shannon isn't doing anything to you. You're doing it all to yourself.

Michael I beg your pardon?

Omar Michael, I want you to go home and write down a list of every nasty thing Shannon has ever done to you, and then cross out each instance of the word 'Shannon' and replace it with the word 'I'.

Michael Are you joking?

Thomas and Desmond re-enter.

Thomas Hey, you're here! Sorry, I was just showing Desmond something.

Thomasina Oh, that's all right. We were all just getting acquainted. Thomas and Desmond, this is Michael. Michael, Thomas and Desmond.

Thomas (*to* **Michael**) It's nice to finally meet you!

Michael It's nice to meet you, too! (*To* **Desmond**.) Hey, what's up.

Desmond (*coldly*) Hi.

Thomas Can I get you guys something to drink? I have cranberry and vodka, rum and Coke, gin and tonic, wine, beer . . . I can make a martini.

Thomasina I'm okay. I've been trying not to drink so much lately.

Michael Really? Me too!

Thomasina No way! Isn't it amazing how much better you feel?

Michael It's great!

Thomasina I'm even considering going to AA. All of my friends go and they love it.

Michael I've been thinking I should go to AA too!

Thomasina We should go together!

Michael What's your schedule like next week?

Thomas WHAT IS WRONG WITH EVERYONE?

Omar There's nothing wrong with not wanting to be an alcoholic.

Thomas Who said anything about being an alcoholic?

Okay. Here's what's going to happen.

He gets glasses and pours scotch.

I'm going to pour everyone a double shot of scotch and everyone here is going to drink it down. Including you, Omar.

Omar Thomas, I really can't! My system is hypersensitive to stimulants of any kind.

Thomas Fuck you, Omar, you're drinking.

Thomas pours.

Thomasina Is everything all right, Thomas?

Thomas I'm fine! It's just that this is a party and everyone has to drink! I'm sick of this bullshit.

Desmond *takes a glass, oblivious. Everyone else stares unhappily at the glasses on the table while* **Thomas** *glares at them threateningly.*

Thomasina (*reluctantly*) All right then, let's drink.

Michael This is an awfully nice scotch.

Omar Thomas, I am telling you right now that if I drink any of that I'm going to fall into a very deep depression starting tomorrow.

Thomas Omar, do you really want to be the only person at this party who's not drinking?

Omar *looks around at everyone. Everyone stares back at him. He snatches up the glass angrily and walks away from the group.*

I didn't think so.

Thomas *lifts his glass.*

To alcohol! Alcohol, I love you. I love the way you look in the glass, so amber and exquisite. I love the way you feel sliding down my throat. I love the numbness that you bring.

Cheers!

Everyone looks weirded-out except for **Desmond**, *who acts as if this were a normal toast.*

Everyone else Cheers.

Everyone drinks. **Omar** *goes to sit next to* **Thomasina** *on the couch but* **Desmond** *blocks him with his foot and takes the seat himself.*

Thomasina So Desmond, what were you holed up with Charlie about for so long today?

Desmond I beg your pardon?

Thomasina Was it about the Hopkins account?

Desmond I don't know what you're referring to.

Thomasina What do you mean?

Desmond *laughs hysterically.* **Thomasina** *stares at him.*

Thomas Everyone, I would like to make an announcement!

Everyone looks at **Thomas**.

Thomas Today is my birthday.

Thomasina Happy birthday, Thomas! I wish you'd told me!

Omar I totally forgot. I feel terrible.

Michael Happy birthday, Thomas.

Desmond Happy birthday.

Thomas Today I am thirty years old.

Thomasina Wow, that's huge!

Thomas *exits suddenly.*

Michael Where did he go? Do you think he's okay?

Thomasina Why wouldn't he be okay?

Michael Is this how he usually acts?

Thomasina He's fine. He's just a little tipsy. Right, Omar?

Omar I don't know. I haven't seen him in a long time. I don't really know what he's like these days.

Michael I think he's acting weird.

Thomasina Oh Michael, you act like you've never seen a drunk person before.

Thomas *re-enters with a cheap-looking birthday cake with one big lit candle in the shape of the number thirty.*

Thomas (*singing loudly, as the others awkwardly join in.*) Happy birthday to me! Happy birthday to me! Happy birthday, dear Thomas! Happy birthday to me!

(*Shouting.*) Yeah!

He pauses to make a wish and blows out the candle.

Thomasina Should I get a knife and –

Thomas No!

Thomas *pulls the candle out of the cake, sucks the frosting off, and throws it on the floor.*

He sticks his finger in the frosting and licks the frosting off. He digs into the cake with his fingers and starts eating it with his hand.

Omar Thomas, are you drunk?

Thomas No.

Omar Thomasina thinks you are.

Thomas Thomasina, did you say I was drunk?

Thomasina No, Thomas, I did not.

Omar You're lying! She's lying, Thomas! Michael, didn't Thomasina say she thought Thomas was drunk?

Michael Uh . . .

Thomasina Omar, you're being ridiculous.

Omar I'm not being ridiculous. You lied! To everyone's face!

Michael Hey, does anyone want to play Library?

Omar What's Library?

Desmond It's an extremely boring game.

Omar How does it go?

Desmond It's too boring even to describe.

Omar You know what I hate more than anything in the world is when someone says, 'Let's play a game,' and then people use it as an excuse to do mean things to each other.

Thomasina Library isn't that type of game, Omar. I love Library!

Desmond I would like to play Library.

Everyone stares at **Desmond**. **Thomas** *gets a glint in his eye*.

Thomas Thomasina, how is Jonathan's new book coming?

Thomasina I think it's going well. He works on it all the time.

Desmond Who's Jonathan?

Thomasina Jonathan is my boyfriend.

Thomas How are things with you two?

Thomasina Great. Really, really good.

Thomas *starts snickering*.

Thomasina Thomas?

Thomas *cracks up*.

Thomasina You want to tell us what's so funny?

Thomas (*cracking up*) Have you gotten to the plastic sheet phase yet?

Omar What's the plastic sheet phase?

Michael Thomas –

Thomas When Thomasina gets serious about a guy, she has to bust out the plastic sheets.

Omar Why, does she wet the bed or something?

Horrible pause.

Thomasina Fuck you, Thomas. Who else have you told? Does everyone at work know?

Thomas No.

Thomasina (*getting up*) You know what? Jonathan does have plastic sheets on his bed. Because he loves me. But you wouldn't know anything about that, would you, Thomas?

Thomas You know who else loves you? Desmond.

Thomasina What?

Thomas Desmond, you're in love with Thomasina, right?

Desmond Yes.

Omar (*pointing at* **Desmond**.) But you're married!

Desmond My wife is leaving me for another man.

Thomasina Well, I'm terribly sorry to hear that, Desmond, but I'm in a serious relationship.

Thomas Why don't you tell her how you feel, Desmond?

Desmond I feel . . . all the time, I think about what I'm going to wear. To work. Where you will see me. Where you will see me and what I'm wearing. All the time I think about that. I think about my shoes. I think about my tie. I imagine you seeing my shoes and my tie at work. I can't wait to see you. When you go on vacation, I wait for you to come back. I wait all the time. Sometimes you and Thomas go to lunch. One time I heard you sing, as a joke.

Thomasina Desmond, that was so . . . I don't know how to respond.

Thomas I guess you're gonna need more plastic sheets.

Thomasina What the hell is wrong with you, Thomas? You think being an asshole makes you a man? You're a cowardly little prick who failed at baseball and lives like a child! It's no wonder none of my friends want to date you.

Pause.

I'm sorry, that was mean.

Desmond It's fine! Thomas is a bad person!

Thomasina Thomas is not a bad person! I don't understand why he's doing this.

Thomas Omar is a virgin.

Omar I am not!

Thomas Well that's what you told me.

Omar I didn't! You're lying! He's lying!

Thomas So you've had sex?

Omar Yes!

Thomas Oh boy. What was that like?

Omar It was fine.

Thomas Oh yeah, who'd you fuck?

Omar I don't have to tell you that!

Thomas You won't tell me because the person doesn't exist.

Omar That isn't true!

Thomas Come on Omar, you're a virgin!

Omar I hate you, Thomas.

Thomas It's not my fault that you're a LIAR, Omar!

Omar I'M NOT A LIAR! I'M NOT A LIAR!

Thomasina Omar, calm down, it's okay. No one here thinks you're a liar.

Thomas Omar's not stupid, Thomasina. He knows we all think he's a BIG FAT LIAR.

Desmond Stop it, Thomas!

Thomas Fuck you, Desmond. You're a liar, too. I know what you told Charlie in his office today.

Desmond (*afraid*) I didn't.

Thomas You're a bad person, Desmond.

Desmond No.

Omar Thomas, I'm glad. I'm glad you're doing this. Because ever since we were kids, you've been mean, and nobody knew it but me. Now everyone knows! I'm going home.

Thomasina Omar.

He gets up.

Omar I know that people don't like me. It's always been like that. But I don't know how to be any other way. If I could sign up for a class to change myself, I . . .

Thomas, you've always had so many friends, and this is how you treat them. It makes no sense.

It was nice meeting all of you.

Thomasina No one here dislikes you, Omar. I think we should all go get a drink and leave Thomas here to be an asshole by himself.

Thomas I have a second announcement to make!

Everyone looks at him.

I poisoned all of your drinks!

It should be clear from this point on that nobody believes **Thomas** *poisoned them, with the exception of* **Desmond**. **Thomasina**, **Omar** and **Michael** *can't be a hundred per cent positive that he didn't, but they're pretty sure.*

Thomasina That isn't funny, Thomas!

Thomas I'm not trying to be funny. I poisoned you.

Michael Why would you say something like that?

Thomas Because it's true. You're all poisoned.

Omar Well I don't feel anything. If I drank poison I would feel it. I'm very sensitive to what goes on in my body.

Thomas You're not going to feel anything until (*He checks his watch.*) ten-thirty.

Thomasina Thomas, what the hell is wrong with you?

Desmond My drink.

Michael What about it?

Desmond It tasted like iodine.

Omar That's right! Desmond said his drink tasted like iodine. What did you put in our drinks, Thomas?

Thomas Something I found on the internet.

Thomasina You looked up how to poison us on the internet?

Michael Is this your idea of a joke?

Thomas Michael, I'm truly sorry, I wasn't expecting you tonight.

Desmond I'm not ready!

Thomasina Don't be silly, Desmond. None of us is going to die.

Michael Is this seriously happening right now? Who does this?

Omar Are you really going to make me call an ambulance, Thomas? You want to take things that far?

Thomas *drinks, impassive.* **Omar** *takes out his phone and starts dialing.*

Thomasina You stop this right now Thomas! This is the most horrible thing I've ever seen anyone do!

Omar (*on his phone*) Hello? Can we please get an ambulance immediately at ninety-nine Washington Avenue? Four people have been poisoned.

Thomasina *and* **Michael** *roll their eyes.*

Omar We don't know – the person who poisoned us won't tell us what it is. But he says we'll all be dead by . . .

Thomas Ten-thirty.

Omar Ten-thirty.

Okay, thank you.

She said they'd be here as soon as possible.

Thomas Five.

Omar What?

Thomas Five people have been poisoned. I didn't want to do it by myself.

Desmond I'm not ready!

Thomasina What the hell is going on?

Michael This is fucked-up.

Desmond My drink tasted like iodine!

Thomasina Why would you do this, Thomas?

Thomas Because you're all terrible fucking people, except for you Michael.

Omar What are you talking about? YOU'RE a terrible fucking person!

Desmond I told Charlie that the cocaine he found in my office belonged to Thomas!

Thomasina Oh my God . . . Thomas, what have I ever done to you?

Thomas You're always patronizing me!

Thomasina What are you talking about?

Thomas You do it constantly! Like the other day when you were talking about how the students at Berkeley have *more* access to their professors than the students at Stanford even though their class sizes are twenty times bigger!

Thomasina So? You went to Berkeley and I went to Stanford!

Thomas I don't know! You always manage to make everything sound like an insult, like you needed to console me for going to a less prestigious state school with huge class sizes!

Thomasina That is such bullshit, Thomas! You're totally projecting!

Thomas No I'm not! You do it constantly and it makes me want to fucking strangle you!

Michael He's making all of this up. This guy is crazy.

Thomasina Thomas, are you crazy?

Thomas I'm not lying. By ten-thirty tonight we'll all be dead.

You know, this isn't going the way I thought it would, so I think I'll be heading up to bed.

Thank you all for coming to my party.

Again Michael, I'm very sorry.

Good night.

He exits.

Pause.

He re-enters.

I'm totally fucking with you guys.

Thomasina Thomas!

Michael Thomas, I must say that I'm inclined to beat the shit out of you.

Desmond Do it.

Omar You are such an ASSHOLE!

Omar *attacks* **Thomas**, *who doesn't defend himself, and they fall to the ground.*

Michael *pulls* **Omar** *off of* **Thomas**. **Omar** *kicks his legs in the air and yells for* **Michael** *to put him down.* **Thomas** *remains sprawled out on the floor.*

Michael and **Thomasina** *confer in a corner.* **Desmond** *goes to the bar cart and starts making a tequila sunrise.*

Omar (*on his phone*) Hello? I just called from ninety-nine Washington Avenue. Yes. It was a false alarm. Someone was playing a joke.

Thank you. I'm sorry, even though it wasn't my fault.

He hangs up and addresses the others.

I'm calling a car. Would anyone else like one?

Thomasina It would be great if you could get one for Michael and myself.

Desmond Yes, please.

Thomas WAIT!

Omar Hello, could we please get three cars at –

Thomas *runs and grabs the phone out of* **Omar**'*s hand.*

Thomas Omar, please wait! Everyone!

I'm sorry. I know you all hate me right now and that I did a really fucked-up, horrible thing, and I'm sorry.

But I am losing my fucking mind. I'm losing it. And if you all leave here tonight then I will definitely kill myself.

Omar Fuck you, Thomas! Give me my phone!

Desmond (*on his phone*) Hello? Can you please send three cars to – ?

Thomas PLEASE PLEASE PLEASE PLEASE PLEASE PLEASE PLEASE!

DON'T LEAVE ME! DON'T LEAVE ME! DON'T LEAVE ME!

He grabs a bottle of scotch off of the coffee table and sits cross-legged on the floor downstage, drinking from it.

Desmond (*on his phone*) Never mind.

Michael I guess we shouldn't just leave him here like this.

Thomasina I've never seen him behave even remotely like this before. I don't know what to do.

Desmond When my cousin Edward threatened to kill himself, we had him institutionalized.

Thomasina Well, we're not having Thomas locked up so you can put that out of your mind right now Desmond.

Omar Thomas, what's going on. Why are you doing this?

Thomasina Are you depressed?

Thomas I'm lonely. I haven't been in a real relationship for two and a half years.

Omar I haven't been in a relationship for longer than that and you don't see me threatening to kill myself!

Thomas I'm tired of going to sleep alone and waking up alone. Sometime I need physical contact so badly I think I'll die. You know when you're in bed with someone and they lie right up next to you with their head on your shoulder, and it's like they're a battery and you're their recharger? I need that!

Michael I know, Thomas. My girlfriend Shannon is horrible to me, but I can't break up with her because then we wouldn't be able to get into that battery recharge position.

Thomas And I'm tired of just having sex with people. It would be one thing if they just materialized in my bed and then disappeared right after I came, but it's so much effort to go out and buy drinks and make conversation and work out. I'm getting too old for this! I'm thirty, goddammit!

Thomasina Thirty's not that old, Thomas. I'm almost twenty-six.

Thomas And I'm sick of my job! I hate going there every day. I want to be able to earn a living by sitting at home doing whatever I want!

Thomasina Thomas I'm sure we all feel that way.

Desmond I like my job.

Thomas Also, sometimes when I'm talking to someone, I realize that I've said something I shouldn't have said. And that makes me feel bad. And sometimes I feel bad for a long time after I've said the bad thing. And sometimes I curse myself in my mind or even out loud.

Omar Thomas, I feel like you're trying to copy me.

Thomas What are you talking about, Omar?

Omar You're trying to copy me!

Thomas I'm not trying to copy you, Omar! But you don't have to worry about it because after you leave tonight I'll be dead.

Michael I'm not leaving then.

Thomasina Well I have to leave. Thomas, I have to say I'm really ticked-off at you.

Omar I'm ticked-off, too!

Thomas I AM ALL ALONE!

Thomas *stands up and chugs from the bottle.*

Michael (*to* **Thomasina**) Didn't you say Thomas was your most social and happy friend?

Thomasina He was!

Omar He's definitely my most social and happy friend!

Thomasina So what do we do?

Michael Thomas, I'm going to make some phone calls. We're going to get some help for you, okay?

Thomas Okay.

Michael *exits.*

Thomas *becomes very pathetic.*

Thomas I'm going to the nuthouse!

Desmond Shut up, Thomas.

Thomas Does anyone want to play Library?

Omar We should just let you kill yourself.

Thomas Omar, I'm sorry.

Omar *walks away,* **Thomas** *chases him.*

Thomas Omar! Thomasina, do you want to play Library?

Thomasina I'm not really in the mood, Thomas.

Omar Desmond said Library is really boring.

Thomasina It's actually really fun.

Thomas So let's play! Desmond?

Desmond *doesn't respond.*

Thomas Desmond, I forgive you for what you did to me today. Thanks to you I'll probably get fired. Now we're even, okay?

Thomasina, will you at least explain the rules?

Please?

Thomasina Fine, Thomas.

(*Unenthusiastically.*) The way you play Library is: someone picks a book, shows us the cover, and tells us the author's name and what kind of book it is – like a biography, a novel, etcetera. Then we each have to make up a sentence that sounds like it would be in that book and write it down. And then we vote on which one is the actual sentence from the book.

Desmond You make it sound fun.

Thomas I'm going to go get some paper and pens. Omar, why don't you pick a book? I know you'll pick a good one.

Thomas *exits.*

Omar *contemplates the books.*

Omar I can't believe I'm doing this.

Thomas *re-enters, passing out paper and pens.*

Thomas What did you find, Omar?

Omar *Sexual Anorexia: Overcoming Sexual Self-Hatred.*

Thomas Ooh!

Omar It's a self-help book by Patrick Carnes and Joseph Moriarty.

You have to guess the first sentence of this book.

Everyone writes. **Omar** *collects everyone's slips of paper, snatching* **Thomas**'*s paper out of his hand.* **Omar** *reads aloud*:

'There is no reason to be ashamed of your penis and/or vagina.'

Thomas *shakes with silent laughter. That one was his. Everyone glares at him disgustedly.*

Omar 'They suffer silently, consumed by a dread of sexual pleasure and filled with fear and sexual self-doubt.'

Thomas (pointing) Ooh, that's the one!

Everyone glares at him.

Omar 'Sexual anorexia is a disease.'

Everyone looks at **Desmond**. *That one is his for sure.*

Omar 'People suffering from sexual anorexia tend to avoid sex.'

Thomas You guys weren't even trying!

Okay, that was terrible. We're not even gonna vote on that one. That was a warm-up. Let's do another one, a good one this time.

I'll pick.

Michael *re-enters.*

Michael An ambulance should be arriving within the next hour. Thomas, they'll be taking you to the hospital for twenty-four-hour observation.

Thomas (*crawling on the floor, looking in the coffee table/book shelf for a book*) Great.

Michael What the hell are you guys doing? Are you playing Library?!

Thomas I found one!

Michael SERIOUSLY?

Thomas This is a nonfiction book called *Black Magic* by Yvonne Patricia Chireau. There's a chapter in this book called 'Negro Superstitions' which is made up of a list of black superstitions. You guys have to come up with the first superstition in the list. Your sentence should begin, 'The Negro believes.'

Omar, you're not going to blog about this, are you?

Omar *gives him a disgusted look. Everyone writes.*

Thomasina Oh, I'm going to hell.

Everyone writes.

Thomas Is everyone done?

Thomasina I'm so going to hell for this.

Thomas *reads everyone's slips of paper.*

Thomas 'The Negro believes that cod liver oil cures cancer.' 'The Negro believes.'

Thomasina Yes?

Thomas That's all it says, is 'The Negro believes.'

Hm.

Thomas *looks suspiciously at* **Omar**.

Thomas 'The Negro believes that a pumpkin in an advanced stage of ripeness has healing properties.'

'The Negro believes that a stutterer may be cured by rubbing him up and down with a raw beef tongue.'

Thomasina *looks at* **Michael**. *That one was his. He crosses his arms and shrugs.*

Thomas (*bursting out laughing*) 'The Negro believes that a Negro's hands and feet are white because the moon done touched 'em in Africa!'

Thomasina *cracks up. That one was hers.* **Michael** *starts laughing as well.* **Thomasina** *looks at* **Desmond**, *laughing, and he laughs loudly in response.*

Omar I'm sorry. I'm sorry, but I have to say that I'm really uncomfortable with all of this.

I just don't think we'd be doing this if there were a black person in the room.

Pause.

Desmond I guess that would depend on what kind of black person it was.

Blackout.

End

Diana Son

Satellites

Satellites was produced by The Public Theater (Mara Manus, Executive Director; Oskar Eustis, Artistic Director) in New York City, opening on June 6, 2006. It was directed by Michael Greif; the set design was by Mark Wendland; the costume design was by Miranda Hoffman; the lighting design was by Kenneth Posner; the sound design was by Walter Trarbach and Tony Smolenski IV; the production stage manager was Martha Donaldson; and the assistant stage manager was Sharika Niles. The cast was as follows:

Characters

Miles Kevin Carroll
Kit Johanna Day
Reggie Ron Cephas Jones
Mrs. Chae Satya Lee
Nina Sandra Oh
Eric Clarke Thorell
Walter Ron Brice

Nina, *mid-30s, Korean American, an architect and new mother*
Miles, *mid-30s, African American, an unemployed dot-com casualty and new father*
Eric, *late 30s, Caucasian, Miles' brother, an entrepreneur*
Kit, *late 30s, Caucasian, Nina's business partner, an architect*
Mrs. Chae, *mid 50s/early 60s, Korean from Korea, a nanny*
Reggie, *early/mid 40s, African American, the king of the block*
Walter, *the upstairs tenant, African American, any age. Non-speaking role.*

Place

Various rooms in **Miles** *and* **Nina***'s unrenovated Brooklyn brownstone.*

Time

Now.

NOTE: (.) denotes a barely perceptible (and yet perceptible) pause where a character chooses not to say something. A solidus (/) indicates two character speaking simultaneously and words in square brackets [ ] are the words the character would have said if they had continued speaking.

Scene One

Late night/early morning – they've bled into another. **Nina**, *still tender from a C-section, bounces her two-week-old new-born as best as she can and pats her back, trying to soothe the crying baby.*

Nina OK, sweetie, I'm trying, I'm trying – (*Reacting to harder crying.*) I'm sorry it hurts so much, I never knew gas could be so painful and hard to get out – (**Nina** *pats harder.*) You know, if only it were this hard for adults to fart, riding the subway would be a much pleasanter [experience.]

We hear the tiny pop of a baby passing a puff of gas. **Nina** *reacts with the pride of a mother who's just watched her daughter win Olympic gold. The baby makes a happy, gurgling sound.*

You did it! Oh, I'm so happy for you!

Nina *holds the baby in front of her to look at her face. She gives her an encouraging little shake.*

My little champion!

The baby starts to cry again. To herself, out loud.

Holy shit, don't shake the baby. I'm such a fucking – (*She puts the baby back over her shoulder.*) Mommy didn't mean that, sweetheart, Mommy wasn't shaking you, Mommy was vibrating –

Miles *walks in, wearing pajamas.*

Miles I can't believe I didn't hear you guys, I was out cold. Did she want to nurse?

Nina (*not ironic*) No, she wanted to watch *The Godfather*. Did you know that *The Godfather* is on every night? On different channels at the same time. If you turn on your TV after midnight, you have no choice but to watch *The Godfather*.

Miles You want to watch it now?

Nina Why don't you take her, so I can go back to bed. (**Nina** *carefully puts the baby in* **Miles**' *arms. The baby starts to cry* *harder.*) Look at her, Miles, chocolate skin, almond eyes . . . she's the best of both of us.

Miles . . . I hope so.

Nina What do you think about hiring a Korean woman to be her nanny? So she could speak Korean to her.

Miles (*distracted by crying baby*) Is that important to you?

Nina I just started thinking about it. I can't speak Korean so she's not going to hear it from me.

Miles Alright, sounds like a good idea. (*Re. baby.*) You want to take her?

Nina Why don't you try singing a song? Like a lullaby or something –

Miles (*sings*) 'The eensy-weensy spider went up the water –'

Nina That's not soothing.

A bang from the apartment above.

Miles Aw, come on, man.

Nina Fucking asshole. (*To upstairs neighbor.*) My baby has gas, man. I'll kill you, motherfucker.

Miles Hopefully we'll close on the house next month, and finally be able to move in.

Nina It's impossible to have a baby in this cramped little tenement. We've outgrown this apartment, this whole neighborhood.

Miles Remember when we used to have wakes for our friends who moved to Brooklyn?

Nina They're laughing at us now from their hundred-thousand-dollar brownstones. Still, as much as we paid, it'll be worth it.

The baby wails, the neighbor bangs on the ceiling again.

Miles You'd better take her.

Nina *opens her arms. The baby quiets down a little.*

Nina What should I sing? (*Miles thinks a beat.*)

Miles 'Hush little baby –' (**Nina** *joins in, a beat behind, singing what* **Miles** *sings.*)

Miles and **Nina** 'Don't say a word, Papa's gonna buy you a mockingbird . . .'

Miles 'If that –'

Nina 'When that – '

Miles and **Nina** '. . . mockingbird won't sing, Papa's gonna buy you a – ' (*They look at each other, unsure what the rest of the words are. Finally –*)

Nina I can look up the words. I found this website that has the lyrics to all the –

Miles (*sings, cues* **Nina**) 'Rock-a-bye –' (**Nina** *joins in.*)

Miles and **Nina** (*singing*) ' – baby, on the treetop.
When the'

Scene Two

Miles *and* **Nina's** *brownstone. It's dark, lit by a standing lamp near the kitchen. The living room blends into the kitchen, a stairwell leads to the bedrooms above, another connects to the garden level office below. Many moving boxes are piled on the floor, some opened, most not. There is very little furniture.* **Miles** *carries in a box as* **Nina** *comes down the stairs.*

Nina I just got her down. Miles, that box belongs in the kitchen. It says 'Kitchen' on it.

Miles It doesn't matter. I've been putting things wherever there's room.

Nina Well, I've been putting everything exactly where it's/ gonna go –

Miles But I haven't. We'll deal with it later.

Nina *grabs an end of the box, starts pulling towards the kitchen,* **Miles** *pulls it back.*

Nina You know we won't. Half of these boxes are going to be sitting in our living room for the next year and a half because we're not going to have the time or energy to/move them later.

Miles We'll move them tomorrow. Or next week . . . or next month, it doesn't –

Nina No, we're not. We'll get used to them being there. We'll start putting things on them, like our feet when we're sitting on the sofa. Or our drinks – they'll become end tables. We'll choose the paint color for the walls by whether or not it matches the boxes.

You know we will.

Miles No, we won't.

Nina How many years did we use a plastic shopping bag hanging on the front doorknob as a garbage can? (**Miles** *makes a dismissive sound.*) Seven years. I bought us our first trash can on my thirtieth birthday because I couldn't stand it anymore. Miles, please, let's just move the goddamn box to the kitchen. I need to finish here and go downstairs to –

Miles Stop bossing me around.

Nina *starts to pull him towards the kitchen again,* **Miles** *resists. She stops in her tracks when she feels a cutting pain. She drops her half of the box.*

Nina Ow, motherfuck.

Miles *sets the box down, walks over to her, helps her to sit on a nearby box.*

Miles Honey . . . you shouldn't be doing all this. You need to stop pushing yourself so much.

Nina I'm not pushing myself, Miles.

Miles So, what – I am?

Nina There's no one else to help us. We've burned through all the friends who offered to . . . let's just finish. After I'm done here, I have to go downstairs and help Kit work on the site plan.

Miles You're gonna work tonight?

Nina Kit's been carrying my weight for the past month. (**Miles** *starts to massage* **Nina**'s *shoulders.*) She's been working on the Tillman job and on the Barcelona competition. Not to mention she set up the whole office by herself.

Miles Yeah, well, Kit can do that. She has the time. You should just . . . take it easy, you know? Relax a little. (**Miles** *touches* **Nina**'s *breasts. She wriggles out of his reach.*) Hey!

Nina I'm sorry . . . honey, it's just . . . these aren't mine anymore.

Miles Nina, I've been keeping it all to myself here for the past four months.

Nina What're you – counting?

Miles *tries to nuzzle her.*

Miles C'mon, the baby's asleep.

Nina I can't believe I just told you everything I have to do tonight and you want to have sex?

Miles Yes, I want to have sex! Remember sex? It's how we made the baby and got ourselves into this mess in the first place.

Nina That's seductive.

Miles *lets go of her hand, walks away angry and rejected.*

Miles I'll get the rest of the boxes myself. You just . . . relax.

Nina I don't have time to –

Miles You need to/relax –

Nina I'm not relaxing! –

Eric *runs into the house, shuts the door behind him. His jacket pocket is torn.* **Miles** *and* **Nina** *look as surprised to see him as he is to see them –*

Eric Two fucking guys just chased me for four blocks. They took my iPod and backpack, they had a gun!

Nina Eric! Where did you – ?

Miles Are you OK? You want me to call the cops?

Eric Yeah, no, it's OK, I just –

He walks over to the window, looks out.

Miles Where was this?

Eric Like a block from the subway, by the projects. All of a sudden, these two (.) guys came up from behind me and ripped my iPod out of my pocket –

Nina *examines* **Eric***'s pocket.*

Miles Did they get your wallet?

Eric No, I have a hole in my pocket so it drops down into the lining of my coat. They grabbed my backpack, and then I just . . . took off. I just kept running until I saw Rosa Parks Avenue.

Nina How'd you know how to get here?

Miles You want a glass of water or something? A beer?

Eric In a minute, I just – (*Changing gears.*) Hi, how are you?

Eric *kisses* **Nina** *on the cheek.*

Nina I'm fine.

Miles *and* **Eric** *embrace, clap each other on the back.*

Miles I thought you were in Malaysia.

Eric I just got off the plane. I'm fucking lagged.

Nina Where are your bags?

Eric I put them in a mini-storage near the airport. (*Looks around.*) Get a load of this place. What's the deal?

Miles . . . This is . . . our house.

Eric This is outrageous, man, your other apartment was like a dorm room. How many floors is this?

Nina Four. We converted the garden level into an office for me and Kit, so we're only living on this floor and the one above.

Eric That where the bedrooms are?

Nina Yes.

Eric So how many bedrooms are there?

Nina Three. We use the third one as a family office.

Miles My office.

Eric Sweet, man. Mom and Dad said it was nice but I didn't expect it would be like this.

Miles Why? What'd they say?

Eric Don't sweat it, Miles, they liked it. They were just more into the baby. Where'd you put the baby?

Nina She's upstairs sleeping.

Eric Can I get a peek at her?

Miles Sure.

Nina I don't think it's a good idea.

Eric How old is she, a month?

Miles Six weeks.

Eric Is she sleeping through the night?

Nina (*on the verge of tears*) No!

Miles (*an apology*) The baby gets up every couple hours to nurse. Nina's up all night.

Eric I noticed the moving van out front. You guys need a hand?

Miles You don't have to, man, you must be exhausted.

Eric Getting mugged got me pumped. Let's do it, man.

Kit *walks upstairs carrying a pizza box.*

Kit Your pizza came, they rang the bell downstairs.

Miles (*turns to Eric*) Let's eat something first. (*To* **Kit**.) Kit, you've met my brother before, haven't you? Eric?

Kit *extends her hand.*

Kit Not yet, but I've heard the stories.

Eric Uh-oh . . .

Kit You've been bitten by a rattlesnake and lived to tell the tale, and you sold the Dalai Lama a laptop.

Eric His Holiness is addicted to Tetris.

Kit (*to* **Nina**) Nina, I've started regrading the site plan.

Nina I told you I'd pitch in with that.

Kit We've got to finish this by tonight. We should be cutting out shapes for the model by tomorrow.

Nina We will. I'm going to work all day tomorrow.

Eric (*to* **Kit**) Are you guys doing a charette?

Miles Listen to you and your 'charette'.

Eric (*to* **Miles**, *a frequent joke*) Just because I didn't go to Columbia, like some of us in the room –

Miles (*looking at* **Kit**) All of us, actually.

Nina's *mobile phone rings.* **Miles** *and* **Eric** *help themselves to pizza.*

Nina (*to* **Kit**) Audrey Tillman.

Kit Why's she calling you?

Nina (*into phone*) Hello? Yes, Mrs. Tillman . . . no, I wasn't at the jobsite today but Kit was – (**Nina** *looks at Kit, who nods, yes, I was, everything was fine.*) No, the carpenters are going to fill that in . . . It's going to look exactly as we discussed. (*Brightens.*) Oh, yes, thank you. She's six weeks old, she's just – [Mrs. Tillman could give a fuck.] I'll make sure Kit takes a look tomorrow morning. Thank you, Mrs. Till – (*Mrs. Tillman has hung up.*)

Kit Why didn't she call me? I'm the one who's been holding her shriveled little liver-spotted hand for the past two [months.] –

The baby starts crying upstairs. **Nina** *reacts as if she's been electrically jolted.*

Nina You guys, go ahead, eat. I'll bring her down when I'm done nursing her.

Kit I guess I'll be working by myself after all.

Eric *hands* **Kit** *a slice of pizza on a plate.*

Eric Here you go. (*He goes to the fridge to get her a beer.* **Miles** *touches* **Kit** *consolingly.*) So, do you live in Brooklyn too?

Eric *hands her a beer.*

Kit Ha! Thanks. Noooo. Look, Brooklyn's great, it's beautiful and cheaper, but . . . I want to be able to drop off my dry cleaning, go to a gallery opening, see an eight-hour

Hungarian movie, then drink overpriced green apple martinis – all within a block of my house.

Eric That's what's great about New York, right?

Suddenly, we hear a smash – the sound of glass being shattered and falling on the floor.

Miles What the –

Kit *grabs a flashlight, they see glass pieces on the floor and a jagged hole in the window.*

Eric Shit, man –

Miles What just happened?

Kit *walks towards the window, surveys the debris. Finds a rock, picks it up.*

Kit It's a rock. Someone just threw it at your window.

Miles *walks over,* **Kit** *shows him the rock.*

Miles Why would someone do that?

Eric You've got a stereo, TV, all kinds of computer equipment . . . people in this neighborhood probably saw all that gear and thought Puffy was moving in.

Kit Or, maybe they weren't trying to steal anything. Maybe they were just trying to send you a message. (Goes for phone.) Want me to call 911?

Nina *walks a few steps downstairs.*

Nina Miles? What was that? What broke?

Miles Stay upstairs, honey. There's broken glass down here.

Nina, *holding the baby, walks down, sees the broken glass on the floor.*

Nina Fucking motherfucker. Who broke my fucking window?

Miles I'm checking it out, don't worry. Go back upstairs where it's safe.

Nina *takes a few steps into the living room.*

Nina It's going to take weeks to get a fucking replacement glass . . . what are we supposed to do with a fucking hole in our house for three fucking weeks?

Miles I don't know. Just take the baby upstairs, OK? (*To* **Eric**.) Her first word's gonna be fuck if Nina keeps –

Nina What?

Miles Just please take the baby upstairs.

She goes upstairs.

Kit You should call the cops, Miles. (*Beat.*)

Miles I don't want to do that. We're new here. I don't want people to get the wrong impression.

Kit What would that be?

Miles I don't want to dwell on this. The most important thing to do is cover up that hole.

Kit Home Depot's open twenty-four hours. You can buy a four-by-eight piece of plywood and some hardware to anchor it to the wall.

Eric I'll go. Will you come with me so you can show me?

Kit I'll get my jacket.

Miles *shakes his brother's hand.*

Miles Thanks, man. Can you believe this happened?

Eric *looks out the window, at the sky.*

Eric It's a full moon. Maybe it's a sign of good luck. Getting all the bad things over with first.

Miles Or it's a sign that moving my family here is the biggest mistake of my life.

Kit *comes back with her jacket, she and* **Eric** *walk out, leaving* **Miles** *alone and feeling it.*

Scene Three

Early morning. **Miles** *tries to set the plywood into the wall, manual labor is not his forte.* **Eric** *sleeps on a nearby couch. A man walks by on the street,* **Reggie**, *his clothes not quite clean, his hair in need of a comb. He stops in front of the broken window. The hole still uncovered.*

Reggie Oh, shit! What happened, man?

Miles *looks at* **Reggie**.

Miles What happened? Somebody smashed the window.

Reggie And you ain't hardly even moved in yet – that ain't a way to welcome a brother to the neighborhood.

Miles – a small reaction to 'brother'.

Miles It's not exactly a pie on the stoop, is it?

Reggie That's what I'm saying! You done a lot of work on this house, man.

Miles Well, we bought a door and . . . we put glass in the –

Reggie We got all kinds of people up in here now, building new condos and renovatin' these old brownstones . . . You see that house over there? Two homosexuals bought that, fixed it up to historical accuracy, and all that. I'm glad you came to the neighborhood, man. What you do, you a lawyer or something?

Miles I'm . . . an interactive producer.

Reggie A producer! You know Biggie grew up two blocks from here, right? I used to send that punk to the store to buy me Milk Duds.

Miles Actually, I produce websites and DVD-ROMs for corporate clients. But, I like Biggie.

Reggie I'm glad you came to the neighborhood, man. This glass was custom-made, wasn't it?

Miles (*a little surprised*) Yeah, it was.

Reggie 'Cause 'round here all the brownstones have one seventy-two-inch window or two thirty-six-inch ones. That was the style in the 1870s when most of these buildings was built. But this one here is eighty inches, only one like it. I know they charged you a lot of money for that piece of glass.

Miles *waits to see where* **Reggie***'s going with this.*

Reggie Mm-hm, a lot of money.

Reggie nods *gravely*.

Miles You seem to know a lot about my house –

Reggie I got a guy I can go to – he'll cut that glass for you cheaper than you paid for.

Miles Thanks, but my wife's got her sources. She's an architect so she has reliable [vendors.] –

Reggie (*insistent*) Listen, man, you don't know me. But, I'm telling you – (*Extends his hand.*) I'm Reggie, I live across the street from you, I lived on this block for – matter of fact, I was born on this block. I'm forty-two years old – I got three grown kids, they live with they moms, but everybody 'round here know Reggie. If you need something, I'm your boy.

Nina *walks downstairs carrying the baby.*

Nina Miles, you take the baby. Kit's going to be here any – (*To Reggie.*) Hi, I'm Nina. (*She can't offer her hand because she's holding the baby.*)

Reggie Alright.

Miles This is Reggie, he lives across the street.

Reggie (*to* **Miles**) Like I said, you make up your mind, you come to me.

Miles, *feeling awkward, turns to* **Nina**.

Miles Oh, I should tell you, Reggie mentioned that he, uh, he has a glazier that he recommends.

Nina He's done work for you?

Reggie (*a nod*) Mm-hm.

Nina Do you have his card or can you give me his phone number?

Miles (*to Nina*) I thought you would want to use Frankie again.

Nina I'll call Frankie, but if this guy's in the neighborhood –

Reggie *sees someone offstage.*

Reggie I gotta talk to this – Hey, Mo! You need to settle up with me, son. (*To Miles.*) Look, I'm a go get my boy's card and you talk to him. Whatever you want, he'll do it.

Nina Thanks, Reggie. (*To Miles.*) I don't know what kind of work this guy does, I'm just saying let's get a price from him.

Miles Doesn't it seem weird to you, this guy who's always hanging out on the corner, coming up first thing in the morning, telling us, 'I got a guy who can fix that for you . . . '

Nina So?

Miles And where were those guys last night? They're always out there, doing whatever they're doing, selling whatever they're selling, but last night – they're not there. Where were they?

Nina What – you think Reggie or one of those guys broke the glass? (**Miles** *gestures – I'm just saying.*) . . . I don't think Reggie did it. Why would he do it?

Miles Maybe he gets a fee. Whenever Reggie finds some sucker to give this guy business –

Nina And what's the deal with your brother? He tell you how long he's gonna stay?

Miles No. But he usually stays a week or two – you have a problem with that?

Nina *turns to the baby for unconditional love.*

Nina (*turns to baby*) Look, she's dreaming. Look at how her expression changes every couple seconds. (*Narrating the baby's thoughts as she goes from a smile, to a frown, to tears, to a smile again.*) Flowers . . . car alarms . . . mmm, Mommy's nipples . . .

Eric *comes downstairs.*

Eric Alright, let me see her. (*Looks at baby.*) She's beautiful.

Nina She's the perfect mix of the both of us, don't you think?

Eric She's herself. You, on the other hand, seem to have turned into a completely different person. Didn't I just hear you talking baby talk?

Nina I was giving voice to her thoughts.

Eric Can I hold her?

Nina *hesitates.*

Miles Of course, man.

Nina Just – make sure you support her neck.

Nina *gingerly hands the baby to* **Eric**.

Eric Ohmigod, it's so much responsibility. If I don't hold her right, her neck will break off.

Miles *goes to get a camera.*

Miles Hang on a second, let me take a picture of you two.

Nina Miles – don't put him on the spot.

Eric I don't mind.

Eric *smiles for the camera.* **Miles** *clicks the shutter.* **Nina** *responds to the sound of the downstairs door being opened.*

Nina Shit, Kit's here. I'd wanted to get a head start before she showed up. Miles, take the baby.

Miles Eric's got her.

Nina (*to* **Miles**) You said you'd watch the baby today –

Miles I will. But, just today. Remember I have an interview at Poseidon tomorrow –

Nina *heads downstairs.*

Eric You guys don't have a nanny?

Miles Not yet. But we'd better soon, because I can't go on interviews if I'm stuck here taking care of the baby.

Eric Look at you man, you've got a wife, a kid, a house . . . Not just any house, a Brooklyn brownstone.

Miles Yeah, but it needs a lot of work, man. I mean, this kitchen is like, from Sanford and Son. This linoleum floor . . . I was gonna fix it but then we ran out of money.

Eric What do you mean you ran out of money – look at this place, you're swimming in bucks.

Miles Look at this place, exactly. I don't even want to tell you how much we paid for it. I had to cash in the last of my stock options for the down payment. If it weren't for the income we get renting the top-floor apartment, we couldn't afford to live here.

Eric There's another apartment?

Miles On the fourth floor. Eventually, we hope to take it over but right now we need the money.

Eric You've got something set aside, I know you, Miles. You've probably got ten thousand dollars in quarters all rolled up and stuffed inside a pair of tube socks upstairs.

Miles Dude, InTech laid me off six weeks before the baby was born. Nina's the only one making a steady check now –

Eric *holds the baby with one hand, undoes his pants with the other.*

Eric Check this out. This is what I got for spending three months in a tropical Asian paradise.

Eric's *pants crumple around his ankles, revealing small piles of blue currency rubber-banded around each leg.*

Miles What the hell are those?

Eric Ringgits. I sold hot dog carts to street vendors in Kuala Lumpur. This is my take home. Twenty-two thousand ringgits. Which is about five thousand U.S. dollars.

Miles What're you, waiting to deposit them in Chicago?

Eric Oh. Did I say I was going back to Chicago? My building went co-op so they kicked me out. How are the rents in this neighborhood? Think I could find a one-bedroom in the six-hundred-to seven-hundred-dollar range?

Miles Aw, no, man, maybe three years ago but now –

Eric Fucking yuppies coming in, jacking up the rents so that even a guy like me can't afford to live in the ghetto.

A smile, he pats **Miles** *on the back.*

Miles It isn't exactly the [ghetto.] –

Eric I'm just kidding, man.

Miles I know it's still rough around the edges, but, it's got a good history. A lot of families have been in these brownstones for six or seven generations. You've got teachers, artists, musicians – Biggie grew up a couple blocks from here.

Eric OK, I get it.

Miles It'll be good for Hannah to grow up around (.) . . . all kinds of kids.

Eric It's a great place to start a business. What does this neighborhood need?

Miles We have to drive two neighborhoods over to get organic milk.

Eric What else?

Miles You know – pasta sauce, good cheese, bread . . .

Eric So, a place where you can buy upscale groceries, sit down and get a good cup of coffee, and – meet other people like you in the neighborhood.

Miles Sounds good, man, I hope someone opens one.

Eric Why not you?

Miles The thing I need to do right now is get a job. Bring some money into this house. Starting a business costs money.

Eric That's what investors are for.

Miles Plus, it's risky.

Eric Man, don't you know you're taking a bigger risk waiting around for the right position to open up in the right company? Starting a business gives you control. Look, I've got these ringgits. We can use them to get us off the ground.

Miles OK, I'll . . . think about it, man.

Walter, *the tenant, walks down the steps and out the door. He tries not to notice* **Miles** *and* **Eric**, *standing there in his underwear with the ringgits.*

Eric Who the hell is that?

Miles That's the tenant, Walter.

Eric He walks through your house to get to his apartment? That is weird, man. Come on, let's take a walk around the neighborhood. Scope out some old storefronts. I'll carry the baby.

Miles We can't leave with the window like that.

Eric It'll be fine. We'll be back in ten minutes. We can work on it then.

Miles *picks up the BabyBjörn.*

Miles You want to wear the Björn?

Eric No, man. I don't want that thing. Think about it – two dudes walking down the street with a mixed-race baby in a BabyBjörn? It's not like people are gonna guess we're brothers. I'll just carry her like this, OK?

Eric *holds Hannah in the football hold.*

Miles She hasn't made a peep this whole time, she likes you.

Eric Of course she likes me, man. I'm crazy Uncle Eric. She needs me.

Miles For what?

Eric To be everything you're not.

They exit.

Scene Four

Nina, *holding Hannah, sits across from* **Mrs. Chae**, *who is dressed neatly and paying a little more attention to Hannah than* **Nina**.

Nina I didn't expect to have to go back to work so soon. The good thing is I get to work at home – unlike other working mothers who have to go to their midtown [offices.] –

Mrs. Chae (*Korean accent*) Yes, I know. My daughter is lawyer and she [works.] –

Nina But, most working mothers get three months' maternity leave and I have to start working after only six weeks. My partner and I have made it to the finals in a major design –

Mrs. Chae These days, woman has to work. My daughter says –

Nina – A major design competition for a new arts center in Barcelona. (*She looks to* **Mrs. Chae** *for approval, signs she's impressed. She gets none. Clearing throat:*) Arts Center in

Barcelona. It's an international competition and only four groups made it to the final. It's an honor and a huge – (**Mrs. Chae** *makes clicking noises at the baby.*) Anyway, the deadline is in six weeks so that's why I need a nanny to start right away –

Mrs. Chae Can I hold her?

Nina *unconsciously hesitates.*

Nina Yes, of course, just – be careful of/her [neck.] –

Mrs. Chae (*soothing to* **Nina**) I know . . . I know . . .

Mrs. Chae *takes the baby, while saying in Korean, 'Oh, look at you, you're such a pretty girl'. This unexpectedly touches* **Nina**.

Mrs. Chae Your mommy and daddy must be very happy.

Nina I think my dad liked her, it's hard to tell.

Mrs. Chae But your mommy, she was so proud.

Nina No, mommy's dead.

Mrs. Chae Tsk tsk tsk. You take care of baby, your mommy supposed take care of you.

This moves **Nina** *again. The baby makes a sound.* **Mrs. Chae** *immediately soothes her by patting her on the back and saying a few words in Korean.*

Nina She's smiling at you.

Mrs. Chae Babies love me. And I love the babies too. The family I worked for before? Husband got the new job in Ohio. They ask me to move with them, 'Please, nanny, come with us'. But I cannot go. I have my family here. I have a grandson, did you know?

Nina Oh, how old is he?

Mrs. Chae My daughter, she work at big law firm, they have daycare center in building. I told my daughter, 'I quit my job to take care of him, he's my grandson'. But she say, 'Mommy, don't be selfish, I want him near me'.

Nina Her name is Hannah, did I tell you?

Mrs. Chae I think maybe you name her Hannah (*Pronounces it huh-NAH.*) because she's first one born.

Nina Actually, we just liked the name. And it's HA-nah, not huh-NAH. That would be weird, wouldn't it? Naming her 'number one'?

Mrs. Chae You know Huh-nah?

Nina (*counts in Korean, pronunciation shaky*) Hana, tul, set . . .

Mrs. Chae Oh. Because when you tell me you don't speak one word of Korean, I think you don't speak one word.

Nina I do know one word. I know 'hana.' Actually, I can count to ten, my parents did teach me that. I just don't know how to say . . . eleven or twelve. I don't know any Korean lullabies, or how to say 'koochie koo –'

Mrs. Chae (*starts to sing; insert first couple lines from 'Koyangi Pom'*) Your mommy sang this to you.

Nina (*moved, wishing she wasn't*) Yes, I think she did.

Mrs. Chae (*looking at Hannah*) She has the curly hair.

Nina Yes, from my husband. I'm thrilled.

Mrs. Chae *looks at the baby again.*

Mrs. Chae She looks like . . . your husband?

Nina I don't know. My family thinks she looks like my husband and my husband's family thinks she looks like me.

Mrs. Chae Your husband . . . he is . . . architect too?

Nina No, he's uh . . . he's a computer guy.

Miles *hurries in.*

Miles I'm sorry I'm late, the interview went long –

Nina So, it must've gone really well. What did they –

Miles I'll . . . tell you later. (*To Mrs. Chae.*) Hi, I'm Miles. (*He goes to shake* **Mrs. Chae**'*s hand, she bows.*)

Nina Oh, uh, Miles, this is Mrs. Chae. Mrs. Chae, this is my husband Miles.

Mrs. Chae (*not skipping a beat*) Congratulations. She is beautiful baby.

Miles Thank you, thank you.

Mrs. Chae So, you don't mind? Nina says she want the Korean nanny to speak Korean to Hannah. You don't worry?

Miles No, I – I think it'd be great. I think it'd be wonderful for Hannah to understand Korean. You thought I might be worried?

Mrs. Chae Maybe some American parent don't want the child to get confused or handicapped.

Miles No, no, I think it's one-hundred-percent a good thing.

Mrs. Chae *looks at Hannah, then* **Nina** *and* **Miles**.

Mrs. Chae She is lucky baby.

Miles *smiles, puts his arm around* **Nina**.

Miles Hey, why don't I take a picture of you three together?

Miles *gets his camera.*

Nina Um . . . Miles? It's a little premature –

Miles It'll be nice.

Nina *stands next to* **Mrs. Chae**, *not quite committed.* **Mrs. Chae** *holds Hannah closer and smiles into the camera.*

Miles That's great.

Flash. The doorbell rings. **Nina** *turns to* **Mrs. Chae**.

Nina Thank you for your time. Let me walk you to the door.

Mrs. Chae Should I call you tomorrow?

Nina I'll call you, thank you.

Miles You guys look great together!

She opens the door to let **Mrs. Chae** *out, sees* **Reggie**.

Nina Oh, hi Reggie. Um, come on in.

Mrs. Chae *leaves as* **Reggie** *comes in carrying a large, ornate chandelier.*

Reggie (*to Miles*) Check this out, man. I just bought it for fifty bucks, I sell it to you for seventy-five.

Miles Where did you get that?

Reggie I told you, I bought it. (*Looks at their ceiling.*) I see you got a hook where one used to be. All you got to do is slip it on. You got a ladder?

Miles Listen, Reggie, thanks but, we don't want to buy that.

Reggie It ain't gone be that hard, here –

He hands it to Miles, who reluctantly takes it. **Reggie** *moves some boxes underneath the hook.*

Reggie I could probably reach it like this.

Miles Can you get down, please? You're stepping on some fragile electronic equipment.

Reggie You got some computer stuff in here?

Miles Can you just come down?

Reggie *steps down.*

Reggie (*to* **Miles**) So, I talked to my boy over at the glassworks, I told him it was a eighty-inch window and he says he can do it for fifteen hundred dollars.

Nina (*to* **Reggie**) Oh. Did you get his card? 'Cause I should talk to him about some details.

Reggie *digs through his pockets.*

Reggie I got his card, I got his card, here – (*He hands her a folded piece of paper then turns back to* **Miles**.) But if you want to pull the trigger on this, tell me. I'll set it up for you. Even with my fee, you ain't paying what you'd pay if you walked in there yourself.

Miles *looks at* **Nina**.

Miles Your fee. That's part of the fifteen hundred.

Reggie (*goes to fridge*) Oh, shit. You still got that fridge? That ugly-ass fridge been here since the seventies.

Reggie *opens the fridge.*

Miles Do you mind?

Reggie You know, I been in your house before. Yeah, I been in here before. Had some good times up in here, man. The night of the blackout, 1977, city was coal-black. People were running around crazy, smashing store windows, grabbing up anything they could get – bananas, turntables, diapers . . . Me and my friends climbed through that window, lay down on our backs, and looked straight up, man, saw stars we never get to see – the constellations. Aquila the eagle; Cygnus the swan; Hercules the warrior – he took on the labors, man. He brought down the lion, the hydra, Cerberus himself. After the riots is when the monsters took over this neighborhood – drug dealers, gangs, robbers. Hercules should've stuck around, we coulda used him. But when the power came back on, all the stars faded away.

Miles *hands* **Reggie** *the chandelier.*

Scene Five

The office. There are two drafting tables and stools, a desk with a computer and printer. **Kit** *and* **Nina** *are building the landscape their model will sit on.* **Kit** *finishes gluing on a layer of gator board and is waiting for* **Nina** *to cut out more shapes. Meanwhile,* **Nina** *is looking for something.*

Kit Nina, I'm ready for more shapes. What're you doing? What're you looking for?

Nina A green and yellow receiving blanket. It was mine when I was a baby. I have this picture of my mom holding me in it . . .

Their office phone rings. **Kit** *checks the caller ID.*

Kit Don't get it, it's Mrs. Tillman. She's called three times already.

Nina Not about the wall again.

Kit The first two calls were about the wall. The third call was about the bathroom. She said the light made the wall tiles look 'too shiny'. I am so sick of these overly-entitled, ignorant, tantrum-throwing rich people.

Nina Me too. I just want to be one.

Kit I want to be in a whole new league. Get the hell out of residential work, be rid of these idiots forever.

Nina I wonder what Mrs. Chae is doing to try to soothe her.

Nina *listens, hears nothing.*

Kit Hannah's not crying.

Nina She is, they're upstairs in the bedroom.

Kit You're saying you can hear them two floors above? I can't hear anything.

Nina (*standing up*) I'm gonna go up there and offer to nurse her –

Kit (*also standing*) Nina, don't. Just . . . leave her, it's disrespectful. If the baby really needed you . . . or your breasts . . . the nanny would bring her down here. I don't even think she's crying.

Nina I hear her. Being a mother has given me superhero powers. And Hannah – Hannah can smell me from twenty feet away.

Kit You measured?

Nina I read it and I tested it. And her crying – it triggers my milk. I was in the bathroom yesterday and she started crying, and milk shot out of my nipples. Smacked right into the back of the door. Sometimes my milk attacks her.

We hear **Hannah** *crying.* **Mrs. Chae** *has brought her downstairs to the living room.* **Nina** *looks at* **Kit**.

Kit No, Nina, concentrate. We blew the first two months of our deadline already. We have six weeks to do what all our competitors have had four months to do. I didn't mean blow.

Nina I couldn't stand up –

Kit (*to Nina*) I know, honey.

Nina Any woman who has a planned C-section is a fucking moron.

Kit I like the image of the doctor grabbing your intestines by the handful and piling them on your stomach, then shoving them back in after she gets the baby out. You know, I think you've broken some kind of sacred code of silence by telling me the details of your horrible birth experience.

Nina Are you afraid to have a baby now?

Kit Hell yeah! Not that it's an option right –

Eric *comes downstairs, puts a set of keys on* **Kit's** *desk.*

Eric Thanks for letting me borrow these, Miles made a spare set for me.

Kit No problem.

Eric Hey, you know that radio station you told me about? I tuned into it this morning. They play some great music.

Kit I figured since you lost your iPod . . .

Eric I appreciate it. Well, I'll leave you gals to your work.

Eric *heads upstairs.*

Nina What the hell was that about? You loaned him your keys?

Kit Yeah. What's wrong with that?

Nina I don't want him getting too comfortable. I don't want him to be here at all. Eric is not the kind of person Miles should get into business with.

Kit Why not?

Nina He's never done anything legit, he's never had a proper job . . . and he's never been able to commit to a relationship.

Kit That was unsolicited.

Nina Stream of consciousness. The thing is, I think Miles is using Eric and this business as a way of avoiding having to spend time with the baby.

Kit If you think that there's some guy out there who's going to do more than what Miles is doing . . . you're nuts.

Nina Fucking Joe.

Kit You think Joe's a shit because he wouldn't marry me after six years, but I think Joe's normal. Every guy in the world is like Joe. You've had it lucky Nina, you don't know –

Nina How hard it is out there? It's hard in here. This is hard. (*Beat.*)

Kit Last night, I went to a Salvadoran restaurant with this guy. I kept telling him in a nice way 'It's not El Salvadorean food. It's Salvadoran'. But all night he kept saying 'I've never had El Salvadorean food before', 'I have to tell my friends I went to an El Salvadorean restaurant'.

Nina Sounds like another online loser. Where was the restaurant?

Kit Deepest Queens. To get there we had to take the Z train. The Z train to Jamaica Center. Then we had to walk twelve blocks to get to this little piece of shit restaurant that served the most heavenly pupusas made on the planet.

Nina You bring some back for me?

Kit No. Hot off the griddle – the crust was crisp and toothsome and when you bit into them the cheese and pork oozed out –

Nina (*putting out her hand*) Stop –

Kit *reaches into her desk, pulls out a bag of pupusas, tosses them to* **Nina**.

Kit They're not going to be as good cold, but –

Miles *comes downstairs*.

Miles Nina, have you seen my camcorder?

Nina What? No.

Miles I know I put it on the bookshelf yesterday but now I can't find it. I wanted to shoot some video of Hannah on her first day with Mrs. Chae.

Nina You know what, Miles, there's a new rule. I want you to spread the word that this office is off-limits to anyone who doesn't work here.

Miles What – ?

Nina We're on a serious deadline here.

Kit Yes, and it's ticking away every minute that you stand there arguing with your [husband.] –

Miles This office is part of my house, Nina –

Nina Our house. But, Kit and I pay rent here.

Miles You have to throw that in my face?

Nina This is our space, Miles, and I don't want anyone else down here.

Miles That is so –

He storms off.

Nina (*calling after him*) Except Hannah and Mrs. Chae! They're still allowed to [come.] –

The office phone rings.

Kit (*into phone.*) Hello? What?! Javier, I told you twice before I left last night those pipes had to be flush with the I-beams – Alright, look, just tell Mrs. Tillman to put her ass on ice, I'll be there in an hour. (*Off his reaction.*) I'll take a cab, but I'm in fucking Brooklyn.

She hangs up the phone, dials another number.

Nina Want me to call a car service?

Kit I'm already doing it. (*Into phone.*) Yeah, can I get a car at 127 Rosa Parks Avenue? Thanks.

Nina I'll finish the shapes for the foundation by the time you –

Mrs. Chae *walks downstairs carrying the crying* **Hannah**.

Mrs. Chae I'm sorry, Nina, I try give her pacifier, I try my finger, I play nice music –

Nina (*looks to* **Kit**) Can you try taking her for a walk outside? Could you try that?

Mrs. Chae OK, yes, OK. I'm sorry I interrupt –

Nina It's OK.

Nina *looks at Hannah. Feeling she might lose her resolve, she turns away. Sound of a car horn outside.* **Mrs. Chae** *starts to leave, Hannah cries harder.* **Kit** *grabs her bag.*

Kit That's my car. If you finish the layers by the time I get back, we might be able to stay on schedule.

One quick look at **Nina**, *who continues working, then* **Kit**'*s out the door. When* **Nina** *hears the door close, she stands up. She starts for the stairs – then stops, starts – stops . . . then runs upstairs.*

Scene Six

Afternoon. There are fewer moving boxes – the place looks more settled. The window is still broken, a piece of plywood has been anchored to the wall to cover it. **Reggie** *walks in carrying two boxes of ceramic tiles and sets them down on the kitchen floor, near another open box, of a different shape. He can't resist looking into the other box.* **Miles** *walks in carrying another two boxes, sees* **Reggie**.

Miles Can I help you, man?

Reggie I see you got a Xbox. I can get you some games that go with it real cheap. They still in the plastic, let me show you what I got –

He starts for the door.

Miles It's alright. I don't have time to play games these days.

Reggie They factory sealed. They ain't no cheap-ass Chinese –

Oops. **Reggie** *does a quick scan for* **Nina**.

Miles She's not Chinese. And if they're meant to be sold in a store, how'd you get them?

Reggie I got a guy, he works in a Circuit City. He say sometimes they order twenty-five copies of a game, they get twenty-six.

Miles So, they're stolen.

Reggie How's it stolen, the store ain't paid for it!

Miles If you take something from a store without paying for it. you stole it!

Reggie Man, who lives like that?

Miles (*trying to get rid of him*) Yeah, right, thanks for your help, Reggie, I can get this from here.

Reggie You got ten more boxes out there.

Miles I can handle it.

Reggie Where you gone lay them tiles down anyway, the kitchen?

Miles *hesitates, he knows where this is going.*

Miles I've got it all taken care of.

Reggie That will look nice, man. But you gotta take up all that linoleum, then you gotta patch up the holes and put something smooth down to glue the tiles to – you can't do all that by yourself.

Miles Well, I have the time right now so I think I'll be alright.

Reggie We done did this in my mom's house in the eighties, man, I'm telling you – you gone need some help. Pulling that old stuff off piece by piece – ain't nothing for that but a pry bar. I don't mind an honest day's work. You hire some guy in the phone-book, he gone charge you two bills a day. I'll do it for half.

Nina, *wearing the baby in a sling, walks in carrying plastic bags loaded with groceries in both hands.*

Nina What's this – you bought tiles? How much did they cost?

Miles *glances at* **Reggie**, *wants to get rid of him.* **Miles** *reaches into his pocket and hands* **Reggie** *a five-dollar bill.*

Miles Here you go, man, thanks.

Reggie *looks at the money.*

Reggie That's alright. We do it another way.

Reggie *heads out the door.* **Miles**, *embarrassed, puts the money back in his pocket.*

Miles Eric paid for the tiles, says it's his housewarming gift to us.

Nina Miles, take the baby. You haven't held her since yesterday.

Miles No, I don't want to wake her.

Nina What about your interview this morning?

Miles I went. (*Opens a box of tiles.*) Look, I got those tiles that you circled in the catalog –

Nina Miles, how'd it go?

Miles I don't want to take a job that I'm going to resent going to every day. You know what I really want to do.

Nina Open a store with your brother? Miles, we make fun of your brother and his ridiculous schemes.

Miles This isn't a scheme, it's a good idea.

Nina I don't trust your brother, Miles. I'm sorry, but I don't. He doesn't have the experience –

Miles He has tons of experience!

Nina He's never opened a business here. He just goes to these Western-worshipping little Asian countries with his all-American good looks and he bamboozles them. He sells them shit.

Miles How can you talk like that about my brother?

Nina You don't need your brother. If you really want to start a business, then why don't you start something yourself?

Miles Start a business – what business? With what? I don't have any ideas –

Nina Look what Reggie does. Reggie doesn't have anything but he's out on that street corner, paying attention to what's going on, looking for opportunities –

Miles I'm not one of the guys on the corner, Nina. Are you telling me to stand on the corner with the rest of the unemployed black guys?

Nina No.

Miles This store is my idea. It's how I want to present myself to the community. A lot of these families living in these brownstones, they stayed committed to the community during the rough times. And now people like us are moving in and I want to be connected to their history. I don't want to be the intruder. I want to bring something.

Mrs. Chae *walks in.* **Miles** *and* **Nina** *brighten like schoolchildren.*

Nina *and* **Miles** Good morning, Mrs. Chae.

Mrs. Chae *makes a beeline for the baby.*

Mrs. Chae She's asleep? You give me whole sling. This way you can work and I can keep Hannah while I do her laundry. And I do your laundry too.

Mrs. Chae *picks up a few stray pieces of dirty clothing lying around.*

Nina Oh, you don't have to do that.

Mrs. Chae I do this for my daughter too.

Mrs. Chae *starts picking up stray laundry from around the living room.*

Nina . . . Do you . . . cook for her too?

Miles Nina –

Mrs. Chae Yes, of course. She and husband spend every weekend at my house. I cook a lots of food – chap chae, bulgogi, kim- chee chigae – then Sunday, pack it up and they take home.

Nina Man, I haven't had home-cooked Korean food in a long, long –

Mrs. Chae You like the Korean food? Even the stinky kimchee?

Nina I love kimchee. But I used to have to sneak it because my mom wouldn't let me eat it. She'd say, 'You'll never have an American boyfriend'.

Miles Unless he also eats kimchee. (*Re. laundry.*) Let me get you something for that.

He heads upstairs.

Mrs. Chae Your mommy want you to have American boyfriend?

Nina That's all we had where I grew up. Except for this one Filipino boy.

Mrs. Chae I see. That's why she don't teach you the Korean language.

Nina I don't think she knew I'd live in a place where I could speak Korean every day. Where every time my local Korean deli got a new cashier, I'd have to explain no, I'm not Japanese, I'm Korean, I just can't talk to you.

Mrs. Chae If you want, I teach you the Korean words I speak to Hannah.

Nina Yes.

Mrs. Chae That way you both learn together. And maybe someday I make kimchee for you. You work hard all day.

You spend evening with Hannah instead of cook, clean and do laundry, eh? Hannah misses the mommy.

Nina Do you think?

Mrs. Chae She love the mommy and daddy. She talk about you all the time.

Miles *comes downstairs with a laundry bag.*

Miles Here you go, you can put things in here.

Mrs. Chae Oh, thank you, Miles. Such a good husband, hm? My husband, he never touch the laundry, never change the diaper, but Miles . . . he does so much.

Mrs. Chae *touches* **Miles***'s cheek, then goes upstairs.* **Eric** *opens the front door. Pushes in half a dozen large pieces of luggage.*

Miles You need a hand with that, man?

He goes over to help.

Nina What's going on, Eric?

Eric Miles was running out of clothes that fit me. Plus it was costing me twenty-one bucks a day to have this stuff in storage.

Nina You took all of this to Malaysia?

Eric I was there for three months. I wanted to have my options.

Miles I don't know if all that's gonna fit in the upstairs office.

Eric What about the basement? I don't need to put my hands on all this stuff every day. A bunch of these bags can go downstairs.

Nina How long do you plan on staying here, if you don't mind my asking?

Eric To get a store off the ground could take a few months. But, I don't have to stay here the whole time –

Miles Where else are you going to stay?

Eric I can get a sublet –

Nina It's just that we're still trying to get settled here –

Miles I don't want you to do that, man. You're family.

Nina Miles –

Miles I asked him to stay here and help me launch the business. The least we can do is offer him a place to stay. We have the room –

Nina No, we don't. That's supposed to be our office –

Miles You have your office downstairs. The upstairs is my office and I say Eric is welcome to stay.

Eric I'm sorry, Nina, if I'd've known you were against me staying here, I wouldn'ta brought all my shit –

Nina This isn't personal, Eric, you just happen to have shown up at a time when we're . . . we're still trying to figure things out ourselves and . . . I just need to put my family first.

Miles (*to* **Nina**) Eric is family. (*To* **Eric**.) Come on, man, let's get these things upstairs.

Scene Seven

Night. **Eric** *sits at* **Nina's** *desk,* **Kit** *stands with her coat on, she's just come into the office.*

Kit Does Nina know you're down here?

Eric No, she's asleep. Why?

Kit Well, she said she didn't want anyone else down here anymore.

Eric Oh –

Kit Anyone except for me, her, Mrs. Chae and Hannah, of course . . . which only leaves you and Miles.

Eric *turns to the computer.*

Eric I didn't know. I'll close my document right now.

Kit (*stopping him*) So – what were you working on? Something to do with the store?

Eric I was drafting a proposal. Miles scoped out a great location. So, what do you think of our idea?

Kit S'pretty good. Neighborhood's changing . . . yuppies love their pesto and their lattes, I know I do.

Eric You know, I don't know why Miles never had the idea to run his own business before.

Kit It's a lot of extra work. And it doesn't always pay off. You know this.

Eric I just wonder if Miles leans on Nina too much. If she ends up holding him back. Because Miles –

They hear a sound from the floor above.

I should get out of here –

Kit Go on.

Eric Miles can do anything, man.

Kit He's smart and hardworking, he's creative –

Eric What? He's way more than that, man. Miles came into the world a four-pound, undernourished, heroin-addicted, premature little bird you could hold in the palm of your hand.

Kit Miles was a heroin baby?

Eric His birth mother was some junkie, shot ten bags of dope to induce her labor. Then after she gave birth, she snuck out of the hospital. My parents adopted him when he was still in the pediatric ICU.

Kit I've known Nina and Miles for fifteen years, I've never heard that story.

Eric Ask Nina. When Miles was a kid, he had to go to physical therapy, occupational, speech . . . he rode the little special ed bus to school with the retards. And then in the fifth grade, pow! He just shot up and shot out. Next thing we knew he was doing karate, playing piano . . . writing code on the Commodore computer I got for Christmas.

Kit Your parents were cutting edge.

Eric All I did was play Pong on it so they ended up giving it to him. That's why I say Miles can do anything. And it's just . . . weird to come here and see him so . . .

Kit Well, getting laid off right before you have a baby isn't exactly an ego booster.

Eric You're right.

Kit I've watched Nina and Miles' relationship for a long time. They try to pass the power back and forth between them, but one person always ends up holding the ball. That's true with most relationships, it's true with two women. (*Beat.*)

Eric This is so embarrassing.

Kit What?

Eric I'm such an idiot.

Kit Why?

Eric Are you gay?

Kit No!

Eric I thought . . . because you said two women –

Kit I'm talking about my friends Stephanie and Laura.

Eric OK, good.

Kit So I take it you're glad I'm not gay.

Eric Considering the fact that it's just you and me down here, in the middle of the night . . . yeah, I am.

Scene Eight

Office. The sound of scraping and prying from above – **Miles** *and* **Reggie** *working on the floor.* **Kit** *and* **Nina** *work on the model – they are gluing a cantilevered roof onto its beam.* **Kit** *applies the glue as* **Nina** *balances the top-heavy roof piece.*

Nina It is already? What's today's date?

Kit The third.

Nina I completely lost track of time – OK, Thursday, your birthday. Is it . . . are you gonna be [forty?] –

Kit Let's not touch on that.

Nina OK. OK, what do you want to do? Do you want me to throw you a party?

Kit (*roof*) Press down harder on this side.

Nina Dinner with a bunch of our friends?

Kit No.

Nina Kit, you gotta ring it in. Your fortieth –

Kit Do not speak the number.

Nina You can't do nothing.

Kit I don't want to do nothing. I want to go out to a nice, quiet dinner, just you and me. We can go to that new French place on Smith Street. It's close enough to here, you can be home in time to nurse Hannah.

Nina You sure you don't want to go somewhere fabulous in Manhattan?

Kit With you constantly checking your watch, worried that your breasts are going to explode?

Nina I guess you're right.

Kit *finishes, leaves* **Nina** *holding the newly-glued-on piece.*

Kit So, Hannah being such a big baby and all, I was wondering – were you a big baby?

Nina Normal. My body was skinny but my cheeks clocked in at about a pound each.

Kit Miles must've been a big baby, then, huh?

Nina Mm . . . no.

Kit, *having hoped for a longer answer, fishes for more.*

Kit Have you ever seen pictures of him as a baby?

Nina I have a picture of him when he was about one year old in my desk.

Kit Can I see it?

Nina Uh . . . sure. It's in my top drawer.

Kit *opens* **Nina's** *top drawer, sifts around to find it. Looks at it.*

Kit Well. Looks like a perfectly healthy one-year-old to me. Perfectly healthy.

She puts the photo back, goes to her desk, silently kicking herself for believing. **Nina** *watches her, unsure what this is about.*

Nina Actually, a normal one-year-old should weigh about twenty pounds and Miles only weighed seventeen.

Kit *turns to* **Nina** *– enthused.*

Kit Tell me more.

Nina His mom said he was a fussy eater –

Kit's *disappointment is visible.*

Kit . . . Right.

Nina He wouldn't drink milk or eat cheese, which are good sources of fat.

Nina *looks at* **Kit**, *trying to read her reaction.*

Kit That makes sense. (*Beat.*)

Nina Plus he was addicted to heroin for the first two months of his –

Kit Yes!

Nina You're in love with Eric! He told you about Miles. That's Miles' big secret.

Kit It came up in conversation.

Nina Pillow talk.

Kit Eric and I haven't even gone out yet, let alone slept together. (*Half-beat.*)

Nina Don't trust him, Kit.

Kit What do you resent so much about Eric? Has he ever hurt you or Miles? (*Beat.*)

Nina He's never there when it counts, you know. He didn't even come to our wedding. Then out of nowhere, he just swoops in and inserts himself into our lives.

Mrs. Chae *carries downstairs a tray with two bowls of soup.*

Mrs. Chae It's lunchtime for the hardworking woman.

She means 'women'.

Nina (*smelling, just saying it fills her*) What is that? Seaweed soup?

Mrs. Chae *places a bowl on* **Nina***'s desk.*

Mrs. Chae Mi yuk guk. I write it down for you. Very good for the mommy after delivering the baby, because it has iron and protein. Good for you now because of the breastfeeding. You need the strength.

Nina Thank you! I'll have it as soon as –

Mrs. Chae *places another bowl in front of* **Kit**.

Mrs. Chae Good for you too, because it also helps to make the baby.

Kit *gently pushes the soup bowl away from her.*

Kit Hmmmm . . . Thanks . . .

Mrs. Chae *notices. So does* **Nina**, *she's embarrassed.*

Mrs. Chae Your husband don't want the children?

Kit My husband . . . uh uh, he says he's not ready.

Nina *flashes her a look.*

Mrs. Chae You cannot wait for him. The man is never ready for the children, he is still his mommy's baby. But, having the child will make him a man.

Nina You can still eat it, Kit, the soup won't impregnate you.

Mrs. Chae (*to* **Nina**) If you like, I teach you how to make it.

Nina God, I would love that.

Nina *looks at the soup, she still can't move her hands. To* **Mrs. Chae**:)

Would you mind moving that a little closer to me?

Mrs. Chae Of course.

Mrs. Chae *does so.* **Nina** *leans her head down, without moving her hands, trying to get her mouth close enough to the bowl. She manages a sip.*

Nina Mm, smells fantastic.

She blows on it. **Mrs. Chae** *watches* **Nina** *struggle to drink the soup.*

Nina I'm dying to eat it but I can't move my hands until the glue –

Mrs. Chae *picks up the bowl, scoops up a spoonful of soup and blows on it before offering it to* **Nina**.

Mrs. Chae (*in Korean*) Eat well.

Nina Oh, gosh, um – (*Takes a sip of soup.*) Mm, that's delicious.

Mrs. Chae *continues to feed* **Nina**.

Mrs. Chae Soon it will be Hannah's paek il. We must have a big party.

Nina Paek il?What's that?

Mrs. Chae Paek il is for one hundredth day because back in old times, when a baby did not die by one hundred days, we have a big party. We say now she will live long life.

(**Mrs. Chae** *feeds* **Nina** *another spoonful.*)

Kit Where's Miles' camera when you need it?

Nina Gosh, I really appreciate this but . . . you don't have to feed me.

We hear **Miles** *and* **Reggie***'s voices in disagreement.*

Mrs. Chae It's OK. Hannah is sleeping and I am in the way upstairs. Miles and his brother are working so hard.

Nina Eric's helping?

Mrs. Chae Yes.

Nina *looks at* **Kit**.

Nina I thought he was going to the realtors – wait a second. Who do you mean by Miles' brother?

Mrs. Chae The man, his brother. The one who's helping him.

Nina Is he black?

Mrs. Chae Yes.

Nina That's not Miles' brother.

Mrs. Chae Oh –

Nina You met his brother. Eric. Eric's his brother. Reggie's . . . just some guy who lives on our street.

Kit *notices* **Nina's** *tone of voice.*

Mrs. Chae Oh, I see . . . (*A beat.* **Nina***'s uncomfortable.*) Miles is adopted?

Nina Yes.

Mrs. Chae (*a Korean sound*) Oh . . . (*Tsk tsk tsk.*) Such nice parents.

Nina . . . They're nice because they're white people who adopted a little black baby?

Kit *tastes the soup.*

Kit Mmmm, Mrs. Chae, this is good. What kind of seaweed is this?

Mrs. Chae We call it mi yuk.

Nina Because actually, I think Miles' parents were – they did things that were kind of . . . like raising him in an all-white neighborhood, sending him to schools where he was the only black kid –

Kit I thought you liked your in-laws –

Nina Miles was teased a lot. The reason he'll be emotionally enslaved to Eric the rest of his life is because Eric would beat the shit out of kids who picked on him.

Mrs. Chae But Miles grew up so nice. Clean and smart, handsome.

Nina Did you just say [Clean.] –

Kit Mrs. Chae, you mentioned your daughter has a child Hannah's age. Maybe he and Hannah can have a playdate! (*To* **Nina.**)It'd be good for Hannah to have another kid she can speak Korean to because . . . you don't really have Korean friends . . .

Mrs. Chae (*hesitates*) I don't think –

Nina What – you're afraid your daughter won't let him come because Hannah's black?

Kit Nina –

Mrs. Chae Hannah is not black. If you look at her, maybe you cannot tell. People cannot tell the daddy is black. She is just beautiful baby.

Miles *walks in through the outside door.*

Miles Nina, I've got to use your computer for a minute.

He sits at her desk, launches a web browser.

Nina Why can't you use your computer upstairs?

Miles I told Reggie I was going to the hardware store to get something. I hid a little webcam so I can watch him. Mrs. Chae, do you mind staying down here for a few minutes?

Kit Watch him do what?

Miles Steal from me.

Mrs. Chae (*a Korean expression of shock*) Aigu.

Nina Miles, you have no reason to think that Reggie stole your –

Miles The man openly offered to sell me stolen goods, Nina. This is what he does. He insinuates himself into people's homes, and then he takes things he can sell. The gentrification of this neighborhood is the best thing to happen to him in years. (**Miles** *checks the web browser.*) See that – look, he's looking in one of our boxes.

I put my portable DVD player in there on purpose.

Nina *looks.*

Nina This is wrong. I'm going upstairs to tell him –

Kit Nina, don't let go of that –

Nina *starts for the stairs.* **Kit** *rushes to the model to grab the roof.* **Miles** *goes after* **Nina**.

Miles Nina, stay. I want to catch him.

Nina You've set up a trap.

Kit Look at it this way. If he doesn't take anything, you'll have won.

Nina You approve of this?

Kit No, I think it's sick but I admit it's pulled me in.

Miles *looks at the browser.*

Miles He's looking around . . . he's walking towards my iPod . . . he's picking up a pry bar – (*We hear the corresponding sound on the ceiling.*) And . . . he's pulling up the linoleum off the kitchen floor.

Nina I am so embarrassed, Miles.

Miles Well, someone took my camcorder.

Nina You should go up there and apologize.

Miles I'm not going to apologize. But I will let him keep working for us. And keep my eye on him.

Miles *goes out the front door.*

Mrs. Chae Can I . . . go upstairs now?

Nina Yes.

Mrs. Chae *goes upstairs,* **Nina** *takes over the job of holding down the roof from* **Kit**. **Kit** *goes to her desk.*

Kit Do you want . . . me to feed you the soup?

Nina No, I don't want it anymore. Do me a favor and throw it away.

Scene Nine

The next day. **Reggie** *holds one end of a tape measure while* **Miles** *pulls the rest across the length of the floor.*

Miles One hundred and thirty-five inches. Divided by two, that's sixty-seven and a half inches. (*He walks to that number on the measuring tape, then makes a mark on the floor.*) So this is the center of the room.

Reggie Why you doing this the hard way? All you have to do is start at this wall – (*Walks to border with living room.*) – get your tiles going across, then whenever you run into your fridge or your stove, you just cut the tile to fit. That's it.

Miles No, if you do it that way then that's the only line that will look like full tiles. It's better to start in the center. That way I can distribute the error factor around the periphery of the room. (*After a beat.*) I'm going downstairs to ask Nina to take a look at –

Reggie Man, why do you have to – (**Miles** *turns to him.*) alright, alright, I get you, man. Now, I get you. I ain't never been married yet so I wasn't feeling you before, but now I am.

Miles What?

Reggie 'Cuz I notice how you talk to your female, see what I'm saying. 'Cuz you always saying 'I gotta ax Nina this', or 'I can't 'til I ax Nina' – and I've been thinking, 'What is this brother, hen-pecked or some shit?' But now I know that's how you do her to do you right. I'm'a try that shit myself. /

Miles Man, Nina's done this before.

Reggie I done this before! I keep telling you!

Miles Nina's done this hundreds of times before. Not just once in her mother's house. Anyway, why are you still living in your mother's house?

Reggie She getting old, she need somebody.

Miles Yeah, but, you never moved out, right? So, who's taking care of who?

Reggie I got four brothers and three sisters, seven nephews and eight nieces, we all there.

Miles All living in that house?

Reggie We family, man. We got seventy-seven years' history in that house. Ain't no yuppie gone come up in here and buy us out.

Eric *walks in.*

Eric I tracked down the owner of the diner, he's this Hasidic guy who hangs out with his buddies in this bakery in Williamsburg. I made an appointment for Friday so you can meet him.

Reggie *starts arranging the tiles the way he wants them. Not gluing them, just placing them down to make a point.*)

Miles Awesome.

Reggie 'Awesome, dude.'

Eric The landlord said another party approached him about the space last week. They want to open a tea lounge.

Miles A tea lounge? Who around here is going to go to a tea lounge?

Reggie I would. I drink tea.

Eric To get an edge on these guys, I think we should put down a deposit. Are you ready to do that?

Reggie He gone ax his wife.

Miles It's your money. If you want to be that aggressive –

Eric That's how you compete, little brother. You have to be fierce, you have to use that big brain of yours to think – how do I get the advantage? What idea can I come up with that no one else could.

Miles I can do that.

Eric I'm gonna go to the bank tomorrow, convert my ringgits.

Eric *heads for the stairs just as* **Walter** *comes down. Once again, he goes straight out the door, without acknowledging anyone.* **Eric** *gives* **Miles** *a look – weird. As* **Eric** *goes upstairs,* **Nina** *comes up from the office.* **Reggie**, *having placed a few rows of tiles on the floor, seizes the opportunity.*

Reggie (*to* **Nina**) Mommy, look at this here. How this looks? You walk into the room, you see one solid line. That's the way to do it.

Nina You're . . . right, Reggie. That is . . . a way to do it. But –

Reggie You hear that? She said I'm right. She said I'm right and she know more about this than you. But you ain't never said nothing like that.

Miles Oh, Nina's your hero now?

Nina Miles –

Miles I've been telling you since the minute I met you that she's an architect. But you keep treating her like she doesn't know anything.

Reggie (*to* **Nina**) Is that true? That ain't true. You the one who act like I don't know anything. I done did this before and you ain't. But you gotta be like one of them new niggas who always think –

The baby starts crying upstairs. **Nina** *can't decide whether to get the baby or stay with* **Miles**.

Miles No, man. No. I'm not any kind of nigger. You hear me?

Reggie Man, I ain't mean it like that. Over here when somebody say new nigga we mean somebody who turn they nose up at something 'cause it ain't new or good enough –

Miles I don't care what you say it means, man. I don't want to hear it in my house.

The baby's cries become jagged and intense. **Nina** *can't take it anymore, goes upstairs to soothe the baby.*

Reggie Man, you all new niggas to me, buying up these here brownstones for a million dollars when they done sat here for decades all boarded up – shit, city couldn't give these buildings away.

Miles Don't try to give me that back-in-the-day bull [shit] –

Reggie This house that you living in now had been abandoned so long it had a tree growing out of it – right through the roof. When we was little kids, we called it the tree house – (*Walks to window.*)We used to climb through that window and sit under the tree – (*Points to a spot on the floor.*) Right here – and smoke cigarettes, kiss, party, you name it. This was our house.

Miles Man, don't try to make it sound like it was better back in the old days 'cause I know this house went on to be a shooting gallery and a crack house before the city took it over.

Reggie I ain't saying it was better. Shit, I got shot walking down my street just going to buy some chicken wings at the Chinese restaurant. So I ain't saying nothing 'bout no back-in-the-day. All I'm saying is – this is the way you do your tiles, son. You get them going across, ain't nothing else to worry about.

Miles Reggie, man, if you want to help, I'll pay you. But we're gonna do it the way I want it. OK? It's my house now. (*Beat.*)

Reggie Alright. (*Checks watch.*) I gotta go check on my girl, wake her ass up otherwise she ain't gone get to work –

He goes out the door. **Nina** *comes downstairs carrying Hannah.*

Nina Miles, is everything OK?

Miles Where's Mrs. Chae? Why isn't she here taking care of the baby?

Nina I told her to come in a little later this morning, I wanted to talk to you about her. I think we have a problem.

Miles What're you talking about? She seems to be working out great.

Eric *hurries downstairs carrying a pair of boxer shorts.*

Eric This is fucked up, man. This is out of line, this is fucked up.

Miles What's going on, man?

Eric My ringgits are gone.

Miles and **Nina** What?

Eric *holds out his boxer shorts.*

Eric I hid the money in here – I folded these up and put them underneath the mattress in the sofa bed – not the most inventive hiding place, I admit, but I figured we were all family here.

Miles Man, what is going on around here?

Eric You got a lot of new people coming in and out of this house. The tenant passes by all our bedrooms to get to his floor. He's got a lock on the door to his apartment, but all our rooms are wide open. Maybe he took your camcorder. What do you know about that guy?

Miles Not much.

Eric If you ask me – you guys need to close ranks. Clean house. How much is he paying in rent?

Nina Twelve hundred a month.

Eric I could pay that. Or close to that. I've got some money in the bank, plus I've built in salaries for me and you in the business proposal.

Nina *looks at* **Miles** *– you're not going for this, are you?*

Miles We can't just kick him out, we gave him a two-year lease.

Eric I should be part of this community too. It'll be good for the profile of the business.

Miles We'll see what we can do to make that happen, man.

Nina We will?

Eric Let me go upstairs and have another look. (*He goes upstairs.*)

Nina (*to* **Miles**) We need twelve hundred for the upstairs apartment. I cannot meet our mortgage payments without – I can't take it on, Miles. I can't have one more thing on my back.

Miles It's not going to be on your back. Eric said he's going to pay rent.

Nina No, he's not. Eric came here with the intention of getting us to give him a free place to live.

Miles He just got off a plane! He came here to meet the baby.

Nina We haven't seen or heard from him in months –

Miles That's usual for him.

Nina Then on the day we move in, he shows up at our doorstep with no place to live. He comes up with this business idea, says he's got the money to get it started, gets you all riled up about it, then all of a sudden – the money's gone. He never had the money, Miles.

Miles You never saw it, but I saw it.

Nina He probably bought it at a party store with a pack of tropical drink umbrellas. What bothers me the most, Miles, is that we've always laughed at your brother . . . together, we've indulged him, we'd listen to his stories and wink wink at each other knowing that it was all a big show . . . but now I look over at you, and you're rapt. You're like a kid listening to his con man uncle and hanging on every word. (*Hannah starts to cry.*)

Miles You really think that I'm that gullible?

Nina I think you're . . . vulnerable, I think you think you're cast out in some way . . . and that your brother's going to bring you in. But you're not cast out. Hannah and I are your family, now. Why don't you hold her. She'll stop crying if you do. (**Nina** *tries to hand* **Miles** *the baby. He doesn't take her.*)

Miles No, she won't. She only cries harder.

Nina Only when she senses your fear. Just focus on how much you love her, and she'll calm down.

Miles You know she's going to reject me.

Nina No, she won't.

Miles She only wants you. I don't have anything she needs.

Nina Miles, take her –

Miles No, you want me to fail. You want me to. (*He storms off.* **Nina** *turns to* **Hannah**.)

Nina It's OK, sweetie, Daddy loves you. Daddy loves you.

Scene Ten

Office. **Kit** *is working,* **Nina** *is nursing Hannah.*

Kit Nina, you can't take time away from work to look for a new nanny. I won't let you.

Nina It won't take that long this time, I'm not going to hold out for a Korean woman. I'll take anyone who isn't going to poison my baby with racist thoughts.

Kit I think you're blowing this whole thing out of proportion.

Nina I'm not. I know that as sure as someday Hannah's going to fall off her bike and scrape her knee, that someone is going to call her a chink, and a nigger –

Kit Cover her ears!

Nina I can't stop it. I can't protect her from it – I can't stop it from happening to me as a grown woman. Last month, I was standing in the front lawn of my childhood home, where I used to play cowboys and Indians, and ride my banana seat Schwinn, and eat Creamsicles from the ice cream man, and some teenager shouted from a car, 'Go back to Vietnam –'

Kit It's horrible, it's embarrassing, but I still think that's completely different from what Mrs. Chae –

Nina My whole bright idea about hiring a Korean nanny was to give Hannah a reason to be proud to be Korean. I thought if she could, I don't know, speak the language, have some sense of belonging – it would help those names bounce off of her. We had the same reasons for wanting to raise Hannah in a mostly black neighborhood.

Kit Look, you guys are making great choices for her –

Nina No, we're not, we're failing in every way. The Korean nanny's denying her blackness, the black neighbors are throwing rocks through our window . . . Miles won't hold our baby and . . . I see how hard you're working and I'm trying my best – I know I'm not pulling my weight – but I swear I am giving this everything I have left. And all I ask from Miles, all I want him to do . . . (*A beat for* **Nina**.) . . . is to be in it with me. (**Nina** *covers her mouth to hide that she's crying – something she saw her mother do.*)

Kit Hey – (**Kit** *walks over, kneels in front of* **Nina**.)

Nina But instead, he wants to know when we're going to start having sex again. And I can't – I swear, Kit, I don't have anything left to give. (**Nina** *hides her face by nuzzling Hannah.*)

Kit When we're in Barcelona, I'm gonna take you to this fantastic little tapas place I read about. We'll eat little plates of fried octopus eyes and beef snout on toast while we watch them build our building. We're going to make the deadline, I'll make sure of it.

Nina *nods but aims all her need at Hannah, kissing her, holding her close.* **Kit** *goes to touch* **Nina** *supportively, but* **Nina** *has closed the circle – there's only room for her and her baby.* **Kit** *stands up, walks back to her drawing table. She draws for a minute.*

Nina Eric tell you about the missing money?

Kit I heard about it.

Nina What do you think? Do you think someone really stole it?

Kit I think it's a ghost. I think that first night when your window got smashed, the ghost of all the neglected communities past – who couldn't get the city to fix their sidewalks, or keep their electricity going on hot days, let alone provide them with a local source of organic half-and-half – wafted in here and is trying to spook you into leaving.

Kit *puts something down on the table,* **Nina** *picks it up – a matchbook from a restaurant.*

Nina What's this?

Kit It has the restaurant's name and address on Smith Street. The food was good, you and Miles should go there some time.

Nina What? Ohmigod. Oh please God, please please please let it not be –

Kit It's new, so it's not that crowded yet. They let me sit for a while.

Nina You waited for me? Why didn't you call?

Kit I have some dignity, you know.

Nina Why didn't you remind me during the day?

Kit Just, let it pass, Nina.

Nina No, it's totally my fault. I can't believe I forgot to show up for your fortieth birth [day] –

Kit Just stop talking about it, OK? I don't care that you didn't show up, I don't care. I ate dinner, went to a bar, I fucked a guy in the bathroom – it was perfect. The best birthday ever. All I want from you, Nina, is for you to do your work. Fucking do your work. I can't finish this model by myself, not with less than six weeks left. I waited for you, Nina, I could've started two months ago without you, but you told me to wait.

Nina I shouldn't have done that. It's just – I never . . . it's like this feral – this animal drive to take care of my daughter. I can't even apologize for it, it fucking feels right.

Kit So you shouldn't be trying to work.

Nina I want to work. I don't want to be a stay-at-home mom. I know it doesn't add up, OK? But I still love my work.

Kit Look, Nina, you're a good mom – my mom, she took Dexatrim when she was pregnant with me because she didn't want to get fat. And I – I don't think women should have children if they're not going to be like you. But this work is all I have and I fucking want to win this competition.

Nina I do too.

Kit Don't say that.

Nina I know it doesn't make sense to you –

Kit Nina, I'm forty years old, I already don't have what I thought I would have by now but I know I can make beautiful buildings. It's not fucking fair for you to hold me back. Between Mrs. Tillman's unreasonable demands and your constant distractions, we're way behind already.

Nina I'll take care of Mrs. Tillman.

Kit No, you won't.

Nina When she calls today, tell her I'll meet her at the house.

Kit That's nice of you to finally offer, but Mrs. Tillman isn't going to call today because I told her we quit.

Nina What – ?

Kit This morning, she insisted I go all the way to the Upper East Side just to show me some dust from the living room had 'penetrated' her bedroom. And I just – I fucking had it.

Nina You quit – you – . . . you quit before she finished paying us?

Kit Now we can focus on the model.

Nina Kit – how could you do that to me?

Kit We need to concentrate on the model.

Nina Mrs. Tillman is my livelihood. That money is what my family lives on.

Kit We split the money but I do all the work.

Nina I designed the plans with you. I did my share until the baby was born. (**Nina** *thinks a beat, looks at the baby, then picks up her bag. Calling upstairs:*)Mrs. Chae? (*To* **Kit**.) I'm going to apologize to Mrs. Tillman.

Kit Go ahead.

Nina (*yells*) Mrs. Chae! (*To* **Kit**.) I'm getting this job back, Kit.

Kit Fine, you can run up there every time a nail gets hammered in crooked.

Nina Mrs. Chae! (**Mrs. Chae** *rushes downstairs*.)

Mrs. Chae Sorry, Nina, I could not hear you.

Nina I need you to take Hannah right now.

Mrs. Chae Yes, yes, I will take. (**Mrs. Chae** *reaches for the baby, says in Korean, 'It's OK, baby, Mommy is very busy so Grandma will take care of you'.*)

Nina What did you just say?

Mrs. Chae Mh?

Nina What did you say to her?

Mrs. Chae I say you are very busy, so I will take her upstairs –

Nina Did you call yourself 'halmoni'?

Mrs. Chae . . . Yes?

Nina Grandma?

Mrs. Chae In Korean language, a child will call any woman my age –

Nina When I come back, we need to talk. (**Nina** *flies out the door.*)

Kit I'm sorry –

Mrs. Chae (*consoling herself, but aiming it at Hannah*) It's OK, it's OK, I know everything will be OK.

Mrs. Chae *heads upstairs as* **Eric** *walks in through the front door. He walks up to* **Kit**, *stands close to her.*

Eric Hey.

Kit Hi.

Eric Now I know why you take a car service, it's a bitch to get here from your house by train. Do you feel hungover?

Kit Eric, I don't have the money.

Eric You didn't get to stop by the bank on your way in?

Kit No.

Eric Well, you still have a couple hours –

Kit I'm not going to loan you any money. I'm sure both of us said things last night that we don't intend to follow through on. We were drunk, we were having a good time –

Eric You called me up, lured me to that restaurant with your sob story –

Kit I invited you to join me, you ordered the most expensive thing on the menu, I picked up the tab . . . everything that happened after that was fun, but it wasn't worth five thousand dollars. You're just going to have to tell your brother you never had the money.

Eric I had the money. I had it until last night.

Kit Well, I'm sure you'll find a way around it, Eric, you're fast on your feet.

Scene Eleven

The next day. Living room. **Miles** *comes downstairs in a suit and jacket – he's missing a tie. He starts looking through some boxes, pulling out kitchen utensils from one box, winter clothes from another . . .* **Eric** *comes downstairs wearing a dress shirt and tie.*

Eric You look sharp, man.

Miles I'm looking for my ties –

Eric You don't need a tie, you look crisp without one.

Miles *lifts a box off the top of a stack and looks in the box underneath it.*

Miles I want to make a strong appearance. Those tea lounge people probably wear thrift store T-shirts and flip-flops.

Eric Don't bring up the tea lounge unless he brings it up first. As far as I know, they haven't put down any money so we'll be on even ground.

Miles *pulls his camcorder out of a box.*

Miles My camcorder . . . that's what I did with it. I put it in here after Reggie came in with his chandelier and was roaming all over the place.

Eric Well, alright. That's great. (*A beat.*)

Miles So, if my camcorder was never stolen . . . what happened to your ringgits?

Eric I don't know, man.

Miles Eric . . . tell me straight up. Were those ringgits real?

Eric Of course they were real.

Miles Where are they, man? I don't believe Walter took them.

Eric Oh, I think he has them.

Miles Eric –

Eric What you want to do is watch his checking account. You have all his information from his credit report, right? Watch his account for the next couple weeks and you just might see a deposit for five grand show up. (*Beat.*)

Miles Then, what, he's going to tell me he's moving out?

Eric Could be.

Miles Is that what you did with the money, Eric? You wanted me and Nina to think Walter stole it, but really you paid him so he would move out? (*Beat.*)

Eric I offered it to him, yeah.

Miles Man – that money was supposed to be for our business.

Eric You want me to commit to this business but what're you doing for me? You own this whole brownstone, but you'd rather price-gouge a stranger than give your brother a home.

Miles We're not making decisions right now based on preference – we need to make ends meet.

Eric You always make ends meet, Miles. Why're you acting like you don't know that everything's gonna turn out your way – it always does.

Miles You think things just snap into place – ?

Eric Nina's gonna win her competition, the store's going to be an instant success, Hannah's gonna be the poster baby for the new Benetton campaign . . . you're going to have it all, like you always do – why do you have to deny me a piece of it?

Miles Man, I've earned what I have. This is what I've always worked for. But you've been flitting around the world, cobbling together this little job with that one, never building anything, never digging roots, and now you're looking at me and saying 'I want some of that'?

Eric You don't think I want a house, a steady career and a family? What do you think I am, a circus performer? A pirate? Of course I want those things but I've never been able to work for them because I'm not allowed to have what Miles has. Miles is the super-baby, the poor little black boy left on our doorstep who goes on to save the town, and my job in life is to make sure I never over-shadow him.

Miles Mom and Dad gave you every chance they gave me. They cut everything straight down the line.

Eric I can see why you'd want to remember things that way, but they weren't. You were always the golden boy, the miracle . . . I could never live up to it, Miles.

Miles Did you try? All you had to do was try.

Eric What, you think because I'm white, because I know who my biological parents are, because I can walk down the street of our hometown without some old lady calling the cops – that every door in the world is open to me? But they're not, Miles. The doors are for you.

Miles You want what I have? Do you know what it is like for me to look at my baby, and see her brown skin, and curly hair, and long eyelashes and know she got them from me – but I don't know who I come from? What am I giving her? What have I passed on? I don't know. Maybe there's some disease that skips a generation, and I've given it to her. Or maybe my great-great-grandfather was a Civil War hero, but I'll never be able to tell Hannah about it. All I can do is take her to Mom and Dad's house in Indiana, where Mom can explain every little tchochke and how it was handed down to her . . . and dad can break out the family albums going back seven generations – but when she looks at those people in the photographs, she won't see herself, she won't see me.

Eric You think I see myself in those old pictures? All I see are a bunch of old people in stiff suits who had sixteen children and were half-dead from lung cancer by the time they were our age.

Miles That's how you make it hard for yourself, Eric. Trying to invent yourself from scratch.

Eric You did. Why don't you think your history enough for Hannah?

Nina *walks upstairs, notices the camcorder.*

Nina You found the camcorder.

Miles . . . Yeah.

Nina Where was it?

Miles . . . Where I put it.

Eric I'm gonna go to this meeting, man.

Nina Miles, I want to fire Mrs. Chae this afternoon.

Eric If you want to catch up with me . . . (Eric leaves.)

Scene Twelve

Living room. **Mrs. Chae** *crosses the living room to get to the door,* **Miles** *sees her.*

Miles Mrs. Chae, are you leaving?

Mrs. Chae Yes.

Miles You left your lunch –

Mrs. Chae Not my lunch. It's jap chae for you and Nina. You have it for dinner. (*She heads for the door.*)

Miles You'll still be with us for two more weeks, right?

Mrs. Chae I am old woman with nothing to do. Husband is dead, no job, what I'm going to do?

Miles I – I don't know what to say, you've been wonderful to Hannah . . . but –

Mrs. Chae I try so hard, I want to make you and Nina happy. What have I done so wrong?

Nina *walks upstairs from the office, having overheard the last part.* **Mrs. Chae** *takes a step towards her.*

Mrs. Chae Nina – (*Without thinking,* **Mrs. Chae** *speaks to* **Nina** *in Korean:*) Nina, you're such a good girl, hm? Give me another chance. I'll do everything right.

Nina I don't – understand you.

Mrs. Chae You are good girl, such a good mommy, hm? Best mommy. My daughter, she hire the British nanny to take care of my grandson. She tell me she don't want Mommy to take care of grandson. She don't want grandson to speak the bad English like Mommy. Kyung Soon say when she was little girl, she speak the English like Mommy, go to school and say 'preejing', it's 'preejing outside. And children laugh laugh.

Nina . . . Pleasing?

Mrs. Chae So cold, it's preejing and Kyung Soon come home and say, 'Mommy, you are dummy. You are such dummy!'

Miles . . . Kids . . .

Mrs. Chae So, she hire another nanny, not me. British nanny take care of my grandson.

Nina You said your daughter has her son in daycare at her firm?

Mrs. Chae Now I am telling you. British nanny comes at seven o'clock in morning, stay until eight o'clock at night. Then, Tibetan nanny comes on weekend, so Kyung Soon and husband can play golf.

Miles She has two nannies?

Mrs. Chae Yes.

Miles That's a lot of nannies.

Nina So . . . you've been lying about all of that?

Mrs. Chae I tell you the truth now. Before, I want[ed] you to hire me, I see nice family, two good parents – happy baby . . . I want[ed] to be in this house, I want[ed] to be in this [family.] . . .

Miles *turns to* **Nina**.

Miles Nina, maybe firing her isn't the right thing to do.

Nina (*to Mrs. Chae*) I know people like you. Some of my mom's friends, they came to this country in the sixties, people taunted them, told them their food stank, their faces were flat, called them gook, chink, chingaling –

Miles (*to* **Nina**)Whoa –

Nina Made them feel like shit for what? For walking down the street, for sending their kids to school, for starting a business. For that they got beaten up, their stores got vandalized, right?

Mrs. Chae . . . Yes. My husband and I had a gift store in Yonkers. Somebody paint all over the windows.

Nina So what did you do?

Mrs. Chae We cleaned the windows. My husband and I scrubbed the paint off with our hands –

Nina You went looking for someone you could feel superior to. And you picked black people.

Miles Nina, I think you need – you need to take a step back.

Nina It makes me mad, it makes me ashamed of being Korean, fucking racists.

Miles Mrs. Chae is new to this country, she's from another generation . . . I don't like what she said to Hannah but I don't think she's a racist –

Nina Bullshit. My mom was all those things and she never said anything like that. Even in that shitty little town we lived in. Mrs. Chae is from Queens, she has no excuse.

Miles Well, she'll learn –

Nina Who taught my mom? Nobody. It was in her heart. (*Half beat.*)

Miles Oh, I get it. I get it now, Nina. It's like you hired Mrs. Chae to be your mom. And you fired her because she's not.

Nina Geezus, Miles, is it too much to ask you to take my side?

Miles Side – ?! What do you want this to be, Nina?

Nina I want you to . . . I want you to defend me.

Miles *looks at* **Mrs. Chae**, *who has kept her head down, turns back to* **Nina**.

Miles Nobody's attacking you!

Nina That's not the point.

Miles (*to* **Mrs. Chae**) Excuse her, Mrs. Chae, Nina's under a tremendous amount of press[ure] –

Mrs. Chae She is working very hard. (*Moves towards* **Nina**, *who turns to* **Miles**.)

Nina Don't fucking apologize for me.

Miles You just said you wanted me –

Nina Not to apologize. I want you to – Christ, if you think I'm being unreasonable –

Miles Yes!

Nina Then, fucking . . . hold me or something.

Miles You're not making me want to hold you.

Nina I have to do something – ?

Miles Well, you're not making me feel like it –

Nina So, making all the money for the family doesn't qualify me for a hug?

Miles Why d'you – (*Looks at* **Mrs. Chae**.)Why d'you have to say that?

Nina Because I'm tired of having to tiptoe around your ego. My work is totally stressful, I'm not giving the baby the time I want – but at the end of the day, I don't get to vent to you. If I say anything about the pressure that is fucking crushing me – you think I'm trying to make you feel bad.

Miles So, what, you're discounting the fact that most of the down payment for this house came from cashing in my stock options?

Nina I'm not counting money. I could give a shit about the money, Miles.

Miles This is obviously about money. You resent me for not being able to provide for my daughter. Look at this house – it's crumbling down around us. We can't afford to fix it, we can't afford to live in it. This is no way to raise a baby. We never should have . . . we were not ready to have a baby.

Kit *walks upstairs.*

Kit (*to* **Nina**) Is everything OK?

Nina You're blaming me because we have a healthy, beautiful baby?

Miles No, I'm blaming you because we have a baby that I don't deserve.

Nina She needs you to love her, Miles.

Miles It's not enough.

The doorbell rings. **Reggie** *appears on the other side of the broken window.*

Reggie Hey yo, son, I got the guys with the glass, they gonna install it.

Nina (*looks at* **Miles**) Now? They were supposed to have come at two, here they are at six-thirty.

Mrs. Chae That's Korean time.

Miles You deal with this, Nina, I'm – (*He heads upstairs.*)

Nina (*calling after him*) You're what? (**Miles** *continues upstairs.* **Nina** *looks at Mrs. Chae.*) Fuck him, man, fuck all of you. I had this perfect, precious baby and all anyone wants to do is blame me for how she's changed our lives. Of course she's changed our lives. What was so fucking good about them before?

Reggie *knocks on the front door then opens it.*

Reggie (*to* **Nina**) Yo, mommy, they gone have to take the rest of that old glass out first. So I'm'a have to put some drop cloth down there so you don't get no glass shards on the floor.

Nina OK, Reggie. (*A beat.*)

Reggie I'm'a go to the hardware store, so, you gone have to hit me so I can get the drop cloth.

Nina (*handing him a twenty*) Here.

Reggie I'm'a need sixty.

Nina Sixty dollars for drop cloth?

Reggie OK, forty.

Nina I don't have forty dollars, Reggie.

Kit I have forty dollars. (*Reaches into wallet.*) Oh, no, I don't.

Nina (*to* **Mrs. Chae**) Do you have any money?

Mrs. Chae Sorry.

Nina Just – fuck it, Reggie.

Reggie Alright, thirty dollars, I'll get the cheap stuff.

Nina Forget it – forget the whole thing. Tell the guys they have to come back another – (*Smash. The sound of the workmen smashing the glass to make way for the new window.*) Goddamnit – !

Reggie What the fuck! Stupid motherfucker!

He heads for the door. Another smash. **Nina** *releases a sound – something between a growl and a war cry. She picks up a prybar and walks to the window and starts smashing the glass as* **Kit** *and* **Mrs. Chae** *watch.* **Reggie**, *on the other side, backs up.* **Nina** *takes several whacks at it until there's little window left. The sound of Hannah crying.* **Nina** *takes a breath, her demeanor changes.* **Mrs. Chae** *also responds to the sound. They both head for the stairs –*

Nina (*to* **Mrs. Chae**) I'll get her. (*She just gets to the stairs when* **Miles** *appears at the top of the stairs holding the baby.*)

Miles I got her. (*He walks downstairs towards* **Nina**. *Knows the words.*) 'Hush little baby, don't say a word. Papa's gonna buy you a mockingbird. If that mockingbird won't sing, Papa's gonna buy you a diamond ring.' (*He meets up with* **Nina**.) You want me to teach you the rest of the words?

Nina Yes.

Miles (*sings*) 'If that diamond ring turns brass. (**Nina** *repeats after him as they walk towards the window.*)

Nina (*sings*) 'Turns brass.'

Miles (*sings*) 'Papa's gonna buy you a looking-glass.'

Nina (*sings*) ' – looking-glass.'

Miles (*sings*) 'If that looking-glass gets broke –'

They stop at the window. They look out into the street for a while. We start to hear the sounds of the neighborhood. Indeterminate voices in conversation. A basketball being bounced, music from a car stereo.

Nina You know what I think that rock coming through our window was?

Miles What?

Nina A meteorite. A chip off of some billion-year-old comet that came crashing through here to let out all the ghosts, all the stories, all the history . . . To let us know . . . we can make up the words ourselves.

The sounds from the street swell as Nina and Miles look out.

End

Property list

Boxes of stuff
Pizza
Plates
Cell phone
Beers
Rock
Plywood, tools
Camera
Blue currency
BabyBjörn
Chandelier
Paper
Computer
Architectural model, model pieces, glue
Keys
Bag of food
Purses
Boxes of tiles
Plastic bags with groceries
Wallet, money
Laundry, laundry bag
Large suitcases
Photo
Tray with two bowls of soup, spoons
Tape measure
Boxer shorts
Matchbook
Camcorder
Crowbar

Sound effects

Baby crying
Gurgling
Bang
Cell phone
Glass smashing
Doorbell
Office phone
Car horn
Scraping and prying
Street noises

Section III
The Distant Present: History, Mythology, and Sexuality

Marcus Gardley

. . . And Jesus Moonwalks the Mississippi

'A play is a poem standing up.'

Federico Garcia Lorca

'I've known rivers:
I've known rivers ancient as the world and older than the flow of human blood in human veins.
My soul has grown deep like the rivers.
I bathed in the Euphrates when dawns were young.
I built my hut near the Congo and it lulled me to sleep.
I looked upon the Nile and raised the pyramids above it.
I heard the singing of the Mississippi when Abe Lincoln went down to New Orleans, and I've seen its muddy bosom turn all golden in the sunset.
I've known rivers:
Ancient, dusky rivers.
My soul has grown deep like the rivers.'

'The Negro Speaks of Rivers,' Langston Hughes

'. . . A slave does not abide in the house forever, but a son abides forever. Therefore if the Son makes you free, you shall be free indeed.'

Jesus Christ, John 35–36, The Bible

Key:

–	Interrupt previous dialogue
/	Overlap dialogue
CAPITALS	Singing or verse
Italics	French

Characters

The Quilter

Miss Ssippi *is a beautifully large, Black woman. She gives new meaning to the word elegance although she appears over-worked and always on the 'run'.*

The Threads

Free Girl *is ten, half Black, half White. Her face is caked in white powder and her hair is always tied up. She wears a tea dress.*
Blance Verse *or* **Blanchie** *is also ten, White. She wears short pants and an old army vest, which hangs loosely on her.*
Cadence Marie Verse *is Blanche's mother. She is White and old enough to be embarrassed by her age. She is always dolled up: blush on the cheeks, rouge on the lips and gin on the tongue.*
Jean Verse *is White, thin and a romantic. He wears a white silk shirt, Confederate slacks and a dark fedora. His voice is like the wind, it caters to the trees.*
Demeter *is old enough to die wise. She is Black, her hair as silver as trout and her skin just as smooth. She is built like a good man, one who's been fighting all her life. She even walks like one, women notice her. Men pretend not to. She wears a tattered petticoat, ripped slacks and a head scarf. Perhaps, a man should play her.* **Damascus** *is her former being.*
Yankee Pot Roast *is juicy with lots of fat hanging off him. He is White and red all over – a bundle of joy and naiveté.*
Jesus *is Black, a warm beauty. He wears sandals and a robe. The actor that plays him plays* **The Great Tree**.
Brer Bit, *the house Negro.*

The stage
The world is a quilt and each story a thread. Sometimes the threads overlap.

The time
May 22, 1863, the siege of Vicksburg, Mississippi and May 25, 1865, Proctorville, Louisiana. The action takes place simultaneously on these two days and in the span of 24 hours.

1. The Word – a promise, the gospel

Dusk.

In the distance there is a wood with trees that reach up like black, incredible arms praising God. To the right, **The Great Tree** *stands bowing his head in shadow while dusk, red as southern clay is seasoned over the field. It reveals* **Miss Ssippi River** *who is black, blue; her quilted dress wide as all get out of town.*

Miss Ssippi River The hot, hard dusk hangs like ear bobs of blood from meat
Cripplin the half moon into a crescent, chipped tooth
Tremblin some gum tree like voo doo bones 'bove my belly.
M. I. crooked letter, crooked letter I. Crooked letter, crooked letter I.
Suh Sippi: I be Miss Ssippi
Though due south they call me Sip
For I'm simply a taste and not a swallow.
Though thick as God's thigh I'm merely a wink of water blue
Mostly mud, mostly immovable
Moved mostly to wrap my big river ways round your waist
And tease you a taste of a tale long untold old.
A tale without a tail, without a head
The gut of somethin
A stream
A thread of history needin to be needled-in
Knotted into your know-how
A Poem
Ripped from the ripples of an ancient rock throw
Hear it. Here it comes
Crumblin from a cloud.
A drop.

A thread falls from the sky.

A splash!
A patch of your past stirs closer

Come, lean in quietly closer
And I shall quilt it into your ear
With this steadfast yarn.

Stroke of lightning.

Hold steady! There pierces the needle.

Roll of thunder.

Hold fast! There spins the thread.

Damascus, *a runaway, rises from her spread.*

Miss Ssippi River A touch of man makes our material.
To seem the inseam of this seamless spread . . .
Arms.
Spread legs. Like Christ across the cross
He lays upon my low tide
Stroking liquid muscle into undulation
Pullin, paddlin through my 'hind parts like the crocodile
Half his head hung above black water
His sharp Egyptian eyes cutting through the night,
through the wood
Wading, waiting for some whistle, rustle of death
Whooo . . .
The old owl rattles her fat neck.
Whooo . . . this here be?
Awl hushhhh
I gush: he be Damascus Free
He be the hunted, not the hunt.
Hidin. Man been ridin my tide way back where
Arkanzest met Ten'see
He be babe in my breast till he reaches Ocean
Till my last wave beaches: 'bye you'
Down. Delta bound where I open my mouth he'll
spew like down home blues do
'Out of your belly' and rooted
I'll plant him: a tree by the rivers of this war-torn earth
For it's far as I can cradle him
Rocked in the hymn of Louisianne's skirt.
I hope he'll sleep.

Miss Ssippi *rocks as if in a rocking chair.*

Creak.
        Rest child.
Creak.
        Dream . . .
Creak.
A choir ah crickets grease their legs . . .
Paws. . .
And feet creep along my muddy spine
Kickin' clumps, clod pockets into my spread
Whooo . . .
The old owl wobbles her fat head.
Flit and flap! Flap and flit.
She takes off in flight.
Blood hounds sniff . . .
Soldiers breathe.
Shotguns cock   a light!
A light bright as death unveils him in the night

Two soldiers shine lights on **Damascus** *in the arms of* **Miss Ssippi River**.

Faces white and coats grey
Canons crownin' a city wall
And we be stuck in the moat, in the mud
'Get out the wata nigger!'
Them soldiers shout.
I scout for a way out, babe clutched in arms
But there be no where to flood.
I weep deep. I wail!
Tides wide as my waist weigh him down
Drag him 'neath my dress!
Hold him!
I hold him sweet Jesus
Till I can wade pass this Vicksburg fortress.
Blood hounds bark!
Shot guns spit bullets into my breast
Bugle horns blast!

And
he
sinks . . .
Folds, unfurls inside my thick-ass mesh
Fightin, reachin for his last breath
He tries to swim
(If I were his momma I'd drown him.)
But I be just rivers: fathers of rivers
Mothers of livin waters
It's my nature to release.
So I set him Free
Knowing he won't find peace or sleep.
I set him Free

Time. **Miss Ssippi** *releases him.*

And he rose
Like the Son
Rose through waters: petals, thorns and stem
Rose into them Confederate arms.
Singin':

Damascus (*singing*) PO'EM

Miss Ssippi As they snatched him from round my neck.

The soldiers drag **Damascus** *away.*

Damascus JUST WANNA GET MY GIRL

Miss Ssippi He sung
As they dragged him into the wood
Bawling, wet.

Damascus NO MATTER I GOT T'SEARCH THIS WHOLE WORLE . . . PO'EM. (*repeats as he is dragged off*)

Miss Ssippi He sung . . .
Till I heard the last lilt of his song.
But there's more story to this quilt chil'ren
So hear it, add your thread to it, then pass it 'long.

She pulls a thick thread from her quilt.

2. Line – a verse, a stitch

Evening.

Free Girl *grabs the thread and uses it as a clothesline.*

Free Girl (*singing*) EYES AH SEEN THE GLORA OF THE COMIN' OF THE LAWD
HE TRAMPLIN' OUT THE VINTAH WHERE DEE GRAPES OF WRATH AH STORE. HE HAS LOOSED DUH FATEFUL LINGHTNIN' OF HIS TERRA-BOWL SWIFF SWORD. HIS TROOF IS MARCHIN'

Miss Ssippi *exits revealing a pasture of dead soldiers. Lights fade over* **Free** *and come up on* **Yankee Pot Roast**, *a Union soldier (lantern lit with a bugle hung over his breast) covers a grave with his shovel. Enter* **Jean Verse** *hiding in shadow.*

Jean Verse – On hook moon nights like dese. Dey say its bad luck t' bury dead.

Yankee Pot Roast Whose there? Show yourself.

Jean Verse Can't show myself. I'm wiiiind. I'm just breezin' by to whisper dis in your Yankee ear: deys watchin' you. Duh ghosts.

Yankee Pot Roast Ghosts? I don't believe in ghosts.

Jean Verse Dey believe in you. Just look, one's crawlin' up your leg as I speak –

Jean *blows air up the boy's leg.*

Yankee Pot Roast – Ho-hey, where?! I don't see no ghosts. Show your face sir!

Jean Verse Ain't got no face. Told you, I'm wind. I'm all mouth. But I see things people don't wanna see. I tell stories people don't wanna hear.

Yankee Pot Roast And I don't want to hear you. Go! Blow away –

Jean Verse – You're not getting my drift boy, dey see you. Stench of dese dead and echo of your shovel brought em to banquet. Now they circlin, preyin over your fat ass body, whisperin: who wants his leg?! Who wants the Yankee's thigh?!

Yankee Pot Roast I'm not afraid, I said! I have only the fear of God. And I will not leave till I bury these men. They've waited three days in the hot sun – their flesh reeking for peace. I will not part till they're beneath this earth!

Jean Verse Then you will part the Earth. You will die –

Jean *moves toward him.*

Yankee Pot Roast – Hold, I hear your feet. You come closer. I'll cut your heart out with this shovel.

Yankee Pot Roast *raises his shovel.*

Jean Verse Can't cut me, I'm air. It means I don't scar. I simply . . . embrace.

Jean *grabs him.*

Yankee Pot Roast Let go! Release me or I'll smite thee Satan with my sword!

Jean Verse Hush ya maw and give me dat horn.

Jean *takes the bugle.*

Yankee Pot Roast No . . . THIEF! You're a thief!!!

Jean *covers the boy's mouth.*

Jean Verse Hush, I said! Confederate soldiers twelve o'clock. Two got rifles, one a musket. You wanna get ate, keep squealin'. You wanna live to kiss ya momma, lie in dis mud like a pot belly. Lie in dis mud! –

Yankee Pot Roast *bites* **Jean**'*s hand.*

Ah Moan Dieu, you bit me you –

Yankee Pot Roast – Give me my horn!

A shot echoes in the night.

Jean Verse – Dang blasted!

Yankee Pot Roast Oh a shot! They shot a shot!

Jean Verse – You bit me, you son of a – !

Yankee Pot Roast – Guns! They got guns. I'm going to be shot.

Jean Verse You're going to be strangled.

Jean *squeezes the boy's throat.*

Yankee Pot Roast Oh . . . no . . . AIR!

Jean Verse Shhh. Dey runnin'. Let em play river.

Yankee Pot Roast I . . . need . . . air . . .

Jean Verse Shh, I said. Dey passin'. Let em pass. (*Time.*) Now dere. Dey done passed.

Jean *releases the boy who coughs.*

Yankee Pot Roast You could have killed me/you

Jean Verse /You one noisy Yank, you know dat?

Yankee Pot Roast I'm a bugler. I blow the bugle. It's my duty to make noise. Give me my horn!

Jean Verse Not on your life, it's my booty now. I'm ah add it to my treasures and sell it for high profit like you Yanks do when you barter southern goods. Taxin and tariffin' us farmers while ya live high off the hog thinkin we gone feed on ya scraps. Well, not moi. Not Jean Verse. I'm ah take my debt off your dead till I'm plump with just desserts.

Yankee Pot Roast Stealing from dead soldiers? But that makes you a grave robber, sir?

Jean Verse Well, somebody give dis boy a cookie. I'm also a deserter and a mean drunk.

Yankee Pot Roast I should turn you in. I should run and tell those Confeds on picket duty who you are Mr Wind. Give me back my horn or I'll do it.

Jean Verse No you won't. Cause you gone be my pig: my Yankee Pot Roast. I'm a call you dat cause ya my dish and the name'll remind ya your edible. And I'll eat ya if you try and turn me in. Now get up! You gone crawl through the mud and carry my bags home. I done had enough of dis war, now its time to fetch my Po'em.

Jean *ties a rope around his neck and drags him off through the mud. Lights return to* **Free** *who is hanging clothes.*

Free (*singing*) IN THE BEAUTIES OF THE LILACS CHRIST WAS BORN ACROSS DEE SEA. WID A GLORA IN HIS BOSOM DAT TRANSFIGURE YOU AND ME AS HE DIED TO MAKE MEN HOLEE, LET US DIE TO MAKE EM FREE HIS TROOF IS MARCHIN –

The Great Tree *lifts his head. He is a black god with terrible wooden limbs that arch from his back like wings, his hair is long and locked with coral shells.* **Damascus** *hangs from his limbs by a noose.*

The Great Tree – On horseback they hoisted him high
'gainst my haunch!
This man-child who held to pride like hate.
Lovingly, leisurely with the noose taut round his neck
They pitched the twice stitched, kneaded cord
And curled a knot into the night's blood.
String! Draw! Heave!
They strung him from the steed's bare back
The cord snatching at his neck carved a cut in my bark
And I screamed: SAP!
Bowed. Bending before this prince of God and Black.
The nerves in his neck numbed
Splitting his song and he hummed
Hung. Hung-round like heaven in all his glory
Hung-round like hallelujah on the tongue

Hung-round like happy tears caught in the crevice of an eye
But he did not break. O! The Black prince did not break
Some curse for trying to crucify him without a crown, I'll testify
How ignorant. How southern.
Trust. He could've killed them each with the poetry bleeding from his bottom lip.
Could have called them each by name
You! Mister! Master! Liar!
You! Killer. Massacre. Fucker of Mother!
You! Father! Father with my eyes!
Nature shall rot out your root.
But he remained humble.
Not even a hard man's weep was heard
As his song, softly began to unknot the noose.

Damascus (*singing*) PO'EM.
JUST WANNA GET MY GIRL.

The Great Tree This song, this neck: not quite 'nigger'
It had beauty wide and Black
And strength that broke into the rope like an epiphany into the poet's ponder
Unknotting its history it split and uncoiled
And cried: AHHHHHH!
A cut! Quick in rage! A solider cut the prick
Cut the balls and boiled the blood
It spun, the spew spat out in flame
Frightened them out of their skins
And fell into the night like a wicked stream.
The soldiers fled.
His seed fell at my roots as the cord cracked
His body fell 'cross my trunk, my limbs
This piece of love lied like a child
In my limber lap.

The Great Tree *rocks* **Damascus**.

Damascus (*fading*) A wind raps against this tree . . .

The Great Tree Rest, child.

Damascus A warm breeze billows . . .

The Great Tree Dream. Beneath this quilt of leaves.

A blanket of quilted leaves falls over him.

Damascus Poem! Where's my Po'em?

The Great Tree You must rest.

Damascus I don't want to be dead. Please. Not before I say goodbye to my daughter.

The Great Tree Drink. Lap. Healing waters flow from the tips of my high branch. Dew drops drip. Lap and rest. Sleep.

Damascus Sweet. The water's so . . .

The Great Tree Dream. Dream of the waters and the way.

Damascus What . . . are you?

The Great Tree I am the tree of life. Tree where they crucified your Lord. Tree by the rivers of waters. I speak through wind. I reach through roots. I give rest. Now sleep.

Damascus No! I won't sleep. I got to say goodbye to my girl first. I got to give her my song so she'll know who I am and from where I come. Please . . . just let me see her.

The Great Tree You aren't long for this world. Your body is tired. Wounded.

Damascus Don't matter, I gots to see my child and if God be good . . . you'd let me see her. You'd let me give her my song.

We hear his song in the distance.

Voice of Po'em (*offstage, singing*) NO MATTER I GOT TO SEARCH THIS WHOLE WORLD FOR 'EM.

Damascus *falls deeply into dream.*

The Great Tree When you wake you will no longer be Damascus, the old road, for you have fallen deep, you have seen the way. You are a new creature with a new body. Like Saul arose as Paul when you arise you will be Demeter. A woman resurrected from a tree. You have only three days before your body rots then you must come home to me.

We return to **Free** *still hanging clothes.*

Free (*singing*) GLORA, GLORA HALLELUJAH
GLORA, GLORA HALLELUJAH
GLORA, GLORA HALLELUJAH
HIS TROOF IS MARCHIN ON!!!!!

Free *marches back to the house but trips on fishing wire. A net falls over. Enter* **Blanche**. *She carries a stick and chews black root.*

Blanche – Got ya, ya Yank. Ya Lincolneer. Ya yella-belly cockroach. Got you in my net. Now you sticky, stuck in my net. Try and get out I'm a stick you in the gizzard.

Free Girl (*nonchalant*) Let me outta dis snare, Blanche.

Blanche Blanche ain't my name girl! I'm a General in God's Confederate Army. The South call me Stonewall. I'm a wall. I'm a wall of stone. Just look at these brick muscles. You couldn't break deez bricks with a canon blast.

Free Girl I'm gettin mad Blanche. I'm gettin' real mad right 'bout now –

Blanche – Hush yer fussin! You'ze my prisoner. *Zhay te preeze*. You get mad when I tell ya to get mad, ya Billy Yank.

Free Girl I ain't no Billy Yank. Ain't never even seen no Billy Yank! I'm Free Girl and you knows it.

Blanche *May* how I know it's Free Girl and not a Yankee an *dee-skeeze – hunh*?

Free Girl Cause Yanks don't dress up like lil girls, doin' other folks laundry at night! Let me out of this net or I'm a tell maman ya been in the shed gain makin' booty traps!

Blanche *Ah . . . den calm twa*. Was just playin wit ya. *Jeez*. Ya no fun Free: *Free-yah*. I'll Free ya, gone tell tattles on yer own sis. Best friend in duh whole worle just for testin nets. Makin sure dey surefire.

Free Girl You want to test nets, net up yer pot belly *Monsieur de Bon-Bon*. See if that hog like it. Look at dis mess. /You got my dress dirty gal.

Blanche /Bon-Bon's borin. I need you *ma sore*. I need you to help me set traps to protect *la maison* gainst the Union.

Free Girl Can't you get it through yer brick Blanche? Ya just a *fee-yah*. Ya won't even take baths, how you gone take a Union army with booty traps. If the Yanks come we need to hide in the trees like *maman* told us.

Blanche And what *maman* know? Woman always soggy on dee drink, runnin' round da place in gowns, talkin' to herself – she can't even feed us Free. What she know about hidin in some trees and we starvin?

Free Girl *Mon Pere* be back before your stomach growl 'gain girl. Long for dee Yanks get here anyway – he promised.

Blanche What if he dead though?

Free Girl Don't say dat! He ain't! My Jesus woulda told me if *Mon Pere* was dead.

Blanche Ya invisible Jesus don't know ev'thing Free. If *Pere* dead we got take care us-self.

Free Girl I said *Mon Pere* ain't dead!!! He promised me.

Blanche Cause he grown. Dat's what grown folks do. Promise ya moon and star – den give you two nickels and tell ya go buy a cow. Now he ain't wrote me back in six weeks, Free. If he ain't dead den where is he?

Jean *passes in another world, dragging* **Yankee Pot Roast** *like a slave. They exit.*

Blanche *Ash*, don't cry. Ya makin ya powder run. And ya know how *maman* gets when ya not made-up and ya burnt features show. Come ere and let me cake ya.

Blanche *takes a brush from* **Free's** *pocket and pats powder on her face.*

Blanche Now, I ain't sayin *Pere is* dead. But we got to protect *la maison* just in case he don't get here fore the Yanks do. We *fee-yahs* but we still got nerve Free. Girls keep they nerves unlike the womens. Dee womens loose they nerves when they have the chillens – like *maman*. She need us to guard the house cause we got lots of nerve. And Pere knows it, dats why he left the protectin to me. He knows *maman* ain't got no nerve and I'ze full of it. But I need ya, *ma sore*. I need you to be me *dee-pu-tee*.

Free Girl What's in dis for me? You gone help round the house? Wash that hog of your'ins dat smell like dah doo doo? Stop makin fun of Jesus?

Blanche *Alors*, I won't make fun of ya invisible Jesus. Jeez. Just be me *dee-pu tee*.

Free Girl Fine. But I ain't gettin my dress dirty and I ain't playin wid no mud and I specially ain't touchin no guns or no spit. I gots to keep my face powdered –

Blanche *hawks-a-loogie on her hand.*

Blanche Just once den. We got to spit and shake on it.

Free Girl Nawl, I said. I ain't touchin' your mouth-water, Blanche Marie Verse. I know you be kissin' dat hog like he good luck. Best keep ya yuck over dere.

Blanche Just stop bein' such a girl and hawk a wad!!!

The girls shake and exit. Miss Ssippi puts on her Sunday dress for church.

Miss Ssippi (*singing*) GONNA PUT ON MY WIDE ROBE
DOWN BY THE RIVER SIDE.
DOWN BY THE RIVER SIDE.
DOWN BY THE RIVER SIDE.
GONNA PUT ON MY WIDE ROBE
DOWN BY THE RIVERSIDE.
AND STUDY WAR NO MORE.

Demeter *walks along* **Miss Ssippi's** *skirt.*

Miss Ssippi Say what you know good Miss Demeter?

Demeter Demeter? How you know that name?

Miss Ssippi Honey, don't you know trees gossip. Why you think they always shakin they heads when ya pass. It's cause they know all your business. And when they see ya, they thinking bout the time you did such and such and they gets to laughin and carryin on. Trees is some cruel creatures. That's why God don't let em move none. They play too much. Ya wanna ride? I'm on my way to a church revival.

Demeter No. I rather walk. I like the feel of the Earth on my feet.

Miss Ssippi You'll never get there in time walkin', Demeter. God gave you three days to find the child and you done already slept through one. Come on, let me carry you to the hem of my skirt. It's pretty there. It's made of alluvia lace.

Demeter I said I'm walkin'. And don't call me Demeter. My name's Damascus.

Miss Ssippi Well look who's mannish. You sound like another Jonah: small head but mouth's wide as a whale's. I had to drop that boy in the Ocean to make him mind. What's it gone take you?

Demeter I don't need nobody's help! I got me a quilt that leads me to my girl. It's the only thing in this world I trust and I'll find her for long –

Miss Ssippi – Then you got a long-legged journey. God don't play second fiddle even in a two-piece band. But if you think you can get there in time walkin', then walk on Demeter –

Demeter – I said my name's Damascus!

Miss Ssippi *raises her skirt.*

Miss Ssippi – HUSH YASELF!!! You're Demeter! Look at your spirit in this water girl! Your body was changed. YOU ARE NOW WOMAN!

Demeter *sees her reflection.*

Demeter No . . . God. (*Beat.*) What happened to me?

Miss Ssippi Nature happened. The Father changed your winter into spring. It wasn't just a dream. Men cut off your manhood and tried to pluck you from Earth. But God replanted you. He fell in love with your song and gave you a chance to put it inside the child. But you got to get there in time Demeter. Now let me help you . . .

Demeter No, I said! I don't need you! I DON'T NEED YOU AND I DON'T NEED GOD!

Demeter *walks off into the night.*

Miss Ssippi You'll never get there in time. Your daughter's lost! And so is you.

Miss Ssippi *continues to dress for church.*

Miss Ssippi (*singing*) I AIN'T GONNA STUDY WAR NO MORE.

Enter **Jean** *still dragging* **Yankee Pot Roast** *by the rope.* **Jean** *stops before the river to wash his face. The boy manages to get up and grab the gun.*

Yankee Pot Roast Make another move, sir, and I'll blast your brains half across the Mason Dixon.

Jean Verse Sho you will, piggy.

Yankee Pot Roast My name is not Piggy! It's Arthurius Jefferson Johns.

Jean Verse Then go ahead and shoot if ya think your ball sack is big 'nough. Just know the echo of that gun will arouse soldiers on the Vicksburg wall. They got canons. They'll blast ya from here to kingdom come.

The boy takes back his bugle.

Yankee Pot Roast – Not if I blow a spiritual with my bugle first. Soldiers won't shoot a Christian, sir. Especially not one that can really blow. Before my infantry was killed, I was known as little boy blue note. I can blow the bluest song you ever heard. I can even take down this wall with half my breath if you tried me.

Jean Verse – Wait a stink! I thought ya was familiar. You that fool bugler who blew the noon's charge three days ago?

Yankee Pot Roast No, not a charge. It was an advance. I blew that morning's advance –

Jean Verse Hoggish, I watched from atop the wall. Dat morning's charge was blown by a skinny and you'ze a fat. You dat boy who blew the wrong song. Dat's why you broke rank and is buryin ya dead. You killed em. Your captain gave you the sign for retreat and you blew a charge. You ran your infantry right into harm's way.

Yankee Pot Roast I did not! It wasn't me!

Jean Verse You must be the dumbest solider on dis whole field.

Yankee Pot Roast Quiet! Quiet or I'll blow my horn and get us both killed.

Jean Verse Never mind not havin' a big 'nough ball sack. You ain't even got a peck. You just a puss.

Yankee Pot Roast *blows his horn.*

Miss Ssippi (*singing*) JOSHUA FIT DE BATTLE, DE BATTLE OF JERICHO

Jean Verse Wait, I was just foolin' –

Miss Ssippi (*singing*) JERICHO! JOSHUA FIT DE BATTLE OF –

Jean Verse Hush dat horn! –

Miss Ssippi (*clapping*) JERICHO! JERICHO! AND THE WALLS CAME TUMBLIN' DOWN.

Jean Verse We're gonna die!

Miss Ssippi AND THE WALLS CAME TUMBLIN' DOWN!

Yankee Pot Roast I'm not afraid of death –

Miss Ssippi AND THE WALLS CAME TUMBLIN' DOWN!

Yankee Pot Roast – Long as you die. Death is Heaven.

Miss Ssippi – AND THE WALLS . . . CAME . . . TUMBLIN' / DOWN!

Jean Verse /I'll see you in hell den.

Canons blast loudly. **Jean** *grabs* **Yankee Pot Roast** *and jumps into the river. An explosion of light.* **Miss Ssippi** *exits, dressed for church. She claps up a waltz.*

3. The Stanza – a room

Midnight

A chandelier falls. Enter **Cadence**, *the middle-aged mistress of the plantation. She wears a gown and holds a flute of champagne.*

Cadence (*singing*) *BEE'AN-VA-NEW* . . . WELCOME TO . . . MY *CHALM-BER*
COME-VA-TO? . . . HOW ARE YOU? . . . I'M CHARMED, SIR.
ALL THE BEAUX OF LOUIS'ANNE ARE HERE
ALL DEE BELLS RINGIN IN MY HEAD.
WHO WANTS A KISS FROM A CAJUN COUNTESS
THE HUSBAND'S TO WAR, GUESS HE'S DEAD.

She raises her glass as she waltzes.

HERE'S TO YOU . . . *BOO VAN-A-VOO* . . . MY LOVERS
PASS THE BOOZE . . . *BWEE-SAN-COME-TROOZE* . . . WHO'S SOBER?
NOUS DAWN-SAWN DE-VAWN BOO-FAY JEAN-TEE.
WE'RE SOPPING OUT MOUTHS WITH NO BREAD.
WE'RE STARVING BUT WALTZING, AND WALTZING
IS LIVING LET'S DANCE AND LET'S DRINK WILL WE'RE DEAD!

In the backyard, **Demeter** *pulls clothes off the line then dresses as a woman.*

You see the story is, my gents.
The old man's gone to fight for his southern brothers
A group of clowns called the Confederates.
Southern buggers, cotton farmers, porch dogs and the like.
He's gone to die and left me alone with our *fee-yahs* Blanche and Free.
He left us to starve.
Well, lucky for me,
Lucky for y'all, the old man wasn't much of man, much of anything
So I don't feel no guilt about drinkin myself into death
Or layin with some young piece just to break his heart
In fact, I am a heart breakin machine
I AM *LA FEMMA FA-TALE*.
KISS ME AND FALL IN LOVE

LAY WITH ME AND FALL FOREVER
Fall forever but don't fall on my floor
It hasn't been washed since the two slaves fled.

She laughs.

O! Would you look at this
My flute is empty.
Kell cat-tass-strof. How will we play?
Pod-pro-blem, I am the host
I will retrieve the joy water and we shall toast
To *la fraternité, l'egalité*, and to *l'amour*!

Enter **Brer Bit**, *the house negro. He plays the fool but he is a trickster.*

Brer Bit Mad-damn! I heard a noise in the cellar. O Lawd, send the word, send the word. Over there! Over there! The Yanks is comin! The Yanks is comin!

Cadence Good God, Brer Bit stay in one place. I told you bout hoppin round like that. Now what are you tryin to tell me?

Brer Bit I'm tryin to tell you the Yanks is here ma'am. I heard a noise in the cellar. And I seen the canons near the river. They here mad-damn. O Lawd it ain't right. It just just ain't right.

He blows his nose on her dress.

Cadence *Ash*, silly rabbit, those canons will never cross the river. Not before the Confederates crush them into crumbs, trust me. I know my army. They cannot be defeated.

Brer Bit (*an aside*) Piss. You must be drunker than a skunk's rump. Your army's bout half dead cause of the Union.

Cadence What's that you say, Brer?

Brer Bit Well, I says madame your army bout half bled the Union. Shucks. We gone win this war just yet.

Cadence *Ben suh*. But we must do our part for the war effort and help our men home. Here. You take this knife and join the Confederacy. You fight amongst our brothers and kill as many Union soldiers as you can.

She grabs a rifle.

Me: I'll take care of our visitor in the cellar. Now go, Brer! And be of great courage.

Brer Bit O. But I don't know how to fight, ma'am. I don't even know how to leave duh house. Member . . . dats why they calls me the house Negro cause I tends to duh house. And you knows I gets the frights when I goes out. All I knows is this. This white house is my mistress.

Cadence That may be so but I'm you're massuh. And I said go join the army! We'll be fine here: me and the girls. We don't know how to cook or clean but we'll manage because we women. And women are made to cook and clean.

So . . . go Brer Bit!

Brer Bit I want to, ma'am, but I can't seem to move my feets. Dey love duh house so dey don't know how to step off her.

Cadence If ya don't go now I'll shoot square 'tween the eyes. Go!

Brer Bit No.

Cadence What did you just say to me?

Brer Bit No, ma'am.

She slaps him hard.

Cadence You know I never take no for an answer. I'm going to the cellar Brer. And when I get back you best be gone.

She exits. He touches his lip – finds blood.

Brer Bit Well, looksy here: S'blood.

Figures. Only one gal could love me anyplace.
She: this house, my mistress. She never mishandles my pretty black face.
And soon, together, we will breed a new race.

Snickering, he cracks his neck.

For in two days: When hot-headed Phaethon
Has trod his father's chariot twice round earth's eternal womb
And lured lightning thin as a serpent's tongue from God's vengeful hand.
The massuh's great white house
Shedding its cotton bright skin from violent whispers of wind and rain
Will turn black as the slaves who have raised it, and fold.
Like the player round the table who has no play
A full house will turn on itself and pockmark a poker'ed face.
O how rosey, that I should hold a flush as bright as the loud mouth moon
And know the hands of all
And like that old white eye, climb to a high point to watch their cards fall.
For only then will I show my hand, revealing the fortune writ on my palm
Which my mother herself once read.
Though I bet she didn't wager I had the courage to cleanse the house
In a royal blood bath. And feed on the Verses – dead.
I COME FROM KINGS!!!
And was born to oversee, not be made limp or blind.
Clothed in new garment, new flesh and nesting upon new nest
Even if it'll cost me my soul, yes. I'll trickster rank for this kingdom, fine.
For the white house is dutifully mine.

He exits. In a tree house, **Free** *wakes* **Blanche**.

Free Blanchie! Blanchie, gee'up.

Blanche I'm sleep grll.

Free Ere's a *bru-wee*, Blanche. Ya alarm gone off – downstairs.

Blanche Was just *ma mere* – drinkin. Breakin glass. Ya know how she gets.

Free What if it's the Yanks? What if they hurtin her and we can't hear er? What if em Yanks stick they knives in er and make er bleed ri-vah? Make her die. We alone den, Blanche. We alone and the Yanks gone feed us to theyz dogs and chillen. Decorate us like a tree, Blanche. Make you take a bath –

Blanche Would you look at this face, Free? It's a sleepin' face. Let it dream grrl.

Free *Maman* dead den and we gone die.

Blanche Good. Then I'm a really get t'sleep.

Free Fine, I'm goin' down. By my lonesome. *Joosta moi. Moi* and *Jesus*. And I'ze just a *fee-yah*. Goin by herself. A brave lil girl. Bye, Blanche.

Blanche Bye ya, Free.

Free *Adieu*, Blanchee.

Blanche *I do too, Fee-yah*!

Free If I 'ont come back, you take care my dolly. Lil Some'um. Tell 'er, her ma la 'er. (*Time.*) *Attend*! Wait. I can't do it. I can't do it, Blanche. I got t'take Lil Some'um wit me. I'ze her only ma. Means ya got t'be alone *ma sore*.

Blanche *snores*.

Free Alright, Lil Some'um. It's me and you. Me, you and Jesus. And we got t'do dis, OK?

Free *climbs down and onto the field*.

You ready, Jesus?

Jesus *slides down the tree.*

Jesus Lo, I am with thee. Till the ends of the world.

He holds a Moxie (the oldest American soft drink).

Free Alright, now hold Lil Some'um. She won't cry if you keep her close to you. Follow me. And don't be fraid none neither, Jesus. Them Yanks can't do nothin to ya cause they can't see ya. So you be strong.

Jesus I am strong. The strength of your life. A lamplight unto your feet.

Jesus' *feet glow.*

Free Ooo, pree-tee. You should go first den. I'll hold the baby.

They creep towards the cellar.

Allon-zee, Jesus. One foot at a time.

In the cellar, **Demeter** *eats.* **Cadence** *sees* **Demeter** *and raises her rifle.*

Cadence Take one more step, mister and I swear to God I'll rip ya open like childbirth.

Demeter Hold it. Who you?

Cadence Jesus Christ in a nightie. I got a long-arm cocked, pointed at your manhood. You make a move I break bread.

Demeter Be Christian, I'ze just a woman. Just a woman passin' through –

Cadence – Trespassin' through. And you don't smell a woman.

Demeter Still it's what I am. And old. If ya listen ya can hear my age in my voice.

Cadence Turn round. I trust my eyes more an my ears. (*Beat.*) Ah . . . turn leisurely, casually as a woman.

Demeter Here. Here's the face of old and female.

Cadence I see. What leads ya here?

Demeter An empty gut. Been searchin' for food.

Cadence You come alone?

Demeter Yeah. And been so in life.

Cadence Followers? Ya bein chased?

Demeter Just by death. But he won't get at ya . . . (*Beat.*) Less ya cross me.

Cadence I might have to siderin you trespassin on my plantation. You a runnin-slave gal?

Demeter I ain't nobody's gal but my ma and she dead so I b'long merely to God. Ya can call me Demeter. It's what I now call myself. What I lets myself be called. And I'ze a free woman. One runnin to not from. And after my daughter.

Cadence Well, she ain't here – all two of our servants fled.

Demeter Damn shame. You seem kinda kind for a white woman with a rifle –

Cadence – Quiet! Let me see what's in your hand.

Demeter What for? It's a good hand. Won't blame it for tryin to steal. Was my stomach had the cravin'.

Cadence Well I could shoot you there – in the stomach. Kill ya cravin'.

Demeter You can try. Though I might have something up my sleeve.

Cadence Could shoot you in the sleeve then. In the arm.

Demeter Go 'head. Still might have somethin' 'nother in my pocket.

Cadence Silence! You talk mighty high for a Negress. I don't like that. Don't like you.

Demeter Figures. I make you shake.

Cadence Ya don't. Ya don't make me shake.

Demeter And I make you lie. No wonder you don't like me.

Cadence I'm not alone!

Demeter I know. You got a daughter and half-colored girl that's sleep. I been spyin' on ya –

Cadence – Got a husband too.

Demeter He must ain't been round in a while. Been watchin the house from the trees. Lookin through the windows from the moon –

Cadence Well, ya missed him. He's here! Just there in the other room – listenin.

Demeter Ya don't say. Call him over.

Cadence Look, he don't need to be at war.

Demeter Well, he need to be somewhere. What kind a southerner sittin' round let his plantation fall to pieces. Lettin' his wife guard the house –

Cadence – He's here! –

Demeter – Garden embraced by weeds, pieces of wood lying round like rotted fruit. What?! Is ya a ghost, sir? Maybe missus ya man just housed in ya mind.

Cadence No he ain't! I'll call em!!!

Demeter Best hurry, that gun's getting mighty heavy in your hands. It's startin t'faint. I could hold it up for ya, while you standin there, tryin t'makin me nervous with that mean face.

Cadence Don't sass me. It ain't heavy. I'm just lettin it droop, aimin it at different parts of ya. I might shoot you in the leg. Shoot you in the arm. Shoot you in da –

She accidentally pulls the trigger.

Free – Jesus!

Jesus *runs and snatches the bullet with his left hand.* **Cadence** *and* **Demeter** *scream.*

Demeter I must be a wonder.

She takes off her headscarf.

Free Jesus, you alright?

Cadence Free, get behind me.

Demeter I'm lookin for a girl named Po'em. She was sold here some years back from Ten'see. You ever hear of her?

Cadence *Non.* I ain't never heard no Po'em. You at the wrong place so get.

Demeter She sent me this quilt in a chest 'long the river. This quilt reads like a map. And this map lead me here. So I know she been here. I'll leave when you tell me where she is. Or where you sold her.

Cadence I told you, I ain't never heard of no Po'em.

Demeter Hm. The nature of lies woman, is that they grow off one another. Be the only way they stay alive.

Jesus *rises.*

Free Jesus, you risen.

Jesus Do not let your left hand know what the right is doing.
That your charitable deed may be done in secret
And he shall reward you openly

Jesus *blows away the blood on his hand.*

Free Pree-tee. *Maman,* Jesus just healed hisself.

Demeter Whose girl is this?

Cadence She's mine! Free, stay behind me.

Free I'm Free.

Cadence Stay behind me, I said.

Demeter (*to* **Free**) I'm Demeter. Don't mean ya no harm. Just passin through . . . those eyes. Where you get dem eyes from girl?

Cadence Leave woman!

Demeter I ain't gone do nothin to her, missus. I just wanna see dem eyes up close.

She reaches for **Free, Cadence** *stops her.*

Cadence Free run now . . .

Free *runs out of the cellar.*

Demeter Wait, girl!

Cadence Run fast, Free!

Miss Ssippi (*singing*) I'VE A CROWN IN THE KINGDOM, AIN'T THAT GOOD NEWS.

Demeter WAIT!

Miss Ssippi I'VE A CROWN IN THE KINGDOM, AIN'T THAT GOOD NEWS.

Demeter *goes after* **Free**.

Demeter Come here!

Cadence – NO!!!

Cadence *knocks* **Demeter** *in the head with the butt of her rifle.* **Demeter** *falls.*

Miss Ssippi (*singing*) I'M GOING TO LAY DOWN THIS WORLD GOING TO SHOULDER UP MY CROSS I'M GOIN' TO TAKE IT HOME TO JESUS AIN'T THAT GOOD NEWS.

4. Rhythm – time, flow

Dawn.

Miss Ssippi *hums the rest of the song as she reaches into the sky and crowns her head with the moon. It is a church hat.* **Jean** *wades in the water carrying an unconscious* **Yankee Pot Roast** *who's covered in soot and burns across his face.*

Jean Verse Ya lookin good, Sip. Say, if I wasn't already in love, I'd give you a run for your water.

Miss Ssippi It be a short a race, Jean Verse. Even on a good day, you ain't half the man that could keep up with me. Who's that babe in your arms?

Jean Verse Dis ain't no babe, it's a Yank. I'm holdin to him cause I ain't been able to reach shore yet. He got a horn on him I'm gone sell. Ya think ya could tide us to the land.

Miss Ssippi Depends. You plannin' on shovin' this boy back in my water once I do it? I don't want to walk into church with a dead Yank dangling from my gown.

Jean Verse Nawl, I'd never do dat, you know me.

Miss Ssippi Yeah, you wish-washy like the dance of my ass. That's why I asked ya.

Jean Verse Come on now, Sip, I coulda just left him to drown. This horn is the last of the treasures I earned from being in dis war. Ya know I didn't want to go. Served as I much I could and now I need just a lil booty to top my fortune. I plans to buy Po'em a dress and run away with her.

Miss Ssippi Doubt if you get far. Best put sassafras and honey oak on that boy's face. He looks like he got kissed by a cannon and lost his blush – poor chile.

Jean Verse Tough, he ain't my boy. I'll get him out the water and to shelter but dats it. I gots to get home for the Confeds realize I deserted. I'm in a hurry.

Miss Ssippi That boy is some mother's child, Jean. Now you know I don't take sides in this war but right is righteous. You need to take him and put a salve on his face. Then build a fire and find him some food.

Jean Verse I'm already up a creek without paddle. Union on one side, Confeds on the other. I haven't even reach Louisianne yet. I'll get killed tryin to keep dis boy from death. If the devil want his soul then who am I to whistle Dixie.

Miss Ssippi Well, obviously you ain't much. But that ain't news to nothin' with a nose. Hell, from what I recall you ain't never been sweeter than cat piss no hoot. Robbin' dead, whipping slaves, beatin' your wife. And that's just what you do when you get bored playin near my waters. Ain't no tellin' what hell you raise in your house. Now normally I bite my lip. Being one whose stuck in her ways but . . . well you the worst kind of rabied-mouth dog, Jean Verse. Tell ya, if God didn't keep his eye on me, I'd drown you 'tween my thighs for the pure pleasure of it. Then carry ya dead body to church and throw it in the collection plate as a free will offering. That's if the church would even take ya for the building fund.

Jean Verse I've changed, Sip. You might can't tell but dats why I'm going back home. Dis war has changed me.

Miss Ssippi That sounds pretty but in my long stretch upon this Earth men don't ever change. God's reserved that trait just for seasons. Nevertheless hold on, I'll carry you to the belly-lead bayou. But after that, your way is up to you.

She takes them away. In the cellar, **Free** *and* **Blanche** *gaze on an unconscious* **Demeter** *whose head lies in* **Jesus'** *lap.* **Jesus** *pours water into her mouth.*

Blanche I just advise we hurry dis looksy. *Maman* still sleep but God knows she'll be up before we know it.

Free My, she's beautiful, Blanche. Her skin got a glow: dark and full of stars.

Blanche Ya thank she dead?

Free Don't know. How 'dead' s'pose to look on a face?

Blanche I ont know. Somethin like dat I figure. Only seen on a kitty.

Free She probably is sick is all. I could feel something ill in her when she looked at me off strange before. Felt like she walked into my eyes with her eyes. Felt like she was tellin me a story I couldn't read or . . .

Blanche We should listen for breath. Figure dat's how ya prove the livin' ain't livin'.

Free And how we gone do dat? How's breathin 'even s'pose to sound?

Blanche I 'ont know. Like wind . . . but softer some. Let me see.

Blanche *puts her ear to* **Demeter's** *mouth.*

Free What ya feel? What ya hear?

Blanche A faint breeze – hard to tell. Let's check her stomach. See if her heart still dancing that two step.

Free *Ah wee, may* how we gone check dat?

Blanche I ont know, figure we gone have to be improper and loosen dis shirt.

Free *Ash.* Not *moi.* Not Free . . .

Blanche Den stand back, girl. Leave it to me to save the worl'.

She unbuttons the shirt.

Blanche *Un. Duh. Twa. Cat. Sank et cease. Ooo, kesk-ka-say* dat dere?

Free It's a *coeur-set*!

Blanche A *coeur-set*?

Free Yeah. *Maman's* got some in pink. It's to hold a woman's bosoms so they don't go shakin hands.

Blanche Ick. I never's gone to wear one of dose. *Coeur-sets*. Don't care if I got dee shakers or not. Looks awful itchy. Best check her heart now though.

Blanche *listens.*

Free What ya hear?

Blanche Ooo . . . deres a smell. Something's got my stomach.

She sniffs and finds apples.

It's . . . it's here . . . *les pums*! *Le vwa-lah*!

Free *Pums*! Oh my! *Lay pums*!

The girls ravage the apples turning their back to **Demeter**. *She wakes and rises over them.*

Demeter Those were mine.

In sync the girls slowly turn around then scream. **Demeter** *grabs them and takes them away leaving* **Jesus**. *He waits. Looks around and takes a boom box from inside his robe. He presses play and 1980s hip hop plays.* **Jesus** *takes off his shoes and tries to moonwalk. He tries his hardest again and again but it is to no avail. He gets frustrated, turns the music off and walks into the kitchen where* **Demeter** *cooks and the girls wait in hungry anticipation.*

Demeter When was the last time you seen her? My daughter.

Blanche Don't member, ma'am. It's been months. She fled when the other slaves did. She didn't even wave good bye.

Free She said bye to me. She even left me something –

Blanche Shht, Free!

Free *bows her head.*

Blanche Say, Miss . . . is that grits you makin'?

Demeter Sho is.

Blanche Ooo, I sho am hungry.

Free Me too.

Demeter That so? Well, where she say she was going then – my girl?

Blanche Don't know. She didn't say.

Demeter You sure? Try and member and it might help the food cook faster.

Free Ooo, try and member Blanche!

Demeter She ever mention her Paw?

Free Yeah. You know him?

Demeter Knew him. But he long gone now. Died.

Blanche O dats sad. Can we eat now?

Free Yeah, now can we eat?

Demeter Sho.

Demeter *puts food in front of them.*

Enter **Cadence**.

Cadence What's goin on here? What's this mess? Dat smell? You!

The girls freeze with guilt.

Demeter Me. Name's Demeter.

Free Miz Dahmeetah.

Jesus I'm Jesus.

Cadence How'd you get in my kitch?

Demeter Ya girls invited me. They told me my daughter Po'em was their mammy. Where'd she go, missus?

Cadence Don't know. Get out! You ain't got no business here.

Demeter I'll leave after I get the truth and fix these childers they meal. This one here took care me this morn. Gave me water for my throat. Bandage for my head.

Cadence Free, you didn't.

Free Blanche helped.

Demeter You nearly knocked me into next Tuesday with that gun butt. But I got somethin' for your hide soon enough.

Cadence You stay back from us. Come on children, let's part.

The girls continue to eat.

Demeter Not to worry. I'll get you when you least expect it. I like to surprise folk, come at em like birthday cake.

Free and Blanche We love birthday cake!

Demeter Let 'em close they eyes, make a wish. Then I blow out they lights. You hungry?

Jesus Jesus is hungry.

Cadence No, you a crazy. She's a . . . he's a crazy. Y'all come on now.

Free But its real good, *maman*. Don't you want some meat and grits?

Jesus Jesus wants some meat and grits.

Free Jesus wants meat and grits, Miz Dahmeetah.

Cadence No, it's poison! It's all poison. Ma Blanche?

Blanche Hmm?

Cadence What this woman do'in in my kitch?

Blanche Cookin'. I tried to stop 'er some but the food just started smellin and tastin so good, I had to do somethin'. So I'm eatin it. And if ya gone whip at my hide ma go a head. Just don't touch my grits, they so good. They like a hug in your gut, they so good.

Cadence She's a witch with spells!!! Y'all can't see that?! A man dressed in a dress. No tellin what's in her brew. No tellin' what whammy this she-man conjured –

Free But *maman*, ain't you starvin' some?

Cadence Starvin'! What I got to care bout starving for? This woman ain't got no business messin in my kitch. I ain't eatin dis mess.

Jesus *prepares to eat,* **Cadence** *grabs the bowl and tosses it toward* **Demeter's** *feet.*

Free But dat was for Jesus.

Blanche Can I have some more meat, Miz Dahmeetah?

Demeter Sho sugar!

Cadence No, Blanche! Don't eat her poison!

Free Can I have some more meat, Miz Dahmeetah?

Demeter Sho honey.

Cadence Free! I mean it!

Free I mean can Jesus have some more meat, Miz Dahmeetah?

Demeter Jesus can have whatever he wants.

Free And Jesus wants more grits too. /Jesus loves grits.

Jesus /Jesus loves grits.

Cadence *Arretez*! No more grits, no meat, no Jesus! LEAVE! NEGRO! NOW!

Jesus (*to audience*) Negroes don't grow from their knees. They don't need to grow, or grow up or grow in need. The Negro is an Argentine river that flows, blue as it pleases into the Atlantic Ocean. The Negro is a river.

Free and **Blanche** We love grits!

Demeter Like I said, I'll leave once you feed me truth. Now sit woman. I don't like people standin' over me while I'm servin'.

Cadence *sits.*

This is for Jesus.

Demeter *puts grits in front of* **Cadence**.

Jesus Jesus is over here. On the main line.

Free No, Miz Dameetah. Jesus sittin over here. 'Member. He sits on my right.

Demeter Course.

Cadence *Ben*. I'll eat one course, one meal. Then ya best get.

Just before **Jesus** *eats his grits* **Cadence** *grabs it and eats*. **Free** *hands the savior her grits*. **Jesus** *kisses her on the cheek.*

Demeter I will. Soon as I get the truth.

Demeter *eats.*

Blanche Where's Bon Bon? I ain't seen him all mornin'.

Free Dat's her nasty hog.

Blanche He ain't nasty.

Demeter Sho he ain't. (*Beat.*) He taste good to me.

Everybody but **Demeter** *freezes. She eats.*

Free Lawd Jesus!

Cadence She's left, there I said it! Your Po'em went South three months ago. She's gone.

Demeter That can't be. She wouldn't have left without telling me . . . or left some sign.

Cadence Don't matter, she ain't here. So get!

Demeter Best not be lyin to me Miss. Or trust, I'll be back here.

She exits. The girls look at **Cadence**. *Just beyond the plantation,* **Jean** *drags a sick* **Yankee Pot Roast** *to a tree near a post office box.* **Brer Bit** *watches from the tree.*

Jean Verse Here piggy! We're home! Taste the air, boy. We just in time for duh first yawn of spring. You can tell by the way Miss Ssippi sweeps 'tween the banks, risin' and spreadin' over the levees. She gets so heated dis time of year she runs to church in her Sunday best just to get baptized in the ocean. Lawd and when she does . . . woman floods the bayou in brown gumbo. Trees tremble like sweaty thighs, birds hop on each other's backs to beat wing, frogs jump bones and the sea cums in crabs, catfish and shrimp. Get up boy you missin' it. Look over yonder, you can see rows of my tabacca field – hangin' like rotted bills. Even beyond dat, the tall, white columns that hold up my southern castle. I'm Home! Wait till you see my kingdom piggy. I got so many mules, hogs, and chickens, your stomach gone growl like a dog. Got girls too, beautiful babies: Blanche and Free. And a wife. And a love named Po'em. And peace. My God . . .

He holds back tears.

I'm going to have peace.

A Voice (*offstage singing*) TRAVELIN' SHOES LAWD GOT NO TRAVELIN' SHOES . . .

Jean looks off into the distance.

Jean Verse Po'em? Po'em is dat you?

He freezes. A knock. The girls run to the door. **Cadence** *follows.*

Free It's *Mon Pere*! I know that knock anywhere. It's *Mon Pere*!

Blanche Naw it ain't! Man your stations, it's the Yanks!

The girls run to the front door.

Cadence Don't open it may *fee-yahs*! Let me answer it first!

Free It's okay *maman*, it's *Mon Pere*!

Blanche No it not, it's the Yank!

A Voice (*offstage*) TRAVELIN' SHOES LAWD. GOT NO TRAVELIN' SHOES.

Cadence It's neither. O God, it's . . .

Cadence *opens the door. We see a figure.* **Cadence** *freezes.* **Demeter** *approaches* **Miss Ssippi** *enraged.*

Miss Ssippi Mercy, look what the cat done spit up. Demeter. Lord, I prayed you'd find your way on the right side of righteousness. And hallelujah, look at God. Did you give the child your song?

Demeter Nawl, I ain't found her yet.

Miss Ssippi What you mean 'ain't found her'?! She was right there at the house . . . Lord, I don't know why you always giving hard-headed folks second chances when they ain't worth the first. I know two preachers up near Magnolia who'd had the job done already and be givin a benediction.

Demeter You know she wasn't there, Sip. Not my child: my Po'em. You and your God is up to no good –

Miss Ssippi Nawl woman, this be for your own good. God led you down this road cause it's the only way your song could find Freedom. That's why he chose you. He fell in love with your song. And now you got to set it Free.

Demeter I ain't got to do nothing but find my girl. She's mine and this is my song –

Miss Ssippi It comes from your ancestors! You don't know it cause your powers been sleep for three hundred years but you are the descendant of Goddesses who bathed in the Nile. Their tears flow in your veins deep as the Euphrates and in your daughter's veins. If you don't plant the song in the child and get her to sing it, the song will be forgotten. And so will your daughter.

Miss Ssippi *reveals a piece of her dress. It is a missing section to the map-quilt.*

Demeter Where'd you get that? It's another piece of Po'em's quilt . . .

Miss Ssippi It fell in my folds three months ago. It fell when she fell . . .

Demeter What you mean? Where is she? Take me to her!

Miss Ssippi Are you commanding me?! It's bout to get real wet out here!

Demeter Please, river! I need to know what happened to her.

Miss Ssippi Fine. But once I do this, you got to give the child her song. No matter how painful it might be, you take this quilt and pass it long.

Demeter I give you my word.

Miss Ssippi *opens her gown to reveal a figure standing at the end of a road. We hear the same voice again.*

A Voice (*offstage*) TRAVELIN' SHOES LAWD
I GOT NO TRAVELIN' SHOES.

Demeter Po'em? Daughter, is that you?

Demeter *freezes. The voice becomes louder as it walks toward us.*

A Voice (*singing*) DEATH WENT OUT TO THE
SINNER'S HOUSE
COME AND GO WITH ME
SINNER CRIED OUT, I'M NOT READY, LAWD
AIN'T NO TRAVELIN' SHOES FOR FREE
TRAVELIN' SHOES, LAWD
GOT NO TRAVELIN' SHOES
WON'T GO TO YOUR HOUSE
SHOUT AND DANCE ABOUT
WITH NO TRAVELIN' SHOES UPON MY FEET

We see **Brer Bit** *in a dress, sitting in* **Miss Ssippi's** *chair.*

Brer Bit Well, don't dis beat a dead dog clean.
Ev'rybody wants a poem so I gots to dress up like a gal and sing.
Yet and still it's a part of my well-made plan
To uproot the plantation and reclaim my ancestor's land
And once I do, I'll raise the crops and burn down the shack
And lo after that, I'll paint the white house black!!!

He blows out the sun. All goes dark.

A Breather: intermission

5. Poem – a made thing

Noon.

Near the mouth of the Ocean, beyond the plantation, **Miss Ssippi** *pours libation over* **Demeter** *who weeps in the river's dress.*

MISS SSIPPI (*sings*) TAKE ME TO THE WATER
TAKE ME TO THE WATER
TAKE ME TO THE WATER
TO BE REVIVED.
I GOT ON MY WIDE ROBE
I GOT ON MY TRAVELIN' SHOES
I GOT ON MY CROWN AND I'M GOIN'
TO BE BAPTISED.

A chorus of voices as if at a church sing while **Miss Ssippi** *speaks and anoints* **Demeter's** *head.*

Your daughter is no more for this world, Demeter. She has gone to the seas of her mothers to bathe in the waters of Oshun. She is a goddess, worshipped in the land of your forefathers and she is content there. You must not mourn for her. For her child and the future children of this child need her story. You must plant it inside of her. Tonight. Before dusk. Before you die.

Brer Bit *crawls from around* **Miss Ssippi** enticing **Demeter**. **Miss Ssippi** *watches, pissed.*

Brer Bit (*singing*) JUBA DIS AND JUBA DAT,
JUBA KISSED DA YELLOW CAT, JUBA JUBA.
YOU SIFT DUH MEAL, YOU GIMME DUH HUSK,
YOU COOK DUH BREAD. DEN FEED ME DUH CRUST,
YOU FRY DUH MEAT, DEN GIMME SKIN,
AND DATS WHERE MY MOMMA'S TROUBLE BEGIN.

How'll do?

Demeter I don't.

Brer Bit O, but you will. You Demeter.

Demeter Maybe. Who's askin'?

Brer Bit Ain't askin'. Tellin'. Cause I know. I seen you move in duh river. Every man can't move in duh river, you got to know her sway. It's got to be taught to ya. Three months ago . . . I saw a girl named Po'em who had your gift. She too moved in the water.

Demeter Not so. She drowned. She couldn't swim cause I didn't teach her –

Brer Bit – It wouldn't have done no good. She drowned cause she was killed.

Demeter Killed? By who?!

Brer *scratches his head then knocks on it.*

Brer Bit (*an aside*) Bruh, you hear dat rap tat on your block. Sound like an opportunity tryin' to knock.

Demeter By who I said?!

Brer Bit What's this? Misses Sip didn't show you how she was tricked. I watched her come to the river every night to move it. She even started comin' with duh massuh afterwhile. And when the river wouldn't move. Dey moved in it. And kept movin' in it. Till dey got dirty.

Demeter Dirty? What's this trouble you cookin'?

Brer Bit Hold on, I ain't put the fire under ya yet. Let me finish stirrin'. This serving's goes down your ear. The madame caught em, one time see. Came out to fetch her *mari* and saw him, laying Po'em down on the water, watching her float, though he wasn't holdin her up. And they was naked.

Demeter Lies! My gal would never lay with a man like that . . . she was probably trying to get Free –

Brer Bit – Shucks, how you think that gal came to be? She got your Po'em's eyes, don't she? When Po'em got pregnant Jean hid her off the land then told Mad-damn Cadence he found a babe on a road and wanted to raise it like his own. As a white. As one who is Free. Course the madame knew whose it was. She might play drunk but she drinks everything in. She decided to raise Free just to spite Po'em. Madame powdered her face white to redden Po'em's skin. But it soon wore off. And Po'em took the stabs like they were pats on the head. Well . . . till she ended up dead.

We hear canons in the distance.

Rat tat a tat tat, it's so sad no one ever takes the white mistress for a snare.
I spose its the way southern bells toll that makes most think she is fair
High strung from school houses and houses of prayer
She dangles when rung, and sways when she rolls
While underneath her bodice sits a hollow, murderous soul.
And lo, her hates been brewin
Since Po'em and her husband went lustin in the riverbed
When massuh went to war, Po'em crossed the river tryin to get free
So the mistress shot her square in the head
But fortune's pendulum might sway and turn things in your direction – see.

Demeter *pulls frogs from* **Miss Ssippi**'*s dress.*

Demeter (*angry*) Hm. It's time I fed the mistress my croak soup.

Demeter *exits and* **Brer** *dances, bows before* **Miss Ssippi** *then exits.*

Miss Ssippi (*as if looking into the future*) NOBODY KNOWS THE TROUBLE I SEE
NOBODY KNOWS BUT JESUS
NOBODY KNOWS THE TROUBLE I SEE
NOBODY KNOWS . . .

Miss Ssippi *puts on her church gloves.*

6. Alliteration – to letter

Afternoon.

Near the plantation, **Jean** *cleans while* **Yankee Pot Roast** *tends to his wound.*

Jean Verse My Po'em's just a stone's throw away now, Pot Roast . . .

Yankee Pot Roast If I had a stone, I know what way I'd throw it –

Jean Verse Bully, you be nice to me pork bottom. I saved your life.

Yankee Pot Roast You should have left me to die!

Jean Verse *Ash*, don't be such a stick in the mud. I'll set you free once you write me a letter. Here. Pen me this prose.

He throws pen and parchment at the boy who writes.

1221 Rue Mont Blanc, Proctorville, Louisianne. (*Beat.*) Cadence, *Ma Femme*. (*Beat.*) Forgive this shivering quill for forging its black blood in foreign calligraphy but my fingers tremble with a great fear. A fear so buried in my bosom that only the threat of death has forced me to free it. And alas, no longer its slave I shall die a defector: a man for complete and utter emancipation. No longer can I admit to loving you with a whole heart and no longer can I admit to wanting to join this war as much as wanting to be free from you. You are my love but love, I loathe you because I never truly loved you and never will. And being forced into your heart has made me your harlot. I felt fragile as a woman inside you for my love is forever for Po'em. I have loved her long as the days are blue, the nights black and star-studded. And I have whispered her name to God and to the graves of my grandfathers as I traveled the streets of Orleans and tossed rue upon their sepulchers. And wife, I have felt shame until now for this love. For today, I am proud to have the poetry of her eyes blinking upon my every thought like all of the constellations in all of the heavens. And her love has made me her runaway or rather a runner to. For I am runnin' to be with her forever. And Free, the girl that was left on our doorstep, the one we took in, she is mine and Po'em's child born the same day as Blanchie. They are sisters, and they are what I leave you – a child of love and a child of legacy.

The girls run into the garden.

Free It's *Mon Pere*! It's *Mon Pere*!

Blanche Naw it ain't! Man your stations, it's the Yanks!

Cadence *follows them.*

Cadence Y'all come back here! Women don't run!

Free It's okay, *maman*, it's *Mon Pere*!

Blanche No it's not, it's the Yank!

Cadence It's neither. It's . . .

Demeter *enters.*

Demeter Me.

Free Miz Dahmeetah. You come back.

Demeter *enters carrying two dead frogs.*

Demeter Yes'm. I come back. I makin your maw a soup.

Blanche Ooo, is dem froggies?

Cadence Soup? What I want a frog soup for?

Demeter For supper – course. You look ill. You childers grab them garden tools. We got to scavenge for vegetables to add to the soup.

The girls exit to gather tools.

Cadence Smell like you up to something woman . . . What's this you cookin'?

Demeter Soup, I said. I just feel bad for judging you, Missus. You was right, my girl did leave . . . I found another piece of her quilt in the river –

Cadence – O . . . she musta drowned.

Demeter Drowned?! What an odd thing to say. Here! Go boil these in a pot. Cook em good too . . . or you'll croak.

She throws the dead frogs at **Cadence** *who screams and runs into the house.* **Demeter** *goes outside.*

Demeter Alright, now I need y'all to help me gather. Lil Free get me a basket and a picker. This soil is nice and wet. I'm get y'all stocked up. Baby white, get me a pail of water.

Blanche My name is Blanche. And there ain't no more vegges, Miz Dahmeetah. All our greens done turned black.

Demeter Not when I put my hands on it. I got a way with greens that's golden. Now fetch me that pail.

Blanche Naw, you fetch it. I'm a white.

Demeter Yeh, a starving white. Free, hand me that pail of water.

Blanche Free, don't you move. We ain't servants. Know your place woman! You fetch it.

Demeter Ooo, ain't you brave? Talkin' large and I got this pick axe in my jerkin' hand. Free ya best tell ya half sister to stay on her side. I might have to scratch an itch.

Blanche She ain't my half sis, we twins!

Free Yeah, Miz Dahmeetah, we was born dee sameday. We'ze identicals.

Demeter Who told you that? Girl ya got blackness all on ya. Even under dat powder I can tell ya got Black. Come here!

Blanche *forces* **Free** *behind her.*

Blanche *Non* said, she's a white! *Maman* says she's just dark some cause the sun got the hots for her. But she's us. She's my same.

Free *Maman* say dat? She say I dark?

Blanche She used to. Fore you start gettin made up.

Demeter Yeah, before she start coverin your beauty. Come here Free!

Demeter *fetches a pail and approaches* **Free**. **Blanche** *stands in the way.*

Blanche You want her. Best come through me!

Demeter Ya know, I just might be scared if ya muscles was as big as your mouth is. Move!

Demeter *lifts* **Blanche** *with one hand. She grabs* **Free** *and wipes her face.*

Demeter Now you look at ya face in dis water Free. Catch ya reflection and tell me what's there. Look deep now.

Free *looks at her face, powder drips off her almond skin.*

Demeter Tell me what you see . . .

Blanche No, Free, you is one of us. You is a white.

Demeter What you see, Free?! You see who you really is?

Blanche You is me, *ma sore*. I on't care what she say. You my same.

Free *is stunned, she sees Po'em's face.*

A Voice (*distant, singing*) FREE . . .

Free Is this my face?

A Voice JUST WANT YOUR LIFE TO BE . . .

Free I 'member this face. This my ma'am's face.

A Voice FREE . . .

Free We got the same face.

A Voice GOTTA GIVE YOU UP GIRL

Free and **Voice** SO YOU'LL BE FREE

Demeter How you know that song? Who gave you that song?

Free NO! I don't want to talk bout it . . .

Free *throws the pail and runs off.* **Blanche** *follows her.* **Demeter** *picks up the pail and looks into it. It conjures the following:* **Demeter** *takes seeds from her pocket and plants them.*

Demeter Ev'thing dat grows 'gins with water.
Water wets the soil, softens it from rock to mud
Mud in da hands can be made to mold.
Mold 'en to a muscle with grooves, rows of holes.

Demeter *makes grooves in the soft soil with her toes, she drops in seeds from her pockets, then covers the holes with her toes. It is a slow dance.*

Holes is made to sprinkle seeds.
I cover 'em kindly with my toes.
Ah, look see the sun is all ready ready to bake 'em.
Won't be long now 'fore this garden grows.

The sun seems to be bathing in blue. **Cadence** *screams from inside the house.* **Demeter** *exits. We hear the sound of crashing pots. We return to the field where* **Jean** *unties* **Yankee Pot Roast**.

Jean Verse You gone put this letter in duh post box just 'fore the sun sets. By then me and Po'em be long gone from here. Now I know you and I didn't start on the right foot but . . . well piggy, you turned out to be alright in my book. Here. I want you take your bugle back and get yourself home, hear? Just promise me, you'll put this letter in the postal box. You promise me boy.

Yankee Pot Roast Of course sir, I promise. I'll do whatever you say.

I've learned so much today 'bout southern hospitalit-tay
And though we differ in politics we still have the same face.
Let us bid adieu Jean, with a civil embrace.

Jean *embraces him as he grabs a knife from Jean's coat and stabs him in the back.*

Jean Verse JESUS!!!

Yankee Pot Roast Yes. Pray Jean. Pray for your soul.

You made me your slave: and now you know slav'ry is wrong.

Jean Verse I curse you piggy. I curse you with the last of my breath
You will squeal . . .
O! You will turn pink and plump and you shall shrill
At the sight of your fat ass rump, piggy.

He laughs, spits up blood.

I will be dead but . . . at least I can boast
You will live your final days: as a Yankee Pot Roast.

Jean *dies. The boy drags him into the arms of the river.* **Brer Bit** *watches from a tree.*

Brer Bit Well, look at dis. Dere goes the first Verse
Didn't even require me to pull a rabbit from my purse
Now I got to get rid of the chillen and the wife
So I'll be mastering the house tonight
And once I do, I'll free the mule and burn the shack
And lo, after that I'll paint the house black.

Miss Ssippi *hums over* **Jean's** *bloody body.*

In the kitchen, **Cadence** *and* **Demeter** *are chatting.*

Cadence I can't even boil water! I'm just dumb.

Demeter Yeh, but don't apologize for it, Missus. Being dumb is natural. It's like being ugly – ain't nothin' you can do about it but scratch your head. God got it fixed so that everybody come in this world is dumb. We all come here dumb babies with nothin' but a world of joy and hope in all our lil ole bodies. That's till some smarty get a hold of us. Put all they fear and ignorance into us so we can be smart like them. Yes Lawd, too smart for our own good. That's why it's alright to be dumb . . . just don't be stupid. Being stupid is shameful. It's like being ugly but goin around thinking you pretty and got one tooth to your name. It's just sad and shameful. Being stupid. Here. Let me help ya.

Demeter *boils water and cooks the frogs.*

Cadence Mighty kind of ya to stick around here. We probably woulda starved if you didn't come back. Look at me: what kind of mother can't even boil water?

Demeter Your kind. You got to light the coals here under the stove. See.

Cadence O, that's where they are. Silly me.

Demeter Hm. You ain't silly. Sit down! (*Soft.*) I don't mind servin' you.

Demeter *slaps a bowl before* **Cadence**. *Then she takes the scarf from around her neck and cooks.*

Time.

Cadence That mark on your neck. It looks like fingers . . . reachin' out.

Demeter Yes'm. Reachin' to form an 'Arah'. It's a scar. I'll cover it if it bothers you.

Cadence Naw. It could probably use some air. How'd it happen?

Demeter Death . . .

Cadence I don't understand.

Demeter Yeah. I don't understand death neither –

Cadence – No, I mean, I don't understand how –

Demeter Why? Don't I seem hard to kill? (*Beat.*) They were foolish to get at me. To bring death into the pact. I took care of them and death. And he was weak. I broke the noose alone just by singin' my song.

Cadence *rises.*

Cadence Here . . . let me put an ointment on it. I can at least do that.

Demeter Better not. It might bite you.

Cadence Oh . . . then I'll leave it. You somethin' strong. Just like your daughter.

She was my dearest friend: Po'em. I miss her . . .

Demeter Funny. A bunny told me you killed her.

Cadence Naw, but I won't tell you I didn't want to.

Demeter Then how'd she die? Give me the truth.

Cadence It won't make it easier.

Demeter Don't matter, I need to know her story.

Cadence Well, it ain't what you been hearin'. She didn't get her life snatched and was carried to hell or . . . got bit by a snake and drowned in the river: all those are lies. The truth is she loved him. She loved my husband so much, so hard that after while, when she didn't hear word from him or get anymore letters. Her poor heart rotted inside of her and she took ill and died. Right in my arms, she went to the otherworld . . . after her love.

Demeter *takes a spice from her pocket and seasons the soup. We return to the field where* **Yankee Pot Roast** *is putting the letter in the postal box.* **Brer** *comes from behind a tree.*

Brer Bit Evenin', suh. And how you be?

Yankee Pot Roast Why, I be fine, and yourself?

Brer Bit Fine, cause I got my health but you sir . . . you skinny enough to take a bath in a gun barrel.

Yankee Pot Roast Ha! Which leg of mine are you pullin'? Me? Skinny? No, I'm just pretty.

Brer Bit Yes siree, Yankee, ya pretty skinny cause I can see your ribs and your stomach and both of em mad enough to chew nails. You need to eat a porkchop sand'mich or some croak soup. Fact some is cookin nearby. Can't you smell it?

Yankee Pot Roast No. I don't smell a thing.

Brer Bit Well, they say it's the first thing to go when you starvin': your sense of smell. Then you lose your hearin'. Then your taste don't bud. And then ya stomach swell up like you with child. And then chile, you start to stink like homemade sin but you don't know it cause . . .

Yankee Pot Roast You ain't got no sense of smell.

Brer Bit That's it! See: that's why you need to eat you some soup. You see that white house over yonder?

Yankee Pot Roast Yes, I know it well.

Brer Bit Well . . . there's a big pot of soup cookin' on the stove with your name on it in that house. You take your big rump over there and I bet you get a bowl. Fact, ain't nobody there but the mistress and her last slave. Bet if you march your big rump over there and put your foot down you could be the massuh!

Yankee Pot Roast Oooo, I could be a massuh. I likes that. But you said big rump. I thought you said I was skinny –

Brer Bit Ooo, best hurry. Sound like you startin' to hear things too.

Yankee Pot Roast *runs off as* **Brer** *smiles. We go to the river where* **Jesus** *enters beat boxing and wearing sunglasses. He walks upon the water.*

7. Onomatopoeia – making a name

Dusk.

Enter **Blanche** *and* **Free** *in their trunks.* **Miss Ssippi** *leaves a trail of her blue skirt for them to swim in.*

Free Sploosh, splosh,
Watery, splash.

Blanche Wish! Wash!
Weze washin our ass.
Slop! Sloshed!
I pass you a crash!

Free Stop. Slop!
I'll give you a lash.

Blanche Dash. Hop!
You best be fast.
I flop like a fish.
I blast like a brass.

Free Swoop! Whoop!
You ain't so fast.
I flap like some fins.
I'm on the glass.

Blanche But can you dive! Plunge.

She goes under water.

Free Plunda! Sponge!

She goes under water.

Blanche Lunge.

Free Dig!

Blanche Bubble

Free Big!

Blanche Bubble!

Free Burst.

Blanche Gobble! Beg!

Free Rotten! Egg!

She soars to the surface, lifts her head.

Air!

Blanche Air!

Free Breath!

Blanche Breathe! Push!

Free Leave!

Blanche No! You Go!

Free No! You leave.

Blanche I was here first.

Free I was here first.

Blanche Whiner!

Free Dummy!

Blanche Cry baby! Mom-my!

Free Stop it.

Blanche Sorry.

Blanche hugs her.

Time.

Free *and* **Blanche** *lay back, floating on their backs looking at the stars. And* **Jesus** *moonwalks the Mississippi.*

Blanche So, what you see in that pail, Free? Where'd you learn that song from?

Free Ma'am. She taught me. I think I got Po'em's face, Blanche.

Blanche You silly! Just cause you look different don't mean you not my same. *Mon pere* be mad if he find out you actin' like you not family. You got to be wit us dat know ya. Dat love ya big.

Free I knows, Blanchie. I knows.

Blanche Good. Now I'm going to the box right now to see if *Pere* showed up. You go home and see bout *maman.* Promise me.

Free *Ah – oui. Je promesse.*

At the house, **Cadence** *sits at the kitchen table alone. She starts to eat the soup but suddenly* **Yankee Pot Roast** *barges in salivating from the mouth.*

Yankee Pot Roast Nourishment! I need nourishment!

He grabs **Cadence's** *bowl and scarfs down the soup. She screams. He grabs the pot from the stove and pours the soup over his face. Suddenly, he turns into a pig. He charges after her and grabs her by the waist. She tries to fight him off and reaches for a lantern to hit him against the head with. Instead it falls to the ground and catches fire. Canon blasts speckle the sky. Near the river* **Blanche** *talks to the postal box.*

Blanche *Mon Pere*? You in there? It's ya *fee-yah*, ya Blanche. I come to see if you've come home. Not in the form of *une lettre*, of course. I don't expect ya to fit in dere postal box, paw but . . . it's sho be good to know when you comin'. It's been so long since I've received a sign from you. I search this box everyday cept Sundays waitin' for a word or your whistlin' to come rustlin' down the road and you behind it. I can't fix you out my head, *Mon Pere*. I can't keep you out of my cryin'. For I miss ya like I'm dyin' to have ya. Though I know you are not dead – can't be. You're too brave for death. And I figure postage routes are rough – and hardly ever reaching out to Proctorville – the most dusty town in *La-wheezy-ann*. But I can't help . . . can't help but need a piece of proof. Cause I'm scared.

She weeps.

I don't know if I can keep my promise and protect *maman* and Free . . . dere's a Negro at duh house, Po'em done run off and Brer too, I hear canons and . . . I just wish ya was here. Home. Here to hug my neck and kiss my nose.

Blanche *opens the box. There is a letter.*

Paw?

She reads it. Nearby, **Brer** *sits in a tree.*

Brer Bit Y'all listen close, hanging from this post I spit the second Verse:

Mistress Cadence has gone the worst.
A bowl full of croak soup is upsetting her gut
And every time she tries to upchuck the poison it quickly rushes
Her soul closer to death and death's glorious light.
Fore long I'll be mastering this kingdom tonight.

Blanche *runs toward the house.*

Brer Bit Well mercy me, and right on time. It's the last bit of Verse left to spit.

Dis gives me another reason to rhyme: how bout dis . . .

He jumps from the tree. **Blanche** *screams.*

Blanche Bruh bit, where you been? You spose to be servin' the army.

Brer Bit Yes . . .

But like late Revelation that rouses a church
And lifts folks from wherever they sit.
I am full

Blanche Yeh, full of shit.

Brer Bit (*an aside*) Note: the wisest fool always plays the part of the poet.

(*To* **Blanche**.)

Brer Bit Come in the house, Blanche, I've made a mess and am dying to show it.

He grabs her by the throat, she tries to fight but it's to no avail.

Forgive me, while I spit some poesie: this one will be free of Verse

Though I shall do it freestyle, for tis sweeter and terse.

Blanche *struggles to get away.*

Brer Bit Ah, don't go nowhere, you need to hear it first
Precious Blanche, your paw has drowned in the Mississippi
Your mother should've croaked a bowl of frog soup
And soon your sister will be Ocean-deep
Which will put an end to all Verses 'cept you.
Due to the occasion, I'll let you pick you poison:
I could smother you like chops or snap ya neck till it cracked.
Either way it go, I'm paintin' the white house black.

They arrive at the house – it's on fire.

Blanche Flames! Fire! The house is on fire!

She kicks **Brer** *in the knee and runs in the house.*

Brer Bit My Mistress? My love you're burnin'? The devil's tongue is lickin' your bones. Painting you with moans and brushes dipped in blue heat with gold tips. Flames! Red as my hate! Give me chills . . .

He dances out flames.

Hold on mistress, I'll save you or I'll grill.

At the river, **Jesus** *baptizes* **Free**.

Free Jesus? Who am I?

Jesus You are Free, Free.

Free Yes. Course, Jesus. But who is my father?

Jesus I am. I and the father are one. I'm your father.

Free Don't be silly, Jesus. Then who is my mother if you're my father?

Jesus I am. I am a joyful mother of children. I am your mother.

Free Jee . . . zus . . . ?

Jesus Yes, Free girl.

Free Who am I really? Be real.

Jesus You are Free. You are my child.

He opens his arms – his robe is like angel wings.

Come to me . . . Freedom.

Free *embraces him.*

Free I love you, Jesus. (*Beat.*) I don't really understand you but . . . I love you just the same.

Jesus One day you will. One day you will fit into your name.

Free *washes* **Jesus'** *feet.* **Blanche** *helps her mother out of the burning house as they cough, covered in soot.*

Blanche Where's Free?

Cadence Don't know. Why is she not with you?

Blanche Cause I sent her home. She was spose to come here.

Cadence I told you to watch her! You weren't suppose to leave her!

Blanche I ain't her mother!!! You're her mother – *maman*.

Cadence Am I? Free don't have my eyes, Blanche. She don't have our skin. You done let her run off with that Miz Dahmeetah.

Blanche I had to go to the post box.

Cadence You always got your head in dat box! You were suppose to watch her! You need to just face it: ya paw ain't writin you cause he dead. He dead and we all that's left. Figure you need to know so you don't be going around with a whole in your heart expectin him to glue back the pieces. Your paw's dead.

Blanche *looks at the letter.*

Blanche *Non*, he ain't dead, *maman*. He just better off.

Blanche *runs off.* **Cadence** *sinks down into her dress. At the river,* **Demeter** *appears right behind* **Free** *– and scares her.*

Demeter You look like a bird –

Free – Miz Dahmeetah! You scared me.

Demeter Who you talkin' with?

Free Jesus. He say hi.

Demeter Tell him I said hello. Where'd you find this Jesus anyway?

Free Don't know. Don't remember.

Demeter Well, what he look like?

Free Like Jesus. Like you . . . but he got magic.

Demeter Your Jesus Negro then. Your real momma musta give you that Jesus.

Free I on't know. I on't know and I don't want to talk about it.

Demeter I think your momma was my girl which means you're mine.

Free My momma?

Demeter You my child, Free. I want you to come with me.

Free Can't. I told Blanchie I'd go home directly.

Demeter These ain't your family girl. I'm your'ins. I'm your grand. I'm goin to take you to see your momma.

Free Den you and momma can stay wit us. Don't leave us, Miz Dahmeetah. We good –

Demeter – My time is runnin' out. You got to come with me. We got to leave this cruel world.

Free No. No I ain't goin' –

Demeter – Yes, you is. Come on now, Free. Be good.

Free Let go of me, Miz Dahmeetah.

Demeter Hush! Don't fight this!

Free Let go of me!

Demeter carries her off.

Demeter You all I got left. Hush your mouth!

Free *reaches out to* **Jesus**. **Jesus** *has to turn his back. She begins to pray. In shadow we see soldiers fighting and the house in flames. We see a history of pain and grief and finally blood. Then a canon blast.*

Miss Ssippi *enters, her church clothes are covered in blood.*

Miss Ssippi MASTER!!!

Suddenly violent, bloody and muddy fabric hurls in and covers the stage.

Master!

Jesus *walks upon the water, listening and answering prayer.*

Miss Ssippi Son of Man . . .

Jesus Shhh . . .

Miss Ssippi Son of Man, my dress. I need to speak to you about my dress, sir.

Jesus I'm a midst prayers, river.

Miss Ssippi This is pressin'. Stained. I got blood in my dress that won't wash 'way. Skirts of blood that won't wash. I need your baptism.

Jesus I'm cryin' on you. I'm sendin' rain . . .

Miss Ssippi It's not enough. My folds are filled with bodies. Bodies of children, blood of baby boys died in war, bones of chill'ren who died enslaved. You must do somethin'. They're just babies.

Jesus Flood then, river. Give them somethin' to wash in. Tomorrow a change's gonna come. FLOOD!

Miss Ssippi (singing) OH WASN'T THAT A WIDE
RIVER, RIVER OF THE JORDAN LORD.
WIDE RIVER, THERE'S ONE MORE RIVER TO
CROSS . . . ONE MORE RIVER TO CROSS . . . ONE
MORE RIVER TO CROSS . . . JESUS . . .

Her flood extinguishes the house.

8. METAPHOR – to carry across

Evening.

At the mouth of the ocean **Demeter** *holds* **Free** *tightly. The wind blows fiercely.* **Jesus** *waits.*

Demeter Come on, Free . . . I'm takin' you home. Don't you wanna see your momma?

Free Yes'm.

Demeter Then come on . . .

They step into the water.

Free But the water's so cold Miz Dahmeetah. *Maman* don't let us play near the Ocean.

Demeter Don't matter, I'm your family now. You gots to come with me. Your momma's waitin' for us.

Free I wanna see momma but Jesus say it ain't my time. He say best let me go.

Demeter *takes her deeper into the ocean.*

Demeter Tell Jesus: been letting go all my life. Lettin' go is how you lose love, daughters and your mind.

Free The water's too deep Miz Dahmeetah!

Demeter LET'S GO!

She snatches her, **Free** *screams.*

Jesus Leave her. This child is mine.

Demeter No. She got my blood. Which mean she belong to me.

Jesus It's my blood that frees her. I said, let her go.

Demeter Can't. I can't be left alone no more. This one's mine. This one thing belongs to me.

Jesus Let her choose, Demeter. She is neither your property nor mine. She is free. Let her choose.

Time.

Demeter Well? What will it be little one? Are you going back to that cruel world. Or you comin' with me?

Free *looks into the direction of the ocean floor then to the land.*

Free I can't go with you, Miz Dahmeetah. You my grand but I gots to fit in my name first.

Demeter *gives* **Free** *Po'em's quilt.*

Demeter Then here. These the pieces to your momma's quilt. Now you can add your thread to it, and pass it long.

Free *takes the quilt and embraces* **Demeter**. **Miss Ssippi** *nods to* **Demeter**. *In the distance we can hear* **Po'em** *sing. She beckons for* **Demeter** *who goes deeper into the ocean as the sea walls close in behind her.*

PO'EM.
JUST WANT TO GET MY GIRL

Free MOMMA
JUST WANT TO BE YOUR GIRL

Demeter and **Free** NO MATTER I GOT TO SEARCH
THIS WHOLE WORLE

Free MOMMA. . .
JUST WANT YOUR LIFE TO BE

Demeter PO'EM
JUST WANNA HEAR YOU SING

Free I'M FREE!
MOMMA, I'M FREE!

All goes dark except the moon as **Demeter** *leaves her song with* **Free** *and disappears into the sea. The moon shines on* **Brer Bit**, *sitting in a burnt rocking chair, on the burnt porch of the burnt house. He is smiling and clearly has lost his mind.*

Brer Bit Well: here's a quick spit of the last Verse: a vicious anti-venom
To cure the poison of dis rabbit's curse put in em.
The Gods are still godly, the Yankee is dead.
Demeter's sleep on the Ocean bed.
The mistress is heated, the massuh's drowned.
Their daughter's carry the weight of an antebellum crown.
The help is still 'round and you know where the river's at
But good news . . . the house is now black.
You think I'm upset but this be my point of fact.
The massuh's house has burned a beauty
That can only be described as Black.

He smiles as the moon moves over **Free** *and* **Blanche** *standing by the ocean, looking at the quilt.* **Free** *realizes that her dolly Lil Some'um is the final piece of the quilt. The doll is made of quilted patches. She adds all the parts together. They hold each other as they sing. Eventually a chorus joins them.*

Free and **Blanche** (*singing*) WEIGHED IN THE WATER
WEIGHED IN THE WATER CHILLREN
WEIGHED IN THE WATER
GOD'S GONNA TROUBLE THE WATER. . .

Miss Ssippi *speaks over the song.*

Free WEIGHED IN THE WATER
WEIGHED IN THE WATER CHILLREN . . .

Miss Ssippi Weighed on his bareback
the atlas of the star-crossed zodiac creeps
As he crawls blindly over blue day
Dusk:
A trail of blood that bleeds upon the war-torn world
A way to the river that weeps toward one's home
A wave that returns from the end to diverge the night
Above a road, in a wood, where they –
Blank and Free of Verse
Found themselves lost in the patchwork of a quilt
where a stitch led them through poet-trees
and grew out under the undergrowth of lies
So truth could live final, indefinitely
Here –
In this nature
Where roads shake hands
Having come together like the threads of this tale
Wanting to weave into one good, thick rope.
To hang history
Here
Where they hold in their hands the needle and know-how
To unstitch the sex of his story
Her story hangs here –

Where the thread pokes through the eye of a thought
To let the letter live or let it lye or let it sleep.

A rip
While the child looks into the fabric of night
Another rip
She rips it . . .
Line by universe
Word by World
Letter by tree
Ripping it . . .
Lifting the pieces to freedom
A burst of paper wings – tossed
Tossed like God must have tossed the stars

Letting them take wind and drift
And fall into my fold
I: River. Water. Woman. Mother Sippi.
Though due North they call me The way to Freedom.
Full of tales
Full of heads
Full of body.

The song rises then we hear ocean. Lights fade to black.

THE END OF THIS ROAD

Robert O'Hara

Antebellum

Characters

Sarah Roca
Edna Black Rock
Oskar von Scheleicher
Gabriel Gift
Ariel Roca

Setting

The living room of the Roca Household in a 'Plantation' home. Atlanta, late 1930s.

Connected to the library of Commandant von Schleicher in a Detention Center. Germany, late 1930s.

It is important that the two settings 'read' as one home. An Atlanta and Germany 'bleeding' into one another in the late 1930s.

Act One

<u>Winter</u>

Sarah *sits in her living room, reading* Gone With The Wind.

After a moment. There is a knock. **Sarah** *looks at her front door.*

'Knock, knock.' Stronger . . .

Sarah Who is it?

Silence. **Sarah** *goes to her front door.* **Sarah** *sees* **Edna**. *She carries two nondescript suitcases in her hands . . .*

Sarah May I help you?

Edna Excuse me, ma'am, but could I bother you fo' a lil' spit of water?

Sarah Well, I –

Edna I've been walking along this road fo' 'bout an hour or so and I just needed to –

Edna *collapses into* **Sarah's** *arms.*

Sarah Oh my goodness . . .

Sarah, *slightly overwhelmed, holds onto* **Edna** *and thinks a moment then pulls her into the room and over to a couch.*

Sarah Sit here . . . I'll go get some water . . .

Sarah *looks out to see if anyone has seen anything, and she closes her door quickly and then exits.*

Soon. **Sarah** *enters and hands* **Edna** *a glass of water.*

Sarah Here you are.

Edna Thank you ma'am.

Sarah You're welcome . . . If you need another minute or two to –

Edna This is a beautiful home, ma'am.

Sarah Thank you.

Edna (*awed*) Beautiful.

Sarah I had nothing to do with it actually. It belongs to my husband's family.

Edna Your husband, is he home?

Sarah No. He's at work . . . Are you from around here?

Edna Yes and no.

Sarah What does that mean, yes and no?

Edna *turns to* **Sarah**, *smiling.*

Edna Well, aren't we **all** from around here? . . . At some point, ma'am . . . didn't we **all** come from around here?

Sarah (*strange*) I guess . . .

Edna Please don't mind my asking, but when is your husband due back, ma'am?

Sarah He should be here soon.

Edna Do you think he could drive me into town, ma'am? I'd be much obliged . . .

Sarah Where in town are you going? Are you visiting folks?

Edna . . . Kinda.

Sarah You just passing through?

Edna Yes ma'am.

Silence.

Sarah May I ask you a question?

Edna Surely, ma'am.

Sarah How old do I look?

Edna Ma'am?

Sarah Guess.

Edna Twenty . . . something. Twenty-five.

Sarah Next week!

Edna Really, ma'am?

Sarah Yes.

Edna That's just wonderful ma'am –

Sarah Sarah.

Edna Sorry, Mrs Sarah. I'm Edna.

Sarah That's a lovely name.

Edna Thank you. I didn't have nuthin' to do with it.

Sarah (*laughing*) Yes, I know.

Edna So you don't think your husband would mind takin' me to town? I'd be much appreciate'd of it.

Sarah (*confused*) I didn't – did I say that?

Edna Well not exactly –

Sarah We do have to go into town. Tonight's the big night. The whole town's going to be lit up like the constellations. We're going be dressing up like in the good ole days.

Edna The good ole days? Didn't you say you just now turnin' all of twenty-five?

Sarah Come Monday morning . . .

Edna Well what you know about them 'good ole days', Mrs Sarah? Old days fo' you and me was just round the corner, they same as **new** days, I don't see no rockin' chair and walkin' canes up in this heah house, and here you come out with the 'good ole days' . . .

Sarah *is a little taken aback.*

Sarah (*laughing*) . . . When I said the town was dressing up like in the good ole days I meant, you know, Before the War.

Edna . . . Oooohhh . . . Before what war?

Sarah The war between the States . . .

Edna Oh **that** one . . . Colored folks dressin' up like Before the War too?

Sarah Some of 'em, of course, somebody gotta cook the food don't they? I mean –

Edna (*smile*) That's alright, I know what you meant. Better than **you** know what you meant.

Sarah It is true though, we're going to have us a catered meal in a big ole tent . . . with all those Movie STARS and folks are going to be taking photos and all that . . . I've been listening to the radio and they said that Airplane just took off from Hollywood, it should be here shortly, might even be little early.

Edna Folks dressin' up like Before the War just cuz Hollywood comin'? Is they tryin' ta' just **remember** it or bring it **back**? . . .

Sarah Bring what back?

Edna . . . The 'good ole days' . . .

Sarah Edna, where have you been living, under a rock somewhere?

Edna As a matter of fact that's exactly where I have been livin', under a rock, somewhere. My full name is Edna Black Rock.

Sarah (*fascinated*) Really?

Edna So, I've been living under a rock for all my life, seems like . . .

Sarah You'd **have** to be under some rock to not know that *Gone with the Wind* is having its World Premiere right here in Atlanta tonight.

Edna Gone With the **What**?

Sarah Gone with the **WIND**? How could you have missed all the flyers . . . and buttons and flags . . ..

Edna I don't know nuthin' 'bout no wind goin' no where. I was just outside and the wind seem the same as it was yesterday.

Sarah It means like a changing of the times . . . or like something that's **gone** and you can never have it back again – like, uh . . . love . . . or like a bad feeling or –

Edna In my book, love is a bad feelin' . . . and ain't nuthin' 'bout it **gone** . . .

Sarah You're funny . . .

Edna (*smile*) So are you . . .

Sarah This WIND is going be a Picture Show! Like the ones they have at those movie theaters? They took that part in the book where Atlanta burns down – I have my edition right here. I have been trying to re-read it all before tonight . . . This book. BESTSELLER from here to kingdom come. They made a picture show out of it. And they are having the first Screening right here tonight. Before even them folks up in New York see it we're going to get to see it, even before Hollywood see it, we're going to be the first . . . **A World Premiere.**

Edna You say they burn 'Lanta in this here book?

Sarah Burn her to the ground.

Edna And folks dressin' up to watch them burn they city down to the ground in a Picture Show? . . . That don't seem right, do it?

Sarah That part about Atlanta is mighty right. That's **true** history. They burned this entire city to the ground and we built it right back up again.

Edna What part you take in it?

Sarah Well . . . my family helped to build it back up.

Edna Oh . . .

Sarah It's the biggest picture show that has ever been made before and I've heard they have more than a **thousand** extras to film all the parts. And the **BURNING** . . . that is suppose to be a spectacle beyond your **wildest** dreams.

Edna (*pepper*) Not beyond **my** wildest dreams.

Sarah What?

Edna (*sugar*) Could I bother you for another speck of water, Mrs Sarah?

Sarah . . . Of course.

Sarah *takes the glass that she'd given* **Edna** *earlier and goes out of the room, not really used to doing for a Colored person.*

<u>**Winterlich**</u>

Oskar *reads a magazine while sitting in his library.*

After a moment there is a knock.

Oskar *looks up at the door leading off his library.*

'Knock-knock'. Stronger . . .

Oskar *exchanges the magazine for a journal.*

Oskar Herein.

(Come in.)

The door opens and there stands **Gabriel** *in a nondescript detainee uniform.*

Oskar Du hast dich verspättet.
(You're late.)

Gabriel Entschuldigen Sie mich, Herr Kommandant, ich habe mich verspätet, weil ich Wasser holen musste.
(I'm sorry, sir. I had to get water –)

Oskar Wie hast du mich genannt?
(What did you call me?)

Gabriel Est tut mir Leid, Oskar.
(I'm sorry, Oscar.)

Oskar Das ist besser. (That is better.)

Ich dachte, dass wir miteinander Englisch sprechen würden.
(I thought we had agreed to speak English to each other.)

Gabriel Aber zuerst sprachst Du mit mir Deutsch und es war verwirrend.
(But you spoke German to me first, and so it was confusing.)

Oskar Sagst Du, dass es meine Schuld ist?
(Are you saying that it is my fault?)

Gabriel Ja. Nein. Ich meine, ich hab's vergessen. Den ganzen Tag spreche ich Deutsch mit den anderen, deshalb hab ich's vergessen. Tut mir Leid.
(Yes. No. I mean . . . I forgot. I speak German with the others all day – I'm sorry.)

Oskar Du bist der einziger mit dem ich Englisch sprechen kann, Gabriel.
(The only time I can practice my English is with you Gabriel.)

Gabriel Ja. Ich weiss.
(Yes, I know.)

Oskar So. Englisch?
(So. English?)

Gabriel Englisch.

Oskar You're late.

Gabriel Sorry. Oskar.

Oskar I am never late.

Gabriel I know.

Oskar It is a condition weak.

Gabriel Yes.

Oskar You must try harder.

Gabriel They stop me along the way.

Oskar Leave earlier.

Gabriel They give me chores . . . obstacles.

Oskar Do them faster.

Gabriel Yes.

Oskar There is no open lunch –

Gabriel Free lunch.

Oskar What?

Gabriel No free lunch. Not open lunch.

Oskar Are you making joke of me?

Gabriel No. But if I were, I'd be making fun of you, not joke of you.

Gabriel *smiles*.

Oskar *does not*.

Gabriel (*saving*) . . . Oskar, you ask me to teach you English. I can not teach unless I correct your mistakes.

Oskar Yes. But you do not have to smile when you do it.

Gabriel Sorry.

Oskar I am not a toy. I am not dumb. This is not my first English.

Gabriel I know that.

Oskar Then act like it. You are not correcting a child . . . You believe you are better than us. Better than me.

Gabriel I do not, Oskar.

Oskar You ARE not . . . If you were, I would be standing and you would be seated.

Silence.

Oskar *picks up a book.*

Oskar Shall we begin.

Gabriel . . . Yes.

Oskar *uses his fingers to scan a journal.*

Oskar A is for Apple.

Gabriel Yes.

Oskar B is for . . . um . . .

He scans the book again. He locates a word.

B is for Boss-ton-i-an Bostonian.

Gabriel Bostonian.

Oskar (*repeating*) Bostonian.

Gabriel Yes. Someone who lives in Boston.

Oskar Is that near Mad-hattan?

Gabriel Man-hattan.

Oskar Sorry.

Gabriel Don't be sorry. You're doing well.

Oskar *smiles at* **Gabriel**.

Oskar . . . Will you sing for me?

Gabriel Not today . . . my throat is strained . . . go on . . . C is for?

Oskar You said that last time.

Gabriel It was strained then too. Next letter. C.

Oskar *doesn't look at the book this time.*

Oskar C is for . . . Clever.

Beat.

Gabriel Spell it.

Oskar C. L. E. V. E. R.

Gabriel *smiles.*

Gabriel . . . Put it in a sentence.

Oskar This is a Dangerous place for a **Clever** Man.

Silence.

Gabriel . . . I will sing for you next time, Oskar. I promise.

Silence.

Oskar *reads.*

Oskar (*reading*) 'They have announced the next stop will be Zoologischer Garten. In mere moments, my dreams will appear before me. Outside this very window. I will plant myself here a while. I hope my expectations are matched and tripled . . . Something grand is waiting for me here. I can feel its music. Oh. There. The Whistle. The Brakes. The Steam . . . Berlin.'

Silence. He looks at **Gabriel** *who is staring off . . . lost.*

The Good Book

Sarah *stands with water and a sketch of an antebellum dress.*

Edna *is looking over the house.*

Sarah (*giggling*) This is my dress. This is the dress I'm going to the Premiere tonight in.

Edna Which one of yo' chil'ren drew that up?

Sarah **I** made this sketch.

Edna Oh.

Sarah We don't have any children just yet.

Edna . . . Oh.

Sarah Matter of fact my husband is bringing my dress home to me this very afternoon. I haven't seen the final product. I sketched it and he had his people put it together for me. I would fuss back and forth every time he bring a piece of it home. Fix a collar here, fix a hem there. I use to be one of the girls making those dresses but now, I just sketch the kind I like to wear and somebody else does the making . . .

Edna Ain't that nice.

Sarah But it's still hard work here **sketching**, Edna Black Rock. That there is just the early idea of it, I went through lots of sketches for tonight's dress. This one tonight has to be **Grand**.

Edna What you say yo' husband's name was, Mrs Sarah?

Sarah (*quick*) I didn't say.

Edna . . . Oh. I thought you did.

Sarah I didn't . . . His name is Ariel.

Edna . . . That's a Beautiful name. Mrs Sarah and Mr Ariel. Beautiful names for a Beautiful House. And you gon' have you a Beautiful Dress.

Sarah (*excited*) You think so? You really like it, Edna Black Rock?

Edna I like it, Mrs Sarah. Now it's not my style you know. That ain't the way I like to creep but I like it good enough for you.

Sarah (*happy*) It's like a **costume**, isn't it? It's like a costume right out of a picture show. I thought of it all by myself. I put my own touch to it. All those samples from the Constitution were just completely dreadful.

Edna The **Constitution?**

Sarah Oh, The Atlanta Constitution, that's one of our local papers. They have been putting out samples almost everyday on how one might dress for tonight. I wanted mine to be different. Extravagant. Something **worthy** of what they would wear in *Gone with the Wind*. Some of these other people, I'm sure, are just going to throw anything they can find together. But I plan to win that contest. You see, there's a contest for the Best Dressed Couple. And the competition is steep. I told Ariel to make anybody who saw my sketches, **swear,** not to reveal an **inch** of its pattern. I put some time and thought into mine. Isn't it **different?**

Edna Well **that** it sho'ly is. But you might want to thank about somethin'.

Sarah What is that, Edna Black Rock?

Edna You see them big-ass hoops running all up and down from the middle to the bottom there, Mrs Sarah?

Sarah Yes.

Edna How long this picture show suppose to be?

Sarah I don't know.

Edna (*lifting the book*) This book heah is bigger than the Bible. This book 'bout the size of two Bibles if you ask me.

Sarah Looks that way.

Edna Now how long you think it would take for them to do a picture show about **Two Bibles**?

Sarah What?

Edna You read yo' Bible, Mrs Sarah?

Sarah Of course.

Edna You go to church?

Sarah I go to Temple.

Edna How long temple last fo' you, Mrs Sarah?

Sarah About three hours . . .

Edna Alright, now how many of them three hours you reckon yo' Preacha Man spend preachin'?

Sarah (*smiles*) None. We don't have a Preacher Man . . . We have a Rabbi . . .

Edna How long yo' Preacha-Rabbi usually spend Rabbitin'?

Sarah (*giggles*) About a Half-hour . . .

Edna A Half-hour? What ya'll do for the rest of the time, Mrs. Sarah?

Sarah Pray.

Edna For two and Half Hours ya'll prayin'?

Sarah Yes.

Edna You and Mr Ariel got that much to pray about?

Sarah Well, Ariel doesn't go in for Temple and all that.

Edna I see . . . well . . . how much of the Bible do yo' Preacha Rabbi usually take up Rabbitin' about in that half hour?. . .

Sarah . . . A sentence or Two . . .

Edna What?! . . . You mean to tell me that ya'll sit there for a half-hour with him Rabbitin' about **TWO** sentences. And **then** ya'll pray a sing-a-long for two and half mo' hours?

Sarah (*laughing barely able to speak*) Something like that . . . And –

Edna (*laughing*) And what, Mrs Sarah?

Sarah Come to think of it, I really don't know what mostly I'm praying about when I'm at Temple.

Edna Why is that?

Sarah Because it's in **Hebrew**. . .

Edna You got to be kidding me.

Sarah I'm telling you the god's honest truth, Edna Black Rock.

Edna (*laughing*) On top of all that, they make ya'll pray in a **foreign** language?

Sarah (*laughing*) And all the women have to sit up in the balcony –

Edna (*laughing*) I always have to sit up in the balcony.

Sarah (*laughing*) Oh . . . you're right. I guess it is like what they have for the Coloreds . . .

Edna (*encouraging*) . . . Now think to yo'self, Mrs Sarah. If the Rabbitin' combined with the Prayer Sing-a-longs, take three hours with only thirty minutes of that being devoted to two Sentences in the Good Book, then **fo' a full year of Sundays** that Preacha-Rabbi ain't even covered nuthin' but 'bout a few Chapters in that whole Bible, and this Book you got here about Somebody Blowin' Wind is **two times** worth of a Bible Picture Show, agreed?

Sarah (*completely lost*) I guess.

Edna Alright, so you liable to be in that Picture show 'bout how long you reckon? Fo' 'em toget **alllll** that stuff they got in this heah book to up there on that screen, includin' them burnin' down 'Lanta beyond yo' wildest dreams? How long you reckon it gon take them to get through that whole book with a Picture Show type of **style**, Mrs Sarah?

Sarah . . . Well . . . About fifteen years?

Laughter. They both enjoy each other.

Edna Mrs Sarah, you simple.

Sarah I know.

Edna You know?

Sarah I been called simple all my life. Folks called me Simple Sarah since I was nothing but a tot. I use to like to **touch** hot things . . . all the time . . . So they started to call me 'simple' . . . Put on a kettle . . . and I would touch it . . . Stick my fingers in hot tea . . . I didn't need a spoon for my porridge, my mother would just put it in front of me steaming hot and I would gobble it all up . . . Simple. Simple Sarah . . . I guess it stuck.

Edna Does Mr Ariel call you simple?

Sarah *pauses. Thinks. Smiles.*

Sarah . . . Only when I upset him.

Edna (smiles) Hmph . . . Well, Looka heah, Edna Black Rock and Simple Sarah. That has a ring to it.

Sarah (*laughing*) Yes, it does.

Edna (*laughing*) We goin' on the Road with them names.

Sarah (*laughing*) On the road? I can't leave here –

The two stop and look at each other and then burst into laughter over the last line.

Edna (*smiles*) That WINDY picture show gon' be at LEAST four or five Hours and you talkin' about ridin' up into town and going to a **feast** ova' here and spending time lookin' at movie stars gettin' they photos taken ova' there and you think you gon' sit yo' ass up in all them HOOPS runnin all through you and you ain't gon' have to **scratch** nuthin' or **relieve** something else? . . . You are indeed Simple Sarah . . . That dress there, ain't nuthin' but a Headache . . .

Sarah . . . You think so?

Edna **Unless** you got you a maid to go wit chu. And help you out.

Sarah (*sad*) . . . We don't have a maid.

Edna And why not, ya'll livin' up here high on the hog without no children to help do no chores and no maid to help look after ya'? How ya'll livin' all up in here like this fo' with no help?

Sarah We can't afford it.

Edna What you mean you cain't afford no maid with this big ole house heah you livin' in, when I was walking pass this heah house I thought to myself they must got them a MAID gonna answer that door ta' this house heah and she might be kind enough to give me a glass of water befo' I fall out, that's the first thing I was thinkin' when I saw this heah house that's the first thang **anybody** would be thankin' when they see somethin' like this and walked as far as I don' walked to see it . . .

Sarah Ariel says we can't afford a maid. I don't mind doing the work to keep it together. We both do the work. I grew up doing chores, that isn't anything new to me.

Edna But when you was growin' up you was **suppose** to do the chores Mrs Sarah, cuz yo' Daddy was payin' the note and yo' Mama was cookin' yo' food weren't they?

Sarah I guess.

Edna Ain't no guessin' to it. You ate food and slept somewhere so unless you remember siftin' wheat and building houses as a lil' girl then **somebody** had to have been providin' for you. . . and that would usually be yo' Mama and Papa, but most likely yo' **Maid**.

Sarah We did have a Mammy now that you mention it. When I was little, we had one.

Edna Mammy. Maid. Same Difference. When you get all growned up and get yo'self a **MAN** who payin' yo' bills and **YOU** doin' the cookin' and you ain't got no chil'ren yet around to do no chores then that's the point when you needs you a Maid. . . And when you do get ta' havin' chil'ren thats when yo' Maid usually turn into yo' **Mammy**. Least that's the way it was done in them 'good ole days'. . . . Wit a dress lak that one there Mrs Sarah, you needs you a Mammy or a Maid or whatsinever you wants to call her.

Sarah . . . I guess you're right . . . But we can't afford it.

Edna I'll do it.

Silence.

Edna *holds her newly empty glass out to* **Sarah**.

Edna Could I have a drop mo'?

Silently **Sarah** *takes the glass and goes off into the kitchen.*

Küssen sie Meinen arsch

Gabriel *massages* **Oskar's** *back, as the latter now looks over a prisoner chart.*

Oskar Good . . . How were your tests?

Gabriel . . . painful.

Oskar More painful than they are normally?

Gabriel Yes.

Oskar I could talk to them.

Gabriel No please. Don't. They would only take it out on me more when you're not around.

Oskar Are you sure?

Gabriel Yes.

Oskar I have tried to protect you as best I could.

Gabriel I know and I thank you for that.

Oskar You should not be here. These Detention Centers are a waste. We are merely asking the questions to which we already know the answers.

Gabriel *looks to him.*

Oskar There is very little reason for you to be here.

Gabriel We both know that you are the 'very little reason' that I am here, Oskar. And you could let me go.

Oskar You would have me violate my command?

Gabriel (*quiet*) . . . yes.

Silence.

Oskar (*whisper*) Go where?

Gabriel Home.

Oskar You can't think you'd honestly be able to get back home, do you?

Gabriel I would like to try.

Silence.

Oskar (*cooler*) I have heard that you refused to eat three times last week.

Gabriel That's not exactly correct.

Oskar So they are lying?

Gabriel . . . No.

Oskar (*serious*) Are you trying to starve yourself?

Gabriel *is silent.*

Oskar (*too concerned*) . . . What happened?

Gabriel It was freezing –

Oskar That is exactly why you need to eat.

Silence.

Gabriel The food. The food was freezing. They hadn't cooked it. It was still raw.

Oskar You expect them to fry something here? You expect to eat like America?

Gabriel (*soft*) You expect me to eat raw meat?

Oskar . . . I will speak to them.

Gabriel Please. You know what happened the last time.

Silence.

Oskar . . . Let me see.

Gabriel It's fine.

Oskar (*gentle*) I want to see.

Oskar *grabs* **Gabriel** *to him and pulls his pants down around his buttocks.* **Oskar** *studies him.*

Oskar (*soft*) It looks better.

Gabriel It is.

Oskar May I kiss it?

Gabriel *resists.* **Oskar** *holds him tight. He kisses* **Gabriel's** *buttocks as he speaks.*

Oskar You must remember, you are oddity here, Gabriel.

Gabriel I understand.

Oskar Therefore you are made more a subject for ridicule.

Gabriel Yes.

Oskar They know of your talents. They've seen clippings.

Gabriel I know.

Oskar Even I remember seeing you in Club Brisk.

Gabriel And I remember seeing you, Oskar.

Oskar (*smiles*) Do you? Do you really?

Gabriel The day you came through. Mein Leben hat sich verandert.

House and Field

Edna *takes a book down that has a bookmark in it. She stops herself from opening it.*

Sarah *returns.*

Sarah My husband doesn't usually allow folks up through his library when he's gone.

Edna Oh, I was just lookin'.

Edna *puts the book where she got it.*

Sarah He's going to know somebody been in his library. If I so much as tap my toe on that floor over there he'll know I been through.

Edna I'm sorry.

Sarah That's alright. I'll make up something. I always do.

She hands **Edna** *the water.*

Sarah He reads a lot.

Edna Does he?

Sarah (*bragging*) Yes. He has a lot of book learning under his belt. I have a fair amount.

Edna That's nice.

Sarah (*honest*) Can you read? . . .

Edna . . . Yes.

Sarah . . . Ariel traveled the world before we married. I have love letters from across all the seas. Would you like to see one? . . .

Edna (*smiles*) . . . Yes.

Sarah *goes to her novel and removes a love letter from its pages. She hands it to* **Edna**.

Edna *looks over the envelope. Not having the indecency to open it.*

Sarah I keep each one in a different book. As Bookmarks. So while I'm reading, Ariel is always there. Postcards. Gifts. Even telegrams telling me he can't wait to come back and make me his girl.

Edna He wanted a girl, huh. Not a woman?

Sarah . . . I was a girl when he left. When he came back, I was a woman.

Edna I see.

Sarah . . . So you didn't really come here for water did you, Edna Black Rock.

Edna You tryin' to figure me out, Simple Sarah?

Sarah (*smiles*) You need a job.

Edna That I sho'ly do.

Sarah I hope you don't need a man, too.

Edna I gots me a man Mrs Sarah.

Sarah Where?

Edna Rights chere in 'Lanta.

Sarah Is he who you were going to visit?

Edna Yes.

Sarah So why aren't you visiting him?

Edna Cuz he got a wife. And he don't know I'm heah yet. And I wants to have somethin' respectable to be tellin' him I'm doin' with myself befo' I see him.

Sarah Were you not respectable before?

Edna No Mrs Sarah, I wouldn't be able to say I was respectable befo'.

Sarah . . . So you want to be our maid, so you can get respectable?

Edna I could help you in and outta that dress when you need it, tonight. We could start from there. See if you take to me bein' here, doin' thangs fo' ya' and if you feel like I wasn't in yo' way.

Sarah We couldn't pay you much, Edna Black Rock.

Edna We ain't got to get into all that just yet. First we should see if your husband likes the idea and then we'll see what we'll see after that.

Sarah Fine.

Edna . . . Fine.

Silence.

Edna . . . So ain't he suppose to be heah by now?

Sarah He's suppose to be. But he's picking up one of them ole fashion Horse and Buggies, everybody suppose to come Dressed up. We're adding the touch of the Horse and Buggies.

Edna How good your husband know how to drive a Horse and Buggie?

Sarah He doesn't.

Edna Then maybe that's what's keepin' him. Maybe it's the drivin' it and not the pickin' it up part that's keepin' him . . .

Sarah You know you're probably right. I never did think of that.

Edna You ain't suppose to, that's what yo' maid suppose ta' thank of. You ain't suppose to thank when you gots you a maid.

Sarah (*smiles*) I guess you're right.

Edna I **know** I'm right. And you know what? Ain't he suppose to be goin' back to pick up yo' dress fo' ya on his way home?

Sarah No, Ariel's a Dress Maker. That's his Family Business. He's a tailor too. His family run this clothing business in the city. I was the one running the shop while Ariel was away. His father became gravely ill so of course Ariel came immediately back home and took over the whole thing. I had to show him the ins and outs of it all. (*Laughing.*) He was soooo funny, the way he'd walk in and sit down in the back office all day with the door closed, as if the factory workers were gonna come and bite him or something. I personally think he would have much rather sent for me to join him in his travels and let the business go to dust, but frankly, he was the last of the ones able to take it over. Everybody else is either too old or too dead or too something to make it work.

Edna But it ain't makin' no money?

Sarah Not enough, for a maid.

Edna I see.

Sarah So we might not be able to take you on after all.

Edna I told you once already. I'll talk to yo' husband on that.

Sarah Alright . . . You sure you want to live all the way out here off the path like this?

Edna Every place I've ever lived has been off some path, Mrs Sarah.

Sarah . . . I'll tell you a secret, Edna Black Rock.

Edna (*smiles*) I like secrets.

Sarah (*quiet excitement*) It can get a little scary up through here . . . sometimes I think I see **spirits** . . . floating around out there in them fields . . . some times I stand at that window there at night and I think I see them **rising** . . . Ariel doesn't like me to go out in the fields, but sometimes, while he's at work, I take me an **adventure**. Just a couple of steps here and there out along the gate . . . I **discover** things . . .

shackles . . . bolts . . . **footprints** . . . there are scratches on the trees along the edge of the field . . . a hidden alphabet I think . . . figures . . . **signs** . . . etched into **roots** . . . And every so often I think I'm being watched . . . I look around and there isn't anybody there but a couple times I could have sworn there was some **things** trying to talk to me. Trying to tell me something. Most of them seem good but some of them leave you with a chill.

Beat.

Edna *looks toward the window. Then back at* **Sarah**.

Edna (*quiet*) Well . . . If I see one of them 'haints, I'll let you know, Mrs Sarah . . . But I was thinkin' since I won't be able to sit and see this Picture Show with you tonight, you wanna tell me what I **won't** be seein'?

Sarah Oh, it's glorious, Edna. Just glorious. You see, it's about a lot of things but mostly, it's about this girl. Named Scarlet. Scarlet O'Hara.

Edna Nice name there.

Sarah (*elated*) And she take up every bit of ownership of it too. She's in love with this man that she can't have. Because he's married to his own cousin already. So there's this other man that she meets, Rhett Butler, who's just as low down and nasty as he wants to be, and he wants him some Scarlet but she isn't about to be low cut to that kind of man.

Edna I hope this ain't some book about her runnin' around after some man!

Sarah I'm trying to tell you it's about more than that but that's **mostly** how it goes. It's a Romance. A **marvelous** Romance . . . (*Suddenly sad.*) Ohhhhhhh . . . And her mother dies . . . and her father goes crazy . . . and they burn and loot her house . . .

Edna What kinda house she got?

Sarah Something like this but much much **much** Bigger.

Edna I see.

Sarah And so then the War starts!

Edna (*bored*) Is this when it gits interestin'?

Sarah Yes! Her family goes broke and she has to go to Atlanta . . . wait . . . uh . . . I think I'm a little mixed up . . . I don't remember why she has to get to Atlanta but I know there's a **Fire** and she keeps meeting up with Rhett Butler and finally they get together but then something happens and –

Edna Simple Sarah, you ain't read that Book!

Sarah I did read it, I'm telling you the truth . . .

Edna Youse a lie.

Sarah I skipped parts of it this time through but I did so read that book, Edna Black Rock! And GUEST WHAT . . .

Edna What?

Sarah (*revelation*) Scarlet had herself a MAMMY!!!

Edna (*smiles*) Now see there, what I tell you?!

The women look to each other and then suddenly, **Edna** *does a small bounce curtsey.* **Sarah** *giggles and gets an idea. Then she grandly ushers* **Edna** *off into the kitchen.*

Ich Liebe Dich

Gabriel *reads the journal that* **Oskar** *had been reading from.*

Oskar *comes into the room, having just awakened.* **Gabriel** *does not notice him.* **Oskar** *comes up slowly behind him.*

Oskar (*softly*) What would you like for dinner?

Gabriel (*smile*) Hmm . . . Raw Meat again, I think . . .

Oskar Not tonight.

Gabriel What do you mean? Why not tonight?

Oskar Nor any other night. From this moment.

Gabriel Oskar.

Oskar I've made some changes.

Gabriel What . . . changes?

Oskar You will remain here with me –

Gabriel Till when?

Oskar Forever.

Gabriel Oskar, you are such a romantic.

Oskar What is that?

Gabriel Someone who . . . make believes.

Oskar (*serious*) We shall . . . make believe.

Gabriel . . . What are you talking about Oskar? What have you done?

Oskar You will be my house servant.

Gabriel What does that mean?

Oskar (*happy*) . . . You will be my **Maid**.

Gabriel . . . You mean Man Servant?

Oskar I mean **Maid**. You will live here with me. I will provide you with one of the guest rooms on this level and you will be here when I awake, when I come home and when I go to sleep.

Gabriel That sounds like a wife.

Silence.

Oskar *slaps* **Gabriel** *to the ground.*

Oskar You will be my secret.

Oskar *picks* **Gabriel** *up and brushes him off. He holds him.*

Oskar (*honest*) Ich liebe Dich. Gabriel. This is more than you could ever want! This is a dream that those out there would kill for if they had the strength in them. You will not have the humiliation that your skin provokes amongst the guards. You can sing your music in here. You can sing it here and teach me how. We will sing to each other. We will –

Gabriel It is too much of a Risk.

Oskar What risk? I am the Kommandant.

Gabriel Yes, but there have been rumors?

Oskar I do not bend to rumors! This very camp is a Rumor! YOUR being HERE is fucking **Rumor**!

Silence.

Oskar *goes to his window.*

Oskar Come here, Gabriel.

Gabriel *does.*

Oskar Point to the Guard who has started these rumors.

Gabriel No.

Oskar Do it. Point to the Guard who touched you that night and has fed these **rumors** of us.

Gabriel *looks to* **Oskar**.

Oskar (*quietly*) Wer vergewaltigt Dich, venn Ich nicht in der nähe bin?
(Which one rapes you when I'm not near?)

Gabriel *thinks for a moment . . . then points . . . then reconsiders . . . and with a smile he points in another direction . . .*

Oskar *goes into his library, opens a drawer, removes a gun, walks back into the living area.*

Oskar Leutnant Ernst Strasser.

Oskar *shoots the guard.*

'POW!!!!'

He turns to **Gabriel** *and holds the gun to his own head.*

Oskar ICH LIEBE DICH!!!

Silence.

Gabriel (*soft*ly) . . . And I love you . . . Oskar.

Adjustments

From off there is a sound of women laughing and silverware clinking . . .

The sound of horses arrive outside the home.

Sarah *appears racing from off and bounding out the front door.*

From outside the door there are kisses heard.

Ariel (*from off*) Sarah . . . (*Kiss, kiss.*) Sarah . . . (*Kiss, kiss.*) My dear, I'm fine . . . Sarah, it's just a scrape, I did **not** fall . . . I'm perfectly fine . . . Yes, yes, take this . . . Take it . . . Sarah STOP KISSING ME! . . .

Silence.

Ariel *walks through the door with a slightly bleeding forehead.* **Sarah** *runs in after him, holding a large dress box.* **Ariel** *moves towards the offstage kitchen.*

Sarah Wait! Dear, we have a guest.

Ariel A guest? Who?

Sarah Well . . . dear, you know how you kept on telling me that we couldn't afford a maid?

Ariel Ah Sarah you didn't!

Sarah I didn't do anything. She just showed up. Like an angel.

Ariel Like a what?

Sarah An angel. A spirit.

Ariel Are we on to those phantoms again? . . . How many times have I told you to stay out of those Fields.

Sarah Ariel –

Ariel They frighten you, my dear, and I will not have you going mad on me –

Sarah I'm not going mad. She nearly fainted.

Ariel Who?

Sarah Edna Black Rock.

Ariel So there is a real person this time that you've let in the house?

Sarah Yes.

Ariel You're not going to go racing after 'shadows' with that shotgun again are you?

Sarah She's **real**, I'm telling you the truth! She's looking for work . . .

Ariel (*sigh*) Ah, Sarah, whoever this woman is I'm going to send her on her way, we don't need a maid and we can't afford –

Sarah I promised her that we'd at least take her into town.

Ariel Do you know how long it takes one of those horse and buggies to get anywhere? We can't take her into town, I have got to get dressed and ready for that Opening tonight. There's going to be lots of potential business there . . .

Sarah *places the box down with a pout.*

Sarah Then she'll have to stay here for the night. I **promised** her we'd take her.

Ariel Sarah you have got to stop making these promises that include me. Now you promised we'd go to this picture show and you promised we'd pick up Rebecca and Sam on our way there and **now** you're promising a perfect stranger that we'd –

He stops himself. **Edna** *has entered the room wearing a maid's apron over her dress. She doesn't make eye contact with* **Ariel** *but picks up the dress box.*

Edna (*racing in*) Sorry, stew's almost ready. Come on nah, Mrs Sarah, let's get that dress outta that box and pressed –

Edna *begins to exit with the dress box.*

Ariel Stop.

Edna *stops still, looking at the ground, she shakes slightly.*

Sarah Edna Black Rock, this is my husband, Ariel. She likes your name, honey. She thinks both our names are beautiful. Sarah and Ariel.

Ariel Ms Rock, I'm sorry to tell you but we've no use for a maid nor would we be able to afford –

Sarah She said she'd work on the cheap.

Ariel Sarah please don't interrupt, dear. Now Ms Rock we would like to thank you very kindly for your offer but we will not be hiring a maid for some time now. And my wife has informed me that she led you to believe that I would be able to take you into town but I cannot.

Edna *doesn't move.* **Ariel** *looks to* **Sarah** *then back at* **Edna**.

Ariel If you start walking you'd get there pretty close to nightfall. Folks around these parts are as friendly as the next fella . . . should be lots of light out from the Celebrations due to the picture show opening . . .

Still **Edna** *doesn't move.*

Ariel I'll just take this Box and –

Edna *finally looks up at him, handing him the dress box.* **Ariel** *jumps back as if burnt.*

Sarah What's wrong, dear, that's not polite to be jumping back from folks like that, after all Edna done already done for us today . . .

Ariel *is now the one shaking.* **Edna** *looks him deep into his eyes. Her feet give way.*

She faints.

Sarah You've scared her to faint, Ariel! Poor dear probably hasn't had anything on her stomach yet . . .

*__Ariel__ (*terror*) Who is she?! . . . What is this? . . . What are you doing? . . . Don't touch her!!! Sarah, Come Here! Come Here!

*__Sarah__ Help me get her to the couch! Help me get the poor woman off the floor, Ariel.

Sarah *goes to* **Ariel**, *leaving* **Edna** *on the floor.*

Ariel I want you to tell me exactly **when** did she get here?

Sarah Around noonish . . .

Ariel And what did she say?

Sarah She asked me for some water and then she nearly fainted.

Ariel You check her identification?

Sarah Her what?

Ariel Dammit, Sarah! Her identification papers?

Sarah Of course not, Ariel, honey don't be silly. How many coloreds you know that keeps themselves identification or whatnot?

Ariel Sarah, WHERE is this woman from?

Sarah I do not know. She could be one of those spirits from out there in those fields for all we know –

Ariel Not that again, **please** –

Sarah Ariel, I'm just saying that she's a **mystery**.

Ariel (*turns to library*) Has she been over there?

Sarah (*lying*) No.

Ariel (*force*) Someone has been in there, Sarah. Have you been in there?

Sarah Yes. I did some dusting.

Ariel Sarah, I need you to look at me.

She does.

Ariel Sarah has this woman been alone in this house today?

Sarah No.

Ariel You've been with her ever single moment she's been here?

Sarah . . .

Ariel Sarah!!!

Sarah Stop Yelling my Name, Ariel! I told you that for the most part I've been around her, what do you think, she's hiding silverware in her undies?

Sarah *goes to* **Edna**.

Sarah Edna . . . Edna, wake up honey . . . Edna Black Rock . . . Wake up honey . . . Ariel go and bring her some more water would you . . .

He starts off. . .

Sarah Take that cup there. That's the one she's been using.

Ariel What?

Sarah What do you mean what? You want us to have to throw **two** cups away when she's gone. Take that one and fill it back up the way I've been doing – Ariel! Oh my – we have to take care of your head right now, its still bleeding something awful.

She starts to make **Ariel** *leave the room with her as . . .*

Gabriel *enters, reading.*

Edna (inaudible) Er. Kommt . . .
(He's. Coming . . .)

Oskar *comes into the library, dressing.*

Oskar (*to* **Gabriel**) What did you say?

Sarah She's coming out of it . . . let's go and get the water and I'll clean that cut.

She pulls **Ariel** *off towards the kitchen.*

Gabriel . . . Nothing.

Oskar Sing me a Song as I dress, Gabriel, so that I may trap you in my thoughts.

Gabriel **Keep** . . . me in your thoughts.

Oskar Yes. **Keep** you in my thoughts.

Gabriel . . . And what you did to me in there wasn't enough for your thoughts?

Oskar What I did to you? What we did to each other is more correct, isn't it?

Genuine.

You didn't like it?

Silence.

You are not my slave, Gabriel.

Gabriel Am I free to go then?

Gabriel *begins to walk out the front door.*

Oskar (*afraid*) STOP! . . .

Oskar *goes to* **Gabriel**.

Oskar Gabriel, what is wrong with you? Was I too rough with you in there? Did I hurt you? Did we not make good love sex?

Gabriel No Oskar. We do not **Make Love.**

Oskar What do you call it then?

Gabriel FUCKING.

Oskar Do you not love –

Gabriel Will you please STOP ASKING ME IF I LOVE YOU? Does it really fucking matter, Oskar?

Oskar Keep your voice down.

Gabriel For what?! I have not left this building for months, Oskar. Only for my **tests** and back again. I see no one but you. You think they have not noticed this? . . . You think that if you shoot one guard the others will go deaf and blind? You think that they don't know what those **sounds** you were making in there mean, Oskar?

Oskar It means I love you!

Gabriel You think that you're the first Kommandant to fuck a Prisoner?!

Oskar I have told you not to speak of yourself in those terms.

Gabriel What **terms**?

Oskar A prisoner.

Gabriel I am a Prisoner, Oskar!

Oskar I picked you from amongst the others and gave you my attention my care my love my –

Gabriel **COCK. C is for COCK. C. O. C. K.** You picked me from amongst the others because you'd never fucked a Colored before –

Oskar That is not true, Gabriel!

Gabriel (*rant*) You said so yourself! And now you expect me to **SING** you out the Door. Every time you leave you request a Song . . . or a Story . . . You want me to **re-live** MY past . . . for **your** sake . . . you would have me **IMAGINE** my life before this . . . imagine what was and would become. While you go out and **live** Yours!!! I am **not** a CLIPPING, Oskar. I am not a **Marquee** that you can post over your Bedroom Door. You can not expect me to **love** you through **force** of words ALONE! In here with you I have nearly no LIFE and you wish **LOVE** to grow inside that?! I will not give you that Oskar! I will play games but I will **not** play that one any longer! You do not love me Oskar! You love the IDEA of Me. And I will NOT **Ravage my LIFE** . . . by **willingly** giving you the scraps of **memories** that I have left. **YOU MAY NOT HAVE THEM!!!**

Silence.

. . . I'm sorry . . . The tests are making me . . . I'm sorry Oskar . . . Forgive me . . . I shouldn't have said that . . . alright . . . A song . . . let's see –

Gabriel *starts to sing a little bit of his signature song.*

Oskar (*interrupting*) You want to come with me?

Gabriel . . . Don't be ridiculous.

Oskar I am not. Would you like to come with me Gabriel?

Gabriel Where?

Oskar To the Sahausspiel?! Tonight.

Gabriel You want me to come and sit with you in the front row of a group of SS as they watch a stupid dubbed American picture show?

Oskar Would you like to come as my date –

Gabriel You are now speaking the language of loons –

Oskar But would you like to? Could you **imagine** That?

Quiet.

. . . There are ways. There are . . . experiments.

Secret.

Gabriel (*soft fear*) . . . I want nothing more of experiments . . .

Oskar . . . Adjustments . . . can be made.

Oskar *slowly exits.*

Edna *awakens now fully, she looks off into the library.*

Ariel *enters with water. His forehead is bandaged.*

Edna *turns to him . . .*

Ariel Wer sind Sie?
(Who are you?)

Silence.

Ich habe Ihnen eine Frage gestellt.
(I asked you a question.)

Edna Edna Black Rock.

Ariel Sie lugen.
(You are lying.)

Edna I am not a liar.

Ariel Warum können Sie Deutsch sprechen?
(Why do you know how to speak German?)

Edna Ich war da für eine kurze Zeit.
(I was there for a brief moment.)

Ariel (*realization*) . . . Who are you?

Edna Wo ist Sarah?
(Where is Sarah?)

. . . Kann sie uns hören?
(Can she hear us?)

Ariel This is not true.

Silence.

Edna Ariel.

Ariel **You are not true!**

Silence.

He turns towards offstage and listens for **Sarah**.

Ariel (*gentle awe*) You cannot be here . . .

Edna I am here, Ariel.

Ariel (*stifle*) You are a fever dream . . .

Edna (*stifle*) . . . So are you . . .

Sarah *enters.* **Ariel** *and* **Edna** *immediately release their gaze and turn so that* **Sarah** *cannot see the blush of their faces.*

Sarah I heard whispers and thought –

Edna Oh, Mrs Sarah, I need to check the Stew . . .

Sarah I've turned it down and kept a watch. Are you alright now, Edna? Drink all that water dear.

Edna Yes.

Sarah I have bad news.

Edna What is it?

Sarah My husband here . . . Well, Ariel, does not believe that we –

Ariel We're in no need of a maid.

Edna Mrs Sarah thinks different, don't you Mrs Sarah?

Ariel Sarah doesn't know what we need.

Edna I wouldn't say all that.

Ariel And Sarah doesn't pay the notes around here.

Edna I was hoping to get to discussing that in private with you, Mr Ariel.

Ariel There's nothing to discuss.

Sarah Ariel, honey. At least let her speak.

Sarah *goes to the dress box.*

Sarah I must go press my dress for tonight.

Edna Mrs Sarah, let me–

Sarah No, you stay and speak to my husband. Let him see how funny you can be . . .

Sarah *leaves, smiling encouragement at* **Edna**.

Ariel Are you here to blackmail me?

Edna With what? Love?

Ariel Yes.

Edna . . . No.

Ariel You could be killed if anyone found you out. Dressed like that.

Edna Dressed like what?

Ariel A Woman. This is not Berlin. This is Atlanta.

Edna Believe me. I know where I am. I am simply dressed as I should be.

Ariel What?

Edna . . . I've been adjusted.

Oskar *walks back into the library. He is now fully dressed in evening wear. He moves to the front door to leave.*

Gabriel Adjustments? . . . Oskar.

Oskar I instructed them to give you 'hormones' . . .

Gabriel You **instructed** them?

Edna At first they told me they were testing my blood.

Gabriel They told me viral tests.

Ariel Do you mean what I think you mean?

Edna What do you think I mean, Ariel?

Oskar At Club Brisk –

Ariel You were so beautiful.

Edna At Club Brisk.

Oskar You were grand.

Gabriel I was an Opening and Closing Act. It was **make up** and **artifice**! How long have they given me Hormones?

Oskar It was determined before your detention.

Ariel How long?

Oskar Since your arrival.

Edna I was detained.

Oskar Because of your inherent feminine qualities you were thought a perfect –

Gabriel (*horror*) Perfect?! How dare you!

Ariel You were perfect.

Edna (*soft offences*) For Political Insurgency. For Homosexual Behavior. For Color. For Height. For Voice. For being Flat Footed. For waist for hair for lips for buttocks.

Oskar For Science.

Gabriel Fuck You!

Oskar Exactly. That is the point.

Ariel (*weak*) What have they done to you?

Gabriel You have been **adjusting** my body?!

Oskar Yes.

Gabriel You're a **horror** to me!!

Edna (*stifle*) I waited.

Oskar And you are an impure dog. Who will bark . . . or quack . . . or fuck . . . upon my command.

Edna I waited . . .

Oskar Wait up for me. I won't be too late getting back. Make yourself ready. I've bought perfume. It is in the bath. A Gift . . . for my little **rumor** . . .

Sarah *runs in from off wearing her 'Antebellum' dress.*

Silence.

Ariel *looks to the dress and he begins to slowly laugh.* **Sarah** *smiles with him* . . . **Edna** *joins in slightly with them* . . .

Ariel's *laughter turns into weeping. He catches himself before throwing up* . . . *And races out* . . .

Edna *and* **Sarah** . . . **Oskar** *and* **Gabriel** . . . *remain.*

End of Act One

Entr'act

1935. Club Brisk

Gabriel *sings his signature song.* **Oskar** *and* **Ariel** *watch in wonder.*

Don't Say You Love Me . . .

I was raised by a Woman
Who was raised by a Man

And together we raised Hell
As only 'family' can

Her name was Lillie
But folks called her Ms Anne

All my life I heard her tell
One man after man

Don't say you love me
I just might believe it

Don't say you love me
My heart might receive it

Don't say you love me
Your voice might make it true
Don't say you love me
Till I say I love you.

Now Lillie was a Mother
But Ms Anne was a friend

And when I took her Lover
That friendship came to an end

I kept trying to explain
That the men wanted me just the same

But to her it was a shame
On what use to be a good name

She told me,

Don't say you love me
I just might believe it

Don't say you love me
My heart might receive it

Don't say you love me
Your voice might make it true
Don't say you love me Till I say I love you.

Finally it came time
For Lillie to take her last step

In the one room that she owned
I found her out of breath

Surrounded by all the men
With whom she'd committed so many sins

They sang to Lillie and Ms Anne
As I walked slowly in . . .

Don't say you love me
I just might believe it

Don't say you love me
My heart might receive it

Don't say you love me
Your voice might make it true
Don't say you love me
Till I say . . .
. . . I love you.

Act Two

Winter

1935. Berlin.

Gabriel *stands on a balcony over looking festive Berlin streetlife. Although it is late, he is only midway through a night filled of boozing and drugging.*

Music plays in the background.

Ariel *soon arrives, holding two colorful drinks. He hands one to* **Gabriel**.

Ariel Cheers.

Gabriel Cheers.

Ariel You must know Berlin adores you.

Gabriel (*smiles*) They tolerate me . . . Barely . . . (*Sighs.*) My falsetto, it **confuses** them . . .

Ariel They do more than tolerate.

Gabriel Maybe a little . . .

They laugh.

Beat.

Gabriel Sooooo. I bet you've never seen that position those two are in back there, have you?

Ariel *looks behind him . . .*

Ariel (*lie*) . . . I've done **that** before . . .

Gabriel Oh, really? . . . They teach that in 'Georgia' . . .

Ariel (*laughing*) Something like that.

Gabriel *watches* **Ariel** *in wonder.*

Gabriel Ariel **Roca.**

Ariel Rock . . . My father useta tell me our family was like a valley of Rocks . . .

Gabriel And 'Ariel' . . .

Ariel Lion of God . . .

They smile at the thought . . .

And 'Gabriel'?

Gabriel Man of God . . . our parents were Optimistic . . .

Laughter. . .

Ariel Yes . . . Being the first grandson, I took my grandfather's name . . . almost fifty years before him **his** grandfather went to America . . . they went South . . . built a business . . . and so forth . . .

Gabriel And so forth?

Silence. **Ariel** *drinks.*

Gabriel So. Is there precedent for **odd matings** in your family . . .

Ariel Precedent . . . a resounding yes . . . My grandmother . . . oh god was she **odd** . . . but she had moments of lucidity . . . very **brief** moments . . . Which reminds me . . .

He reaches for his journal in his breast pocket . . .

Gabriel *stops him.*

Gabriel Please, I beg you . . . Don't start that damn Scribbling . . . Every time I open my mouth you start scribbling . . . it's very impolite . . .

Ariel I'm taking notes on my journey . . .

Gabriel Darling . . . 'The journey . . . Is your Destination' . . . Live it. You don't have to **scribble** it.

Ariel My notes are on Life. On Music.

Gabriel But why?

Ariel Because I can't sing . . . I can't play anything. I can barely dance.

Gabriel Tell me about it . . .

Gabriel *pulls* **Ariel** *into a slow dance.*

Ariel But I can . . . enjoy . . . I can savor. . . . And that is worthy, is it not? . . . That is Worthy to share with others . . . to **scribble** about . . . I mean who will know we existed? . . . You existed . . .

Gabriel I hope I'm not about to become extinct . . .

Ariel The world should **know** you exist, Gabriel . . . I want to open you up . . . And mark you like a book . . .

They continue to slow dance.

The theme from Gone with the Wind *is heard . . .*

Sarah *appears on dais at the Gone with the Wind ball . . . She is all smiles and has a sash on around her which reads: 'Most Original'. She beams and waves to the crowd below like the Belle of the Ball . . .*

Soon.

The theme is overlapped with a Nazi rally as **Oskar** *appears.* **Oskar** *raises his right arm.*

The sounds mingle. **Gabriel**, **Ariel**, **Sarah** *and* **Oskar** *all remain a while in their own realities.*

Dancing, waving and saluting.

Then . . . they all disappear . . .

Acceleration

A love song plays as **Edna** *enters into the dark through the front door, breathing heavily, having run for miles.*

She carries a toy-like Confederate Flag on a little stick. She looks to it. Breaks it into little tiny pieces and throws them across the room.

She calms herself.

She turns toward the light in the library. Slowly, she begins to move in its direction.

Ariel *appears in the shadows, dressed in a bit of his own 'Antebellum' outfit. A bottle of brandy is in his hands.*

They stand in silence.

Ariel What shall I call you now?

Edna Whateva' you wish.

Ariel Man of God . . .

Edna Lion of God . . .

Ariel Gabriel. . .

Edna (*as if for the first time*) Yes . . .

Edna *turns toward the library.*

Edna . . . He had your Journal. The one you forgot, at my side that Night. You didn't lose it, Ariel. They took it from me that day and I thought I'd never see it again. He practiced his English through it . . . And I would read it to myself . . . when he was gone . . . or done with me. I would read it . . . and pretend you were there . . . next to me . . . whispering **notations** . . . this ear . . . sensitive . . . to your voice . . .

Ariel *goes to* **Edna** *and stands close to her ear.*

Ariel (*whisper*) This ear . . .

Edna (*weak*) Yes . . .

Remembering verbatim.

'Walking the streets with him is like an after-hours gathering of the circus. Extravagant and misty. Doors opened at his command. A flick of his wrist or a nod or a smile . . . A wink at times. But most often they knew he was coming . . . I don't want this to end . . . But I must go home . . . Before –'

Ariel (*completing the memory*) '– Before I lose myself . . . Or else I fear this city and my new friend shall swallow me whole and abhor the bitterness that will be found there . . .' I remember what I wrote, Gabriel . . .

Silence. They continue in soft close voices . . .

Ariel Wo ist Sarah?
(Where is Sarah?)

Edna I left her.

Ariel You left her?

Edna Your neighbors are bringing her home after the picture show –

Ariel She is afraid of the fields . . .

Edna I'm sure they will deliver her safely . . .

Ariel Did she apologize to Rebecca and Sam for my absence?

Edna . . . Yes.

Silence.

Ariel . . . You smell . . . the same . . .

Edna You don't. You smell . . . better . . .

Silence.

He moves to kiss her.

Edna I waited for you . . .

Ariel *stops.*

I held the show for you . . . I brought my suitcase . . . I stuffed my life under its lid and brought it with me that night . . . I would follow . . . I was prepared . . . to follow . . .

Ariel Your gaze would have stunned me . . . I would have been helpless . . . My resolve would have been useless to your – All of you . . .

Edna . . . I held the show . . . refusing to budge, refusing to breathe even . . . not moving from my dressing booth until word of your arrival. Finally . . . finally, there was no other choice but to go on . . . an hour late . . . a lost realized . . . a promise broken . . . and at the end of my set . . . when I'm normally somewhere near you . . . drunk or **close** to it . . . at the end of that set . . . delayed for a dream . . .

Ariel I'm sorry . . .

Edna . . . a wish . . .

Ariel I'm sooo . . .

Edna A Kommandant arrived . . .

Oskar *enters . . . He is intoxicated.*

Ariel *and* **Edna** *listen quietly to the rest of the song playing . . .*

Oskar *looks around in the darkness . . . He turns to his library and sees.* **Gabriel** *reading by lamp light.*

Oskar Gabriel . . .

Gabriel *says nothing. He keeps reading.*

Oskar *slumps to the floor at his library door.*

Oskar (*crying*) Gabriel . . . please . . . speak to me . . .

Silence.

Oskar I give you everything . . . And you continue to think of only him . . . You continue to daydream upon **his** words . . . **his** . . . English . . . I want to be **good friend** . . . I want to **match** your . . . **expectations** . . . and . . . **triple** . . . them . . .

Silence.

Slowly . . . **Gabriel** *closes the book.*

Silence.

Gabriel I want to . . . accelerate . . .

Oskar . . . Accelerate?

Gabriel Tomorrow. Let's begin tomorrow . . . I am your secret am I not, Oskar?

Oskar Yes.

Gabriel Then let it remain so . . . let's accelerate the process in secrecy.

Ariel (*into* **Edna's** *ear*) Gabriel –

Edna My name is Edna Black Rock now . . .

Oskar Tomorrow?

Gabriel You can bring the strongest medicines to me privately . . . I will remain hidden . . . here . . . your secret . . . until I am completely **transformed** . . .

Oskar I thought you hated it here?

Edna My suitcase was brought from my dressing rooms by the SS. They had indeed been following **me** . . . Not you.

Ariel They assumed **you** were leaving that evening . . .

Gabriel With you I am safe. I want to be complete for you. My body is no longer mine . . . But yours . . . You have enriched it.

Oskar You are my **flower** . . .

Edna I waited . . .

Ariel (*soft*) You **held** the set . . .

Edna (*sadness*) I **waited** for you, Ariel . . .

Oskar (*gentle*) I shall wait for you . . . to blossom.

Edna . . . And now my sweet Ariel, I would like a **real** drink.

Ariel *pauses for a moment.* **Edna** *smiles at him.*

Ariel Your usual?

Edna That would be **lovely**.

Gabriel *helps* **Oskar** *up and out of the library.* **Ariel** *makes* **Edna** *a drink.*

Gabriel *comes back onstage in a robe and we are in 1935 Berlin.*

Gabriel Mr Scribbler, Did you remember to bring my –

Ariel *now bleeds from the forehead as he had earlier.*

Gabriel *is stunned and reacts much like* **Sarah** *had earlier to the bleeding.*

Gabriel Oh my god . . . They did this to you didn't they? . . . Those **fucking** Nazis . . . Roaming the streets . . .

Ariel I'm alright . . .

Gabriel *goes off.*

Gabriel (*from off*) Everyone should just leave this fucking place to those beasts . . . let them have it . . . let them rip each other apart . . .

He comes back in with medical aid of the period. He begins working on **Ariel's** *head.*

Ariel It's not so bad . . .

Gabriel It's not so bad? . . . Ariel, there is **blood** on your forehead and there are signs in the windows . . .

Ariel There are signs in the windows in America.

Gabriel That is my point. This place is turning into Mississippi . . . Alabama . . . Georgia . . .

Ariel I live in Georgia . . .

Gabriel You don't live as a Colored in Georgia . . .

Smile.

I'm telling you. I can smell it. Berlin is turning into the American **South** . . . Only here the Jews are the Niggers.

Ariel You know I hate that word.

Gabriel Which word? 'Jews.' Or 'Niggers'.

Ariel Stop it.

Gabriel Get use to it. I have . . . You know I have friends who have been questioned!

Ariel **Everyone** is questioned . . .

Gabriel Why are you doing that?

Ariel Doing what?

Gabriel Defending them.

Ariel I'm not defending anyone. I'm just saying that a little bruise from some over ripe kids shouldn't mean one needs to leave an entire country.

Gabriel They have SIGNS **barring** entrance into their stores while **they** are boycotting Jewish Stores . . . All over this city.

Ariel We are Americans. They will not harm us.

Gabriel Tell that to your **bleeding forehead!**

Ariel They remember what was done to them before –

Gabriel And they are **furious** over it. They were made the world's **foot stool** and now they allow evil men to preach hate and conquest in beer halls. **Beer halls!!!** For goodness sake, they are inciting **DRUNKS** . . . and the government is not only allowing it but encouraging it . . . They are BEHIND IT . . .

Ariel A bit melodramatic aren't we?

Gabriel Am I? . . . Do you know how most lynchings begin in America my dear? . . . **Drunks** . . . Sitting around a bar, a house, a shack, the sheriff's office, **wherever** they can get

DRUNK and nasty . . . then one of them happens to remember that 'Mrs Anne **mentioned** Mrs Sally **overheard** that Mrs Martha **THOUGHT** she saw **Old Tom's Youngest Boy's Third Cousin once removed** giving her the **EYE**'.

Ariel (*drunken sexual*) Giving her the **what**?

Gabriel . . . I mean, really! . . . How can you not see the parallels? . . . to your own country, your own state, hell, your **home** town . . .

Ariel You are paranoid. No one I know speaks of such things . . .

Gabriel You know **me** and I am speaking of it –

Ariel The Jews and Coloreds are Hated **everywhere** . . . in varying degrees . . . It has **always** been that way . . .

Gabriel Yes but we do not see the SIGNS the same . . . In fact I doubt if you see the Signs at all . . .

Ariel (*close*) I see them . . .

Gabriel You are White first in America, are you not?

Ariel I am Jewish. Everyone for miles around knows that my family is Jewish. We don't hide it . . .

Gabriel You don't?

Ariel No . . . We don't hide it but we don't flaunt it either.

Gabriel And what would **flaunting** it be?

Ariel We **don't** hide it.

Gabriel But the point is that you **can** . . . If you so choose. You can change your name. Shave yourself. Dress differently. Pray secretly. Hell, you can Convert. In America, I am Colored first. I am Colored second . . . and third. I can not clean that off.

Ariel You speak as if you grew up along the banks of the Mississippi. You were born and raised in New York City and it is certainly different there –

Gabriel (*quick*) How would you know, you've never been Colored there **either** . . . you think because we are not hanging from lamp posts in Washington Square . . . that New York is **different**?

Ariel New York has thousands of –

Gabriel **Immigrants.** Who are ALL WHITE . . . They are also some of the most race-hating individuals to ever touch Mother Earth.

Ariel How can you possibly say that?!

Gabriel Immigrants don't see **Coloreds** coming through Ellis Island gates . . . I am not **there** with them getting off of those boats . . . I got off **my** boat a long time ago . . . No one tells those immigrants that that Statue of Liberty they so fondly point to upon their arrival, that they've dreamt of seeing, that they've kept as their beacon of hope. . . no one tells those **White Folks** . . . to **LOOK TO HER FEET!!!**

Ariel Her feet?

Gabriel **'LOOK TO HER FEET', I SAY!** . . . With those **broken** chains around them . . . **THAT** was put there for the **Coloured** folks who are ALREADY **inside** those Stone and Glass Cities that the immigrants seek as refuge . . . they come to New York and look at **ME** as if I am **MUCK** between THEIR **infested** FEET.

Heat.

Those immigrants do not see America's **COLOR** until they land INSIDE its **Villages** . . . and by then, **trust me** . . . they've **learnt** what a **'Nigger'** is . . . and thanked whatever god they give thanks to . . . **that it is no longer them** . . . for once . . . in their life . . . there are others to **blood hate** . . .

openly . . . with encouragement . . . and **signs** in the windows . . .

Ariel . . . **Jews** are not WHITE . . . We are a persecuted people of this world . . . and **beyond** . . .

They laugh.

Ariel . . . Jews are different in almost every aspect from 'Whites', just as Coloreds are, how can you say such a thing as we are White . . . that word, 'White', is **relative** and you know it. I cannot go to Temple in Georgia without the glazed stares of those **WHITES** that you would bond to me.

Gabriel You don't even **Go** to Temple.

Ariel Well, if I did on a regular basis I'd have **'glazed stares'!**

More laughter.

We were slaves just as you were . . .

Gabriel True.

Ariel In harsher times . . .

Gabriel Uh –

Ariel **WE have survived** . . . **WE** are made for survival . . . **WE** are a testament to it . . . we all have to learn to survive somehow . . . Jews have learned one way, Coloreds another . . . everyone learns . . . or dies . . . Have you heard of Leo Frank?

Gabriel Of course. That Jewish man those **hateful** heathens lynched in Marietta. Awful.

Ariel One day I went with my Father to pick up some materials in Marietta . . . on our way into that city . . . there was a man selling postcards . . . and since we rarely went out and away from Atlanta . . . every trip I was able to take I collected a postcard . . . even if it was just to the other town over from ours . . . I would make sure to have saved a little for a postcard . . . that day in Marietta this man approached us with his stack . . . and there, in the center of his box . . . was a picture of Leo Frank . . . hanging from a oak tree . . . I bought it . . . and oddly my father didn't refuse . . . we turned around and left that town . . . without any materials that day . . . and when we returned home . . . I gave the postcard to my Mother . . . she would later die with it in her hands . . . I keep it now in my journal . . . to remind me of my place . . . and who I am . . . there are parts of me that I have hidden, Gabriel . . . but not that part . . . I do not hide . . . that part . . .

Silence. They look to each other . . . **Ariel** *has worked himself up into quite a sweat . . .* **Gabriel** *admires that.* **Ariel** *moves in close as* **Gabriel** *speaks the following.*

Gabriel All I'm saying is that America was built with my people's blood and Germany hopes to **rebuild** with the blood of your people. They have that in common and I can smell it.

Ariel (*close*) What does it smell like?

Gabriel (*close*) **Like the Red Clay Hills of Georgia.**

The two men remain close for a moment, taking in the heat of passionate exchange . . . Soon **Gabriel** *breaks the silence.*

Gabriel . . . You stink . . .

Ariel . . . From my scuffle . . . I guess I need a bath . . .

Gabriel Yes. You do . . .

Ariel Would you care to join me? . . .

Ariel *stands and begins removing all his clothing for* **Gabriel's** *benefit . . . Shoes. Socks.*

Gabriel (*softly*) They are following you.

Ariel (*shirt*) What?

Gabriel (*smiles*) Look outside my window.

Ariel (*unzipping pants*) Don't be silly.

Gabriel Look.

Ariel *walks out of his pants as he goes to the window and looks.*

Ariel That man is a drunk, singing himself down the street.

Gabriel Well that **drunk** was at the Club tonight and has been there every night that you've come to see me. He is SS Kommandant.

In front of the window, **Ariel** *removes his final piece of clothing.*

Ariel Maybe he is following **you**.

Naked. Silence.

He slowly walks out the room.

Gabriel *remains for a moment . . . Soon he begins to clean up the discarded clothing and drink . . .*

He heads out of the room and falls.

Gabriel *is suddenly in pain. There is a blood clot in his legs from the hormones . . . He steadies himself as a hot flash takes him over . . .*

Oskar *enters naked.*

Oskar C is for Come . . . C. O. M. E. . . . Come to bed, Gabriel . . .

Gabriel (*pained*) I can not sleep.

Oskar . . . Are you . . . excited?

Gabriel (*cringe*) . . . Yes.

Oskar Would you like me to **read** to you.

Gabriel (*stifle*) . . . Yes . . .

Oskar *smiles.*

Oskar I shall take a story.

Gabriel (*ache*) **Pick** . . . A story.

Oskar Ah . . . Pick . . . I pick you, Gabriel.

Gabriel (*clinch*) Yes.

He smiles.

I will be there shortly.

Silence.

Oskar Gabriel. Is the pain back?

Gabriel (*lie*) No.

Oskar You are lying.

Gabriel (*lie*) It's okay . . .

Oskar Have you taken your –

Gabriel Yes . . . No.

Oskar Gabriel! You know you must. You can not skip one dose you must continue with the acceleration . . .

Gabriel (*child*) . . . It hurts . . .

Oskar We must increase the dosage. Twenty ccs this time.

Gabriel No.

Oskar . . . Thirty ccs . . .

Oskar *goes to his desk.*

Gabriel *suddenly weeps in pain.*

Oskar *takes out a small lockbox.*

Oskar I am here for you, Gabriel.

He unlocks lockbox.

I will be with you the whole way.

He opens the lockbox.

We have enough here for the duration.

The lockbox is loaded to the brim with boxes of estrogen vials. And syringes.

Gabriel *gasps in pain.*

Gabriel Oskar. You stole too much this time.

Oskar I would steal much more for you.

Gabriel They will notice –

Oskar I am the Kommand –

Gabriel Someone will NOTICE, Oskar. You took too much!

Oskar I do not care!!!

Silence.

Oskar *looks deeply at* **Gabriel**.

Oskar (*strange intensity*) I. Do. Not. Care . . . about anything but **you, Gabriel** . . . let them . . . **notice** . . . I am the . . . Kommandant . . . It is **mine** to take . . .

Gabriel (*frighten*ed) Oskar . . .

Oskar (*eerie*) We must **Accelerate.** A. Is for Accelerate.

Silence.

Oskar *holds out a bit to* **Gabriel**.

Gabriel *hesitates then takes the bit and slowly places it in his mouth.*

Oskar *looks at him a moment.*

Oskar Good?

Slowly, **Gabriel** *nods, bracing for the pain.*

Oskar *fills the syringe with the estrogen.*

Oskar *administers the injection as* **Gabriel** *screamingly bites into the bit.*

Oskar *looks at him. He slowly takes the bit out of* **Gabriel's** mouth. *Then he puts both the bit and the empty syringe into the lockbox. He closes it tight and locks it away in the desk.*

He looks to **Gabriel** *again.*

Oskar I **pick** You, Gabriel.

He kisses **Gabriel**.

Oskar *gathers* **Gabriel** *in his arms and helps him off into the bedroom.*

Ariel *enters with drinks . . .*

He gives one to **Edna** *who has sat and watched the previous scenes . . .*

Ariel I'm sorry, it is an approximation. Our resources are not as rich as yours were in Berlin. I searched but –

Edna This is perfectly fine.

They sit and drink a moment . . . Silence.

Edna (*looking around nonchalant*) Did your family own slaves?

Ariel In Russia?. . . Or Portugal? . . .

Edna This is a plantation, Ariel. . .

Ariel Well, it use to be.

Edna It doesn't stop being a plantation just because there are no slaves left.

Ariel I know.

Edna You did not share with me that your family home was a plantation . . .

Ariel I thought better of it.

Edna 'And so forth?' . . .

Ariel Yes . . .

Edna Yes they owned slaves?

Ariel I do not know . . . But, it was the way of the world . . .

Edna It reminds me of my detention center. It has the same awfulness to its architecture . . . I left one death camp and have ended up in another . . . Sorry.

Silence.

Ariel . . . How was the picture show?

Edna . . . I spoke to Mr. Selznick tonight . . .

Ariel Who?

Edna Mr Selznick. Mr David Selznick . . . I got close to Mr Selznick . . . I waited for Intermission . . . He and the others came out the Back Door, so it's a good thing that's where they made the Colored Help wait . . . He came out and I got right up close to him . . . between the warm velvet of Mrs. Vivien Leigh and her husband, Olivier . . . I got right up into Mr Selznick's face . . . and smiled . . . he smiled back . . . and then I said . . . as politely as possible . . . 'Mr Selznick, how could you produce such a picture show, when an ocean away, your **kin** are being viciously rounded up in the streets and slaughtered? . . .'

Ariel (*awe*) . . . You did not.

Edna And then I **Ran** . . . with a Confederate Flag in Hand . . . I said it . . . and I Ran . . . back here . . .

Ariel Do you **know** what could have happened to you? . . . Going up to a white man in the middle –

Edna I thought Jewish people weren't **white?**

Ariel You **know** what I mean.

Edna Atlanta was on its best behavior tonight, I can assure you . . . There was no fear or hatred in their Costumed hearts . . .

Ariel Does Sarah suspect?

Edna Suspect what? . . . That we were lovers once? . . .

Ariel Yes.

Edna Yes . . . no . . . maybe . . . I don't know.

Ariel I will tell her.

Edna Why?

Ariel She should know.

Edna Why?

Ariel Because it isn't right that I continue to lie –

Edna You've lied for the last four years. Why stop now?

Ariel I did what I had to do to make my father's final days peaceful –

Edna Were they?

Ariel Yes.

Edna Good. So why didn't you come back to me?

Ariel I wrote.

Edna You wrote?

Ariel Yes.

Edna (*flip*) Sorry, I was detained.

Ariel . . . My family needed me.

Edna I needed you!

Ariel To Rescue you.

Edna Yes!!! I needed to be rescued. I needed to have you walk through the gates of that camp as your Moses parted the sea . . . I needed you there holding the other end of your Journal as my hands clenched its outer cover . . . Yes. Ariel I **needed** you . . . to **rescue** me . . .

Ariel . . . I can never begin to make up for –

Edna Try . . . start at this very moment . . . I will detail my every experience . . . let us go to a shore somewhere . . . away from the madness of war and color and **signs** in the windows . . .

Ariel I would in a heart beat . . .

Edna *goes to* **Ariel**. *She takes his hand and places it on her heart . . .*

Edna (*suffer*) Eins . . . Zwei . . . Drei –

(One . . . Two . . . Three –)

Ariel Edna –

Edna Vier . . . Funf . . . Sechs.

(Four . . . Five . . . Six)

Ariel Gabriel . . .

Edna *stops counting . . . Something inside her melts . . .*

Ariel *runs his hand along her face as he had years ago . . . She kisses his hand . . .* **Ariel** *kisses her lips, with unbridled passion.*

Sarah *appears dressed in her 'Antebellum' wares.*

She stands and looks at them as they continue to kiss, not noticing her entrance.

Gabriel *sneaks into the darkness of the library. He is naked.*

Gabriel *finds a letter opener. He looks toward* **Edna** *and* ***Ariel*** *kissing, in his mind's eye.*

Gabriel *cuts himself as* **Sarah** *retreats.*

Gabriel *struggles back offstage.*

Edna *rips* **Ariel's** *undershirt off of him. She feels and remembers the contours of his chest.*

Ariel *discovers* **Edna's** *breasts . . . She stops him . . . Soon. Their hands, lips, hips, tongues, beings, begin a vicious ballet of embrace* *through which we see* **Edna's** *reception and need for aggression . . . and* **Ariel's** *recognition of his ability to give it and like it.*

Soon.

They mold.

Dark Valley

In the darkness there is a roar . . .

Oskar (*voice*) GABRIEL!!!

The lights come up to reveal **Oskar**, *naked, holding a bloody blanket.*

He races to the front door, barking orders . . .

Oskar (*barking*) Holen Sie mir den Doktor! Sofort! Niemand soll dieses Haus ohne meine Erlaubnis betreten! Absolut niemand!

(Bring me the Doctor! Immediately! No one is to enter this House without my permission! Absolutely no one!)

He stops himself and notices that he is naked in front of his guards.

Silence.

Oskar (*mad rage*) Holen Sie den Artzt! Jetzt! Sofort!
(Go get the Doctor! NOW!)

Silence. **Oskar** *races back into his bedroom.*

Wo/Man

Silence. The sound of birds and Southern mornings comes forth.

Edna *and* **Ariel** *have finished fucking.*

She dresses. He does not.

Confident and bold he goes to **Edna** *and takes her breasts in hand.*

Ariel These are lovely.

Edna *looks to her breasts, only recently having been able to see them as something other than foreign objects.*

Edna (smile) You don't mind them?

Ariel I adore them.

Silence.

He holds them. Fascinated.

Edna Ariel get dressed. Your wife will be here soon.

Ariel (*abandon*) I don't care . . .

Edna Well I do. Get dressed.

Beat. He begins to dress. **Edna** *looks out into the fields.*

She laughs at a memory.

Edna Sarah says there are Spirits in these fields.

Ariel *stops and looks out in the field.*

Ariel (*seriously, simply a fact*) There are.

Beat. He continues dressing. **Edna** *looks to him as he continues to speak.*

Ariel (*honest*) Sarah is not the first to see spirit's rising in those fields . . . I grew up here, safe and ignorant of the world . . . But when my mother died . . . it was clear that my father wanted me to go into the family business now more than ever . . . and he wanted me to stay **here** . . . right here . . . I wanted something else . . . I did not want to spend my days overseeing patterns and chalking lines onto cloth . . . I wanted music in my life . . . I wanted art within my grasp . . . I had yet to venture beyond the five points of this town . . . There was always fear in this house . . . but before I left . . . I went down beyond the creek that sits to the right of the fields . . . I had always been told never to cross it . . . that it was not part of our land that it held things that were not to be remembered in this house . . . but after my mother died I went down there . . . soft earth . . . flowers wrenched unto each other . . . the odor . . . it was a cemetery . . . I dug in the dirt . . . fragments . . . burlap . . . faded rags . . . bones . . . It was as if they had been thrown there . . . flung across the creek . . . covered with impatience . . . I looked into the water . . . green . . . brown . . . **violet** to the kiss of the sun . . . And there I saw . . . **faces** . . . millions of them . . . in the water . . . beneath its surface . . . ashen and solemn . . . I realized . . . they were the ones that did not make it to these shores . . . onto these plantations . . . across these fields . . . to the edges of this creek . . . **beneath** my hands of soil . . .

Edna (*soft*) . . . There were many lost in the journey . . .

Ariel (*suffers*) For me . . . The earth **shifted** . . . that day . . . whether **vision** or **fact** . . . something was **disturbed** beneath me . . . and within me . . . that day . . . as I looked into the water of this creek . . . as if it were a **crack** in the middle of this grassy tomb . . . **faces** . . . the dead staring **through** me . . . I knew . . . they had not been **mourned** . . . those that did not last the journey . . . I saw them that day . . . **millions** . . . dead . . . yet to be **mourned** . . . and I knew . . . I knew then and there . . . I had to leave this place . . . It would eat me alive . . . I had to get out of here . . . I had to **leave** . . . in order
to **live**.

Silence. Uncomfortable.

Edna . . . What do we do now?

Silence. Eventually they smile.

Ariel You're a woman now, Gabriel.

Edna Close to it.

Ariel Close enough for me.

Silence.

Edna . . . What are you saying Ariel?

Ariel Let's go north together.

Edna . . . Together.

Ariel Get on The Queen Mary. Go to England.

Edna There is a war.

Ariel There will always be wars.

Silence.

Edna (*excited*) Let's stay in New York for a while.

Ariel You **hate** New York.

Edna I have never been a **woman** in New York. A woman with a man.

Smiles.

Ariel . . . I'm your man . . .

Edna Then I'm your woman . . .

Smiles.

Edna . . . Your marriage . . . Your business –

Ariel I never consummated my marriage with Sarah. She knows the truth. It's time she accepted it.

Edna I don't want to hurt her.

Ariel Neither do I. It was an arrangement. Not a marriage.

Edna I should leave before she returns.

Ariel (*sudden*) No.

Edna I can wait for you in town.

Ariel No. You should never leave me again. I will not risk it.

Edna Ariel –

Ariel Sarah is a child. In many ways she lives still in childish fantasies. I will not hide the truth from her. **You** are the truth. And I want you at my side. Stay.

Silence.

They sit. And wait. Holding hands.

<u>Gone with the Wind</u>

Ariel *sleeps.*

Edna *is gone.*

Sarah *enters . . . Disheveled with dirty stains over her 'Antebellum' gown. She is drunk. She moves into the living room and stands near* **Ariel** *for a long moment.*

Soon he awakens with a start.

Ariel Sarah! Where have you been? I was going to send word to –

Sarah (*venom*) Liar.

Silence. **Ariel** *looks around trying to hide his desperation.*

Sarah Is she still here?

Ariel (*stifled fear*) I don't know.

Then the sound of cooking or frying is heard. And they know **Edna** *is indeed still in the house.*

Husband and wife look to each other.

Sarah We can't **afford** a maid, call her and I'll do the honor. Ariel.

Ariel Where have you been, Sarah?

Sarah . . . Working.

Ariel Working? . . . Why is your dress – Sarah are you drunk?

Sarah If by 'drunk' you mean 'FULL'. Then yes I am drunk. I am DRUNK of YOU. And this fiction of a marriage.

Silence.

Ariel Sarah, why have you been drinking so early in the morning and where did you –

Sarah I suppose drinking at NIGHT is better. Under the moon and stars makes being DRUNK of YOU better? It certainly doesn't make you **touch** me . . . in the night . . . believe me, I've **tried**. Scarlet should have never married Rhett and I should have never married you.

***Ariel** I think you should sit down –

***Sarah** Why did you MARRY ME!!! Why didn't you stay away? Doing your research. Why couldn't you have researched FOREVER . . . You could have kept me in a daydream! I could've continued to read my books and live between their pages . . . where lovers love madly but **honestly** . . . At least one of us could have lived happily ever after.

Ariel Sarah!

Sarah **WHAT WHAT WHAT WHAT WHAT???** . . . I may be Simple. But I am **no** fool. And I am no longer a school girl blushing in delight of the mere presence of the Boss' Son . . . Where is our **MAMMY**!!!

Edna *appears in an apron.*

Sarah (*she sings*) ***GONNA JUMP DOWN SPIN AROUND PICK A BALE OF COTTON***

GONNA JUMP DOWN SPIN AROUND PICK A BALE OF A HAY . . .

Ariel *and* **Edna** *look to her as if she's gone insane.*

Sarah This is a plantation after all . . . You've made numerous references to its **beauty** and the work necessary to keep it up . . . Well, Edna Black Rock, what are you doing in the BIG HOUSE? Shouldn't you be out there in the Field?

Ariel Sarah!

Edna You think I should go out and get to bending. You think you understands quite clearly how these plantations work, don't you **Mrs Sarah?**

Sarah (*direct*) Yes.

Edna That picture show last night showed you a lot of stuff about this house didn't it, **Mrs Sarah**?

Sarah Much more than you could imagine.

Edna Oh my imagination is **quite** large. Did you watch it carefully?

Sarah **Yes I did.**

Edna Well did it **not** teach you that the **Mammy** is allowed to stay indoors and avoid the **Heat** . . .

Ariel Edna, please –

Sarah I want you out of my home.

Ariel Wait, Sarah –

Sarah **I want her out!**

Ariel We are old friends, Sarah. There is much I need to explain –

Sarah (*screaming to* **Edna**) How DARE you look directly into my face. I could have you tar and feathered!!!

Ariel **Sarah stop it!!!** . . . Now. Sarah. There are some things I'm going to tell you that you won't believe –

Sarah Why haven't we had any children?

Ariel I would appreciate it if you would –

Sarah It is a humiliation to be your wife. Showing up last night without my husband. Whispers and hisses like daggers thrown at my back.

Ariel Are you going to listen to me or what? We need to deal with the reality of **this** situation right here . . .

Sarah Reality? What do you know about **Reality!** There is no such thing between us. We are as false as the accents of those English **Actors** pretending to be Southern last night.

Ariel I don't **CARE** about that Stupid Picture SHOW!!!

Sarah What **do** you care about Ariel?! . . . You don't care to have children, you didn't care to come back here and take 'care' of your father, you don't care about the business he and your ancestors built with their blood and sweat, and you don't care about me or you would remove that woman from this HOUSE, **immediately!**

Ariel Why??

She slaps him hard.

Sarah I am your WIFE!! And you want me to spell it out to you . . . you want to make me the vicious ONE to come out with it . . . why can't you be a Man and SAY IT.

Ariel I AM TRYING! Goddamn you, I have been TRYING for YEARS NOW! But you refuse to hear past your own LOVE for me. You think you can change hearts and minds with **DEVOTION???** . . . I left someone when I came back to you.

Sarah Came **back** to **ME???** . . . Your presence was **demanded**! Your father wept for you. Within weeks of your mother's death and you left to go . . . 'explore . . . to find yourself' . . . You did not come back to me . . . you came to bury your father . . . found a girl had turned into a woman . . . and her eyes begged you to **surrender** to a childhood **promise** . . .

Silence.

Ariel Do you want the **truth** or not?

Sarah To hell with TRUTH! Why can't the TRUTH ever be on **my** side! It was better when the world was black and white. Them and us.

Edna My name is Gabriel.

Sarah Gabriel?! Yesterday your name was Edna! You are a **faucet** of lies!

Edna I was once a man.

Beat. **Sarah** *laughs.*

Ariel And my lover.

Sarah *stops laughing. Silence.*

Sarah (*to* **Ariel**) **This** is how you ask for a divorce?

Silence. **Edna** *and* **Ariel** *exchange looks.*

Slowly, **Sarah** *comes to the realization that they are telling the truth.*

She looks from one to the other . . .

Sarah . . . I'm going to be sick.

Edna *blocks her exit.*

Edna (*violent*) As I was sick last night. It is the same sickness!

Ariel Edna calm down. Let me handle this –

Edna I will not CALM DOWN!!

Ariel, *exasperated, sinks into seat and covers his face with his hands . . .* **Edna** *looks at him in disgust.*

Edna I was the very **MODEL** of Calmness last night – Colored folks dressed as slaves singing spirituals to **White** folks dressed like their **Masters** – The **BLOOD** of those Coloreds' ancestors are in the SOIL upon which THEY **STOOD**!!! And they dared to **MOCK** that! . . .

Sarah **AND YOU DARE TO MOCK MY MARRIAGE!** I saw you two. I saw it **ALL**. I ran into the fields . . . to the old shack where your father kept his . . . southern **comforts** . . . I drank . . . and I drank . . . and I **drank** to keep from coming back here and butchering you both as you slept . . . There is hate inside me that reaches between the cords of my veins . . .

Edna (*understanding*) I can smell it all over you . . .

Sarah And I can smell **your** envy. Your quest. Somehow. I knew you had not arrived yesterday by chance.

Edna I thought you'd be busy with the festivities for the Opening . . . I picked yesterday to come, remembering what Ariel had told me of you before his departure, I thought that you'd certainly be one of the followers of the **WIND** . . .

Sarah I knew it!!! A scheme . . . from the very beginning.

Edna (*honest*) I did not want to hurt you, Sarah.

Sarah (*mo' honest*) **Well I want to hurt you!** . . . I want to hurt you both . . . I could go to town at this very moment . . . and on my word alone . . . have you dragged from this house . . . drawn and quartered . . . or stripped whipped and strung up . . . lit aflame . . . tortured until your last breath . . . I could **THINK** it and make it true . . .

Edna It **is** true . . . Already . . . for both my people and yours . . . Hitler will not stop with Europe . . . Oh he's coming here . . . There is Blood Hate in **this** country . . . and like me . . . he can smell it . . . and HE is coming . . .

Silence.

Sarah . . . Edna Black Rock . . . HE is here . . . if his name speaks Blood Hate . . . then he is here today . . . I was Counseled to come to this house and watch after his Father. **HIS. FATHER**. Believing one day I would be the wife of a Gentleman's Son . . . But I was left to live. In a lie. (*To* **Ariel**.) Feeding that **hateful** man, clothing him, bathing him, honoring him . . . Father **and** Son. Forbidding myself the luxury of attention from other suitors . . . Down-playing my looks . . . dressing in grays and blacks . . . **saving** my **virtue** . . . allowing myself to be thought **SIMPLE** . . . in order to have him return . . . broken and false . . . pieced together with tissue . . . willing his eyes to return and HOLD my gaze . . .

Ariel *indeed, can still not hold her gaze.*

Sarah Stupidly replacing his **pity** with **genuine love** . . . imagining children –

(*Suffers.*) . . . imagining complete and utter **comfort** . . . imagining . . .

She stops herself . . . She looks around the home.

Sarah (*quiet*) I can not remember . . . one totally satisfying day . . . since coming to this house . . . not one **full day** in which I did not have doubts about my life and the void that remains here . . . no moment of grace . . . outside of the invention of myths surrounding a Boy who smiled at me once . . . and kissed me . . . kissed me on a rainy afternoon . . .

Slowly, **Sarah** *exits.*

Edna *turns to* **Ariel** *who does not move and appears even more buried under the weight of this life.*

Edna She is right . . . You never came back to her, Ariel . . . You simply ran away . . . from me . . .

Ariel (*desperate*) We can sit and make this right . . .

Edna It is too late for that . . . sitting and making right, I fear . . . is gone with the wind . . .

Silence.

Ariel *stands.*

He has made a decision . . .

Ariel I will go and tell her . . . I am leaving with you . . . **I am leaving. With You**.

Beat.

Ariel *exits.*

Edna *takes a moment and surveys the room. She notices herself in the mirror as* **Gabriel** *appears, looking into the same mirror.*

Soon **Ariel** *re-enters . . . This time in Berlin . . . He speaks to* **Gabriel**.

Ariel (*entering*) I have to go back to America . . . My father is not well.

Gabriel *is completely taken aback. Silence.*

Gabriel When were you going to tell me?

Ariel I'm telling you now.

Gabriel When do you leave?

Ariel Monday.

Gabriel **Monday?** . . . When will you return?

Ariel Soon.

Gabriel How many nights does '**soon**' consist of?

Ariel . . . Don't do this.

Gabriel Do what? What **exactly** have we been doing, Ariel?!

Silence.

Take me with you.

Ariel You know that is impossible.

Gabriel (*threat*) If you leave, I'll follow.

Ariel No you won't.

Gabriel I won't?

Ariel No. You won't. All that about 'everyone should leave everyone should get out' means nothing to you. You are **still** here. And you will remain here because they **worship** you.

Gabriel I do not want to be worshiped!

Ariel You **LIVE** to be Worshipped . . . I've seen it!

Gabriel Why are you talking to me like this?

Ariel There is **business** that I must attend to.

Gabriel **Family** business.

Ariel Yes. There is that –

Gabriel That?

Ariel Someone.

Gabriel You told me it was over, that it never got started.

Ariel She has moved into my family's house.

Gabriel How long ago?

Ariel It does not matter –

Gabriel **How long ago?!**

Ariel My father has taken her under his wing in hopes that I might return. She takes his messages to and from the shop because he is too frail to do so. He writes to me that she reminds him of little Mary Phagan . . . The little girl that Leo Frank – My **father** . . . is obviously very sick! . . . **delusional** . . . And . . . He has flowered her dreams with thoughts of . . . She has been allowed to expect –

Gabriel She expects what Ariel? What have **YOU** allowed her to expect?

Silence.

Ariel You can not come with me. It would not be right. There are **Signs** . . . in the windows . . . remember?

He starts to leave.

Gabriel (*fury*) I have remained here only for you! I perform that show through **clenched** teeth ONLY for you!

Ariel (*nasty*) . . . Then go to **New York** but do not come to the **South**. It is not for you. Your words and manner would destroy you. Your talents will not be appreciated. Your intelligence will become a disease. Your beauty will be suspect. There is **nothing** there for you –

Gabriel **You** will be there!!

Silence.

Ariel (*tremble*) **You** have the gifts, Gabriel. **You** have such wonders . . . your voice . . . **That** is your gift . . . I know it so well. I have **nothing**. I have **no** such thing as that. I am the son of a Tailor. Born and raised on a simple farm (*Pause.*) **I have no gifts** . . .

Gabriel **I love you.**

Ariel Don't say that.

Gabriel It is **truth**. It is undeniable **fact**. This place has linked me to **you** . . . I feel it evermore because . . . you . . . you . . . **you are in my blood.**

Ariel (*lost*) . . . I have never felt such things before. For neither man nor woman. I do not know if I ever will again. You have been witness and companion to my life here. Whatever **love . . . What. Ever. Love** . . . there is in me to give . . . **You have it** . . . But my family needs . . . My father . . . You may **not** come South with me. I will return. No matter what. This is not our ending.

They kiss.

Long. Passionate.

Finally, **Ariel** *gathers all the strength he can muster to remove his lips from* **Gabriel's**. **Ariel**, *crying, goes toward the door.*

Gabriel (*crying*) Come to my show tomorrow.

He turns to him.

Ariel (*crying*) . . . I will.

Gabriel Promise.

Ariel . . . With all my heart.

Ariel *exits.*

The library door opens and **Oskar**, *disheveled, in a robe and holding a suitcase, enters . . .*

Gabriel *notices that* **Ariel** *has left his journal. He goes to it . . . Picks it up and begins to read it as he goes off . . .*

Oskar *sees* **Edna** *at the mirror and smiles . . .*

Edna *wipes away the tears that have fallen over the recognition that she is no longer and can never again be a man.*

Oskar *places the suitcases near the front door.*

Oskar You are startling . . . You are my **open** secret . . .

Edna Are my papers in order, my darling?

Oskar Yes. It has all been arranged . . . Josef will arrive in mere moments . . . he has all the instruments for your safe journey and no one shall know of my involvement.

Edna Will our house be as large?

Oskar Yes.

Edna How am I to pass the Guards? . . .

Oskar Simple. I have given them the weekend off . . . Have you not looked out . . . I have requested a man walk the perimeter once at noon and then at dusk . . . there is no danger about . . . they are happy for the holiday before the new Commandant arrives . . .

Edna Why must I go before you, my love?

Oskar It is safer if we travel separately . . .

Edna Safer for whom? . . .

He takes her head in his hands . . .

He kisses her lips . . . He touches her inner thigh.

Oskar I thought I had lost you . . . You could have been **ruined** . . .

Edna I did it for us . . . How shall you spend your days while I am gone?

Oskar . . . I shall read, of course . . . and dream of **you** sitting near me . . . listening . . . in **Englisch** . . .

Edna Oskar . . .

Oskar Yes . . .

Edna I have chosen a name . . .

Oskar What is it?

Edna Edna . . .

Oskar (*smiles*) Edna . . .

Edna Edna Black Rock . . .

Oskar Odd isn't it? . . .

Edna (*big smile*) Yes . . . Indeed . . . very very **very** odd . . . but **solid.**

He kisses her again . . .

There is a car horn . . . Outside . . .

Oskar Do not delay . . . Josef has been instructed to not speak or inquire, but only to drive you to the Border . . . There is a path through the wilderness there . . . You will have one hour to get through and the guards will return . . . It is steep and you must take care as you run.

Edna I learned very early how to **Run** in Heels . . .

He holds her . . .

Oskar You . . . You are the contradiction that has stapled my heart. It had been severed very early in life. I was not the most 'gifted' child. I worked hard to keep my place. In school. In work. In the Reich. But I can no longer remove you from my mind's eye. I read reports and records and lose thought and time. I have never been so happy with indecision. I have never been so well taken care of. I believe the Fuhrer is correct. We are a perfect race. We have within us the only truth. We shall lead the world one day. But I disagree on one note. **You**. You are that note that plays inside me. You are so perfect. You have been perfectly manufactured. For me. There is no other gift I shall ever dream of receiving . . . I picked you on sight. I followed your voice as if a lullaby. It determined my schedule. It placed my day in order and became my blanket in slumber. I had to have you. I had to taste the creature who created such . . . vibration . . . within me . . . You were my destiny . . . and you can not be impure . . . because WE are perfect . . . together . . . my love . . . there is nothing you shall ever need to be afraid of again . . . It will all go off as planned.

Silence.

Oskar *looks deep into* **Edna's** *eyes . . . He kisses her one last time.*

Edna *goes to her suitcase.*

There is a 'click' and **Oskar** *now holds a Lugar under his chin.*

Silence.

Oskar Ich Liebe Dich.

Car horn.

Gun shot.

Edna *screams and immediately covers her mouth. Biting her own hand as she looks on in horror, barely able to catch her breath . . .*

She takes the gun from **Oskar's** *hands.*

Car horn.

She kisses him gently.

She notices that **Ariel's** *journal is in* **Oskar's** *robe pocket. She takes it.*

She puts the journal in her coat pocket . . . She opens the front door as ***Ariel*** *enters behind her.*

His voice stops **Edna** *. . .*

Ariel I have told her –

He sees her at the door.

Edna (*sorrow*) . . .The moment Sarah opened this door . . . I knew . . . why you stayed . . . my questions . . . were answered . . . you were the love of **her** life . . . you sat there in her eyes as she stood before me . . . she would die on your command . . .

Ariel I have told her. I have made my **choice**.

Edna Ariel –

Ariel Wait for me.

Edna I am not even here Ariel . . . I am not the someone you left . . .

Ariel (*suffer*) Then why did you come . . . why did you cross oceans to come here . . . to **crucify** me and leave? . . .

Edna (*stifle*) I came because of Gabriel . . . He sacrificed **himself** for a chance to see you again . . . And I owed him that . . . that **moment** . . .

Ariel It can **exist** here . . . We can find another **moment** . . .

Edna Berlin is **dead**.

Ariel I am **here.**

Edna (*realization*) Gabriel is **dead.**

Silence.

Ariel I have just given up **everything!**

Edna *touches his face.*

Edna (soft) . . . **So have I.**

Edna *takes the journal out of her coat pocket . . . She kisses the front and back covers . . .*

Ariel *weeps at the sight . . .*

She hands it to him.

Finally, he slowly reaches for it.

It is extremely difficult for **Edna** *to let the book go but she does.*

She returns to the open door, picking up her suitcases . . .

Ariel *rushes to her. He falls to his knees holding onto her for dear life.*

Ariel . . . **GABRIEL!!!** (*Full.*) . . . I'm lost without you . . . I love you . . . from my very **root**, I love you . . . Beyond every creed or color or distinction between us . . . **I love you. . .**

Edna (*suffer*) And Gabriel loves you. But **Edna** must go.

Edna *pulls herself away from* **Ariel**.

Sarah *appears with a shot gun.*

'POW'.

Edna *falls . . . dead.*

Silence.

Ariel *is stunned still.*

Sarah *lowers her shotgun and turns to* **Ariel** . . . *She is newly intoxicated . . . Her eyes are bloodshot.*

Sarah (*haunted*) . . . There is blood hate in this house . . . It haunts me . . . I've stood at that door and seen the spirits . . . rising . . . inside. . . and out . . .

Silence.

Slowly, darkness comes. . .

Das Ende.

Section IV
Re-Imagining/ Re-Engaging Africa

Danai Gurira & Nikkole Salter

In the Continuum

"varying by degrees" - fm experience but similar related - episodic structure
"congruent whole" - collective concious? related across distance
"progression or sequence" - over time, across space, across age, across cultural moments

· can perform these roles because they are accessible to those in the continuum of post-blackness?

· what is it a continuum of? => continuation of a cycle perpetuated by double standards & opression. world view, process of disillusionment of the American dream from a want for opulence to a want for simple survival. continuation of opression through victim blame & silencing - women victim of women (= darnelle's mother, next woman hurting next woman by being quiet). cultural understanding & stereotypes surrounding aids. black women are in the continuum of aids.

· we are still in the continuum of AIDS being silenced & being judged by sexual identity

· call to be an advocate if you've been victimized bc victim is a passive role

· USA - resturaunt, club, hospital, house - not a safe place

In the Continuum received its World Premiere in September 2005 at Primary Stages (Casey Childs, Executive Producer; Andrew Leynse, Artistic Director; Elliot Fox, Managing Director) in New York City. It subsequently moved to the Perry Street Theatre in November 2005, where it was produced by Primary Stages in association with Perry Street Theatre (David Elliott and Martin Plait, Co-Dircctors), Patrick Blake, Cheryl Wiesenfeld and Richard Jordan. The production was directed by Robert O'Hara, Associate Director was Gus Danowski with the following designers: Set, Peter R. Feuchtwanger; Costume, Sarah Hillard: Lighting, Colin D. Young; Sound, Lindsay Jones; Props, Jay Duckworth. Production Stage Managers were Kate Hefel and Samone B. Weissman with the following cast:

Abigail and others	Danai Gurira
Nia and others	Nikkole Salter
Understudies	Tinashe Kajese and Antu Yacob

The original production toured from April 2006 through August 2007 to the following venues: Harare International Festival of the Arts, Harare, Zimbabwe; Baxter Theatre, Capetown, South Africa: Market Theatre, Johannesburg, South Africa; Traverse Theatre, Edinburgh, Scotland; Woolly Mammoth Theatre Company, Washington, DC; Cincinnati Playhouse, Cincinnati, OH; Center Theatre Group, Los Angeles, CA; Yale Repertory, New Haven, CT; Philadelphia Theatre Company, Philadelphia, PA; Goodman Theatre, Chicago, IL.; and the Grahamstown National Arts Festival in South Africa.

In the Continuum was work-shopped at The Mud/Bone Theater in New York City, Michael Wiggins, Artistic Director, and developed in part at the Ojai Playwrights Conference. Robert Egan, Artistic Director.

Place
South Central, LA and Harare, Zimbabwe

It is suggested that the play be performed with no intermission.

A note from the playwrights

In the Continuum was born of our profound concern for the experience of black women in the present fight against HIV/AIDS. Black women currently represent the highest rate of new infection both in the US and Africa and this is a story told from that perspective. Developed during our third year of NYU's Graduate Acting Program with an invaluable artistic community of students and teachers, it is a representation of the humanity behind the statistics and an invitation for more unheard stories to be brought 'In(to) the Continuum'.

Prologue: Back in the day

Children playing together – **Child #1** *in South Central, Los Angeles, CA;* **Child #2** *in Harare, Zimbabwe.*

***Child #1** Come on! Com' on! I wanna play . . . I wanna play hopscotch! C'mon! Hopscotch! Just get some chalk! No, get a brick! Just bang it out. Then draw a circle. Yeah! (*Draws circle on the ground with a 'brick'.*) All the way around. I'ma show you how to play like this alright! But I'ma go first cuz I drew the circle. Huh? Okay, okay . . . One! Two! Three!

She throws her marker in to the circle.

***Child #2** Okay saka, totamba chi? Totamba nodo here? Va! Saka une chalk here? Saka hauna? Oh, ndaiwona pano, mirai, – ngatigadzire circle rakadai, rakadai (*Draws circle on ground with chalk.*) Okay, ini ndotanga, one, two, three . . .

Throws stone in the air, tries to catch it and it flies behind her.

Child #2 Oh, shiiit.

Child #1 What?

***Child #2** Aiwa, richiri jana rangu, aiwa. No man, it's best of three! Iwe waka pusa! Ahh, saka hapana achatamba, hapana achatamba!

She rubs our the chalk with her feet.

***Child #1**. No! It's got to land in the middle of the circle. That's not the way you play the game. You stupid! Fine! (She rubs out the chalk with her feet.) Then nobody's playin' this game then! Ain't nobody playin'!

Both children; *singing and dancing together.*

TOMATO SAUCE, SAUCE,
SAUCE, SAUCE, SAUCE, SAUCE (2X)
ELIZABETH, ABETH,
ABE, BE, BE, BETH (2X)
CHIPIKINRINGO, GO
GO, GO, GO, GO (2X)

COUSIN'S ON THE CORNER IN THE WELFARE LINE
BROTHER'S IN THE SLAMMER, HE COMMITTED A CRIME
PREACHER'S IN THE CLUB ON THE DOWN LOW CREEP
AND YO' MAMA'S IN THE GUTTER SCREAMIN' H-I-V

The children separate into their distinct worlds, no longer playing together.

***Child #1** What you say about my mama?

***Child #2** Saka wati amai vangu vari HIV?

*** Child #1** Yo' mama got HIV.

***Child #2** Amai vako ndivo vari HIV.

***Child #1** Yo' mama, yo' daddy, yo' whole generation got HIV!

***Child #2** Amai vako, nababa vako, nevese vemumhuri menyu vari HIV.

***Child #1** You stupid! And you got HIV! And yo' mama got a cauliflower growin' out of her pussy!

***Child #2** Iwe waka pusa, newewo uri HIV; futi Amai vako vane maronda panaapa.

Bother children Ewww!

One: In the beginning

The two actresses continue separate conversations in their separate worlds as **Abigail** *and* **Nia**. **Abigail** *takes a seat and commences reading a news report at Zimbabwe Broadcasting Corporation Studios.* **Nia** *is in a stall of a bathroom in a hip-hop night club, hovering over the toilet.*

Abigail Good evening and welcome to the 8 o'clock main news bulletin. I am Abigail Murambe. Harare. The minister of agriculture comrade Nixton Chibanda warned against any reports by the biased and slandering Western Media which assert that Zimbabwe is facing a famine. He further commented that these irresponsible journalists and their evil cohorts have been the source of Zimbabwe's expulsion from the Commonwealth as well as the crippling sanctions imposed by the United Nations. He asserted that contrary to such reports, Zimbabwe will in fact produce a surplus of agricultural crops in the coming harvest. He admonished against nastyers who . . . Ahh, ahh, what is nastyers? Naysayers? Whooa, ah, but it says nastyers ka. And what is naysayers, someone who says nay? Ah. hey, are we in Shakespeare or what. Okay, why can't they just say liars or something? Ahh, ahh, look at all these typos man! And since when was the vice president's name Janet Mujuru? Its Joyce Mujuru man, you want to get me fired?

Nia (*she vomits*) It feel like I'm dying. No, I'll be okay. Just give me a second. I haven't had nothin' to eat – I keep throwin' everything up. Nasty cafeteria food. All I had was a Long Island iced tea. I know I should eat something. Just give me a second. I'll get it myself. I don't know, Trina. It mighta been in the weed – I ain't the weed expert. They was passin' it, it was free, I took just some. (**Abigail** *sits at mirror – touches up makeup with tissue.*) I think it's somethin' else. Cuz nothin' taste the same, don't nothin' smell the same – I ain't old! Just cuz you popped outta yo' mama coochie yesterday don't make me (*Starts to throw up.*) – Trina, just pass me some tissue!

Abigail Ewe, wait, is there any shine here? Okay. (*Dabs side of face. drops tissue to the floor,* **Nia** *picks it up.*) Thanks. And, can I have the rest of the report please?! (*Perusing report.*) Hey. It's getting harder and harder to even say this crap man. I can't believe – Huh? No I wasn't saying anything. But, Evermore, have you gotten your pay check? Ah, NO I haven't, its been six weeks now, how am I supposed to pay school fees with air? Right now I am near penniless. This is what we get for working for the government, ini I want to move into the private sector, South Africa man! SABC! Real money, shamwari! Ah, I am just as good as them, probably better! Then from there CNN!!! Why not, I bet I am just as good as them, probably better. (**Nia** *flushes the toilet and exits the stall.*) Where is my tea by the way, Evermore, can you please, please bring me my tea BEFORE we start, I need to calm my nerves. Four sugars.

Abigail *sits – jots notes on her tasks for the day on news report.*

Nia My breath smell like raw fish and old tacos. No, I don't wanna go. (*Looking into an imagined full-length mirror.*) I got all dressed up so I could celebrate with Darnell, so that's what I'ma do. 'Cause, I don't see him everyday no more, so when he get here I wanna look good. (*Fixing her hair.*) No, he just be out, doin' his college thang, but in two more days, all this scholarship stuff will be done. We been together ten months and three weeks, I can wait two more days. Huh? Yep, it's almost been a year. He practically my husband. (*Fishing out lipgloss.*) 'Cause we been through so much! Like last summer, when he got jumped by them Piru niggas; girl, I was so scared! But I was the first one to visit when he got home. And when everything went down with my mom's I would run away from the foster homes and Darnell would let me sneak and stay with him 'till got my spot at Good Shepherd. And if that ain't love, – He even came to see when I won that poetry contest. (*Applying lipgloss.*) Girl, yes! They gave us a big banquet; I got $500 – and a plaque. And the judges said I was – what they call it? – 'full of potential'. I know, I didn't have no potential before, but now that I can talk they poetry language, I'm 'full of potential'. (*Closing lipgloss.*) It ain't hard, all they have you do is follow a pattern and write it out – A pattern! – Okay, like: (*Using the lipgloss to count the syllables on her fingers.*) bright ass sun-ny day – 5 syllables. Burn-in' the shit out-ta me – 7. I wish it was cold – 5. See. No, I think about them all the time. It just come to me. It's easy. It's just like flowin'. Try one. Just try one. Alright, I'ma start you, okay? Okay. Dir-ty ass, skank . . . humm? – (*Waitingfor* **Trina** *to fill in the blank.*) Hoe! Good! Wit yo' crun-chy hair – (*To*

Trina.) wit yo' fake weave? – no, no, wait I got it. Wit yo' crun-chy ba-by hair – 7. Leave Dar-nell a-lone – 5.

Begins fishing mascara out of her purse.

Abigail By the way, before I forget, I next time I want to be dressed by Truworths – because Edgars keeps bringing these clothes that make me look like I have grandchildren or something. Thank you for that Evermore, I know I am a married woman, that doesn't mean I have to look like I am selling vegetables paroadside. Next time they bring such things I am just going to say no, they must know I am their model, saka they're supposed to make me look good.

Nia (*applying mascara*) Shut up, Trina! I always look good. Please! I look better than those groupies! Did you see that girl that had on the – So. (*Putting mascara away*.) So what! So, Darnell looks at them, so what! Girls walking around with they titties hangin' out tryin' ta get looked at. (*Fixing her clothes*.) He might look at them but he goin' home with me. Don't worry, tonight, I'ma just let him celebrate. But Saturday night, after his scholarship ceremony (*Imitating female video dancers in hip-hop music videos*.) I'ma give him somethin' to look at. (*She laughs*.) Huh? What, my new purse? Yeah, it was a gift – courtesy of Nordstrom. (*Fishing for and applying perfume purse*.) Girl, please. A playa like me don't pay fo' nothin'. (*Pretending to steal the purse*.) Everything I got on was a five finger discount. Wait! No! Cuz the way I see it, it only cost fifty cents for these companies to make; they only pay Javier and them ten cent to put it together; they pay me five wack ass dollars an hour, then they go sell it for a hundred and fifty? Do I look like a dummy? Please, me takin' this purse is part of my community service. I wish I would pay a hundred and fifty!

Abigail Mmm, mmm, Evermore, forget about that tea. I am not feeling well. Ahh, we better do this thing quickly guys. Where's the cameraman? Oh oh oh, is Gibson not here yet? Finish. But shame – he told me he has no transport, hanzi he has to wake up at 3 am to reach here by 7! (**Nia**

returns to the bathroom stall.) Ahh, times are hard suwa. MunomuZimbabwe sha. Oh, is he still feeling sick? He wasn't looking very well. Shame . . . But Evermore, you are looking plumper these days, where are you finding sadza munomuZimbabwe? Please can you direct us all there? No, no tea please, I'm not feeling well . . .

Nia I never get sick. No, never! When have you seen me –? I don't be sick for real at school. No! I be fakin'! Yeah. I guess I'ma good actress – liar, actress, whatever. Like you ain't never lied about havin' cramps to get outta sex ed. Shoot, when I realized that worked, I would be havin' my period like two, three times a month. I mean, it's not like they gon' check! What they gonna do, look? – Oooh! Hay! Shh! Be quiet. You hear that?

Abigail Ahh, I think I hear Gibson out there.

Nia That's my jam. Me and Darnell always dance to that. They would play our song when I'm on the toilet.

Abigail (*gets up*) Yes Gibson, muri right? / Are you feeling better – good good. / Evermore checkai for lint! / Let's go. (*Looking in the mirror.*) / Yes I am ready! / Wait where is my special ballpoint?! / (*Finds it in her hand.*) Oh, it's right here. / Totanga kat I Let's go!

*__Nia__ Trina . . . ? / Trina, why you so quiet? / You takin' a dump? / You don't take a dump in a public bathroom! / You nasty! / (*Looking in the mirror.*) Yeah, I guess I feel a little better. / Do me a favor: go get me a breath mint or somethin'. / Hurry up!

Gunshots. **Nia** *runs out.*

Blackout in both worlds

Abigail Oh, no tell me your joking, another powercut!! This is the third one today! We won't be finished till night time! Twenty minutes? Okay please, ndapota. AND can we get some sort of lights here please! (*Sits back down.*) Better be twenty minutes, last time it was three hours. Ha. It's bad enough we had to work so late all last week, you know ma in-laws they start to say marara – 'hey hey that is why she only has one child' – imagine! 'We want more children here, Simbi is getting lonely! You mustn't work so much!' This coming from in-laws who have never given me a bubble gum or a fork at my wedding. But, (*Looks around.*) they can shut up now Evermore, baby number 2 is on the way! Ya! Pururudza! Tofara tese! Hmmm? I just found out on Monday! Stamford doesn't even know yet, I am going to tell him and that family of his at Simbi's birthday party on Sunday. Ya, he's turning seven, he's a big boy now – time for another, one that looks like the mother. Simbi? He looks just like his father man, with that big nose – shame. Stanford? He's fine . . . he just keeps doing too much of those late nights I told you about – I don't like it man! These men, they want to play away and have us at home at the same time – he's got to stop that. But, you know, I think another baby will make him act better; Auntie always said showing the husband you are a good and fertile wife will keep him indoors.

Oh, by the way Evermore – you chased your man out when you caught him with the other woman? Ah, no, that's not the answer man – no it's not, because then that other woman, hure that she is, will get everything you have been working for! Ah no me, I realized the solution: men are like bulls searching for pastureland, you show them greener grass and they stay put, and this baby is greener grass. He's going to stay put now. Hey, Stanford, he wants to forget how hard he had to work for me! ME? I was known as the Ice Queen! Hmmmhmm! No one could get near me – I was very, very picky. I used to go to those house parties and I was the best dancer – EH HE, suwa. (*Gets up, begins to dance.*) Wonai, wonai – ha, I've still got it! Ah, Evermore! Do you remember this one? This one? It was big around '92, '93 – I hated it but it was so popular I had to know how to do it – WELL. Do you remember what it was called – ABORTION! Imagine!

So nasty hey! And the men wanted to come from behind! Ha, no me I would say 'Just look hey, don't touch!' But then along came Stamford Murambe – ah, with him I was like (*Bending over.*), 'You can touch, please touch!' (*Laughing.*) Ya, ya he won me over, fair and square, but he had to persevere! With maletters, flowers! Me I didn't come easy ka! (*Sits back down.*) . He wants to forget all of that. He'll come around, he just needs another boy. A girl?! What am I going to do with a girl in this world? No, two boys that's perfect. And they're going to grow up in Chisipiti or Glen Lorne, – no we can't stay in Hatfield anymore, ahh, it's too filled with strong rural types, too many muboi! I am sick and tired of living next door to people who keep chickens and goats in their backyard, I want to be around the poshy! Those who know how to eat with a knife and fork. And our new house will have a swimming pool, DSTV, maybe a tennis court. Stamford can drive the Pajero because I'll drive the benz. And the kids will go to St John's prep or Hartman House and learn the best these whites can teach, and I have a good feeling about this one. (*Points at stomach.*) He could become the next Kofi Anan, or Bill Gates – why not! And Stamford will love this one so much; hmmhmm, he will take one look at him and never forget where home is again. (*Phone rings.*) Oh, that's mine! I thought I turn it off! Oh, let me take this Evermore it's the clinic . . . Hello . . . yes . . . this is Mrs Abigail Murambe . . . (*Exiting.*)

Two: Nia's dream

Nia (*looking behind emergency room curtains*) Trina . . . ? Trina . . . oh, sorry! (*Sucking her teeth.*) My bad. Trina? Hey. (*Entering into* **Trina's** *space.*) How you doin'? Good. Did you do what I told you? Lemme see your wrist – Why not? I said don't give them your real information! You did give them your real name! You such a scaredy cat. What they gon' do, spank you? Cuz! Now they gonna call Good Shepherd and then everybody gon' be all up in our business. Has the doctor even come in here yet? Be right back? Please, if we was dyin' we'd already be dead. Lemme see it. (*She looks at* **Trina's** *wound.*) At least it not bleedin' no more. (*Sitting.*) Me? I think I got to get some stitches. Yeah. No, wait, the doctor was like, 'How did you get glass stuck in your side?' I was like, 'Duh! They was shootin', people was goin' crazy! You get knocked over and stomped on you while you lyin' on a floor full-a shot-up glass and see what happen to you!' Yeah, you laughin' now (*Beat.*) but you looked fucked up then. I ain't gon' lie – all I saw was blood, you know, and I got scared. I was like (*Like an exaggerated mother crying over a child's coffin a la BOYZ IN THE HOOD*) Oh, Lawd! (*In a Baptist Church breakdown.*) Don't let Trina die! Please don't let Trina die!!! Lawd no! (*Laughing.*) You shhh! *You* silly! Okay, lemme see it again. At least it's gonna make a cute scar. I'm just glad you okay. Nothin'. Okay. But if I tell you somethin' Trina, you promise not to go tellin' everybody? Okay. No, the doctor wanted to give me this x-ray to see if I like broke a rib or somethin', but she made me pee in this cup to see if I was pregnant first, and . . . I am. I know I'ma get kicked out. I don't know what – She just gave me all these pamphlets, and did all these tests. Now I'm supposed to come back tomorrow but – Of course, I'm gonna tell Darnell! Yes, I am! I'ma go right up to his practice . . . and I'm gonna take his hand and put it on my stomach, look up at him and say, 'Darnell, I'm pregnant'. And he gon' look down at me and say, 'For real?' and I'ma say, 'ummm, humm'. (*Laughing.*) Then, he gon' get on his knees and put his ear against my belly and listen. Umm, humm! And then he gon' look up at me and say, 'My son in there?' and I'ma say, 'umm-humm.' Then, we're gonna get married. Umm-humm. And move into a big-ass house cuz he gon' play for the Lakers and I'll just be – Oooh, shut up! Oh, I'll be rich doin' somethin'. Watch! (*Getting her cell phone out of her purse.*) I'll call him right now. I will tell him! Just watch and learn. (*She dials.*) Voicemail? Darnell! Where are you? It's Nia. We was at the club waitin' for you – you will not believe what happened. I'll tell you all about it when you come pick us up – me and

Trina at the hospital. We need a ride. And, uh . . . (*To* **Trina**.) Shut up, I am! (*Into the phone again.*) I . . . I got somethin' to tell you. Just call me back. No! Why haven't you called me? That's what's more important! It's been like four hours –!

Three: The diagnosis

Nurse Mugobo (*steps out banging clip board*) Please, this is a clinic.

Nia (*as if the nurse has chastised her for her cell phone usage*) My bad. I just –

Nurse Mugobo Please, can you control your children, they can't run around like eh . . . monkeys!

Nia I'm comin' back! Dag! I got to go, this lady trippin' talkin' 'bout I can't be on my cell phone. Call me when you get this message. I love you. (*Putting away her cell phone.*)

Nurse Mugobo (*looks at clipboard, talking to* **Abigail**) Right, Mrs Choto? You are not Mrs Choto. Mrs Choto, Mrs Choto!

Nia That is my real name. Why would I – Can I go!

Nurse Mugobo Ha, and vanhu vatema vanonetsa. (*Flips to next chart.*) Mrs Murindi? Murambe, ya, sorry, Abigail? Right. (*Looks through chart.*) I have your chart here . . .

Nia My chart? Ya'll gon' call – ? (*Sucking her teeth.*)

Nurse Mugobo Everything looks fi – oh.

Nia What?

Nurse Mugobo You have tested HIV positive. This means you have the virus that causes the Acquired Immune Deficiency syndrome . . .

Nia I'm sorry what?

Nurse Mugobo . . . there is no cure for Aids, it is generally transmitted through unprotected penetrative sex, anal or vaginal // with a person infected with HIV. And unprotected sex means sex without a condom, male or female to protect the sexual organs and in Africa that is generally through heterosexual contact.

Nia // You trying say I'ma hoe? Do I look like a junkie? Do it look like I'm gay? Do I look like I'm from Africa? No! Every time we come in here ya'll try to make us feel like we're dirty or stupid or something. (*Pulling out her cell phone.*) You don't know what the fuck you're talkin' about – s'cuse you – no, S'CUSE YOU! (*She exits.*)

Nurse Mugobo We therefore recommend that from now on (*Eyes follow* **Nia** *– to passing orderly.*) Ewe what are you doing? Yes I can see that – but can't you see those are dripping on the floor? Take them to the back, those are contaminated. Yes they are! You barance wemunhu. (*Eyes follow him out. Back to* **Abigail**.) We therefore strongly recommend your practice abstinence from now on; but if you must, please can you protect others, there are three condoms, sorry we have run out. If you want we can show you how to use them on a banana in the next room. (*Eyes wander.*) But then you will only have two. Excuse me. Eh, Sisi Getty, are you going to the shops? Please Sisi help me sha, I am so hungry can you just buy me a sweet bun ne a coke? Thank you Sisi. Aiwa, I have the money, mirai. (*Looks over at* **Abigail**.) Ah Miss, Miss – (*Looks at chart.*) Miss Abigail, why are you crying? No, aiwa, you must think clearly mange. I see here you have a son? Bring him in, we can test him also. (*Finds no money in bra.*) Ahh, sorry Sisi I forgot my money – Oh . . . thank you Sisi you are a life saver – surely, every time! (*Looks after* **Sisi Getty** *smiling, returns to* **Abigail**, *smile fades.*) Right, so, we must see your husband in the next few days – he must be formally informed and tested. Ah, AH Miss, Miss Abigail – there are no exceptions for that – I know it can be dangerous to tell him, many women are scared he will beat them and take the children – what, what, even though usually it's coming from him, but, sorry you tested first. SO – you must tell him and bring him for testing. Even with the risky business of it. And we must see him as soon as possible, nhasi riri Friday saka on Monday, latest; we can make the appointment right now. (*Looks down at chart.*) Ah. (*Stops, puts down pen.*) You are pregnant? Ah . . . you women. You go and get this HIV then you want to have a baby or two? It's not good, munoziwa, it's not good. (*Goes back to chart.*) Drugs? Ah we don't have them here, if you have money you can try to find them, they are very, very expensive. Otherwise, change your diet – eat greens, negrains, nemeat. And don't breastfeed. We will test the baby soon after it is born. So we will see you and Mr Stamford Mirindi, sorry Murambe, on Monday, 10am. Please amai, if you don't come I will be forced to call him. Right. (*Flips to next chart.*) Mrs Choto, Mrs Cho – (**Nia** *rushes in – referring to her as though she if* **Mrs Choto**.) there you are, you are late, can you sit down. Ha, and vanhu vatema vanonetsa.

Four: Nia's denial

Nia Trina, get your stuff. Let's go. Just get your stuff! I called Patti, she gon' give us a ride, but leavin' right – Yes, I called Probation Patti – to get us a ride, Trina. Who else was I gonna call? My mama? What for? She don't care about me. Why don't you call yo' mama? – forget Darnell. He not comin' – Whatchu yellin' at me for? How is any of this my fault? You the one said you could hang. You the one begged me to come – If you didn't go – get yourself shot we wouldn't have this problem. Did I stutter? You was the only idiot walkin' around when people shootin'. Ain't you ever heard gunshots before? You supposta get down. Duck, stupid! *You* messed everything up! We was supposed to sneak out, go to the Club, have some fun, sneak back in – nobody was gon' know. Now I gotta listen to Patti's bougie mouth, all for what? Yo' bullet scratch and a couple-a stitches that you won't even see after two months with some cocoa butter?! I'm the one brought you here and made sure you got taken care of. I shoulda left yo' stank ass there. And just went back by myself. Then I wouldn't be here. I ain't even supposed to be here – ! Nothin's wrong!

I'm pregnant stupid. Whatchu think?

I don't see what you so worried about, Trina. All they gon' tell you is not to sneak out no more. I'm the one who can't go back to Good Shepherd. If anybody should be mad, it should be me. And I figured Patti was gon' find out anyway cuz you used your real name – So if we gon' get caught, we might as well have a ride! Just get your stuff. Let's go.

Five: Have mercy

Abigail *on the street, trying to flag down a ride.*

Abigail (*to street kids*) Fotsek! You kids get away. NO I don't have any money. Don't touch me! I'll beat you like your mother should have. (*Pause.*) Just go away. Please (*Phone rings.* **Abigail** *starts, petrified, she pulls the phone out of her purse.*) Hello Stamfo –. Simbi. (*Laughs, cries – relieved.*) Hello my big boy. How are you – no mummy is just happy to hear from you that's all – but what did mama say to you about calling her cell phone from the landline? NO, I said it's very expensive so you mustn't. What's wrong my beby, why are you calling me? Is daddy home? No don't put him on. No, no, no, no, mummy doesn't need to speak to him right now, just don't put him on. Don't. Okay. (*Trying to flag down omnibus taxi.*) No, I am catching a commuter omnibus, so let mummy go so that I can catch one okay. (*To street kids.*) Ewe fotsek, I said I don't have any money. No, no not you baby. What? What did you put in my handbag? Simbi, I don't have time for this – okay, okay, okay. (*Finds folded paper in handbag.*) What is this Simbi? This is beautiful, did you draw it yourself? Okay, so who is the first person? Quickly, quickly. That's deddy, okay. And who is this one in the middle?! That's mummy? Okay! And who is the last one? That's you? Simbi you are funny! Why are you bigger than everyone else Simbi? But Simbi this is beautiful, we will to put it on the fridge when I get home. But Simbi, next time you draw mummy don't draw her with hair that's going all over the place like that! Mummy's hair doesn't do that beby. Just draw me with simple hair, one, two, three, four, five neat little strokes that's all. But beby this is beautiful. (*To pestering street kids.*) Fotsek, go away, you kids, where are your parents . . . (*Slowly turns back around to street kids.*) Fotsek, go away, please, get away, just go. (*Flagging down ride.*) Simbi, Mama has to go now, okay, now you go to eat; see I just stopped one, I have to go. Mommy's coming.

Six: Chatter heads

Patti Gosh! I cannot believe, at the peak of rush hour I had to – Nia!

Petronella (*more British than the British*) Abigail!

Patti Not you Trina, you wait inside!

Petronella Abigail Moyo!

Patti Nia, you get in!

Petronella Get in, get in! It's me, Petronella Siyanyarambazinyika!

Patti (*to driver*) The 105 (*One o five.*) to the 110 (*One ten.*) 405 (*Four o five.*) to Beach Avenue and Centinela, please. Yeah.

Petronella How are you my dear? I haven't seen you since – is it high school? Oh, my gosh it's been too long! AH, but you're looking well, kept that figure. Just tell Lovemore where you want to go. The city centre? Is that safe Lovemore? Okay. Good.

Patti I am not angry, Nia. Did you think I was angry? 'Cause I'm not. I'm dumfounded, I'm worried, I'm completely devastated! We've been through Independent Living Classes, Life Skills Assessment, Job Readiness Training – we were getting somewhere, Nia! What was so important at this club that it was worth giving up everything we've worked for? And I tell you, if I miss my flight to Milwaukee for the second part of the Journey toward Self Discovery Conference I'll –

Petronella And did I hear correctly that you married Stamford Murambe? HAA, well done my dear, he was gorgeous! What a bloody catch! Oh, you still have him right? Whew! But good work my dear everyone wanted a piece of him! I too have officially joined the married club! Mmmhmm, just two years ago, do you remember Farai Mungoshi? Prince Edward, headboy, captain of the rugby team, a real feast for the eyes? No, I married his younger brother Richard.

Patti . . . Yes, but you tell the universe exactly what you want to experience by the choices you make every moment. And I know we don't always make the best choices, but – Yes, even me, I don't always – Okay. Like yesterday, I was having lunch in the cafeteria and I had not one, but two helpings of macaroni and cheese. Not the best choice, no, but not going to drastically change my life. You take the good job I found you at Nordstrom and chose to get fired by stealing – again. I've given you the easiest course curriculum developed for continuing education yet you throwaway your chance at a diploma by ditching. You take the free housing in Westwood I gave you, and was asked to leave because you wouldn't keep curfew. I've even violated the state's abstinence only policy and given you condoms! Now you're telling me that one night of hangin' wit the homies, rockin' your phat gear and sportin' your big chain with the medallion of the mother land and shakin' your booty with some boy at some club is worth getting shot at? (*Beat.*) Okay. Good answer. So: with my choices, I'm telling the universe that I . . . want . . . to be fat. But, so what, big deal, we're talking about you! You're telling the universe that you want to be an uneducated, unemployed, homeless, kleptomaniac, soul train dancer. Is that what you want? If you were in my shoes, what would you do?

Petronella . . . oh you got those here? They look just look just like my Stella McCartney pumps. I know her personally actually, she gave me a pair – she couldn't give them to her step mum – she's only got one leg! Did you say you worked ZBC? Oh, (*Laughs.*) no, I am sorry, I just got back home so I am still adjusting to all the lingo, and someone the other day called it Dead BC. Good for you though hey! You were always a great public speaker! Me, oh, well . . . went abroad soon after high school, to study at London School of Economics, I was there for both my undergrad and my masters, International Relations with a focus on Human Rights and Gender Development, and I am still there mostly, I work as a consultant for big organizations, the UN, OXFAM, stuff like that. Right now, I have been really focused on HIV and Southern African women and of course all the big organizations abroad are going to hire me right? I am like this perfect poster child – but I can't complain, I've been working with DATA – oh come on you know – Debt, AIDS, Trade, Africa – Bono – he's a rock star – he has an organization. (*Car swerves.*) Careful Lovcmore!

Patti Ah, pardon, sir –

Petronella God, the way people drive in this country!

Patti Yes, but that clearly said, 'no left turn' –

Petronella In England he would have been arrested on the spot!

Patti It is illegal! – I should write down your number and report – It's just that it's a very risky turn, sir, and we have precious cargo. Yeah! Thanks. (*To* **Nia**.) Perfect example: there are many ways to get to Inglewood, but making an illegal short cut turn here is not one of them. There are no shortcuts in life, Nia! The laws are designed to keep us safe. And I hate to burst your bubble, but, no matter where you go there will be rules. On this road there are rules, gangs have rules, even in the wilderness there are rules. And there are consequences in choosing to violate the rules. Are you listening to me? Nia!

Petronella . . . there's not even any bloody petrol! This is not the country we grew up in. How do you survive? Anyway, concerning the whole AIDS issue – I was actually trying to get some statistics –that's why I was at the clinic – naturally the head nurse was on a two hour lunch or something! Zimboes! And of course you have to get the highest statistics possible in order to get them to do anything. That's when they get all aghast and say, 'Oh those poor Africans who can't help themselves – let's bring them our great answers' – which are WHAT? Okay – they are manufacturing some drugs here, but believe me they aren't the best kind and how is anyone supposed to be able to afford them long term in this economy? It's a bloody mess! And you want to know why? You want to know why? I'll tell you why. It's because we've been programmed. Yes! Because we look to them as our source of hope and redemption. Meanwhile we have the answers and we don't know it. I have been thinking a lot about our own traditional AFRICAN healing and I – No! I am not saying we have the cure or whatever, but there is something in it, you can't argue that. Do you remember Sisi Thembi?

Patti . . . the value is not in material things. Nia, I don't know what I can give you that's more important than the opportunity to lift yourself up. That's what I did. Yeah. It may not look like it, but I'm from the 'hood – well, Ladera Heights – but I drove down Crenshaw every day – It doesn't matter! It doesn't matter your race or your gender or where you're from, it's where you're going. But I think you want to stay in the ghetto because no matter what I show you, no matter where I put you, you carry it with you in your mind. Now, you can either take that Emergency Services number, call, and stay in a shelter tonight; or you can pick yourself up, march yourself in there and patch things up with your mother. A girl needs her mother, Nia. You know, my mother and I never got along either – well . . . it's 'cause she never really cultivated my garden of talents, it was either her way or no way, and I know you and your mother are experiencing a rift, that's the connection – okay, okay! I know, I know! I'm all in the 'kool-aid' –

Petronella . . . remember when we caught her talking to trees?

Patti – my bad . . .

Petronella And she used to roast grasshoppers!

Patti . . . I learned that yesterday. // Did I say it right?

Both //hahahahahhahahahahahaha . . . hheee . . . heee . . .

Patti Nia?

Petronella Abi?

Patti Are you alright? Okay.

You know, I was online yesterday, surfing the web, and I saw that the city is looking for poetry to display on the new eco-efficient trains. I think you're work is perfect. Go online, download an application and submit some of your work. If you win, it's more scholarship money for when you – when you decide to go to community college. And your poems won at the Success is Our Future Ceremony, now that's something! Believe you me there are plenty of opportunities out there for a girl like you!! You can still be anything you want to be! (*Light bulb.*) Change the course of history. Don't let yesterday's bad choices keep you from making good choices today. Huh?! But I know you. I can tell, you're gonna do the right thing! Hey, there's no place for you to go but up, HUH?! – Huh? Well, you could go down and spiral . . .

Petronella . . . she was such a mad, mad, MAD, woman – Sisi Thembi! I can't believe she is in the church now! Like every day that sort of thing? Oh what a shame, hey – remember how she swore by witchdoctors? Remember how her . . . daughter, her daughter – had some sickness no one could figure out – she said her witchdoctor – sorry – traditional healer – fixed it! She had to do some strange things but it worked and nothing else did. There is something to it I tell you. What? You want to get out here? Abi there is nothing – ABIGAIL – What are you doing the car is still moving. Lovemore stop the car! (*Getting out of car, yelling.*)

Patti Bye, Nia!

Petronella Abigail, wait!!!!

Patti (*getting out of car, yelling*) Nia, wait!

Petronella You work for ZBC – do you host that show Breaking New Ground?

Patti Tell you mother I said hello!

Petronella No . . . well I really want to be on it, I think I have a lot to say this country needs to hear, I am breaking new bloody ground . . .

Patti I'm an Audi.

Petronella How do you say 'bye' again Lovemore? Oh – CHISARAI!

Patti Five thousand!

Petronella NO, what's the other one – TICHAMBOONA!!!

Patti No, Audi, like the car, but 'out of here'! (*Makes the sound of a car speeding by.*) Never mind . . . just go, go, go . . .

(*Her laughing at herself turns into . . .*)

Seven: Mama

Friday morning. **Mama***'s porch She's calming her crying baby throughout the scene.*

Mama (***Imani**, *a six-month old baby, crying. Sound is made by actress.*) *Hey! Hey! Get offa my grass! Get offa my grass and take your Funyion bag with you. (*To herself.*) Bad ass kids. (*Beat.*) * Well, well, well. I knew you'd come back. Lemme guess: they didn't believe your lies at the Good Shepherd either, huh? You thought it was gon' be easy as that. Well, life is not easy, guess you got to learn the hard way. And now you wanna come back. I'm still goin' to family court off of the shit you pulled; anger management, freakin' parenting classes like I don't know what the hell I'm doin', and you wanna come back just like that? No apology, no nothin'? And then you got the nerve to ask me for $400! I tell you – how you gon' pay me back? You got a job? You lookin' like a damn prostitute, what are you wearin'? It's nine o'clock in the morning, walkin' 'round like you been walkin' the streets. (*Baby talk to* **Imani**.) She walkin' the streets, ain't she? Ain't she? (*Seriously.*) Is you walkin' the streets, Nia? Don't get smart with me! Then what you need $400 for, huh? Probably some Guess jeans. What happened to the money from that poetry contest? Ain't nobody payin' you to put 'ch'a little rhymes together no more? Ain't got no job, no place to live, but spend all yo' time writin' poetry and shoppin' – for $400 Guess jeans. Are they self-cleaning? Do they pay rent? If anybody's getting $400 'round here, 'guess' who it's gonna be – ME. I'm tired of comin' second to ya'll. I can't remember the last time I had me some lotion or some new panties. Besides, you grown, remember? And us grown folk, we pay for our own shit. You old enough. Hell, when I was 19 I was * – And don't think you slick goin' behind my back askin' Marvin for the money. I thought you didn't like him. He ain'tchya daddy, so stop askin' him fo' shit. (*To* **Imani**.) Huh? He's yo' daddy, huh? Yo' daddy! Who's yo' daddy? That's yo' daddy! (*To* **Nia**.) I don't know. You should ask that lil' boyfriend of yours, Darnell, for $400. He'll buy them pants for you . . . since he the one like to get in 'em so often. Don't think I didn't usta hear your little narrow behind climbin' out the window to go oochie coochie with that boy. Like you the first one discovered how to sneak out the house? I invented that shit. I already been everywhere you been, Nia. I was just tryin' to keep your fast ass from goin' to half of them places. OH! But you 'grown'! Well, I'ma tell yo' grown ass this: I know you like him, and he look like he goin' places, * but don't you end up pregnant, Nia. Cuz once you turn this switch on, you can't turn it off, and I'ma be damned if I end up raisin' your kids cuz you couldn't use a condom. Oh, OH! (*To* **Imani**.) She woman enough to do the do, but she can't talk the talk. (*To* **Nia**.) What would you rather I say, Ms. Nia? Look at me. Strap on the jimmy? Pull the balloon over the sausage? I wish somebody had told me about this shit, half-a ya'll wouldn't be here. And now days, you can catch all kinda stuff. Stuff you can't get rid of cuz it gets in your blood. Trust me: three minutes of slappin' bellies ain't worth death. And that's what it is, death. * Because it's a government experiment, it was designed – They've done it before and will do it again. You think it's consequential that we the ones got it the most out of everybody. They been tryin' to get rid of us since the Emancipation Proclamation. First they lynched us, then they got us high so they could put us in prison. Then they got the ones that ain't incarcerated to shoot up each other and now they brought this hopin' that we fuck ourselves to death. And you know they got a cure. What you think the whole civilian rights was about? That's why they really assassinated Martin: to distract us from the monkey fuckers that brought it back from Africa to kill us. And they killed Malcolm cuz, on his pilgrimage, he found out who the monkey fuckers were. You got to know your history. That's what's wrong with ya'll – I know, I know, you love Darnell. Darnell love you. Ya'll invincible in love. Yes, I know. I was in love too, okay. Five times. Remember that. All I had to worry about was gettin' pregnant, but ya'll got a whole slew of other stuff you got to think about. Real love lasts forever, but so do real mistakes. (*To* **Imani**.) Yes, they do, huh? Yes they do! And I'ma tell you, just like I tol' them, yes I am, yes I am! You only got me 'til you're 18. That's it! Count down! * (*To* **Nia**.) That's it. Now you can go on in the back and get $60 outta my purse so that you can get you a room to rent for the night, cuz you can't stay here. I ain't gonna let ya'll run my world forever.

And, uh, you grown, remember? And I ain't gonna let you scare this man away, Shiiit. One down four to go. Look at them. That's exactly what I'm – Hey! HEY! Well, stop sprayin' paint on them walls, that shit ain't art! * (*She exists.*)

Eight: The Church

'Akuna wakaita saJesu' is being sung by the congregation, **Abigail** *rushes in, trying to look normal, greets people and sings and dances along as she searches for* **Sisi Thembi**.

Abigail (*singing along*) Hallo auntie! Muri right? Ya, Stamford is fine thanks! Hi Pastor Manyika! How are you? No, we have had trouble with transport, no petrol ka! Otherwise twice a week I would come to worship! Shit (*Sees* **SisiThembi**.) Sisi Thembi – SisiThembi wuya! Ahh (*Makes her way through the pews.*) Excuse me, sorry, pamsoroi! Sorry baby, don't cry. Excuse me please . . . thanks (*Manoeuvres around a rather large man. Reaches* **SisiThembi** *tries to sing, and look natural.*) SisiThembi, I need the address of the, eh (*Looks up at large man.*) remember that man you said helped you when your daughter was sick? NOO! The man with the eh, eh –herbs – Come on. Okay look at me –the – (*Imitates a witchdoctor possessed.*). THE WITCHDOCTOR MAN!!!! (*Everyone stops, music stops.*) He is the devil! Praise GOD!!! (*Raises arms in the air dancing, after awkward pause, music resumes.*) Come on Sisi – please! 121? Oh I know it, ya, I know it. Thanks Sisi – Thank you. (*Makes her way back through the pews.*) Excuse me, sorry, pamsoroi, sorry baby, pamsoroi . . . (*To congregation member.*) Ha? Oh, I am fine, I just felt the spirit telling me to go see a friend in need – but praise God, He is from where all blessings flow!

(*Rushes out.*)

Nine: Keysha (Short for Keyshawn)

Miss Keysha (*to the waiter*) No, the water is fine. But could you bring some lemon. And sugar. No, I don't want no lemonade. Did I ask for lemonade? If I wanted lemonade I would order lemonade. Thank you. (*To* **Nia**.) Okay. So, should you have his baby? Should you have his baby? Should a dope fiend in a crack house run from the police? Hell yeah, you should have his baby. (*To the waiter.*) Waiter! (*To* **Nia**.) No, I don't, Nia. I really don't see what the dilemma is. It's not like you got pregnant by some ole, dirty, jerry curl juicy, gold-tooth pimp. We talkin' Darnell Smith. Dar-nell Smith. The crem de la crem. Do you know how many girls pokin' needles in condoms tryin' ta have his baby. And here you sit, on the come-up like Mary pregnant with Jesus, talkin' 'bout should you have his baby. Have Miss Keysha taught you nothin'? What else you gonna do? That's Darnell Smith's baby and everybody know Darnell Smith. And these recruiters is lickin' his anus tryin' to get him to go to they school. I'm talking UCLA, Notre Dam-a. Indian-I-A, all of 'em. And you know what's gonna happen when he get outta school? He goin' straight to the NBA. Do you know what that mean? Do you know what that mean? That mean you . . . we 'bout to be set for life. For LIFE. I'm talkin' Malibu mansion. Mercedes Benz. SL class on Sprewells! I'm talkin' Louis Vetton luggage . . . no, no, no. Real Louis Vetton luggage. VIP parties, backstage passes . . . hold on. (*He has an orgasm.*) Ooooo! I can't believe I gave him to you. He was right on the line, he coulda went either way, either way. I was the one introduced ya'll when you was eight cuz I was tired of you followin' me around. Uhh huh. Those were my dark days of darkness – before I became the fine specimen you see before you. We was all staying' wit Auntie Gina – all of us up in that one room; and her makin' me take you with me when I went out, knowin' you would tell if I did somethin' wrong. Why you think I'd have you to go play with Darnell? To get yo' nosey ass out my business. Who knew Darnell would end up a damn star? He about to be so rich. I shoulda went ahead and did him then, with his little eight year old pee pee. (*Acting out what that might look and sound like.*) Speakin' of pee-pee. I gona go tinkle. (*Laughing, he exits.*)

Witchdoctor (*sings and dances complete with fly whisk and headdress*) Mhondoro dzinomwa muna Save. Mhondoro dzinomwa muna Zambezi (*x 2. Sits.*) Don't mind all this. (*Indicating traditional attire.*) I had some whites, matourist, they wanted to see the witchdoctor like the one they see on TV. I didn't know I could do those dances, hey! (*Dances from a seated position a bit.*) But it was good, my daughter, I gave them a show, they give me some money, everyone was happy! But, the spirits are happy to see you my daughter. They were angry at you – because – you have been running to these other cultures for your answers; but now you have returned they are happy. But you must know that this is from where all answers flow. These are your roots. So what's the problem here, eh, don't say anything, the ancestors will speak it to me. (*Throws bones.*) Mmmm, you are a professional woman, very well dressed, what, what. I see you are married, ya. Not enough children, not enough children from you, yah. But your hips are looking like you could have some more if you wanted. Don't tell me you are pregnant – I knew that, I was going to say it! Don't anger the ancestors. (*Whisks himself angrily with whisk. Throws bones, sniffs the air, rubs nose.*) I'm smelling fear, fear of the husband, fear of the husband, fear of the husband – but why? (*Silences her with his hand, throws bones again, looks at them, then at her.*) Why are you so sad, you are pregnant, but you are sad, scared, and sad, scared and sad –but you are pregnant – he doesn't know eh? Yah! But what are you scared of? . . . WHY are you telling me? You are going to bring on the wrath of the ancestors. (*Whisks himself with whisk.*) So you are sick, ahh . . . it's The Sickness? Okay, okay, okay, okay, (*Gathers bones.*) we don't cure that. No one can cure that. There was a time, we thought it was a joke, we would call it American Ideas for Discouraging Sex. But now, now ahh, what we have seen, we know better. But you can come back to me when the illnesses start, I can help you with those symptoms. You can bring your husband to me too, if you tell him, I have a couples' discount. (*Claps his hands.*) Hey! Stop crying! Usacheme mwanawangu! You think you are the only one dealing with this problem? If you go outside you can count, one, two, three – he has it. One, two, three – she has it. You are not special, there are many people who have this thing and still live their lives! As for the other problems I've seen here (*Indicating bones.*) I can help you with those today. For the fear of your husband beating you or leaving you, there is a love potion, a muti. AH – it is very popular these days I am running low. Rub it on his penis thrice a day. He will never leave you or forsake you. DON'T ask the great ones how to do it! That is your concern. But, you women know how to get it when you want it, he he hehehehehe. That one will allow the baby to die before it is born. That way it won't have to suffer. But don't confuse the two or your husband's penis will look like a piece of tree bark by morning. (*Winces continually at the though and whisks himself, Starts singing again.*) That is all. And don't be so afraid my daughter, you are not alone. (*Holds out hand while singing, gets cash looks, holds out hand again, looks satisfied.* **Keysha** *re-enters.*) Sharp. Be gone. (*Keeps singing.*)

Keysha Where is the complimentary bread. I tell you, that waiter got three mo' minutes – (*To* **Nia.**) Stop lookin' so sad. You not dyin', the world ain't over. You ain't the first one to end up pregnant. You should be happy! 'Cuz. you rollin' in the game with the big dogs now WOOF, WOOF! But let me warn you: this is not high school – these girls will be after Darnell and these bitches is ruthless. Don't trust none of 'em. They would fuck yo' man and yo' daddy in the same day. I've seen it happen: sports will turn these men into fools, but it'll turn women into . . . – Halle Berry in 'Jungle Fever': (*Mocking.*) 'Can I suck yo' dick? No? Uh, can I suck *yo'* dick? Anybody dick? Everybody dick?' Just wait 'til he get a little money, a little more fame – I already see that nigga every weekend with his hand indiscriminately placed between somebody's legs. And them girls! Please! They love it. Well, they may cum, but they will go cuz they ain't shit to him. You got his baby. You stayin'. But it won't be easy. 'Cuz he'll be out with two, three of 'em at the same time every night and won't think nothin' of it. Then he'll bring you back some nastiness, his PR person will get involved and the next thing you know, you readin' about how you tried to give it to him to bribe him outta some money or somethin'. Hell yeah, we want to be paid and pampered, but not enough to be catchin' no STD. You remember my roommate Monica? Monica. You know. (*Imitates Monica.*) Yeah her. (*With discretion.*) She had Chlamydia. Girl, yes! Walkin' around with it, thought it was a damn yeast infection. By the time she asked me to help her to the clinic, she couldn't even walk. And when she got there they said she had waited so long it turned into P-I-D – Pussy in Distress, yes. She got that shit from Jerry –that muthafucka didn't even know he had it. He coulda been walkin' around with herpes, shit, AIDS and not even know it. Of course she was afraid to tell him! I had to confront his punk ass and you know what he said? He said, 'I don't know whatchu talkin' 'bout. That's on her', like she gave it to herself. That nigga was on the DL, had Chla-my-di-a and he was still tryin' to make it seem like it was all on her. Like she did it like all by herself. How you even do that? What, you be like (*She imitates what giving herself a sexually transmitted disease would look like.*) – Okay, okay, okay. The point is this: these men don't give a fuck about you. All you are to them is a piece of ass. And I'ma be damned if I'ma let my cousin get used up and then end up with nothin'. If you're givin' it up, then you best believe he givin' it up too. And you sho' ain't havin' no babies for free. That is not prostitution, that's called takin' care-a you. I mean, look-atcha mama! She dated some first class Negroes, had they baby, but still couldn't pay her rent. The last thing you wanna be is some hood-rat, baby-mama, walkin' around with cold sores and house shoes; buyin' government cheese with food stamps when yo' baby daddy in the N-B fuckin' A, and playin' husband to some other bitch and her kids. Then who the one lookin' stupid? Now, at least if you his wife, you get half, even if he divorce your ass; even if you do get Chlamydia. Then, whatever way it go, you won't never have to worry about money, and can do whatever the fuck you wanna do. Write your poetry, be Maya Angelou, whatever. Listen to me: don't let that boy out your sight. Remind him that you was the one at his games before anybody knew his name. Tell his mama you carrying his baby. Mmm-hum. Naw, go 'head, make it a family affair. Didn't you say you met her at they family picnic? See! She probably already like you! And once you have her, it don't matter what he say. Don't stop 'til you get keys to the crib and a ring on that finger! Should you have his baby . . . how else you gon' pay me back for all the shit I did for you? Nia, havin' a baby is a blessing. I mean, think about it. I look better than all ya'll heifers put together, but I cannot have a baby out my ding-a-ling. Whatever you do, I'ma always be your cousin, but remember, we already live in hell. Don't make it so you have to spend eternity there too. God gave you that baby. That baby is yo' ticket out. (*He exits.*)

Ten: Sex worker

Sex Worker (*enters smoking*) Dahling, dahling, dahling. How the bloody hell am I supposed to know how to make a man fall asleep so you can put love potion on his penis? Don't believe those stories about us sex workers stealing the penises of men who don't pay. That's all bullshit! (*Starts to sit, gets back up.*) Just give me a second my dahling, (*Takes out cloth tucked in side of pants, wipes between her legs.*) What a messy bastard . . . that's better. (*Sits.*) Right, shit, you've got yourself into a pot of poo my girl! Who would have thought Miss Priss Abigail would get herself in such a bind! But, let me help you out my sister, since you have come to your old high school chum for advice. You have to face the truth. Your marriage is ova. You think you can make him stay? You know how these men are! He will blame you for everything, even though you got it from him. And the in laws!! Do you remember Elizabeth Chidzero? It happened to her! Sent back to her village, penniless, the kids taken by the bastard and his family, even though she got it from him! Now she is waking up to the cockerels singing 'kokoriko' – dancing at those fucking village pungwes for those old farts, and she bathes in a filthy river, even though she's as sick as a bloody dog hey! You think it won't happen to you? You'll find yourself back in your village, grinding com singing 'dum dum duri, dum dum duri'. Ha, and you were always the one who was going to go to America or something and become rich and famous. What did you say your man's name was again? AHHHH (*Deep in thought, then looks back at* **Abigail**.) All I'll say is I am not surprised. Shame. The best thing I can offer you, my sister, is a new lifestyle. Leave the bastard. Because he gave you AIDS! I can hook you up with a nice beneficiary. Who will take such good care of you, my love, you will never need that man of your again. He will give you enough doughs to get the medicine and save that baby! You can take your son, get your own place – you take care of the man every now and then. BUT – you get the doughs, buy the drugs. And you will live so much longer futi. And no bullshit in law stress. What have you got to lose my dahling? I don't understand the prob – Ohh, ha! You think this lifestyle is planned or something? The economy is shit, my dear. In case you haven't noticed. I was a secretary, couldn't pay for my rent, couldn't pay for my electric, I couldn't pay for my fucking DSTV! And I was NOT going back to watching Dead BC. No offense. So I did it once, did it twice, next thing you know I had a business. Listen, there is NOTHING wrong with being a kept woman. It's the least these bastards can do for us. And it's a fair trade, almost like going back to the barter system. And these African men, they love to flex their dollars, makes their dicks hard. So, it's there for the taking. You have to decide what's more important to you. Remain Miss Priss Abigail, or become a survivor. Because, you can't save both your marriage and that baby. You can keep quiet about it, act as if nothing is wrong and die horribly – watching your kid die too, all because you wanted to remain the perfect little Shona, Zimbabwean wifey. Which many have done. Or you can take care of yourself and your children. Personally, I want to be a mother. I have this one guy; he's a client, but he's a really nice guy hey! He wants me to have his baby. He says, no condoms. Saka, me, I say, why not! It's important to be a mother, it's the one thing we can do that these bastards can't! This is just a hope for me, but you, you have children, so be a mother. And forget about that potion girlie. Those n'angas are mad. If they had anything that worked Africa wouldn't even have AIDS. (*Looks outside.*) Shit! Sorry dahling, it's another customer – and this one needs a little bit more time. He's one of those old government chef bastards. The machinery takes so much longer to oil. I can't even get into it. (*Puts out cigarette.*) Abi, Abigail – think about what I said, you have to do something, you can't keep running around like Speedy Gonzales! This is the best answer you are going to get! (*Straightens out wig and shirt, looks over at client approaching.*) Hi, howzit! ?

Adlibs and overlaps with the **Gail**: '*Hi, howzit . . . I'm fine*', '*Just don't be rough today, Chef!*')

Eleven: Gail

Gail Just be quiet, please! Shhh! Damn it, Darnell! I said to take your medication and use a condom. Use a condom. I told him to – You kids don't think. You don't think beyond your own little circle of existence. You think this is a video game? This is life. Real life. You don't get to start over! 'Cause he's just a boy, he's a baby, how is he supposed to know how to – when you all just keep tossin' yourselves at him! Don't give me that look. I see the way you look at him. Salivatin' with dollar signs in your eyes. You probably thought that if you latched onto him you could ride him all the way to the top. You think you the first one to try to lock him down? Ask his agent: he's already had two paternity claims. Sit down. Sit back down! Why should I have told you anything, Nia? This is a private family matter. You should have kept your legs closed. And I warned Darnell about ya'll. I said, 'Darnell, baby, stay focused. You can't afford to get caught up'. I made sure he played in all the right districts, with all the right coaches, he was seen by the recruiters! Look at his trophies. Look at them! Does this look like AIDS to you? Do you think he would be being recruited if anybody knew? Do you think he would be getting a scholarship? That's right! A scholarship for outstanding athletic achievement – to my son. So, no, nobody knows. It's none of they damn business. You consider what people will think about you if they knew. You think they gon' treat you the same? When you mention it, even the people you thought loved you will have you eatin' outta paper plates. Everybody turns on you; little kids say nasty things to you. Even the people at church! They gon' whisper behind your back; point at you in the pew, sayin', 'That's what happens to people who sin with the devil'. Think it won't happen. Now, I'm trying to help you, Nia, but you have got to promise me – Is this about money? Huh? Cuz I can get you money, Nia. Give me a couple of hours and I'll get you . . . $5,000. (**Maid** *enters, singing, starts cleaning*.) How's that sound? That'll be enough to get you a place, have some money left over to do what you got to do. That's what we'll do: I'll get you $5,000 for now, and we can worry about later, later.

Twelve: Maid

Maid, *on hands and knees. cleaning the floor, singing 'Tauya naye nemagumbezi'.*

Maid Oh . . . Miss Abigail, masikati, Maswera sei? Ndaswer. I have put out the chicken and samosas for Simbi's party, and the man is here with the jumping castles, but he wants to know if you want the jumping castle, kana the jumping giraffe. And that crazy little friend of Simbi's Fungai Mparaza he had to come early – and he has already broken two plates Miss Abi! And Bhudi Gilbert called, he said he was coming with the braaai stand – MissAbi are you okay? My husband? I don't have a husband MissAbigail. No, ya, of course, my family wants me to have one but I don't want. Anyway my family now it's just my brother and aunts and uncles. My mother and father – they died kuma 1998 and 1999, then my sister kuma 2001. They had a long illness. Anyway, me I said, it's better to be alone, love between a man and a woman seems to end in death around here. And people say stupid things to me, but I don't care. Oh, they say things like – 'eh, she thinks she is too good to get married, maybe she thinks she's a man. Eh, you don't want us – you are ugly anyway'. (*Talks to imaginary men.*) I would like to say to them: YOU are ugly anyway and you probably have something then you will beat me and leave me to suffer when I get it from YOU!!! No thanks! But I just keep quiet. Saka, I am alone. I work here and go to night classes – I want to get a degree. Like you MissAbi, you work, you went to school, and you are a wife and a mother futi – I don't want that part but I admire that – then I know I can do it too zvangu. People say, you can't do anything without a husband in Zimbabwe – but I will try anyway. At least like this I can say, Ini I know who I am, where I am going – I know what I am working for. And I am moving (*Gestures.*) forward, forward, forward, not this way or that way but forward. Maybe I stand alone, but I know who I am – Mary Chigwada – not Mrs So and So with the in laws and brideprice, and going to his village to cook at the funerals chi chi – NO – just me Mary Chigwada. AHH, Miss Abi, – your mother and father are coming through the gate – ah, your mother looks so pretty! (*Straightening up.*) I am so glad you are back Miss Abi, there is so much to do, I haven't even put out the drinks yet and . . . Miss Abi – Miss Abi? Oh, maiwee!

Rushes out.

Thirteen: The prayer – bills, bills, bills

Nia It smell like booty. I wish I could fly away. Dirty ass motel. Guess what, baby. Guess what? (*Dumping her purse.*) Today your mommy opened her purse to see how much money she had and she had a five dollar bill and a $5,000 check. $5,000. (*Folding up the check and putting it aside.*) But you know what? We don't need his money. No, we don't! 'Cause mommy will go tomorrow and see if they still want her at Nordstrom. What was they talkin' 'bout payin'? Five dollars. But no, baby, no, we can do it. We just got to budget. (*Tearing a piece of the five dollar bill with each item.*) See this, this right here is for my retirement fund. 'Cause Oprah says you should pay yourself first. This, this is for your college fund, 'cause you going to college. This is for rent . . . on our mansion in Malibu. And my Mercedes. What else? What else you want, baby? You can have anything you want. Oh wait! (*Tearing the last piece in three.*) Gas, water, and lights. What! That's the life right there, baby. You got retirement, college, mansion, Mercedes, gas, water, lights. What! Ooooo! Mommy forgot to put food in the budget! How mommy forget to put food in the budget? But there's no more money. There's $5,000. (*She breaks down in tears.*) Because he knew. He knew. He knew the whole time – And he knows you're his baby cuz he the one made me pregnant. And now she thinks she can just throw $5,000 at me and I'ma just be quiet? $5,000 dollars. I sold myself for $5,000. Nope, baby, that's how much I cost. That's how much you cost. (*Balling up the check and throwing it down.*) No, no, we don't need his money. This is what we gonna do. (*Picking up the pieces of the five dollar bill.*) I'ma take the light money and make it the food money. Cuz we gotta eat. But we don't need no lights. (*A la 'The Roof is on Fire'.*) We don't need no lights let the muthafuckas burn! (*She b-boxes and makes a beat on the furniture.*) Come on, baby. Cuz we got, huh? What we got, huh? What we got?! (*Periodically breaking down and breaking rhythm.*)

We got, we got Sunlight, Insight, Out of sight – out of mind.

Full-time, Lifetime
Out-of-time
I'm outta my mind
We gon' Re-define
Discipline
Undermine that bottom line

(*Applying perfume.*)

Drench myself in Vaseline
Make myself look feminine
I'll be dressed and drapped in Calvin Klein.
And he'll come home at dinnertime.
My womb is free of guilt and grime.
Before this change, before this crime.
Before the fall, before the climb (she begins to pray)
Please keep me from this constant grind
Help me see, although I'm blind
Help me breathe despite the slime
Help me live if you're inclined
Please don't decline my prayer.
I know it's nobody's fault but mine
I won't bitch, complain or whine
If you help me out, one more time
I will not let you down.
I'll give up sex, weed, and wine.
Everything. Everything.
Just plant my feet on solid ground.

(*She sobbs.*) No. No! This what we gon' do. (*Picks up the check.*) Tomorrow we're going to go up to that scholarship ceremony. And I'm gonna make Darnell look me in the face and tell me I'm only worth $5,000. Then, I'm going to stand there in front of all those recruiters, in front of the whole world and I'ma just say it. And then all the girls he been with's gon' know. And all the girls he was thinking about doin's gon' know. And then everybody will know. (*Balling the check up and throwing it down again.*) I'm worth more than this money. (*She begins to exit. She doubles back for the check.*) Tomorrow.

Fourteen: Abigail's prayer

Abigail (*enters, reading an old certificate*) Huh, I won that thing! I won that thing! (*Reading.*) This is to award Abigail Moyo of Malbereign Girls High as the winner of the National Interschools Public Speaking Championship, 1994, Harare, Zimbabwe. I won that thing. What was my speech again? Oh, oh! Of course! (*Steps up on bed.*) The New African Woman – Modernizing and Post Colonizing. I was once number three of four wives – yet I chose to rise. I was once denied usage of the same toilet as you. (*Laughs.*) – I always had to look for a white – yet I chose to rise. In me is the blood of the great Mbuya Nehanda – the spiritual medium who fought and died for this land. In me is the pride of Winnie Mandela who marched the streets of Soweto singing 'Free Nelson Mandela' until they did. In me is the ferocity of the woman freedom fighter who let go of the milk of human kindness to fight for a free Zimbabwe! I am no longer the third of four wives, but the first of the first. And I can become whatever I please. Because my dreams can be a reality . . . (*She breaks.*) He knew, he knew, that bastard. (*Steps down.*) . . . How long . . . how long have you been bringing your hures into my house? Have you been sleeping with them in my Woolworths sheets from Joburg? But I knew it, I knew it all along, with the late nights and the way he was smelling . . . but what could I have done Baba? You are the one who said two become one, two flesh become one – and that's what I did – So how did you allow one flesh to rot into the other when I lived according to your word? And how can this be your plan for my life? You want me to die like a prostitute? That's your plan? That's what you have been building me up to? And don't give me that trial and tribulation bullshit! I have come too far, I have done everything the right way! What more did you want from me?

You've got to help me Baba, you've got to help me, you've got to help – (*Stops to catch her breath, goes silent, drops to her knees.*) Okay, okay, I will tell them. But this is what I ask: DON'T you let them blame me. You make them stand by me. And support me. And you make Stamford stay put. You make him still love me and take care of me. Because he's still mine and I am not giving up everything I worked for. And I want my baby, so don't you let it have this illness. (*Grips belly.*) You have to fight this baby with whatever you have. You just have to fight it okay. And if I must die – don't let me die like Sisi Stella who was convulsing in so much pain they had to strap her to a bed. And don't let me die like Sekuru Lovemore who was covered in so many sores they couldn't even show him at the funeral. And if I must die let my chil – (*Knock on the door –* **Abigail** *starts, sits on chair and composes herself. Cheerily.*) Come in. (*Enter* **Simbi**.) Hello my big boy. Are you enjoying your party? You look so smart, is this the outfit daddy bought you? It's very nice. . . huh? They want to sing 'Happy Birthday' already. Okay, tell them I am coming – tell them Mummy spilt something on her dress and I have to change it. Okay . . . okay so you go ahead baby . . . Simbi, dzoka mwanawangu, dzoka. (*Calls him back.*) Unoziwa kuli mummy loves you? Okay, saka iti 'mummy loves me'. Good boy. Ita futi, 'mummy loves me'. Good, okay, okay, you go ahead . . . mummy's coming.

Fifteen: The end

Abigail (*singing Watinti bafadzi with* **Nia** *– both clear stage of stools.*) Watinta wafadzi watinti mbogoto uzagofa (*x2*) 'Pamsoroi, Baba naAmai, nababamukuru, naBhudi Gilbert, navatete. Tafara, we are happy you have come to celebrate Simbi's seventh birthday with us. In our culture I know the family shares everything, and takes good, good care of one another. So I know I can share this with you and get your support. Stamford, I am telling you this here so we can find a harmony okay. Stamford, we have to go to the clinic tomorrow morning because I . . . you . . . you and therefore we have acquired the acquired immune deficiency syndrome virus HIV and I am pregnant.'

Nia 'Good evening ladies and gentlemen. My name is Nia James, and I'm here to say that Darnell Smith gave me AIDS!' Then I'ma rip up the check. No, I can't say that . . .

Abigail No – that acquired acquired thing is stupid . . . No, no this is good, he can't beat me or throw me out with my parents and Bhudi Gilbert there at his son's birthday futi . . .

Nia . . . no, it's the right thing. Everybody should know . . .

Abigail He will have to beg my forgiveness. 'Okay, okay, I forgive you – but you can't cheat anymore' –

Nia 'He could be giving it to everybody. If I had know, I would have never' –

Abigail 'Now we must plan ahead for us and the children.'

Nia 'I'm not a hoe. Everybody has sex.'

Abigail 'Yes I forgive you – no, no – don't hit him Bhudi Gilbert.'

Nia 'I didn't make this disease. I didn't give this to myself.'

Abigail 'I choose to stay with you but you must find the money for treatments.'

Nia I should have protected myself, but he –

Abigail 'Because you got us into this trouble. Okay!'

Nia I just wanted him to . . .

Abigail *and* **Nia** *face each other in a mirror, bur remain in opposite worlds.*

Abigail 'And you must look at me and see me, Abigail Moyo Murambe.'

Nia 'There's no amount you can pay me to take this away.'

Abigail 'You must treat me like a wife you respect.' –

Nia 'Naw, I don't want yo' apology!'

Abigail 'Because I know who I am!'

Nia 'I'm changing the course of history!'

Abigail 'And I am moving (*Gestures.*) forward, forward, forward – not this way or that. Okay!'

Nia That's fine.

Abigail That's good.

Abigail/Nia So help me God. Let's go.

Abigail Okay kids, go play on the jumping castle!

Nia (*to herself*) Damn, it's a lot of people . . .

Abigail (*faces family*) Pamsoroi Baba, naAmai na babamukuru, navatete naBhudiGilbert.

Nia (*to herself*) There he is . . .

Abigail Tafara, we are happy you have come to celebrate Simbi's seventh birthday with us . . . eh . . .

Nia (*to herself*) Just say it . . .

Abigail In our culture, we . . . move forward, forward, forward . . .

Nia (*to the crowd*) Hey! I have . . . something I want to say. . .

Abigail No, no, I mean . . . with a family . . . eh . . .

Nia (*to the crowd*) My name is Nia James . . .

Abigail We share everything . . .

Nia (*to the crowd*) And I just came to say . . .

Abigail . . . and that's why I know I can say what is happening between me . . . and Stamford . . . here . . .

Abigail/Nia Eh . . . eh . . .

***Abigail** Stamford and I are having another baby! // Pururdza!!! (*Ululates*) Eh, suwa, tinofara! Ha? Ya, that was the news, that was it! Another boy, ya, that's what I was saying Tete! Another boy ya! Well, you were saying Simbi is getting lonely! So it's time, ya, it's time. Sure ya. Maita! Tinofara . . . hehe.

* **Nia** // Congratulations! Oooa, Oooa! Oooa, Oooa! Huh? No, no that's what I came to say. Congratulations. Yeah. His mom's probably real proud, huh?! Hey! Can I get tickets to the games? Just two tickets? One ticket? I'ma get me a ticket, watch! You crazy! Heeee . . .

Both characters laugh in synchronicity into a blackout.

End of play

Shona/Zimbabwe glossary

Aiwa	no
Amai	mother (also used as a sign of respect to a woman)
Amai naba vako nevese nemumhuri menyu	your mother and father and your family
Baba	father (also used to substitute as Lord, God)
Babamukuru	older father (usually refers to an older uncle)
Bhudi	brother
Barance wemunhu	idiot of a person
Beby	baby
Chef	a term used to describe men of power and influence in Zimbabwe
Chi chi	etcetera etcetera
Chisarai	goodbye
Chisipiti	an affluent suburb of Harare
Commuter omnibus	a van used as a form of public transport.
Dahling	darling
Deddy	daddy
DSTV	equivalent of digital cable
Dum dum duri	a song traditionally sung while grinding corn into flour with a large pestle and mortar
Dzoka mwana	come back child, come back
Edgars	major clothing chain around Southern Africa
Ewe	you
Fotsek	an expletive originally used to address dogs
Futi	again/also
Glen Lorne	an affluent suburb of Harare
Hartman House	one of the most affluent boys' prep schools in Harare

Head boy	the top position a student can obtain in their final year of high school. A position of authority, from the British schooling system model, used in Zimbabwe as a result of colonization
Heré	converts a statement into a question
Howzit	how is it going?
Ini	me
Ita futi	say again
Iti	say
Iwe waka pusa newewo uri HIV, futi Amai vako vane maronda panaapa	you are stupid and you have HIV, and your mother has sores here
Ka	a Zimbabwean exclamation – often used for emphasis
Kana	or
Kokoriko	sound used to depict cockerels crowing
Kuma	in
Kumusha	a person's rural homeland
Kwete	no
Maita	thank you
Maiwee	an exclamation or expression of distress.
Marara	bullshit/garbage
Masikati	good afternoon
Maskwera sei	how are you?
mati amaivangu vane AIDS	did you say my mother has AIDS?
Mbuya Nehanda	legendary female Spiritual medium who stood up against the British when they first invaded Zimbabwe in the 1890s. They executed her.
Mhondoro dzinomwa muna Save, Mhondoro dzinomwa munaZambezi	a song describing a lion drinking from the Save and Zambezi rivers.

mirai	wait
Muboi	derogatory term that black people use to describe lower-classed black people
MunomuZimbabwe	here in Zimbabwe
Muri right	how are you (are you 'right')
mwanawangu	my child
na	and
ndapota	please
ndibatsirewo	help me out
ne	and
nhasi ririFriday	today is Friday
nodo	a children's game involving throwing a stone in the air and trying to move other stones out and inside of a circle while the stone is still in the air
n'yanga	witchdoctor/traditional healer
Pajero	prestigious Mitsubishi SUV in Zimbabwe
Pamsoroi	excuse me
Paroadside	at the side of the road
Pururudza	a celebrative expression. Often termed as ululating
Richiri jana rangu	it's still my turn
Sadza	a staple Zimbabwean starch dish made from cornmeal, often word used to reference food in general
Saka	so
Saka hapana achatamba, hapana achatamba	so nobody is going to play, nobody is going to play
Saka wati Amai vangu vari HIV?	so you said my mother is HIV?
SABC	South African Broadcasting Corporation
Sekuru	grandfather/older uncle
Sha	exclamation substituted for 'man', for example 'come on

	man', 'come on sha'. Also short for Shamwari
Shamwari	friend. Also used as an exclamation
Sisi	sister
Suwa	sure
Tafara	we are happy
Tete	aunt; specifically on one's father's side
Tichaboona	see you
Tinofara	we can all be happy
Totanga	let's start
Tomato sauce	children's play song
Totamba chi	what should we play?
Truworths	major clothing chain around Southern Africa
Unoziwa kuti	do you know that?
Usacheme mwanawangu	don't cry my child
Vako ndivo vari HIV	they are the ones who have HIV
Vanhu vatema vaonetsa	black people are a pain
Village pungwe	traditional village meetings conducted in the rural areas
Watinta wafadzi wantinti mbogoto uzagofa	You strike a woman you strike a rock and you will die. (A South African song. Zulu; made famous by a musical production in the 1970s by the same name)
Wonai	Look
Wuya	come here
ZBC	Zimbabwe Broadcasting Corporation ('Z' is pronounced 'Zed')
Zimboes	a term used to describe Zimbabweans
Zvangu	myself – used as an emphasis

J. Nicole Brooks

Black Diamond

The Years the Locusts Have Eaten

Black Diamond: The Years the Locusts Have Eaten received its world premiere at the Lookingglass Theatre Company on April 14, 2007 Chicago Illinois. The cast and creative team were as follows:

Alana Arenas	Colonel Black Diamond/ Mariama Sesay
Jason Delane	Chogan Jim Fox
Tamberla Perry	Born to Suffer, others
Nancy Moricette	Ripley, Olivier, others
Penelope Walker	Clear Heart, Millicent, others
Freeman Coffey	General Dragon Master, Dr. Martin Delany, others
Ericka Ratcliff	Disgruntle, Professor Negro Know It All, others
Victor Cole	Jusu Masali, Kojack, others
Thomas J. Cox	Tristan Monoghan, Thomas Jefferson, others
Adeoye	Colonel Yankee, Commander Cripple Pussy, others
Kevin Douglas	The American Dummy, Ranger One Attack Force, others
Tamberla Perry	Born to Suffer, Condelezza Rice, others.

Directed by David Catlin & J. Nicole Brooks
Lighting Design Brian Sydney Bembridge
Costume & Hair Design Alison Siple
Set Design Sibyl Wickersheime

A crossroad where civil unrest meets the spirit world.

Time and Place: 2003, Zamani (past) and Sasa (present).

Location: Throughout Liberia, New York City, and all dimensions in between.

A crossroads where civil unrest meets the spirit world.

Characters

Chogan Jim Fox	Correspondent for BBC Africa
Tristan Monoghan/ Thomas Jefferson	Camera journalist and friend of Jim Fox/American founding father, third president of the United States, Inventor
The Deities	Ancestral spirits with supernatural powers
Liberian People	Various Liberian orphans, refugees and citizens
Finely the Ventriloquist	A founder of ACS (The Society for the Colonization of Free People of Color of America)
American Dummy/ Anansi	Dummy-puppet of Finley/ West African Deity
Jusu Masali	Godfather to Black Diamond
Millicent Gladwell	On again off again love of Jim Fox
NPFL Soldiers	Soldiers serving President Charles Taylor of Liberia
Commander Cripple Pussy	Commanding Officer
Kojack	Commanding Officer
Mr. Whiskey	Gun/Precious metals smuggler
Scarface	Soldier
Olivier	Soldier
LURD Soldiers	Rebel forces in opposition to President Charles Taylor
General Dragon Master	General of the LURD forces, mentor to Black Diamond
Ranger One Attack Force	Soldier LURD

Choir Stand	Soldier LURD
Colonel Yankee/Ezekiel	Colonel in LURD rebel forces
Colonel Black Diamond/ Mariama Sesay	Leader of WAC rebel forces
Born to Suffer	Master Drill Sergeant
Clear Heart/Asase Ya	Soldier/ West African Deity
Disgruntle	Minister of Defense
Ripley	Soldier
Dr. Martin Delaney	Father of pan Africanism

Principal Acronyms and Abbreviations

WAC	Women Artillery Commandos – a division of LURD
LURD	Liberians United for Reconciliation and Democracy
NPFL	National Patriotic Front of Liberia
ACS	Society for the Colonization of Free People of Color of America
UN	United Nations (AKA Blue Helmets)
ECOMOG	Economic Community of West African States Cease-fire Monitoring Group

Miscellaneous

CO	Commanding Officer
HNIC	Head Negro in Charge
GDM	General Dragon Master
BD	Black Diamond

Other References

Chairman Sekou Conneh Chairman of the LURD rebel forces.

NOTES

All parts (except Black Diamond and Jim Fox) should be multi-cast.

Aura: 1. An invisible breath or emanation. 2. A warning before a seizure.

Some of the dialogue in this play is spoken with a local West African dialect (broken English for the most part), so grammatical errors serve a purpose.

Some of the characters also slip in and out of their tribal dialect. We will hear snippets of the following languages: Mande, West African French, and American Sign Language.

Much of the music can be created with the human mind, body, spirit and soul. Hand clapping, percussion; beat boxing, rap/hip hop, spoken word, indigenous folk, classical and gospel music encouraged.

Dance, movement, combat, flying, climbing and challenging conventional ways of choreography is encouraged.

Combat/martial art techniques may include (but are not limited to): kung fu, kali stick, and krav maga.

Act One

'Hawkeye and Trapper Have A Fight'

Pre-show West African Hi-Life music blares. Sand bags are stacked all throughout the space. The lights flicker on and off, the audio slows down and garbles, all electrical power fails.

The ticking of a clock.

Silence.

Sound and electricity restores; a tight light on Joseph. We hear the voice of Jim Fox, reporter for BBC, interviewing Joseph Karpeh, a Liberian civilian. Actors gently whisper greetings to say 'hello'. 'Ya kunay,' 'Asalaam malekum', various pidgin greetings etc., which builds into Joseph Karpeh's interview.

Joseph Karpeh Hello. My name is Joseph Karpeh. I am a shopkeeper here on Bushrod Island. I love Liberia, have lived here most of my life, but since the war, I have sent my children away to stay with relatives. But I have stayed behind to help my other family members.

Jim Fox And how have things been here for you here?

Joseph Karpeh Well, it's okay when there is no fighting. But when mortars hit, it is chaos.

We had an attack the other day. Government soldiers came, and . . . it was terrible.

Jim Fox Did they do anything to you?

Joseph Karpeh Two men with rifles dragged me out of my shop.

I was stripped naked and a bandage, it was, uh tied across my face . . . they took me somewhere. I yelled with all of my power and voice, not knowing where I was. I began to feel a cold blade on my chest and back. I was for certain that my life was over but, before the blade made the slightest prick in my flesh, God spared my life.

Jim Fox Do you mean you were rescued?

Joseph Karpeh Yes.

I was surprised by how my tormentors so quickly and mysteriously took my place, with their faces tied and arms bound, prostrate on bare earth. Meanwhile I sat trembling in the van that my liberator set me in. That liberator was Black Diamond. Respect for the Colonel.

Jim Fox Thank you for your time, Mr. Karpeh.

Joseph Karpeh *exits. Lights focus on* **Jim Fox**. *He is a thin, very light-skinned black man who can charm the pants off a snake. He has a bandage on his forehead.*

Jim Fox This Black Diamond is something else. 'Respect due to the Colonel', that's what they all say in the interviews. I even talked to some of Taylor's boys who said they have respect for Black Diamond.

Tristan Monoghan, *a well-built Irishman, circulates snapping photographs. He is* **Jim**'*s field operator and close friend. His hand is wrapped in an ace bandage or a makeshift splint. He spots a dead body.*

Tristan Monoghan Got us a jack in the box.

Jim Fox Jesus.

Tristan Monoghan Disemboweled.

Tristan *snaps a few photos.* **Jim** *searches for materials in a nearby garbage can.* **Tristan** *uses his bandana to wipe sweat from his neck. He then takes a sip of whiskey from his flask and offers it to* **Jim**.

Tristan Monoghan The devil's got her legs open today . . . so fucking hot.

Jim *searches for materials. He spots a blue tarp. He pulls it down.*

Tristan Monoghan Jesus fuck Jimmy . . . what are you doin? We can't –

Jim Fox Yes we can. Give me a hand.

Tristan Monoghan I don't – Fine.

They cover the body with the tarp. They have a moment of silence. **Jim** *pours some whiskey on the ground.* **Tristan** *gives an obligatory sign of the cross. They go on about their business setting up for the shot.*

Tristan Monoghan Hey, did I tell you? Spoke to Opal.

Jim Fox How is she?

Tristan Monoghan She says her boobs hang down to her waist and that she has an ass like a baboon.

Jim Fox Pregnancy never sounded more glamourous.

Tristan Monoghan They may have to induce labor.

Jim Fox S'alright. The baby's on Colored People's Time. Taking after his Trinidadian mama.

Tristan Monoghan Maybe I should've married a Jew. The baby would've shown up on time.

Tristan *checks the audio levels on his.*

Wake your face, I'm almost set here.

Jim Fox (*Blowing out his lips, quick vocal warm ups.*) Participle. Parents. Prince Paul. Pied piper.

Tristan Monoghan Good. Hey, how's Millicent?

Jim Fox Ah you know the same.

Tristan Monoghan Get your head out of your ass and marry the woman. Settle down. Get a morning news show –

Jim Fox I move back to the States, that's exactly what'll happen. No thanks.

Tristan Monoghan Can't believe you left a comfortable job at the Post to come here.

Jim Fox (*re: his head*) Bandage on or off?

Tristan *sets up for the shot.* **Jim** *gently begins to peel away his bandage.*

Tristan Monoghan You're lucky it's not infected. On.

Jim Fox How's your hand?

Tristan Monoghan Doesn't matter, I've got another one.

How's your head?

Jim Fox I told you it's fine –

Tristan Monoghan I'm not talking about the gash.

Jim *avoids eye contact with* **Tristan** *and pushes on.*

Jim Fox Come on we're losing day light. In five, four, three, two . . . It's the only African country with the distinction of the label, 'made in America'.

The founding of the Republic of Liberia in the 1800s was created by a small group of American men at an Ivy League institution. The love of liberty may have brought them here, but for decades this country has witnessed struggle between Americo-Liberians and the indigenous people. Americo-Liberians (sometime referred to as Congos) are the descendants of black American settlers. (**Asase Ya** *&* **Anansi**, *two spirits appear*) This tiny nation quickly went from a land of milk and honey to yet another antebellum south. (*He stumbles through the report with impaired comprehension and word difficulty*). Indigenous people weren't even considered chictizens – citizens – For 133 years the cchn, chhh –, the settlers dominated commerce and politics. A coup de tat . . . of the Tolbert – administration – sorry . . .

Tristan Monoghan You alright?

Jim Fox Samuel Doe . . . a native of the Khran tribe . . . 13 officials were publicly executed by a firing squad on the beach –

He goes blank. A bright light illuminates throughout the space. **Asase Ya** *and* **Anansi** *walk to the dead body from earlier.* **Jim** *notices the pair. The woman stretches her hands ceremoniously over the body causing the dead body's spirit to rise (may be done via light, sound, or other visual theatrics.)* **Jim** *is hypnotized by the spectacle. The man, woman and the body exit. The sounds of locusts fly.*

Tristan (*He puts the camera down. Carefully he approaches.* **Jim** *is in a trance*) Christ. Jim?

The man, woman, and the spirit of the dead body disappear. The lumination wanes. He loses mobility in his legs, and plops on the ground. After a moment regains composure.

Have you been taking your pills?

Jim Fox I'm fine.

Tristan Doesn't look that way to me.

Jim Fox I . . . don't look at me like that man.

Tristan Monoghan Well how should I look at you?

Jim Fox Where'd they go? That man, and a woman . . . the body. Did you get them in the shot?

Tristan Monoghan What?

Jim Fox Check your camera; you had to have captured it. Check the footage. That body we covered . . . there was a man, and a woman . . . they took the –

Asase Ya *re-appears. She and* **Jim** *regard one another. Her power emanates.* **Tristan** *reluctantly goes to view the footage.*

Tristan Monoghan (*Looking into the camera.*) You should consider getting back on your meds. Nothing to be ashamed of. Some of the most brilliant people have Epilepsy. Socrates, Dickens . . . also in the epileptic hall of fame . . . Lewis Carroll.

You know *Alice in Wonderland*? If he didn't have a few crossed wires, we wouldn't have that stupid cat in the tree –

She disappears. **Jim** *vomits and coughs.* **Tristan** *turns away.*

Tristan Monoghan You keep getting sick like this, and we'll never to make it to Oz, Dorothy.

Turning back to him.

You need water.

Jim *frantically turns his attention to the 'body bag'. He uncovers it. To his surprise he discovers the body is still there.*

Jim Fox I thought . . .

Tristan Monoghan Gutted this fucker like a pig. Vultures feast, this one.

Jim Fox Would you shut up? Honestly the shit you say sometimes. I don't know why I bother with you.

Tristan Monoghan What does he care, he's dead?

Jim Fox Have some fucking respect.

Tristan Monoghan What would you have me do? Weep? wail? Gnash my teeth like some . . . ? Look. He's DEAD. This guy has no more problems. He doesn't have to worry about – whatever the fuck he was worried about before.

Tristan *goes to and turns to pack his camera bag.*

Jim Fox You're a punk, you know that?

Tristan Monoghan Fine.

Jim Fox Is it really that easy for you to be so disrespectful? We find bodies in ditches, doorways, or the steps of the goddamned Embassy. And all you can say is 'they're dead – no more worries.'

Tristan Monoghan We're on assignment, not a rescue mission.

Jim Fox Let me be clear about something, these are my people –

Tristan Monoghan Your people?

Jim Fox Yes goddamn it. Black people. I'm black, they're black, My People. I'm no different from them.

Tristan Monoghan You that think some 'black unity' passport is going to get you inside this beast? Do you have any idea what you're trying to get into?

Jim Fox You don't know the first thing about what's going on here.

Tristan Monoghan Here's what I know –

These people aren't fighting for nationality. They are fighting because a warlord-turned-president fucked them. That's what I know. You need to have a realistic view. Most of the Western world shares a conservative, economic view of things. They've nothing to gain by helping these people. It's politics.

Jim Fox My last name might be Fox, but you're the one talking like an ultra conservative.

Tristan Monoghan Wait a minute –

Jim Fox This war has been going on for years. Whats been happening in Sierra Leone, Liberia, the Congo – you name it, has been underreported. Fabricated. Omitted from the world at large. So you think, if you can let the world know what's happening here, things will change?

Jim Don't worry about what the fuck I do. You do your job, and I'll do mine.

Tristan Monoghan No no, answer me. Truth? That's what your after?

Jim Fox Yes.

Tristan Monoghan Yes and the truth is relative.

Jim Fox Truth mutates when its reported thru the filter of the seven or eight media conglomerates in North America that chooses which stories to share.

Tristan Monoghan But things are different in the UK.

Jim Fox Not really!

They made sure the world knew about the massacres in Bosnia and Herzegovina . . . but why not here?

Tristan Monoghan I don't have that answer.

Jim Fox Don't worry. I wouldn't expect you to understand.

Tristan Monoghan What exactly are you implying? Because I'm white, you think I don't understand hate and prejudice?

Jim Fox All due respect, but please do not compare the African holocaust to a few Irish and Brits not liking each other. Don't give me that same old, 'the Irish are the blacks of Europe' line –

Tristan Monoghan I wasn't –

Jim Fox Because the truth is, the blacks are the blacks of Europe –

Tristan Monoghan I – you know, Jim, you're just so damned pleasant . . . Being with you in this heat has made me a little crazy.

He begins to pack his back then he stops.

Everyone has suffered oppression. Blacks, gays, whites, women. Every group has a story. You shouldn't assume that *your* struggle is their struggle.

Tristan *attempts to walk away and* **Jim** *blocks his path.*

Jim Fox What do you know about my struggle? Matter of fact, why don't you tell me more about 'every group having a story'.

Tristan Monoghan You need to calm yourself –

Jim Fox Planning to raise your kids with this 'conservative view' of the world? Think you can raise a mixed – black child with this conservative view?

Tristan Monoghan (*He drops his bag.*) You'd better dry up, or I swear . . .

And what right have you? To talk about an unborn child?

This place was fucked long before I started taking pictures here. My allegiance is to my job, nothing more. So if you want to start a crusade then go work for the goddamned Red Cross.

Jim Fox Fuck you man.

Tristan Monoghan And Fuck you! Fuck anybody who looks like you. Good luck saving Africa.

Tristan *packs his equipment.* **Jim** *meanders for a moment.*

Jim Fox Let's get this footage and follow up on the new leads. We're this close to finding Colonel Diamond. I'm not letting up on this story. What?

A swollen **Tristan** *stares at* **Jim**.

Look man I said I'm sorry, but that's as far as it goes –

Tristan Monoghan You have the audacity to bark orders at me?

Jim Fox I said I was –

Tristan Monoghan And what the fuck do you know about the Irish and the Brits not 'liking' each other? You want to know what I know. Their not 'liking' each other killed my father.

Jim *is a bit shamefaced and can't quite find words.*

Tristan Monoghan I've got a family. I'd rather be with them, than some self-righteous, brooding egomaniac, who's caught up in some stupid identity crisis.

Jim Fox Do not mock me.

Tristan Monoghan I promise you, I'm not that much of an asshole. But you seem to be hell bent on proving something to the world. Let me ask you something brother, are you here to be right, or are you here to tell the truth?

Moments pass.

Jim Fox Lets just agree to disagree. Alright, look I'm sorry. There it is.

Tristan Monoghan Well now that's just friendly to hear. Thanks lad.

Tristan *turns to go.*

Jim Fox Tristan come on man, don't . . .

I should've said that. I don't know where that came from.

Tristan Yes you do.

Moments pass.

Jim Fox I reacted poorly. No disrespect to your father's memory. And I . . . I know you've been out in the field for a while. We all survive – handle things the best way we know how. I . . . I'm truly sorry for . . . you're gonna make a great father. Alright. That's all you're getting out of me.

Tristan Monoghan Apology accepted.

Jim *extends his hand.* **Tristan** *smiles at him. They shug. Playfully* **Tristan** *places* **Jim** *in a head lock. They begin to spar.*

Jim Fox You better gone 'fore I stomp you in your lucky charms.

Next time I'm bringing Bono with me.

He's a real Irishman ain't scared of Africa!

Tristan Fuck off.

Jim Fox Let's roll.

In five, four, three, two . . .

As the bloodshed intensifies, calls for international help seem to have fallen on deaf ears.

In 1990, at the height of civil unrest in Liberia, the president of the United States sent 2,000 marines to evacuate Americans and other foreigners, leaving Liberians to fend for themselves.

The likenesses of Bush Sr., Bill Clinton, and Bush Sr. appear in various 'press conferences'. Their respective mates accompany them. Music underscores.

The president declared that –

Bush Sr (*Wearing glasses, suit and tie.*) 'Liberia is not worth a single life of a US Marine.'

It wouldn't be prudent, not at this juncture. Not gonna do it, not gonna do it.

Jim Fox The following administration said –

Lights up on **Bill Clinton** *in the center. He takes a drag from a joint.*

Bubba Clinton Well seeing as how I am the first black President . . . I, Bubba Clinton will help the Liberians. I'm gonna have my intern type of a letter of protest right now.

The intern starts to her knees.

Not now baby . . . keep hope alive.

Jim Fox Ten years later, the current administration has done little or nothing to help the people of Liberia.

GW Bush *appears. He dons a tee that reads 'Fuck Y'all, I'm From Texas. With him is Condelezza Rice.*

Bush Jr The people of Libya are very important to the United States. We –

Condeleeza *clears her throat and whispers to* **Bush**.

Bush Jr Libya is what I said . . . oh, it's Liberia? Well, what's in Liby – Okay thanks Conde . . . I like your shoes. Ferragamo . . . Eh, the people of *Liberia* are important to the United States. They're like distant cousins to us. And we won't stand by and watch them suffer. We will help them – by sending – our prayers. God bless.

The president is whisked away.

Jim Fox This is without a doubt one of the most dangerous places on earth. It's one of Africa's most ruthless civil wars. Ethnic cleansing, rape, torture, and crimes against humanity are committed on a daily basis. It's a war where soldiers get high on brown-brown; smear their faces with mud and makeup in the belief that 'Juju' West African magic will protect them from enemy bullets. Cross-dressing male combatants paint their fingernails bright red, wearing women's wigs, pantyhose, wedding gowns, even Donald Duck masks before committing some of the world's worst atrocities against their enemies. It's a war where child soldiers as young as seven years old carry teddy bears in one hand and AK47s in the other. Welcome to Liberia.

Blackout

'The A Team'

In the dead silence the surround sound of guns being cocked. Fluorescent lights flicker on and off to reveal the warehouse. A female hostage stripped down to her underwear is in a surrender position on the floor. NPFL soldiers **Commander Cripple Pussy**, *and* **Scarface** *are enjoying their new palette of weapons provided by* **Mr Whiskey**, *a European arms dealer sitting at a table nearby drinking whiskey. He inspects coltan with a loop. Ambient street noises and the sound of children playing.* **Commander Cripple Pussy** *is singing a rendition of 50 cents P.I.M.P.*

Commander Cripple Pussy (*singing*) I don't know what you heard about me –

But a bitch can't get a dollar out of me

No Cadillac, no perms, you can't see

That I'm a mother fucking P.I.M.P. (*stops singing*)

Ay mama, you know that song eh? What? You don't like 50?

You don't like Commander Cripple Pussy?

What's wrong, you can't speak? (**Commander Cripple Pussy** *pries her mouth open.*) Open your mouth woman! I ask you question! Hey Mr. Whiskey!

You think she know who I am? Do you think she know Commander Cripple Pussy?!

Commander Cripple Pussy *and* **Scarface** *laugh and give each other dap.* **Mr Whiskey** *is clearly annoyed, but forces a smile and continues his business.*

Commander Cripple Pussy All the mothafucks know we! We are the lords of war.

Ey, I'm fighting for my papay!

Fighting for my papay Taylor . . .

Hey mama, this here is my friend. My brother, Mr Whiskey. He comes all the way from Russia to bring me fire!

Mr Whiskey Да, да. Командир, пожалуйста?

Russian: Da, Da. Commander, pa-ZHAUL-sta?

(*Yes, yes. Commander, please?*)

Commander Cripple Pussy (*turning on* **Mr. Whiskey**) Ey boy, don't interrupt me.

He pulls a gun from a pine box. He cocks the gun. He circles **Ma Korpo**.

You know, I was having a good day.

But then I walk in to see you, going thru my boxes!

Now, why were you going through Commander Cripple Pussy boxes?

No answer. He strikes her. He strikes her again.

Commander Cripple Pussy Speak woman.

Ma Korpo Nanah AAAAHHHHHHHH!

She screams hysterically and stops when **Scarface** *yanks her up like a marionette doll.*

Commander Cripple Pussy (*Mocking her*) Aaahhhhh! I make the girl scream before I even give it to her! They don't call me Cripple Pussy for nothing mama!

Ma Korpo Nanah Please. My— I have children . . . they are outside . . .

Commander Cripple Pussy Oh okay. Scarface bring her children in inside eh.

Ma Korpo Nanah No!

I thought it was food . . . I swear to you Commander. I only wanted to find food –

Commander Cripple Pussy Food that did not belong to you!

He drags her down to the stolen supplies. He takes his knife and slices the bag open. Beautiful red beans spill onto the floor.

This is my food!

Ma Korpo Nanah I was hungry.

Commander Cripple Pussy Well then, let me give you something to put in your mouth.

Commander Cripple Pussy *drops his trousers.* **Ma Korpo** *shoves him away. The laughter is brought to a halt by Ma Korpo's defiance.* **Commander Cripple Pussy** *grabs her and wrestles her to the ground.* **Commander Cripple Pussy** *prepares to rape her.* **Mr Whiskey**, *ambivalent about the situation packs his briefcase to leave. In the midst of this commotion we see two figures lowering themselves from the ceiling on rope [Spanish Web, or harnessed zip lines]. They move like spiders down a web and are in perfect* *harmony.* **Disgruntle,** *Minister of Defense, has crude tattoos and tribal markings on her body.* **Born to Suffer** *Master Drill Sgt. is petite but muscular and attractive. They use the hand signals to communicate non-verbally as they close in on the hostages.* **Born to Suffer** *and* **Disgruntle** *have on wigs, tank tops/hip hop gear and their bodies are decorated with guns and knives. They quickly dismount aiming their guns at* **Scarface** *and* **Mr Whiskey. Colonel Black Diamond** *kicks through the boarded doorway and cocks her hand gun. She coolly stands in the center watching the action. She is clad in tight jeans, a red tank top with a matching Kangol hat. A cell phone attached at her hip wearing brightly colored gold and jewels, and dark glasses. She looks like Mary J. Blige in battle).*

Black Diamond Who is standing on my left foot?

Who is doing business in my territory without my permission?

Long pause.

Commander Cripple Pussy (*He stands.*) Fuck you.

Black Diamond *quickly draws her .357 magnum and shoots him in the head. Blood sprays.* **Commander Cripple Pussy** *drops to his knees and falls face forward.* **Born to Suffer** *holds a knife at the throat of* **Mr Whiskey. Disgruntle** *holds a knife to Scarface's throat.*

Mr Whiskey Please. I will give you anything –

The men are executed. Blood sprays. The corpses are removed. **Diamond** *walks over to* **Ma Korpo. Ma Korpo** *screams.* **Diamond** *holsters her weapon.*

Black Diamond What is your name?

Ma Korpo Nanah Ma Korpo Nanah.

Black Diamond What were you doing here?

Ma Korpo Nanah He rounded me up with the other looters. I am sorry, I meant no harm.

Ma Korpo *grabs onto* **Black Diamond**, *weeps.* **Black Diamond** *reluctantly pats her on the back and gives her a bag of rice.*

Black Diamond Please dress yourself.

Ma Korpo *quickly dresses herself and is escorted out by the two women soldiers. TRANSITION: the room changes to Black Diamond's hut; a stone and wood house painted blue, which also serves as the WAC headquarters. [The set should reveal itself as a study in war anthropology – a mix of graffiti, traditional and found art. NO STUPID MAN ALLOW is spray painted on the wall.] Black Diamond is alone. The room is almost bare with the exception of a clock on the wall and a small television that sits on a wooden crate. Black Diamond goes to the crate to sit and powers on the television which is connect by a large battery. She removes her hat and glasses reflecting on the previous events. The ticking stops and she is startled by the silence. The TV surges and the Liberian song 'Who Are You Baby' plays. She stands and looks around the room when she sees a masked man standing in a doorway. He makes a crude gesture. She whips out her revolver and the gun jams. The music skips. The man remains staring.*

Black Diamond Halas! Halas! Enough of this!

There is a knock, then banging at the door. **General Dragon Master** *runs in with his gun drawn.*

General Dragon Master Colonel? Are you okay?

The man disappears. Lights and sound restore

Black Diamond I was – I'm fine.

General Dragon Master I heard screaming –

Black Diamond It was my TV. We took the weapons from that Russian.

She inspects weapons throughout the box.

General Dragon Master How have you been feeling Colonel?

Black Diamond I don't like some of these weapons. I need automatic.

General Dragon Master Answer my question please.

Black Diamond I am fine. This one, I like.

General Dragon Master Chairman Sekou and I would like you to meet someone.

Black Diamond Yes?

General Dragon Master His name is Jim Fox.

Black Diamond And who is Jim Fox?

General Dragon Master He is a journalist.

Black Diamond With respect due to you, General Dragon Master –

General Dragon Master (*He prepares a cigar.*) He is with the BBC! We are giving him unprecedented access to our troops –

Black Diamond I have assembly to conduct.

General Dragon Master You have a problem with my order, soldier?

Black Diamond I don't need some reporter. He can follow you.

General Dragon Master Most leaders beg for this portrait. Don't you see how incredible this can be?

Black Diamond I can see how foolish –

General Dragon Master Beg your pardon? Are you calling me a fool? Speak your mind, soldier.

Black Diamond Who watches the BBC? English peoples. They will not help us!

General Dragon Master Oh I see. So do you think you can do a better job at running this organization than the

General? I take ordinary civilians and train them in the art of war. I fight to protect our civilians . . . to give power back to the people! This is foolish you say?

Black Diamond You do a fine job, sir.

General Dragon Master I know I do.

Now straighten up.

General Dragon Master *steps out to bring in* **Jim Fox** *and a male soldier.* **Jim** *is wearing a poncho and is soaking wet.*

General Dragon Master Come in brother; prepare to meet the world's finest warrior.

Jim Fox Thank you General. I have been looking forward to meeting him.

Jim *notices* **Black Diamond**. *Confused, he looks back to* **General Dragon Master**. *He lets out a hearty laugh.*

General Dragon Master This is your Black Diamond.

Jim *gazes at* **Black Diamond**. **General Dragon Master** *clears his throat.*

Jim Fox Good after – hello. My name is Jim Fox. I am a correspondent on assignment with BBC Africa. It is an honor –

Black Diamond Why do you look like that?

Jim Fox Oh, ah . . . please pardon my appearance. I had some trouble crossing the border from Guinea and I've been traveling throughout Monrovia and Tubmanburg. It's just been, five rainy days of –

Black Diamond Are you here to speak of your troubles or mine?

General Dragon Master (*Covering.*) Mr Fox has an impressive background. He has studied Journalism and Political Science. He is fluent in French, German; I have even taught him a little Vai!

Black Diamond You are traveling alone?

Jim Fox Yes. My cameraman's wife gave birth this morning, so he went back to England. I decided to stay.

Black Diamond Guess that makes Mr Fox the brave warrior, and not me.

General Dragon Master I have assigned one of my soldiers as your personal guard, and Jusu Masali will be your host for the night. The Colonel is gracious enough to interview with you for an hour –

Black Diamond One hour?!

General Dragon Master One hour. More if need be.

Make yourself at home Brother Fox. And welcome to Liberia.

Jim Fox Thank you General Dragon Master.

General Dragon Master Colonel.

General Dragon Master *exits.* **Black Diamond** *stares at* **Jim Fox**.

Jim Fox May I have a look around?

Jim Fox *looks around the space.*

Black Diamond You work for BBC?

Jim Fox Yes, ma'am I do.

Black Diamond (*She jumps in his face.*) Listen to me boy,
You will address me as Colonel Diamond.
You have a problem following my order?

Jim Fox No, Colonel Diamond.

Awkward, awkward.

Black Diamond My generals seem to think you will be our savior. Have you come to save us Mr Fox?

She puts on her shades and Kangol. She straps more weapons to her body.

I have assembly to conduct. You do not speak unless I say so.

If you look at us the wrong way, we will consume you. Understood?

Jim Fox *nods.* **Black Diamond** *nods toward the soldier and he exits.* **Black Diamond** *crosses downstage and pulls out her cell phone. She dials a number and places a call.*

Black Diamond Gather.

Male LURD soldiers appear with drums and other percussive instruments. The accompaniment echoes that of a 1970s Badass flick and eventually grows into beautiful West African drumming.

The Women Artillery Commandos begin to appear literally out of the woodworks. Some climb down off ladders or webs, appear out of 'secret' places on the stage, through windows etc., Once they congregate it looks like the press carpet at the MTV awards show. The women wear colorful hairpieces, airbrushed nails, wigs, jeans, baby Tee's and accessories. They have all kinds of weapons attached to their bodies. **Black Diamond** *takes a white bucket and places it center stage. The women ceremoniously dipped their hand into the bucket of water and cleanse their faces [libations].*

The women immediately stand at attention in formation. **Black Diamond** *walks through the women closely surveying them.*

Black Diamond Commandos we have a guest. His name is – Savior. Meet your Savior. He is a journalist with the BBC. He has the great honor of bearing witness to the finest warriors in the world. Women Artillery Commandos!

No Monkey Tries It

They perform a military step/chant led by **Born to Suffer**. *Precise and filled with cadence. During the assembly* **Jim** *stands by in wonderment.* **Black Diamond** *mocks him at times with her own war call movements.*

Black Diamond (*Call and Response sequence.*) I'm in my war face! (*x2*)

Tell them: Taylor's a woman, Sekou's a man!

What I am going to say to you today and everyday is never retreat! Never surrender.

No monkey tries it! NO MONKEY TRIES IT.

Who you gonna go for?

All Taylor!

Black Diamond Other than that who you going for? Who you gonna go for?!

All Taylor!

Black Diamond Gather.

The soldiers go to the center and hit the ground to give praise to their respective God/Omnipotent being. 'All praise due to Allah,' 'All praises to Yahweh,' 'For the goddess Ochun,' etc. etc.

Born to Suffer Tell 'em Taylor's a woman Sekou's a man!

The women stomp their way out toting their AK47s.

Black Diamond (*To* **Jim.**) I hope you have saved your energy. You belong to me now.

'Hotel Masali'

TRANSITION; we are now at the home of **Jusu Masali**, *a smallish older man. He is meticulously painting a doll he has crafted. There is a knock at his door.*

Jusu Masali Hello daughters!

Ripley Yakunay Jusu!

Jusu *crosses to his workshop and picks up a small hand-carved animal. He gives it to* **Ripley**.

Jusu Masali For you dearheart. Happy birthday!

Ripley Thank you! But it is not my birthday.

Jusu Masali (*He affectionally palms her face.*) My dear girl, you are reborn everyday. Now off you go.

The soldiers gleefully regard the carved animal.

Jusu Masali And who is this?

Jim Fox My name is Jim Fox, General Dragon Master has sent me here –

Jusu Masali Of course! Come in, come. Bye girls!

The soldiers exit.

Welcome home Mr Fox. Please, hand me your belongings.

Jim Fox Thank you. I'm sorry for the intrusion.

Jusu Masali Nonsense. Let me have a look, now. Aha. You remind me of my own son. How many years are you Mr Fox?

He steps out of the room and takes **Jim**'*s bag;* **Jim** *looks around the room.*

Jim Fox I'm 35 years old, Mr Masali.

Jusu Masali My Samuel is the same age as you.

He is studying at the London School of Economics. He plans to save us all from our economic disaster! What do you think of that?! Ha ha! And what brings you here?

Jim Fox I'm a journalist for BBC focus on Africa sir.

Jusu Masali How often do you come to Liberia?

Jim Fox This is actually my first time.

Jusu Masali A spirit never forgets the road home! Ha ha!

He steps out and returns with a pot with water. He then grabs a coffee mug, and a small basin. He pours some of the water in the mug, and the rest in a basin. He also grabs a hand towel.

The Almighty has found you in favor Mr Fox! I'm quite fortunate to still get a little bit of water.

Jusu *crosses to shelf and in an old cigar box tin he removes a packet of instant hot cocoa and begins to mix it.*

Jim Fox Oh Mr Masali I don't want–

Jusu Masali No no no. Please, call me Papa Jusu. Please, it is fresh water.

Jim *refreshes with the water on his face.* **Jusu** *finishes mixing the cocoa. Takes a whiff and sets it in front of* **Jim**.

Jim Fox Thank you.

Jusu Masali So you are a friend of the Colonel's?

Jim Fox I wouldn't exactly say that.

Jusu Masali Oh well you should look forward to getting to know her.

Jim Fox (*Looking in his cocoa mug.*) Okay.

Jusu Masali Oh you mustn't be fooled by her harsh exterior. I've watched many of the soldiers grow up. I've known the Colonel since she was a child.

Jim Fox General Dragon Master says she's one of the finest warriors he's ever seen.

Jusu Masali General Dragon Master. His given name is called Isaiah. He and I have known each other since we were children.

So tell me Mr Fox, what will you tell the world about us?

Jim Fox Where do I begin? I suppose with the history of Liberia; the colonization that is, by the U.S. and how it relates to this current war; also a deeper look into rebel organizations in post-colonial African politics. Not to mention post Cold War – sorry.

Jusu Masali No, no, no, it – sounds good . . . it seems ambitious. Very ambitious.

Jim Fox I'm sorry, I sound like a talking head.

Jusu Masali This is good. Liberian people are ambitious, always have been.

Jim Fox I get the feeling that the Colonel doesn't like me much. Any advice on getting into her good graces?

Jusu Masali Yes. Do not underestimate yourself.

Jim *looks at a photograph on the table.*

Aminah. My wife. She made her transition last year.

Jim Fox You were a beautiful pair.

Jusu Masali You cannot find a person that did not like her. Please, drink your cocoa.

Jim Fox (**Jim** *stares at the dolls and carvings on the walls.*) What is this? The carvings I mean.

Jusu Masali That is Asase Ya. She is Mother Earth. And her son, Anansi. The trickster spider.

Jim Fox How long have you made these?

Jim *almost becomes entranced with the masks when suddenly he jumps.*

Jusu Masali What is it?

Jim Fox Nothing just a spider –with a sack – a big one too. Excuse me.

Jusu *gently sends the spider back up the web.*

Jim Fox Wow. You just . . . huh, that doesn't – I mean that's a big spider.

I dream about spiders a lot. I wake up in the middle of the night and see dozens of them on the wall . . . or one big one crawling toward me.

Jusu Masali Spiders on the attack or nature conspiring for your freedom? Haha!

Where was I? Oh yes, carving is a great tradition in my family. You can no longer export goods out of Liberia, so I do it for my own pleasure. He is my latest creation –

He shows **Jim** *a black dummy-puppet used in ventriloquist acts.* **Jim** *handles the doll with a bit of unease.*

Jim Fox Yeah . . . okay. Uh, yah. Looks real. Really real.

Jusu Masali I can remove the dolls if they scare you?

Jim Fox Oh no no . . . it's fine. I think the Twilight Zone got me a little wary of . . . these. But its beautifully crafted.

Jusu *laughs at* **Jim**.

Jusu Masali I have prepared bedding for you. I'm certain that you would like to rest?

Jim Fox Yes. It's been a very long day.

Jusu Masali Well, Brother Fox be grateful for this day, for we will never see it again.

Jim Fox Amen.

Jusu Masali *picks up a beautiful doll and removes her head. Inside he pulls out a small hand gun.*

Jusu Masali In case of midnight marauders.

Jim Fox I – uh, I don't –

Jusu Masali I hate them too, but you must understand, Liberia is not what is use to be. Please take it.

Jim Fox Good night. And thank you.

Jusu *exits and* **Jim** *is left alone in the dark. He takes out a vial of pills. He regards the bottle, and decides not to take them. He lies on the bedding preparing for sleep. The lights surge and focuses on the dummy-puppet.*

Jim Fox Great.

'The World According to Finley'

Hours into the night. **Jim** *has fallen asleep. Music. A large spider appears [an actor doing a movement sequence] descends from the ceiling. The spider moves around the room causing a stir which awakens* **Jim***. The spider comes face to face with* **Jim** *and the lights surge and go to black. When lights restore,* **Jim** *looks over to see a deity appearing as* **Finley** *[should be portrayed by the actor playing* **Tristan***] holding the dummy-puppet carved by* **Jusu***. The lights surge again and the puppet has now come to life [portrayed by an actor]. Applause machine flashes prompting cheers and laughter from the crowd for this Vaudevillian act.*

Finley Good evening ladies and gentlemen and welcome to Princeton University –

American Dummy circa 1816!

Finley Thank you Dummy. Please allow me to introduce myself. I am Albert Finley, a founding member of the American Colonization Society. (Affectionately known around these parts as the ACS) Here at the ACS we believe that we should help Negroes that have been treated unfairly because of slavery and indentured servitude. Therefore our goal is to help them *go back to Africa* where we feel they belong –

American Dummy Ahem.

Finley Oh, yes. I'm terribly sorry, how rude of me. Ladies and gentlemen I'd like to introduce you to my faithful companion, the American Dummy. Say hello, Dummy!

American Dummy Hello Dummy!

Finley We are here this evening to present a short play that Dummy and I have written entitled 'A Realization of the Negro's Ambition'.

American Dummy Or as I like to call it, 'What in the hell do we do with these Niggas?'

Niggas

Niggas Niggas Niggas . . .

Finley Uh, sorry folks. Slight glitch . . .

(*He whacks the dummy on his back.*) There we are. Now Dummy remember,

You mustn't use that word.

American Dummy Of course! Thank you kindly for reminding me. Ahem. Where was I? Oh yes 'A Realization of the Negro's Ambition' or 'What the hell do we do with these Nigros?' A comedy with an all-star cast featuring the likes of Thomas Jefferson, the Ku Klux Klan, Marcus Garvey, Willie Lynch, the Church of Scientology, Nat Turner, Kwame Nkrumah, WEB Dubois, Huey P. Newton and the Black Panther Party (Power to the People!), Ronald Regan, Barak Obama, Noam Chomsky and everybody's favorite Head Negress In Charge, Oprah! (Check under your seats ladies!) Pam Grier, Rudy Ray Moore (Closed Captioning for the Jive Impaired) and featuring a score by none other than Nina Simone, Mos Def, and Stevie Wonder with a special guest appearance by: Quentin Tarantino performing his much lauded 'nigger speech!' Djimon Honsou portraying the mighty warrior Afri-can and the entire staff of the Johnson Ebony-Jet magazines.

Finley I say, that's rather exciting! We'll be back after this brief touch with reality.

Laughter, Applause. They take a bow. TRANSITION: The streets of Monrovia. Days have passed. In the BG we see the bustling life of the markets, craftsman, children playing etc. [Production note: Vendors store items for sale in the sandbags from the set, slicing them open to sell goods to the crowds] Vendors haggle, hustle, and lure customers.

Vendor 1 (**Vendor** *slices sandbag open and tiny Virgin Marys spill.*) Virgin Mary! Virgin Mary, praise to God with Mary! Eh baba you!

Vendor 2 (**Vendor** *slices the bag to reveal colorful tracks of hair weave pieces.*) I have for you mama! Red, yellow! Silky see? Long nice hair! La vie est belle yes? So are you! You mama! Come buy!

Vendor 3 (**Vendor** *slices his bag to reveal little jars of cream.*) Fade cream! Darkness gone! Nice smooth complexion! Lighter skin even!

Jim *sits in the background his eyes glued to* **Black Diamond**, *who is practicing Krav Maga (hand combat), moves on a target.* **Ripley** *guides her throughout with the target. She strikes with precision.* **Disgruntle** *and* **Born to Suffer** *sit nearby reading aloud from a book.*

Born to Suffer Sun Tzu believed that the skillful strr-at-tee, straa

Disgruntle Strategist! Here let me. (*She takes over the reading.*) Strategist should be able to subdue the enemy's army without engaging it, to take his cities without laying siege to them, and to overthrow his State without bloodying swords.

Black Diamond The last part. Read that last part again.

Disgruntle To overthrow his State without bloodying swords.

Black Diamond Read more.

Disgruntle Victory is the main object of war. If this is long delayed weapons are blunted and morale depressed. When troops attack cities, their strength will be exhausted.

In a whisper to the others.

Why does she make us read this to her? It's everyday this stuff. It's boring.

Born to Suffer She can hear you lazy cow, and she has eyes in the back of her head. Keep reading!

Disgruntle I am not lazy! You are the stupid one. At least I can read!

Born to Suffer Yeah but you look like a goat!

Black Diamond I can hear you both.

Born to Suffer/Disgruntle Yes Colonel Diamond.

The girls silently shove each other and punch each other on the arm. **Disgruntle** *pulls off Born to Suffer's wig.*

Black Diamond Aaay I swear to God! Read!

Disgruntle/Bush Shaking Waging War. Sun Tzu said: War is like unto fire; those who will not put aside weapons themselves are consumed by them. All war is based on deception.

Black Diamond Again!

Disgruntle/Bush Shaking/Ripley All war is based on deception.

Diamond *stops takes to take a break.* **Ripley** *brings her a rag for her face and some drinking water.* **General Dragon Master** *enters with a fine cigar in his mouth and a foxy woman. She has on a American flag bikini top and super duper short mini skirt.* **Diamond** *rolls her eyes and continues to workout.*

General Dragon Master Mister Fox!

Jim Fox Wow. I mean hi, wow. Uh, hello General Dragon Master.

General Dragon Master *laughs at* **Jim**.

General Dragon Master How is the interviewing with the Colonel?

Jim Fox I – haven't had much time alone with her –

General Dragon Master Is that so?

Jim Fox But I'm looking forward to it.

General Dragon Master You don't have to be polite Mr Fox.

Jim Fox Oh trust me I'm being honest. Some of my best reporting simply comes from observing. I'm patient . . . I'm sure when she's ready we'll speak.

General Dragon Master How is your stay with Jusu?

Jim Fox Couldn't have asked for a more gracious host.

General Dragon Master Jusu I were ward brothers in primary school. We have been friends since we were children picking coconuts from the grove!

Jim Fox Ward brothers?

General Dragon Master A lot of Liberian children are sent to live with families as wards. We were all foster brothers and sisters. But I did not come here to bore you with my upbringing. I thought perhaps you might like to meet my friend, I call her Betsy Ross.

General Dragon Master *winks and nods toward the foxy chic.* **Jim** *blushes.*

Jim Fox Oh, I – uh, haha. I mean no. No. But its great to meet you. Betsy.

General Dragon Master Yessss I pledge allegiance . . .

I brought you dinner.

Here, enjoy this jollof washed down by a cold Heineken!

You will let me know if you need anything?

Jim Fox You bet, thanks again General.

General Dragon Master *crosses to* **Black Diamond**.

General Dragon Master Colonel Diamond! How is the interviewing?

Black Diamond Ask him. I am not the journalist. Excuse me.

General Dragon Master I am curious about something soldier. How does a one hour interview turn into two weeks? And this man, this very important man, he still knows nothing about you?

Black Diamond Maybe he finds me boring. Perhaps Betsy Ross can show him Liberia.

General Dragon Master Are you trying to humiliate me?

Black Diamond I am following your orders. I have given him permission to interview my soldiers.

General Dragon Master It is your portrait!

He came to see *you*, not them. *You* are the focus of the feature.

Black Diamond My life is none of his business.

General Dragon Master It is if I say so.

Black Diamond *wipes the sweat off her brow and tosses her rag at* **Jim**. *She storms off.*

General Dragon Master Sorry about that. She's usually quite pleasant.

Jim Fox Beer?

General Dragon Master Cheers brother.

He takes a long frat-boy swig of the beer. **Jim** *lights* **General Dragon Master***'s cigar.*

So, I hope the girls are not too hard on you?

(*A few of the soldiers stare at him, hanging on his every word*)

Jim Fox No. They're all very, very . . . uh . . . what can I say? I'm glad to be here.

General Dragon Master There's no need to save face, Liberian women are hot blooded!

Shit even I am careful around them! (*He belches.*) Eh baba, watch your ding ding.

General Dragon Master *exits with his chic in tow.*

Jim Fox Yes sir. I will watch my ding ding.

The soldiers stare at him and approach like lionesses.

Disgruntle Look at how pale he his.

Ripley I think he is funny looking.

Born to Suffer What? He's gorgeous. Wavy hair, smooth skin. Look at those arms! Not a gunshot wound on him.

Disgruntle Oh please, he would never like you.

Born to Suffer Why not? I am the prettiest here!

Disgruntle You look like a fake-ass Beyonce!

Born to Suffer Maybe I am Beyonce!

Born to Suffer/Disgruntle Oh please dog face . . . woof woof! Etc., I am the pretty one! Shit breath! Etc.,

Ripley We will ask him. Jim Fox. You settle this for us, eh?

Disgruntle Who is the prettiest girl here?

Born to Suffer Yah who is the juiciest tomato?

Jim Fox (*He looks at their ammo attached to their bodies.*) Uhhh, In my humble opinion . . . you . . . are all lovely, courageous women. Each and every one of you. Simply put. Lovely.

Beat.

Ripley You know, I never be called lovely by anybody. Fuck man, I like that.

Disgruntle Me too! We are fucking lovely.

Born to Suffer Oh my god, I want to give him babies. Lovely babies!

Disgruntle (*To a civilian man passing by.*) Hey boy! I am fucking lovely! Remember that!

Giggling and gabbing the soldiers exit.

'The Science of Sleep'

TRANSITION. Sound bite of a BBC 30-second news report on civil unrest in Liberia. Weeks have passed. In the BG soldiers patrol UN warehouse in Monrovia that LURD now control. Soldiers do various activities. Playing with a soccer ball, game of cards, braiding hair etc., some work on intelligence reports with maps and papers; A Red Cross worker examines a civilian. Enter **Ranger One Attack Force** *a charming 17 year old LURD soldier. He wears a chin-length wavy brunette wig, with a red bandana. He wears baggy jeans and a tee shirt with Brooklyn written on it. He plays with a knife throughout often picking at his teeth with it. He enters with CHOIR STAND his fellow soldier, free styling a rhyme rapping over a beat.* **Ranger One Attack Force** *turns his attention to* **Born to Suffer**.

Ranger One Attack Force (*rapping*) From West Africa, not Nigeria
My place of birth is LIBERIA
Soldier at war, ain't got no fear of ya
Taylor is a monkey and I'm his superior
Girlz check me while I'm on the mic
They love my rhyme cuz I'm so damn tight
Check this cutie to my right
She knows she wants me but she puts up a fight . . .
(*end of rapping*)

Ranger One Attack Force Baby don't be that way! I'm telling you, you stick with me and I have you in the blinging baby! Me and Choir Stand going to sell millions of records! Come on baby!

Born to Suffer You are such a liar! You told Fatuma last week you were going to marry her.

Ranger One Attack Force Owh! Come on baby, don't be this way! Daddy will make it up to you. I promise!

Disgruntle You are too young to talk so much shit.

Ranger One Attack Force I wrote a sonnet for you

Ripley/Disgruntle/All *A sonnet?! He thinks he's a player, bullshit etc. (general mocking).*

Born to Suffer Shut up you heifers!

You. Read my poem. Slowly and make it pretty.

He gets down on one knee and pulls a wilted piece of paper. The other girls giggle and tease them.

Ranger One Attack Force There'll be no darkness tonight, baby our love will shine.

Just put your trust in my heart, and meet me in paradise.

Girl you're every wonder in this world to me . . .

Disgruntle Silly girl. This boy got your nose wide open.

Ranger One Attack Force Hush woman when I am speaking.

Listen to my heart –

Ripley If this is your poem, why it does not rhyme?

Ranger One Attack Force What? It rhymes!

Even when we're old and Gray

I will love you more each Day 'cause –

All You will always be the lady in myyy life.

Ripley That's Michael Jackson's song! Idiot!

Born to Suffer What?

Ranger One Attack Force Don't listen to them baby. I'm going move to New York and I'm gonna take you! These girls are only jealous. Vexing big daddy like that. Mad because they can't have all this hot cocoa!

He gyrates and rolls his hips in front of **Ripley** *and* **Disgruntle**.

Disgruntle Yuk! You nasty boy!

Ripley I swear to God I will cut off your Charlie Browns if you don't get out of my face!

Playfully he struts around the yard like Mick Jagger singing and shaking his hips. The girls laugh and lift him into the air like a sacrificial lamb.

Ranger One Attack Force Ladies one at a time!

I'm a lover, not a fighter!

Jim *secretly snaps photos. After a while* **Ranger One** *takes notice of* **Jim**.

Ranger One Attack Force Who is that?

Ripley Jim Fox. He is the journalist for us.

Ranger One Attack Force Oh shit! He is, he is here for you girls? Bullshit.

Born to Suffer/Disgruntle Yes, for us, not you!

Ranger One Attack Force What? Watch Ranger One work.

Foxy Jim? My main man! What's happening brother?

Jim Fox Ranger One.

Ranger One Attack Force You know me? Oh, yah . . . that's right! You know me. Ranger One Attack Force baby!

Jim Fox I've seen your name tagged on every wall and billboard here.

Ranger One Attack Force Well you know how we do it baby!

Jim Fox Who's this?

Ranger One Attack Force Oh this is Choir Stand! He is my hype man you know? I rap, he sings. Watch this. Choir Stand! Sing Luther!

Choir Stand

(*Filled with riffs.*)

(*sings*) Don't you remember you told me you loved me baby?

You said you'd be coming back this way again . . . Baby, baby oooohh oohhh baaahbbyy . . . (*stops singing*)

Ranger One Attack Force Okay okay. Jesus, he'll go on and on if I don't stop him; all he does is sing. I don't know if this idiot can speak even. Scram, we got business here. (**Choir Stand** *goes away.*) So Jim Fox my main man, you interview me?

Jim Fox (**Jim** *retrieves his recorder.*) Would you mind if I recorded this?

Ranger One Attack Force (*Grabs recorder and uses it like a microphone.*) Yo! Yo! One two, one two!

I am Ranger One Attack Force baby, nah waht I mean son?!

Yo this goes out to all my baby mothas

And my niggas on lock

Neva forget Biggie and TuPac –

Jim Fox I haven't turned it on yet. It's not recording –

Ranger One Attack Force What? Rubbish! Stop playing Jim Fox. You kill my rhyme man. Okay we, we go now? You record, Jim stop playing.

Jim Fox All right, would you start with your name and age?

Ranger One Attack Force Now? Okay. I am Ranger One Attack Force, and I am 17 years old. I'm a fighter with the

Liberians United for Reconciliation and Democracy. We the real army! We gonna catch Taylor and him dress like woman! Fuck Taylor's monkeys!

Jim Fox How long have you been fighting with the rebel forces?

Ranger One Attack Force Since I am 10 years old. Colonel Diamond trained me.

Jim Fox Really?

Ranger One Yes the Colonel is a strong fighter. She is like a green snake in the grass. They always do well on mission.

Jim Fox So you respect the women fighters?

Black Diamond *enters unnoticed.*

Ranger One Attack Force Oh yah. They are trained like the men. We are the same. But they care for civilians and don't loot compared to men fighters. Only a fool would disrespect those girls.

Jim Fox What do you mean?

Ranger One Attack Force I saw a one girl shoot another officer because he raped a woman. I have seen even Colonel Diamond punish her own soldier for not following orders.

Jim Fox How so?

Ranger One Attack Force Well for security it's best I don't say. But I will tell you she uses a rubber hose to beat people. Ooh, another time she knocked a man two times her size on his ass for stealing rice. With her bare fists! She'll off anybody. That's why they say, 'No monkey tries it.' Mannah she crazy oohh! Ah I love it!

Jim Fox So you enjoy the friendships you have with the women commandos?

Ranger One Attack Force Oh yah, but you have to be very careful though. These girls – they can be ferocious. I never marry a female fighter.

Jim Fox Why not?

Ranger One Attack Force Mannah, didn't you hear that girl say she was gonna cut off my Charlie Browns?

They share a laugh. **Ranger One Attack Force** *gives* **Jim** *some dap. After the handshake* **Ranger One Attack Force** *starts to leave then comes back.*

Ranger One Attack Force Hey Fox?

You have picture of me?

Jim Fox Yes, I do my friend.

Ranger One Attack Force You show me off like . . . Jay Z?! Rock-a-fella! Worldwide baby!

Jim Fox I will do my best to tell the world about you Ranger One.

Ranger One Attack Force Yo I live for hip hop! I gonna live forever like Tupac! I gonna turn this blood into platinum. Make way for Ranger One Attack Force (*makes sounds of a roaring crowd.* **Jim** *continues snapping shots.*) Ahhh-frrreeee-kkkaaa! Jim-be careful around this parts baby! Bullets don't know no better!

Ranger One Attack Force *smiles brightly sticks his knife back in his mouth and then exits. On the way out he sees* **Black Diamond**.

Ranger One Attack Force Here she is!

Sings Michael Jackson's 'Liberian Girl'. Does his best MJ impersonation.

(*singing*) Liberian girl! You came and you changed my world

I love you Liberian girl!

Black Diamond (*She playfully pops him in the mouth.*) Go on crazy boy.

Ranger One Attack Force (*Laughs, and gives a full Elizabethan bow.*) Alright then mum!

Ranger One *exits.*

Jim Fox Jester to the Queen.

Black Diamond He likes to run his mouth. Some of the girls call him Diarrhea lips.

Jim Fox I'm sure it's a compliment in his mind.

Black Diamond So, Savior you are still here.

Jim Fox I'm still standing.

Black Diamond Yah I can see that.

Jim Fox Hope you don't mind my saying, but I do believe this is the most we have spoken since my arrival Colonel.

Black Diamond Yes I know, so do not spoil it by talking too much.

Jim *seals his lips.*

Black Diamond Have you eaten today?

Black Diamond (*She tosses him a bottle with a dark fluid.*) Good. You can't fight a revolution on a full stomach.

He takes a swig and coughs.

It's pepper, juice from lemons, and a little water. Its good for you.

Jim Fox Jusu says you're an excellent in the game of chess. Good way to pass time.

Black Diamond If we play, you cannot talk too much.

Jim Fox Think the pepper and lemon juice will take care of that.

Ticking of the clock. Time passes. Lights up on the chess match.

Black Diamond You are terrible at this! I thought a fox was a sly and crafty animal. What's your problem?

Jim Fox I'm not that kind of fox, Colonel. It's a tribal name.

Black Diamond America has tribes?

Jim Fox Not really but, my mom's black and my dad was Indian – Native American.

Black Diamond So what is the tribe?

Jim Fox Algonquin.

Black Diamond What is your tribal name?

Jim Fox Chogan James Fox.

Black Diamond Chogan?

Jim Fox It means 'blackbird'.

What is your tribe Colonel?

Black Diamond Mandingo.

Jim Fox Are you Muslim-Mandingo?

Black Diamond Its best for security you do not ask me such question.

A moment.

But I like to listen to religious music. Choir Stand sings that stuff for me.

They play. Time passes. **Jim Fox** *finally makes a decent move on the chess board.*

Black Diamond What happened to your head?

Jim Fox Oh this? That's nothing – you should've seen the other guy.

My introduction to some of Taylor's soldiers.

Black Diamond You let Taylor's monkeys do that to you?

Jim Fox Well, I'm only an army of one, Colonel.

Black Diamond It's the only army you need.

Jim Fox 'No Monkey Tries It.' What does it mean?

Black Diamond You know monkeys. Treacherous, deceitful; most people are charmed by monkeys. But those little bastards are smart and strong. Rip your limb right off.

Answer my question, what happened to your head?

A soccer ball bounces onto the stage. A young boy enters soon thereafter. **Olivier**, *a boy soldier. He plays with the ball.*

Jim Fox His name was Olivier. He was a soldier in Taylor's boy unit. My partner Tristan and I met him near the border . . .

**A FLASHBACK*

Olivier (*French*) Bonjour, je m'appelle Olivier et j'ai dix ans. Ma famille a été tué dans mon pays Sierra Leone.

Jim Fox Olivier was this kid from Sierra Leone, he was only 10 years old.

Olivier J'aime bien les films d'action et je veus être comme Jackie Chan!

Jim Fox During the fighting in Sierra Leone, he was forced to join Charles Taylor Small Boys Unit. He said he lost track of his parents.

Olivier Je n'y pense pas tellement mais il me manque maman et papa. Je me force d'oublier leurs visages.

Jim Fox To deal with the pain, Olivier said he makes himself forget the faces of his loved ones. Especially his mother and father.

Olivier My job is big. Diamond mining, collecting ammunition in Liberia, looting villages and capturing civilians. I buy drugs at the Liberian border too. They force us to take them.

Jim Fox He said his C.O.s would mix heroin and gunpowder; said they call it 'brown brown.'

Two young women approach **Jim Fox** *and* **Olivier**.

Jim Fox While we were talking these two young women approached us. Warning Olivier not to speak with me and Tristan.

Young Woman Olivier who is this you are speaking with? Don't be an idiot!

I will tell Kojack that you are speaking with outsiders!

She grabs **Olivier** *by the arm. He pushes her down. She gets up and runs away.*

Jim Fox I didn't want to cause a stir so Tristan and I took Olivier away for a meal at the local tea shop. (**Tristan** *captures images throughout.*) He seemed happy to free himself from his bayonet and the business of war, as we talk about simple things a child his age should think about. About what kind of life he wants or rather what life he deserves –

A group of armed NPFL soldiers enters the tea shop. **Jim**, **Tristan** *and* **Olivier** *are surrounded.* **Commander Kojack** *leads the pack. After a moment* **Olivier** *attempts to escape, but is restrained by a soldier. The soldier strikes* **Olivier** *and uses his belt to create a noose around his neck.*

Olivier Ahhhh! No! No! No!

Jim Fox Wait, wait, wait . . . cool it there brothers –

Tristan Jimmy don't get involved.

Commotion. Violence. **Jim Fox** *is butted in the head with a gun from one of the soldiers. He still manages to speak.*

Jim Monsieur, s'vil vous plait –

Commander Kojack (*Halts his soldiers with a gesture.*) Speak English. Who are you?

Jim Fox My name is Jim. Please. He did nothing –

Commander Kojack WHO are you? What are you doing here?

Jim Fox I only took him for eggs –

Tristan We were just leaving Commander. Sorry for any confusion.

The soldiers assault **Tristan** *and break his hand.* **Commander Kojack** *places the gun in the center of* **Olivier***'s head.*

Jim Fox Release him to me.

Release him to me, as . . . as my – I'll buy him from you. I have money. I will be responsible for him. I will give you all that I have. Please . . . brother you don't have to do this.

Kojack What make you think you are anything to me? This pikin is my brother. Not you! What do you know about me? Come on. I know your type. Oh you don't understand? Nigger. What's up nigger? Isn't that how you greet each other Uncle Sam? Now look me in the eye and call me brother. (*He shoots Olivier in the leg. Blood sprays. He cocks gun and turns it on Jim.*) Repeat after me: I have no control here.

Jim Fox I have no control here.

Commander Kojack You go back home and you tell that to your George Bush, yah?

Jim Fox Yes sir.

Commander Kojack Great.

It is settled.

I'll leave your ward for you outside.

Commander Kojack *smiles and drags* **Olivier** *out.*

Olivier Souviens toi de mon visage! I am sorry! I am sorry!

Olivier's *screams are cut short by a rapid succession of gunfire.*

All soldiers exit. **Jim Fox** *stumbles, grabbing his head. He returns to the seat across from* **Black Diamond**. *Back to present.*

Jim Fox I never saw Olivier again. I can't seem to get him out of head.

Black Diamond You shouldn't feel bad. That little boy has been dead for a long time.

She goes back to studying the board.

Jim Fox How long have you been fighting?

Black Diamond Since I am maybe 13 years old.

Jim Fox Do you feel like you've missed out on your childhood?

Black Diamond Because you are young does not make you safe from this war.

If you are angry, you get brave. You can become a master in everything. I have no mother, I have no father, so I don't care. God is my family now.

Jim Fox How do you keep connected with your spirituality in the midst of a war?

Black Diamond At night, I serve God.

TRANSITION: The ticking of the clock. **Jim Fox** *leaves the stage.* **Black Diamond** *is left alone. Garbled sounds of the High Life song 'Who Are You Baby' restores. Her parents* **Mama** *and* **Papa Sesay** *enter the space.*

* *A FLASHBACK*

Mama Sesay

Mariama! Don't just stand there girl. Look what Papa Sesay has for us!

Look at our new table!

Mariama/Black Diamond Mama? Papay?

Mama Sesay It's beautiful! Fit for Kings and Queens!

Papa Sesay I hope my beautiful wife will prepare her best fufu, jollof, yams, chicken and cassava . . .

Mama Sesay Ay, he thinks I will prepare all that food? Go on wicked man.

Papa Sesay Dance with me!

Papa Sesay *smothers* **Mama Sesay** *with kisses.*

Mama Sesay Ah man, go on now! I'm too old for such excitement!

Mariama/Black Diamond Papa it is so beautiful! Oh I love it! Oh mama, I will set table for dinner!

Papa Sesay (*Begins to dance to the music.*) No no, Mariama! Come dance with your old papay!

(*Singing along with the song.*) Who are you baby? Who are you?

Mariama *and her father begin to dance and have a good time.* **Mama Sesay** *goes into the kitchen. A loud scream and the crashing of dishes.* **Papa** *motions for* **Mariama** *to hide, and she runs and hides.* **Papa** *goes into the kitchen. There is arguing heard from the kitchen, that grows louder and louder. Then silence . . .*

Mariama Mama! Papay! Papay!

Mariama, *terrified, calls out to her parents. A solider appears. His white tank top is dripping with blood. His rusted machete drips with blood and matter. He drops it to the ground. He regards* **Mariama**. *Other bloody militia men with machetes enter the space surrounding her. The record skips.* **Mariama** *has nowhere left to turn. She runs but is overpowered. In silhouette we see the men sexually assault* **Mariama/Black Diamond**. *A tight line highlights her face.*

The voiceover plays during the assault.

Asase Ya (V/O) When one has no one left on the earth, neither father nor mother, neither brother nor sister, and when one is small, a little boy in a damned and barbaric country where everyone slashes each other's throats, what does one do? Of course, one becomes a child soldier, a small soldier, to get one's fair share of eating and butchering as well. Only that remains.[1]

Mariama Sesay/Black Diamond I have no mother.

I have no father.

So I don't care, GOD is my family now.

Blackout.

[1] Reference Ahmadou Kourouma, *Allah n'est pas oblige.*

Act Two

'We Came Here for the Love of Liberty: The Fourth Wall's Dream'

The sounds of a TV flipping through stations. Snippet from a rap song singing about diamonds, a gospel televangelist preaching, and finally the music of a Larry King-Live type show. Lights up on two men sitting at a desk. Two deities work as camera operator and producer nearby. The voice over comments are mixed in with the music.

Pat Robertson *GOD HAS A MORAL RIGHT TO KILL AND SO DO WE!*

COMMUNISM WAS THE BRAINCHILD OF GERMAN-JEWISH INTELLECTUALS!

MANY OF THOSE PEOPLE INVOLVED IN ADOLPH HITLER WERE SATANISTS, MANY OF THEM WERE HOMOSEXUAL – THE TWO THINGS SEEM TO GO TOGETHER.

Lights up on **Finley** *and* **Pat Robertson**.

Finley Hello and welcome back everyone! You've just heard the words of Pat Robertson, religious leader of Christian Broadcasting Network and host of 700 Club. He is the controversial televangelist whose comments over the last few years have caused a fire storm! What, pray tell, does the good Lord think of Pat Robertson? We'll let the Reverend Robertson express his views right here on Finley Live. We have a few callers on the line. First up is Professor Marla Watson of Evanston, Illinois. She is a Professor Emeritus of Anthropology at the prestigious Northwestern University. She is also author of the best-selling book –

Professor Negro Know It All 'Don't Call Me African American, Black is Just Fine.'

Lights up on **Professor Negro Know It All**.

Finley Welcome Professor Watson.

Professor Negro Know It All Thank your Mr Finley. Reverend Robertson has forged a relationship with Liberian President Charles Taylor, who has agitated civil unrest throughout West Africa. His soldiers are often sent on missions to attack innocent women and children.

Finley Well I think both sides of these forces are known to torture civilians . . . but go on.

Pat Robertson What's your question Professor?

Professor Negro Know It All My question is how can a so-called man of God support this genocide? And further more the degradation of women by means of –

Pat Robertson This is just a platform for a feminist to say her views. Between the Lord Almighty and President Taylor, Liberia will be just fine.

Professor Negro Know It All Religion will not stop this war, Reverend Robertson. They're not even fighting over religion! This war is a result of wicked, greedy men –

Pat Robertson (*To* **Finley**) See, see the feminist agenda is not about equal rights for women. It is about a socialist, antifamily political movement, that encourages women to leave their husbands, kill their children, practice witchcraft, destroy capitalism and become Lesbians.

Professor Negro Know It All What?!

Pat Robertson Listen, the Christian nations of Africa are right now under assault by Muslims . . . either funded by Saudi Arabia or Libya. But President Bush has asked Taylor to step down. So we're undermining a Christian, Baptist president to bring in Muslim rebels to take over. What appropriation has been made by the US Congress to back up the actions that have been taken to bring down the freely elected government of a sovereign and friendly nation?

Finley Thanks for joining us Professor.

Reverend you have a special relationship with President Taylor, and Mobutu Sese Seko, the brutal tyrant of Zaire. Which brings me to 'Operation Blessing' and 'Freedom Gold Unlimited.' These are your business ventures in Africa. What can you tell us about that?

Pat Robertson Well –

Finley Isn't it true that you purchased rights from Mobutu to dredge for gold and diamonds? You invested 8 million dollars in Freedom Gold Unlimited, your joint venture with Charles Taylor. Isn't that fueling the ongoing civil war?

Pat Robertson Well, uh . . .

Finley What is the purpose of these mining ventures Reverend Robertson?

Pat Robertson Operation Blessing is a humanitarian effort. And Freedom Gold is helping to reestablish the state of Liberia.

Bright smile.

Finley Seems our brother Pat Robertson is global in his financial dealings.

We're going to take a quick break. Later in the hour, focus on the Hip Hop Nation: Diamonds, Rims and Ho's. Do these rappers really know what they're glorifying? Do they care? We'll hear from hip hop queen Dawn Corleone and members of the rap groups Gimme the Loot and Low Riding Vatos. More Blackaphobia when we return to Albert Finley live.

***'Yankee Doodle Came To Town'* . . .**

The waterfront. Nightfall. **Black Diamond** *sits in the sand softly singing 'Who Are You Baby?' She uncovers a small satchel in her pocket. She pours uncut diamonds into her hand. Sounds of locusts. A man approaches.*

Yankee Who can find a virtuous woman? For her price is far above rubies.

Black Diamond Yankee.

Yankee Mariama.

They embrace and nearly devour one another with their passionate hugs and kisses. **Black Diamond** *is nearly breathless and almost loses her composure in his arms. He cradles her like a babe and gently strokes her face.*

Black Diamond Did you bring her?

How is my small diamond?

Yankee No, but she misses you.

Black Diamond Oh God. I miss her . . . and look at you.

How your wounds heal?

She inspects gun shot wounds on his abdomen. She kisses his wounds.

Yankee Oh God, you smell like myrrh.

Black Diamond I knew you would come back! Your soldiers will be so –

Yankee Softly, softly woman.

Black Diamond I am so happy to see you. Have you seen the General?

Yankee Yes I have.

Black Diamond Well? You are re-instated then? Yankee?

Yankee I was just speaking to him about you – about us.

A moment.

Black Diamond I don't want this conversation.

Yankee I want you to go back to Guinea with me.

We have a child who needs her mother.

It is not fair to her.

Black Diamond I fought until I was eight months pregnant on the front line with her. She is probably the only person who understands why I am here.

Yankee You are still a mother and wife. I am a husband and a father. I'm not that soldier boy anymore.

Black Diamond Yankee I cannot leave my women. They need me.

Yankee So does your child!

Black Diamond The only reason you have been with her is because you are injured.

Yankee Soon she will ask questions about her mother, and what will I tell her?

Black Diamond The truth: I am fighting for her right to walk this earth and fear no man but God.

Liberia is my home, not Guinea! I am not some refugee! I was born here, I will die here.

Yankee This is not our war to fight. Taylor started this war and he is the only one who can end it. You may control over those girls, but I control (*he grabs her left ring finger, she snatches her hand away*). Where is your ring?

Black Diamond Here I am soldier . . .

Yankee (*He kisses her about neck etc.*) But what about here –

Black Diamond I have to focus when I am here –

Yankee And here –

Black Diamond I do not want my child to see me this way.

Yankee She will love you no matter what. So will I.

Black Diamond What does she look like now? Is she growing big and strong?

He pulls a small photograph out his pocket and gives it to **Black Diamond**.

Black Diamond My God, she is, she –

Yankee Is the spirit and image of her mother.

She looks at the photograph.

Yankee You are so beautiful.

Black Diamond No I'm not. This war has washed away my beauty –

Yankee Shut up.

He tugs at her hair and lays a fat kiss on her.

Black Diamond What do I look like now?

Yankee What does she look like, she asks?
Well let me rub these sore eyes and look:
She has height of a woman I appreciate.
She who stands 5'6 (*he lifts her into the air*) but is really 8 ft tall.
Legs agile, fast and strong like a cheetah.

She slides down to his waist, and he smooches her neck.

Ooh notice the elongated neck of this goddess (*she giggles*),
and we mustn't forget this, the laugh of the hyena!
She smites her enemies, with a state of calamity
and when I am making love to her,
she simply moans and calls out my name.

Hotness. More Hotness.

Yankee Come home.

She looks away. Yankee breaks away from the embrace, and begins to dress.

Black Diamond Yankee. Yankee, please? We have to fight for our country.

Yankee For what? To watch the wicked take positions in yet another corrupt government?

Black Diamond I am their leader! I will not abandon them. Who dares not to show respect for women in LURD?

We are the forerunners and are respected like man. Feel free to ask anybody.

Yankee Oh save your propaganda!

Black Diamond You go out there and tell my soldiers who were raped, maimed and displaced that they are here for propaganda! All because you want me at home on my back, and to live like some refugee! If you will not fight for us, I will.

Yankee The only war you seem to be fighting is the one within yourself.

Black Diamond Coward.

Yankee Am I?

Black Diamond I don't understand why you are giving up for our struggle.

Yankee Our struggle?!

Black Diamond Yes! Im not fighting for riches or power! Our struggle is a honorable fight.

Yankee You believe this to be all there is for you?

Black Diamond YES! This is my fucking war! And I will kill anybody in my way.

Yankee What would you parents say if they were alive?

Achilles. She slaps his face.

Black Diamond Firm your jaw.

Yankee Your parents –

Black Diamond Are dead! They are nothing to me!

Yankee You can't mean that.

Black Diamond You don't know what I speak of.

They took my ma,

They took my pa. They took me.

I can't breathe without smelling those bastards,

Ripping parts out of me.

They visit me every night. Taking me over and over

He goes to her. He holds her from behind. It stifles her; she struggles to free herself. She hyperventilates and claws at her neck.

Yankee Breathe baby.

Breathe, it's okay.

Breathe.

Sounds of locusts. She wrestles away from him and whips out her gun aimed at his temple. **Jusu Masali** *and* **Jim Fox** *out walking, stumble upon the pair.*

Black Diamond No stupid man allow!

Yankee *raises his arms in surrender. She quickly aims the gun at* **Jim** *and* **Jusu**. **Jim** *raises his hands in surrender.* **Jusu** *unruffled, walks to her and gently removes the weapon from her hands. She realizes what she has done. Horrified turns to* **Yankee**.

Black Diamond Yankee – Ezekiel.

That was not me, I got confused. I WAS CONFUSED. Zeke . . .

Yankee *exits.*

Black Diamond I . . .

Jusu *embraces* **Black Diamond**. *After a moment she takes notice of* **Jim**. **Jusu** *slips away discreetly sometime during the scene.*

Black Diamond What are you waiting for boy? Take my picture.

Jim Fox Colonel.

Black Diamond WHAT!

Jim Fox I can see that things are difficult for you –

Black Diamond Oh is that what you know boy? You been here how long, and all you can say is things are difficult? Whats wrong, take my picture!

Jim Fox I'm not here to take advantage. I care about everyone here. And I care a great deal about you –

Black Diamond I've got a husband to do that for me. I have a husband.

Jim Fox Okay.

Black Diamond I bet you did not know that about me. Don't you dare look at me like that. I don't need you to bleed for me. I can bleed for myself! I don't need help from you. From any of your tribe! We know George Bush will not help us. There are African bodies on the steps of the American embassy as we speak.

Why don't you go interview them, see what they have to say.

We have NO ONE to stand up for us, but us.

How are we supposed to live when we are afraid to die?

We are SICK of war.

I am sick of war –

Jim Fox Then stop fighting.

Black Diamond What did you say?

Jim Fox Stop fighting.

Black Diamond (*she charges towards him and stands nose to nose with him*) I was 11 years old when I was raped! It was many.

Yes. And I cannot remember all the faces.

It made my angry to get (*UNINTELLIGBLE*). It made me to fight (*UNINTELLIGBLE*) because of that . . . to free my country from the hands of fire.

Jim Fox I'm so sorry –

Black Diamond No, no nothing like this (*UNINTELLIGBLE*). No monkey tries it. No monkey tries it.

WOMEN ARTILLERY COMMANDOS! Now!

The women quickly enter.

Tell him. Tell him. TELL HIM your story . . . why you fight.

I told you to save your energy boy, and by God I hope you have. There is no turning back.

She gets on his ear.

Never retreat, never surrender.

She takes her knife and makes a knick in his arm. He bleeds.

Then across hers. She bleeds.

Black Diamond We bleed the same now.

She looks around at the women and takes her leave.

'Suicide is Painless: WAC Stories'

Lights up on the women in different places on the stage.

Disgruntle I am Teo Zubah, I am 18 years old, a fighter with LURD and I am a mother. I became pregnant with my daughter Wendy after guerrilla soldiers raped and sexually tortured me with a piece of cassava.

Jim Fox Cassava?

Disgruntle It's like a potato. I noticed with bitterness that I was pregnant. And I thought, 'this is a child I did not need, a child of my tormentors.' But when herbs failed to abort my pregnancy, I had no choice but to keep her. That is how I have my fighter name Disgruntle. I hope I will not be haunted with the thoughts of killing Wendy's fathers because they all were responsible for making her.

Growing up, I prayed to be stronger than the men. But now, I'll bite any man. They made me a commander because of my hardiness. We wanted to fight so we formed our own lady unit. We shoot better than the men. Much respect to Black Diamond, she is my superior.

Born to Suffer My name is Born to Suffer.

I joined WAC after I survived an attack by Taylor's troops. They hit my feet with an iron stick and made me walk to prison in Monrovia. I was beaten and tortured by the guards. I thought my life was over but, just like in the movies one day it all changed. WAC attacked the prison – Black Diamond freed me and took me to Tubmanburg. RESPECT to her! Even though everything was taken away from me, this nightmare accounts for my success in battle. The memory of them propels me to fight to the finish. Those cowards who hurt me may have a head start, but to them I say: You better run. Because I'm coming after you.

Ripley I join Women Artillery Commando's after I see a Hollywood movie *Aliens*, with the lady who kill monsters from space. I like the way she held the big guns against the monsters, the way the gun goes eh eh eh eh eh eh eh, and the monster goes Raaahhhhhhh! And all through movie, everybody call her name, cuz she can handle it! 'Ripley!!!! Get away from her you bitch!' Oh shit! I love that shit man! She say fuck everybody! Me too, FUCK EVERYBODY! I can take care of myself. That's how I get my name, because of Ripley. She trusted nobody, neither do I. She was smart, strong and sexy woo! Was the last woman standing! I am like her! I see this monster out here and eh eh eh eh eh eh, boom they gone. She fight monsters in space and I fight monsters in the bush. When this is all over, when this all over . . . maybe . . . I make movies about killing monster in Hollywood.

Clear Heart Here I am called Clear Heart.

Three years ago my husband, son and I were coming from church on the way to Waterside marketplace. Some soldiers stopped us. I am not sure if they were government soldiers or not, because sometimes rebel forces torture civilians too. First they demanded all of our money, our food. Laughed in our faces, told us we was trash. They were drunk and cursed. They wanted my son Jacob to come and fight with them. Say he will be their little brother. One soldier jumped down from the truck and offered to teach my son how to use a gun. He was terrified. They tried to make Jacob hold the rifle, told him 'Don't you want to be like us? I have had a woman even. If you stay with your dad you will grow to be a pussy like him'. My husband began to argue with the soldiers. He told them that they were cowards for trying to scare innocent civilians, and they could never have our son. My heart began to beat like never before. But my husband Francis, he never show any fear. That is when everything started to look funny in my mind. I no longer heard the shrill voices of arguing men, but the slow deep wail from my little Jacob. I began to feel heavy and wet. I look over to see that the soldier had wrapped Jacob's little hand around the gun, placed his hand on top of Jacob's and forced him to pull the trigger. Jacob had put bullets into his father's stomach, arm and neck killing him instantly. I remember hearing them say 'He's the real killer boy, yeah!' My body began to shiver from being cold, but I remember it was a very hot day. I did not even feel the bullets enter my own body. I could do nothing, but surrender myself to the earth. I have never been outside Liberia, but for the first time I was able to view the world differently. The world was sideways. Not flat, or round, just lopsided . . . a movie shown the wrong way.

TRANSITION: *Lights.* **Born to Suffer** *escorts* **Jim** *home.*

Jim *looks somber and distracted.* **Born to Suffer** *does her best to keep his spirits up. She chatters endlessly about everything. He quietly takes sips from a flask.*

Born to Suffer Jim you have girlfriend?

Jim Uh, I guess you could say that.

Born to Suffer Is she pretty?

Is she clever?

Is she lovely!

I bet you she cannot beat me in push ups . . .

I can do more push ups than all the soldiers.

Except Colonel Diamond.

Ooh I can even do a back flip! Watch.

Wait, please hold this.

She hands him her gun.

Don't shoot yourself.

Can she do this?

She does a back flip. **Jim Fox** *applauds her gymnastics.*

Jim Fox Nice.

Born to Suffer Aha, I knew I could make you to smile.

Jim Well done. Thank you.

Born to Suffer Hey, heeey! See that building? That's where they made tires.

My dad use to have a job here.

She crosses to the wall.

Me and my sister would wait for him after school outside. We would play hopscotch, jump rope . . . we played here everyday.

Jim Fox Is your family still in Liberia?

Born to Suffer No . . . they are – in a refugee camp. I think.

Jim Fox Why didn't you stay with them?

Born to Suffer I don't know. I didn't like those people. It's like every night, I hear women crying and . . . it's bullshit! These people who were supposed to be helping us – protecting us from war . . . I mean some of them were nice but, some of them were just nasty men, mishandling women. I decided I not want to be one of those girls crying in the middle of the night . . . so I left. I ran away.

Jim Fox You left your family.

Born to Suffer I am sure they are okay. Ohmigod? Omigod! Is here! Hey look! Is still here!

The hopscotch!

She uses her tube of lipstick to retrace the hopscotch map; then she grabs a bullet from her revolver to use as a rock. She tosses it on the hopscotch map. She jumps through.

Born to Suffer Hey look it! Sky blue! I made it to heaven! Isn't that something Jim Fox? I'm back in heaven.

TRANSITION: Ticking of the clock. Lights up on **Jusu Masali** *working on one of his dolls.* **Jim Fox** *arrives at* **Jusu Masali***'s hut. He is a bit buzzed from the whiskey. He enters.*

Jusu Masali Well look who is out and about at this hour! I was beginning to worry about you.

Jim Fox Didn't mean to worry you. I had a guard.

Jusu Masali How are the interviews going?

Jim *stares off.*

Jusu Masali Jim? Jim?

Jim Fox Yes?

Jusu Masali Are you alright son?

Jim Fox Uh, I just got caught in thought.

I'm just thinking about my report.

Jusu Masali Yes, you have been with us for some time now.

Jim Fox Yep. And now it's time to pull up the tent and take the circus to another town.

Jusu Masali Oh. I see. Back to London then?

Jim Fox Back somewhere.

Jusu Masali So. What will you tell the world about us?

Jim Fox I don't know. This report is like opening Pandora's box. I mean it's not like I expected gum drops and unicorns running freely here.

I just can't seem to wrap my head around some of this.

I was silly enough to believe I could changes perspective by giving some, I don't know, new narrative of, of – a war that will never end . . . One man changing the face of a war. How ridiculous is that?

Jusu Masali Make it plain son. Why did you come here? What did you really hope to find?

Jim Fox I don't know.

Jusu Masali Of course you know.

Jim Fox Everyone wants to go back to the motherland, right??

I've come all the way here – only to discover how American I am. That connection I so desperately wanted – these people are killing one another and I don't understand it. And there's nothing I can do.

I've done my job, but other than that . . .

Jusu Masali Yes?

Jim Fox There's no connection Jusu. I don't belong here. I'm not much different than any other journalist that comes to a war-torn region. Tristan was right.

Jusu Masali Far cry from the man I met a few weeks ago.

Jim Fox Well, seems that my 'brothas and sistahs' are doing okay without me.

Jusu Masali Does that include me?

Jim Fox *goes to speak, and* **Jusu Masali** *halts him.*

I have heard what you have to say. Now.

Would you agree that you have kinsmen all over God's earth?

Jim Fox One way of looking at it.

Jusu Masali So this connection, formation if you will, is the work of God. So even though English is not my mother tongue, I still remain responsible and deeply connected to you.

This way of being does not always afford me amnesty either. No one is pardoned.

You cannot stand up for others when it is only convenient for you.

Jim Fox But it's the American way.

We only protect others when we find it convenient.

Too bad there's no oil here, right?

Maybe then the savior nations could protect people right?

Or what about me? I could protect people.

I mean I tried to protect him . . .

I guess I thought –

You want to know the last thing he said to me? 'Don't forget my face. I am sorry.'

Fuck me!

A moment.

I'm sorry. I'm a little. I didn't mean to disrespect your home . . .

Jusu Masali Sit.

Tell me, who are some of your heroes?

Jim Fox Well I like Superman because he can stop bullets.

Okay . . . alright uh . . .

My father. Uhh, Stephen Biko, Ed Bradley, Harriet Tubman, Richard Pryor.

Jusu Masali These people you have named, do you believe they followed precedence? Do you believe that when life knocked them around they decided it was time to quit? Listen, society gives you laws that can obscure you from what you are meant to do.

You see, when a spirit is not bound by precedence, all boundaries disappear.

Once this code is acknowledged, all of the chains will disappear and you will take back those years the locusts have eaten.

He goes back to his sculpting.

Jusu Masali Do you know what happened when Pandora's Box was opened?

Jim Fox Well, supposedly it released all of the sorrow and mischief into the world.

Jusu Masali Yes. Do you know what was left in the box?

Jim Fox No.

Jusu Masali Hope.

I can smell the rain coming.

He leaves. **Jim Fox** *climbs into his sleeping area.* **Jim Fox** *hears sounds of gunshots in the distance.*

Jim Fox Hope.

He drifts off to sleep.

'Sometimes They Hear the Bullet'

Later that night. **Jim Fox** *is in a deep slumber. The silence is interrupted by loud cabaret type music.* **American Dummy** *takes the stage. The commotion awakens* **Jim Fox**.

Voiceover The 'Chronicles of the N-Word' is filmed in front of a live studio audience.

Music, applause, excitement.

American Dummy Well hello boys and girls! Oh, and look who we have here! It's Nigger Jim.

Jim Fox What –

American Dummy *takes a piece of tape and slaps it over* **Jim Fox***'s mouth. It has 'the Nigger' written on it.* **Jim Fox** *is restrained by two deities.*

American Dummy Oh I know we ain't 'sposed to use that word no more, but we ain't 'sposed to be broke down and disenfranchised no more either.

Jim *is distressed and tries to talk thru the tape.*

American Dummy Oh look at him. It really is upsetting to him.

Guess I'd better not say the word so late at night, so he don't wake up early in the morning talkin' bout some 'Niggah, Niggah, Niggah!'

American Dummy *cackles which prompts laughter from the crowd.*

American Dummy Do you think he deserves his emancipation? I can't hear you?!

The crowds cheers: YES! **Jim Fox** *is completely baffled.*

American Dummy Alright then, let's free this brotha!

He removes the tape from **Jim**'*s mouth. He shakes* **Jim**'*s hand and pats him on the back.*

This been a long migration for our little Blackbird y'all. He came all the way here to 'find hisself.' Hey baby brother would you like to lay your burdens down?

Jim Fox If you can't call me by my name, don't call me anything at all.

American Dummy Ohh wee, it's all ways the light skinneded ones ain't it? Malcolm, Huey, and now the revolutionary Chogan Jim Fox.

What you say bruh, No Pigment No Peace? I get it.

Now that you free, I promise never to say the N word. I'm gonna even give it up for Lent!

Here sit down . . . see if I can nigger-rig a seat for you – oops I said it again!

The laughter-applause signs lights up. **Jim Fox** *sits.*

Enough of the Uncle Tom Foolery, we got some business to get down to.

Even got a special guest at our meeting!

Ladies and Gentlemen it is with great pleasure I bring to you an associate of the American Colonization Society.

Author of the Declaration of Independence

And of the Statute of Virginia for religious freedom

And the father of the University of Virginia

My very good friend, Sir Thomas Jefferson!

Jefferson (*played by same actor as* **Tristan**) *storms the stage like Tony Robbins addressing the crowds and eating up the 'adulation.'*

Jefferson Thank you. Thank you. No please, thank you.

Gentlemen, I have been summoned here this evening, and it is a pleasure indeed.

And not because I'm thought to be greatest mind to ever occupy the White House.

Woman We love you Tom!

Jefferson No, no no really. I am here with total disregard concerning my presidential and diplomatic achievements, democratic struggles, my purchase of Louisiana, or my accomplishments in music, architecture, science, law, medicine, engineering –

Dr Martin Delaney Hah!

Jefferson Astronomy, horticulture, mathematics paleontology, literature –

Dr Martin Delaney Slave catching.

Jefferson Eh em . . . I am here for one reason, and one reason only. I am here, because I love America and everything she stands for. And soon, she will have a sister. In a rich land across the pond –

Delaney Across the pond?

Clever one isn't he?

Jefferson I stand before you on behalf of the American Colonization Society, though I am not a charter member, I do share the same vision. The gradual extinction, eh hem – exodus, of the Negro from America. Since successful colonies in Africa and South East Asia have proven –

Dr Martin Delaney Proven what exactly?

Jefferson What's he doing here Dummy? I was promised no obstructions!

Jim Fox I don't understand.

American Dummy See you if you can dig this plot: That's Dr Martin Delaney, the father of Pan Africanism and he can't stand Jefferson. He's one of the free blacks that thought West African settlements were doomed for failure and that white folk was just trying to get rid of a 'dangerous population' as they called it.

Dr Martin Delaney The fate of Africans in America cannot and will not be determined by a group of lewd, pigment challenged, swag-bellied beasts!

Jefferson The American Colonization Society has the best interests for Negro people!

Dr Martin Delaney The ACS? Hah! I say most pernicious; it was originated in the South, by slave holders –

Jefferson But I love my slaves –

Dr Martin Delaney Propagated by their aides and abettors, (North and South) and still continues to be carried on under the garb of philanthropy and Christianity, through the basest deception and hypocrisy.

American Dummy (*to* **Jefferson**) Dang, he told you!

Dr Martin Delaney Tell me, are you afraid that the slaves will finally earn a diplomatic place in Washington D.C.?

Jefferson How can you say that Delaney! I am here to help these people! I wrote the Declaration of Independence! I even wrote in the part about the slaves, but they took it out!

Three black girls skip onto the stage. They are the **Rejects of Monticello**.

Rejects of Monticello Daddy, daddy can we go out and play?

Jefferson Not now, darlings, daddy is working. And you know you're not allowed to play in the fields – Eh, go on.

The girls play double Dutch jump rope. **Jefferson** *joins them.*

Rejects of Monticello Thomas Jefferson was a good ol' man,

He jumped out the window wit' his dick in his hand,

He said 'Scuse me lady, I'm juss doin my duty,

Now bend on over and gimme some booty!'

Jefferson Most outrageous! Go on and find your mother!

The girls exit.

Dr Martin Delaney How is our Miz Sallie Hemmings?

Hahahahahahahahahahahahahahaaaaahhhaaa!

Jim Fox It's only a dream. Only a dream . . .

Jefferson Shut up! Stop that cackling!

Dr Martin Delaney Fair is foul and foul is fair.

American Dummy Oooowwee! You gone let him talk to you like that Tommy?

Jefferson You little weasel. I'm going to destroy you.

American Dummy Well whoever the baddest hit my hand first!

Dr Martin Delaney *and* **Jefferson** *slap the dummy's hand at the same time.* **American Dummy** *turns and sucker punches* **Dr Martin Delaney**.

American Dummy Ooh he hit you Doc!

Dr Martin Delaney *lunges at* **Jefferson**. *Throughout the scene they chase one another, roll off stage, throw things etc.*

American Dummy Oohh wee this is too much fun. Hey I've got a joke to tell. Stop me if you've heard this one. 'The tale of the white man, Marcus Garvey, and the Jew.'

The three of them are shipwrecked on an island, and they find a bottle. So they dusted off the bottle and out come a Genie! Genie says, 'Okay y'all got three wishes. I'll grant one wish to each of yous.' Garvey says: I want to take all the black people of the world and put them in Africa where they can live forever.

The Jew says: I want to take all the Jews of the world and put them in Israel where they can live forever.

The white man says: Wait a minute, you mean to tell me you're going to put all the niggers in Africa, and all the kikes in Israel?

The Jeanie says: Yes.

The white man says: Well, shit you can make me a Martini!

Jim Fox I don't like it. Please I gotta get out . . .

American Dummy I mean I can't take credit for that one, but it sure do tickle me!

Jim Fox I'm losing my mind . . .

American Dummy And what a twisted mind you has. More twisted than an episode of Twin Peaks. 'Cept ain't no midget dancing and talking backwards in this here dream. Nigga's is dying.

Jim Fox Stop saying that!

American Dummy What's wrong Kunta?

Jim Fox Don't call me that.

Jefferson *chases* **Dr Martin Delaney** *off stage.*

American Dummy (*Re: the fight 'twixt* **Jefferson** *and* **Dr Martin Delaney**.) My my, this is getting ugly.

Say you a injun right? Why don't you make it rain, so we can stop this fire?

Jim Fox SHUT UP!

American Dummy You shut up!

Sound of gunshots erupts.

American Dummy Come on Blackbird, make them stop fighting!

I know! Why don't you call your congressman?

Oh that's right, Uncle Sam don't fuck with Africans no more after he got his ass stomped in Mogadishu. Oh I like saying that word: Mo-gah-dee-shu. Sounds like a sistah from the hood. 'Hello my name is Mogahdeeshu.'

He revels in his joke.

Hey ain't that your boy?

American Dummy *snaps his fingers.* **Tristan** *appears with a bloody limb in his hand.*

Tristan (*in an exaggerated Gaelic accent*) Oi boy-o! You've got to come see this! The best fecking footage! Arms and legs everywhere! My god, you were right about these lads! This war IS better than the Brits and the Irish!! I love the African holocaust! Jasus Fecking Christ!

He does a mini jig with the limb.

Tar tee tar tee tar!

Tristan *snaps a picture of* **Jim Fox** *and runs off. The flash disorients* **Jim Fox**.

Jim Fox Tristan! Tristan! Tristan!

The sound of trucks coming to a screeching halt and more commotion grows in the background. Actors climb the walls. Rain builds in the soundscape.

Jim Fox What are they doing?

American Dummy Oh they climbing Jacobs ladder.

American Dummy *puts on a WWII army helmet.*

Jim Fox Make them stop!

American Dummy Okay lets see what it says in the Geneva Conventions . . .

He looks through a small booklet and produces a can of Afro Sheen.

I ran out of curl activator, BUT use the Afro Sheen instead! Spray it on the ground, they'll slip, fall and die! Easy.

Jim Fox You're not helping!

American Dummy *snaps his fingers.* **Olivier** *appears swinging on a rope pendulum style.*

Olivier Jim! Hey Jim! Watch this! Jackie Chan!

Jim Fox Olivier? Wait – don't move. Just stay there. Come back with me.

Another boy appears.

Jacob No! I'm Jacob.

Jim Fox Jacob? Clear Heart's son.

Jacob I'm a murderer! Killer boy yah!

Jim Fox No. Let me take you –

You can be my ward. I will take care of you.

He grabs **Jacob** *by the arm and starts but his path is cut by* **Black Diamond**.

Black Diamond Let the boy fight, he's dead already.

She cocks her gun.

We never retreat! Never surrender!

Jim Fox Stop fighting. Just stop fighting!

Everyone *stops.* **Black Diamond** *lowers her weapon and* **Jim Fox** *gently grabs her by the arm. She then grabs his wrist and shoves the weapon into his hand. She forces* **Jim Fox** *to shoot* **Jacob** *then* **Olivier**.

Olivier I am sorry! I am sorry!

Jim Fox STOP!!!!!

The rope swings back and forth without **Olivier**.

Black Diamond My brother from another mother.

He's a killer boy, yah!

(*She turns the gun on him and places center forehead.*)

What are you standing there for boy?

Take my picture.

She pulls the trigger click of the gun, with a flash of light.

Take my picture.

Sound of the gun: click, click, click.

Black Diamond *fades away into the background and* **Jim Fox** *begins to contort.*

American Dummy Wwwwhat's the mmmatter? Having a seizure? Come on Bambi get up!

Jim Fox *loses mobility in his legs. A deity brings* **Jusu Masali** *on the stage and lays him near* **Jim Fox**. *His clothes are blood soaked and his breathing is shallow.*

Jim Fox I have to leave . . . I won't do this.

Please let me out.

Jusu Jim leave.

American Dummy You want out?

Jim Fox Yes, I don't belong here! I'm not one of them! I'm not one of you!

American Dummy Ooh really? Now why should you get to leave, if they can't?

Jusu Jim . . .

Jim Fox It's not my problem!

Jusu You must wake up . . .

American Dummy Well ain't you juss a complete mothafucker? Blackbird got his story and is ready to fly.

Jim Fox Get me out NOW!

All sound/chaos stops. Light illuminates on **Jim Fox**. *His face contorts and he convulses.*

American Dummy Very well. Wake up.

Jim Fox – –

All Wake up

Jim Fox – – – – –

All Wake up
Wake up wake up wake up wake up
Wake up
Wake up

Jusu Masali Jim wake up!!!!!!

All WAKE UP!

A large explosion followed by gunfire; **Jim Fox** *comes out of his seizure. He wakes from the dream. He stumbles, ducking the cross fire, calling out to Jusu. It is smoky and visibility is poor. He searches desperately and trips and falls. He falls over the body of* **Jusu Masali**.

Jim Fox Jusu!

Jusu Masali The village . . . you must leave, we are being raided!

Jim *rips off his shirt using it as a tourniquet for* **Jusu Masali***'s badly injured leg. He picks him up and runs away from the house. They make it to Colonel Diamond's hut/WAC headquarters where several soldiers are there returning fire.* **Black Diamond** *and the other COs lead the army shouting out orders, and engaging in heavy combat. They are bloody and dirty.*

Jim Fox Somebody please!

Born to Suffer Oh God.

Find General Dragon Master! Tell him it's Jusu!

Jusu Masali Aaahh!

Disgruntle Set the mortars!

Jim stay with him.

She shoves a handgun in his hand.

Don't you let him die!

Ripley, Clear Heart, go!

She runs off.

Jusu Masali Jim, you are here?

Jim Fox I'm not leaving your side.

He coughs blood and begins to shiver.

Jim Fox Everything will be okay. We're gonna walk right out of this.

Gunfire in the BG.

Jusu Masali I'm cold.

Jim Fox Well you just hang tight, and I'll serve you the best cup of hot cocoa you've ever had. Warm you up.

Jusu Masali *coughs gurgling, and spitting up blood.* **General Dragon Master** *runs in.*

General Dragon Master Jusu.

Jusu Masali Mariama?

General Dragon Master No, it's me old man.

Come to give you a ride in my chariot.

Jusu Masali Oh Isaiah, you are the limit!

Gunshots, another explosion. **General Dragon Master** *prepares to lift* **Jusu Masali**.

General Dragon Master Look you have fanfare and everything! Come now man, let's get you going.

Jusu Masali Not out there.

General Dragon Master Jusu we don't have time to argue.

Black Diamond *runs in, dismounting her ammo. She is covered in dirt and blood. Chaos continues in the BG.*

Jusu Masali We use to have the best of times remember?

Jim Fox *backs away from the group.*

General Dragon Master But we have so much left to do. Visit the rainforests of Costa Rica, kayaking with Orcas in the Pacific, walk through the entire Louvre in one afternoon! And you owe me a game of chess old man!

Jusu Masali You have always been all the book in the world. I'll meet you for that game under the coconut grove?

General Dragon Master Sure thing my friend.

Jusu Masali Jim don't leave until the job is done . . . help . . . us . . . help . . . Mariama.

Black Diamond Papa . . .

Jusu Masali You will rise again –

His breathing staggers.

He dies. The soldiers begin to weep and express sorrow.

Black Diamond Back to your post. What are you looking at?!

Shoving other soldiers.

You! You! Fire you! Now! Back to your post. NOW!

General Dragon Master Reload soldiers! Move out!

Soldiers exit.

General Dragon Master *reloads the chamber of his gun. He takes one last look at Jusu and exits.* **Jusu Masali***'s body remains.* **Jim Fox** *stands nearby.*

Jim Fox Colonel Diamond, I tried, I really tried.

Black Diamond He became my father, when I had nothing left. He was my papa.

Jim Fox I know.

Black Diamond *sinks to the ground.*

Black Diamond He is the reason . . . that I survived that night . . .

She sits staring.

**FLASHBACK*

Aminah Dear heart? Can you hear me? Will you nod if you can understand what I am saying?

Jusu, this girl won't speak. She's covered in blood, and I cannot tell if it is her own blood.

What is your name? Who are you, baby?

Jusu Masali I have telephoned Isaiah. He will be here shortly.

Aminah My name is Aminah. This is my husband Jusu. You may stay here as long as you like, but we need to know what has happened to you? She is suffering from shock.

No response. **Aminah** *goes to* **Black Diamond***'s jacket looking through the pockets.*

Stay with her; I'll check her pockets, see what I can –

Aminah *finds the small satchel of uncut diamonds. She stares in disbelief.*

Aminah Jusu? My God.

Black Diamond *springs to her feet and snatches the satchel from them.*

Jusu Masali Okay.

Black Diamond/Mariama We have a new table. Papa bought it for us.

Aminah Where is your papa?

Black Diamond/Mariama We were singing. And they came –

Aminah Yes?

Black Diamond/Mariama Then they came – from everywhere. They broke all our dishes.

Jusu Masali Were they after these diamonds?

Black Diamond/Mariama They took mama and papa.

He was on top of me. They all on me; took turns.

The last one –

I took the dish and I hit him and hit him in the neck until he stopped.

Finally **Black Diamond** *gives over to* **Jusu Masali** *and he holds her. He rocks her gently.* **Aminah** *slips away discreetly.*

Jusu Masali It's alright. Everything will be alright. Papa Jusu is here.

Black Diamond Papa Jusu?

Jusu Masali I am here.

Black Diamond *hugs* **Jusu Masali** *back tightly. He rocks her gently and caresses her face giving his weight over to* **Black Diamond**. **Black Diamond** *is now holding* **Jusu Masali**. *Return to the present. She gently lays his body back down. The deities return for his body.* **Jim Fox** *and* **Black Diamond** *are witness. The deities and* **Jusu Masali** *exit. She stands and she and* **Jim Fox** *look upon one another. She cocks her weapon. And exits.*

The Road Popeye Could Fix (If Only He Knew It Existed)

Ticking of the clock. TRANSITION. Weeks later. Lights up on a black woman sitting in bed. She is swaddled in a robe and sips wine from a glass. She's doing the crossword in the New York Times and listening to Patsy Cline's 'I Fall to Pieces'. Millicent Gladwell is a rich and attractive woman. In the distance we hear the sounds of a shower. After a while, **Jim Fox** *glistening with water appears in a towel.*

Millicent Uumm. If I knew you were coming, I'da baked you a cake.

Look at you.

Jim Fox Two words: Steam shower.

Millicent You look much better. Say thank you Kohler.

Jim Fox Thank you Kohler.

They kiss. He crosses to a window to enjoy the view.

Damn, so this is what the Upper East Side is like.

Millicent Yep. The Jefferson's ain't the only ones who know how to move on up.

She lights a pipe loaded with pot. He pours a full glass of whiskey and starts to suck it down.

Millicent So what's happening in the world Jim Fox? Or should I call you Jim Beam?

Jim Fox Same old shit, different toilet. How are you?

Millicent I could complain, but who the fuck would listen? Oh –

Tristan and Opal emailed me the baby's picture the other day.

Jim Fox Yeah? Cute kid I bet.

Millicent Like all newborns, it looks like a little lizard. But they look happy. So.

How are things at the BBC?

Jim Fox I . . . I handed in my resignation so . . . that's that.

He downs the rest of his whiskey.

Millicent I won't get to see Jim Fox on the telly anymore? Guess I'll have to watch Dr Who, when I'm touching myself then, now that you're gone. Pity.

Jim Fox Bring that Hottentot ass over here.

He pulls her into his lap.

Millicent Jim Fox. Lives in my heart, but pays no rent. Hmph.

They kiss.

Millicent So, now what?

Jim Fox I've got an offer from Free Speech Radio. I don't know . . .

Millicent Pee-uueew. You're going to work for NPR now?

Jim Fox No, not NPR. That's for conservatives and Bush-ites. This is independent media.

Millicent Alright, kind of granola . . . but hey follow your heart.

That little puny, dried up, little heart.

(*Singing along with the song.*) I fall to pieces, each time I see you again. I fall to pieces how can I be just your friend? (*stops singing*)

Patsy sanging like somebody broke her heart. I feel you girl! Sang bitch!

Millicent *continues toking.* **Jim** *stares off touching the scar on his arm where* **Diamond** *nicked him with her knife.*

Millicent Jim Fox. Jim Fox, poised, telegenic good looks, seamless delivery, dedicated to the job, the only fly in the buttermilk . . . is unemployed.

He shrugs his shoulders.

Hell I thought you were living somewhere over the rainbow. Listen.

Since you're moving back to the States –

Jim Fox I never said I was moving back to New York Millicent –

Millicent I could get you a correspondence job at Waif.

We'll do features on Doctors Without Borders, or whatever you want –

Jim Fox Stop stop stop stop stop . . . sweethart just stop alright?

Millicent What's wrong? Can't commit?

Beat. Nasty beat.

Jim Fox It's just not the right time for us –

Millicent What the shit makes you think I'm talking about you?

Jim Fox Alright baby, white flag –

Millicent Oh I know we're not jumping the broom –

Jim Fox Okay –

Millicent No New York Times or Jet Magazine wedding society pictures for us. Nope. I'll just marry some lousy NBA player, and wait for him to leave me for a white girl.

He plants a kiss on her mouth to shut her up.

Jim Fox You're exhausting. Lets go to bed.

Millicent First you leave The Post, now the BBC. Admit it: you have commitment issues.

Jim Fox Millicent.

Look I'm jet lagged, and would like to just . . . not think about any of that.

Millicent Why did you leave Liberia?

Jim Fox (*grabbing her newspaper*) See, what the New York Times says right here? Charles Taylor is in exile. They have a cease fire. ECOMOG and the Blue Helmets have it under control. Pretty soon a group of musicians will make a song to raise funds for them, and everything will be fucking fine.

Millicent So, Liberia has been restored to its glory then?

Should I be booking a vacation there? Jet-setting in the motherland with our brothers and sisters? We could 'shroom, get back to nature . . . then stick our feet in the River Nile, or whatever the fuck people do over there for enlightenment. Wouldn't that be nice?

Jim Fox Liberia does have a beautiful oceanside. Good surfing there. You just have to step over the mass graves to get to the water. Oh and try not to get raped along the way.

Off **Millicent***'s look.*

What'd you think I was on safari?

Millicent No . . .

Jim Fox Alright, so it's done. I'm here now. No more questions. It was another time, another world.

Millicent Well – there's only one world. We're one giant family, right? We just got dropped off in different places . . .

The doorbell rings. She goes to grab her wallet.

Ooo that will be our dinner. I'll be back handsome.

He flashes a smile at her. She exits. **Jim Fox** *deflates the moment she leaves the room. After a moment he looks to the iPod docking station.*

Jim Fox Patsy my girl, you are a Debbie downer.

He changes the music to Morris Dolley's 'Who Are You Baby'? He goes to his luggage and pulls out a blood-stained shirt. He stares at it. He drops it into a trash bin. He then pulls out the carving of Asase Ya and Anasi made by Jusu. A spider descends. He takes notice.

Jim Fox What's happening spidey man? Make you deal . . . you stay out of my way, and I'll stay out of yours. You can hang up there, but if you come near my woman, I'll have to kill you. No. I won't do that . . . you may be one of my ancestors.

Jim Fox *gently places the spider on the floor when he is met by a pair of feet. Light illuminates. He steps back to see* **American Dummy** *standing before him, as the god Anansi in his full arachnid image. He has glorious thick brown spider legs that protrude from his torso.* **Anansi/American Dummy** *holds beautifully crafted small box. He hands the box to* **Jim Fox**. **Jim Fox** *is both terrified and hypnotized.* **Millicent** *re-enters.* **Anansi** *disappears.*

Millicent (*She nibbles on a piece of cornbread.*) You know, I was thinking. If you want to tell the truth, why don't you work for work for Al Jezeera? They show all that fucked up shit. This tastes like Jiffy Mix. I know they better not have made my cornbread with Jiffy Mix. Jim? Hello?? Looks like you just saw a ghost.

Jim Fox Do you believe in spirits?

Millicent I sure do. Ghosts, spirits, orbs, hobgoblins all that shit.

Jim Fox I'm serious. It's like something has a hold of me. I see them . . . I hear them . . .

Millicent Well if you see a haint in the room; talk to it. See what it wants.

Jim Fox A haint? What is that, geechy talk?

Millicent Maybe you're hearing voices because Liberia ain't done with its prodigal son.

(*Singing*) Pick yourself up, dust yourself off. Start all over again.

He hugs her tightly.

Jim Maybe I will go back, and work for your little magazine. Only if you go with me.

Come on princess, let me take you to Zamunda.

Smooching her, biting her legs.

When God made black women, he was just showing off!

Look at these gams!

Millicent Baby the only bush jumpers I like to see are the ones braiding my hair. Now, I don't know about you, but I got some hot plantation food waiting on me. Got some neck bones, black ass peas, cornbread, and peach cobbler, washed down by some grape pop, umph purple! You're gonna be okay, right?

Jim Fox Yeah, I'll be okay.

She exits. **Jim Fox** *sits with box. He stares out.*

Lords of War: The Final Chapter

Meanwhile on the other side of the globe, a cease fire has taken place. President Taylor has agreed to leave Liberia. His farewell speech plays mixed into our score. Liberians celebrate and tearfully emerge from years of war. Waving white tee shirts hugging, singing, chanting etc., speaking with a camera crew. **Black Diamond** *sits near by staring at her assault rifle.*

All We need peace, we need peace.
Oh Liberians, we need peace!

NPFL/LURD Soldiers Is over! No more! See he is my brother! Same skin, etc.,

Ranger One Attack Force I gonna find my mother, and build a big house for her and me too. I gonna build a big studio and drop some fat beats and send my demo to JAY Z!

He exits.

Born to Suffer My family, they are dead. I hope my sisters here will not forget me. They are all I have left.

She exits.

Disgruntle I think we need a palava hut. It's for peace you know? I have hurt people . . . they may not like me anymore. But to them I say: I'm still your child.

She exits.

Tristan (*snapping photos*) I hope this holds, I really do. It's up to the people to make it right again.

He exits.

Ripley I'm still gonna go to Hollywood. I'm a fucking star!

She exits.

General Dragon Master I'm going climb to the top of Kilimanjaro. See if I can peek at the heavens to say hello to my dear friend Jusu.

He lets out a hearty laugh, and sticks a cigar in his mouth and exits.

Yankee The war is over, but I still need peace in my home.

Sounds of wind. **Yankee** *reaches out to* **Black Diamond** *and gently brushes her hair. He walks away.* **Millicent** *runs her finger down* **Jim Fox**'*s back. She walks away.*

The ticking of the clock builds into the soundscape.

Asase Ya When will there be the emancipation of the African girl child?

Black Diamond *runs her fingers along her rifle.*

Jusu Masali What God has fore-ordained no human being can change.

When a spirit is not bound by precedence, all boundaries disappear . . .

(**Jim Fox** *runs his fingers along the wooden box.*)

The ticking continues.

Anansi and Jusu Masali His future could not happen without her past . . .

Asase Ya She survived her past, to arrive in the present.

All (*sans* **Jim Fox** *and* **Black Diamond**) But the locusts have come to destroy their crop . . .

Sounds of locusts cross faded with ticking of the clock swells.

All (*sans* **Jim Fox** *and* **Black Diamond**) Please Mother Earth, do not swallow my child.

Ticking of the clock, stops in both worlds. Silence. **Black Diamond** *and* **Jim Fox** *both look around. Finally they see one another.*

All Release your sorrow, release you pain.

Asase Ya Take back the years the locusts have eaten . . .

Take back those years . . . .

Together **Jim Fox** *and* **Black Diamond** *open the box. A beautiful light shines from within.*

A beautiful light shines from within, transporting ______ to them both.

END OF PLAY